EXPLORING CREATION WITH

PHYSICAL SCIENCE

3rd EDITION

Vicki Dincher

Technical Editorial Contributions:
Chad Snyder

Exploring Creation with Physical Science
3rd Edition

Published by
Apologia Educational Ministries, Inc.
1106 Meridian Street, Suite 340
Anderson, IN 46016
www.apologia.com

ISBN: 978-1-946506-51-1

Exploring Creation with Physical Science, 3rd Edition, is revised and updated from a previous edition authored by Jay Wile.

Cover: Doug Powell
Book Design: Andrea Kiser Martin and Doug Powell

Unless otherwise indicated, Scripture quotations are from:
English Standard Version (ESV)
© 2001 by Crossway Bibles, a division of Good News Publishers.

Printed by Asia Printing Co., Ltd, Seoul, South Korea
March 2020

10 9 8 7 6 5 4 3 2 1

INSTRUCTIONAL SUPPORT

Did you know that in addition to publishing award-winning curriculum, Apologia also offers instructional support? We believe in helping students achieve their full potential, whatever their learning style. When you choose an Apologia curriculum, you are not just selecting a textbook. Every course has been designed with the student's needs in mind.

INDEPENDENT LEARNERS

Apologia textbooks and notebooks are written to students in a conversational tone so that young people can easily navigate through the curriculum on their own. Apologia curriculum helps students methodically learn, self-check, and master difficult concepts before moving on.

AUDITORY LEARNERS

Sometimes students learn best when they can see and hear what they're studying. **Apologia Audio Books** are the complete text of each course read aloud. Students can follow along with the audio while reading.

VISUAL LEARNERS

Sometimes subject matter is easier to comprehend when the topic is animated and presented by a knowledgeable instructor. When available, **Apologia Video Instructional Courses** enhance the student's education with more than 20 hours of instruction, including on-location video footage, PowerPoint lectures, animated diagrams of difficult concepts, and video presentations of all experiments.

SOCIAL LEARNERS

Some students learn best when they are able to interact with others in an online setting and ask questions of a live instructor. With **Apologia Online Academy**, students can interact in real time with their classmates and a professional instructor in a structured virtual classroom. Also, we offer recordings of all our live classes on the Apologia Online Academy Video-On-Demand Channel.

At Apologia, we believe in homeschooling. We are here not only to support your endeavors but also to help you and your student thrive! Find out more at apologia.com.

EXPLORING CREATION WITH

PHYSICAL SCIENCE

3rd EDITION

ABOUT THIS BOOK

You may not realize it, but you are a scientist! After all, science is simply a way of studying the world around us. If you've ever wondered what makes your soft drink bubble after you pour it in your glass, you're thinking like a scientist. If you've ever tried to figure out if you could make a ball bounce higher, you're acting like a scientist. Science is everywhere!

This course will take you on an amazing journey! We'll have a detailed discussion of the world around you and what makes it work. We'll work our way from quarks to rockets and we'll marvel at the majesty of God's creation. Like anything worth doing, this course will require your effort, but I think you will find it interesting and even enjoyable. From the inner workings of atoms to the grandeur of space, be prepared to be awed and amazed with what the Creator has made for you!

Course Overview

This text contains 15 chapter-modules. Each module should take you about 2–2½ weeks to complete, working 4 days per school week for about 45 minutes to an hour. At this pace, you will complete the course in 34 weeks. Since most people have school years that are longer than 34 weeks, there is some built-in "flex time." You should not rush through a module just to make sure that you complete it in 2 weeks. Set that as a goal but be flexible. Some of the modules might come harder to you than others. On those modules, take more time on the subject matter.

To help you guide your study, there are 2 sets of student exercises that you should complete:

- The On Your Own questions should be answered as you read the text. The act of answering these questions will help you know if you have mastered the concepts you are trying to learn. Answers to these questions are at the end of each module. Once you have answered an On Your Own question, turn to the end of the module and check your work. If you did not get the correct answer, study the answer to learn why. You may want to reread the materials in your textbook to ensure you grasp the concepts.

- You should answer the questions in the Study Guide at the end of the module after you have completed the module. This will allow you to review the important concepts from the module and help you prepare for the test. The separate *Solutions and Tests Manual* includes answers to the Study Guide, as well as tests and test solutions.

Important definitions are <u>centered</u> in the text and put in blue, boldface type. You should memorize the definitions or be able to define them in your own words so you know what they mean. Words that appear in blue, boldface type (but are not centered) are important terms that you should understand. You don't have to memorize them, but make sure you are able to understand what they mean if you see them mentioned later.

In this course, you will learn to read and create tables, graphs, and even infographics. Sometimes, these forms of information will be used in the On Your Own, Study Guide, or test questions. Although you do not have to memorize the information in them, you do need to understand the information they present to you.

ACTIVITIES
Experiments
This course contains 2 types of activities: Experiments and You Do Science boxes. The experiments in this course are designed to be done as you are reading the text. Apologia recommends that you complete all the experiments. You do not necessarily have to do all the You Do Science activities, but each one helps you to better understand a new concept or take an idea further.

I recommend that you perform the experiments in the following way:

- When you get to the experiment, read completely through it. This will allow you to gain a quick understanding of what you are to do.

- The *Student Notebook* has specific pages for each experiment. You will write down all of the data taken during the experiment on those pages. What do I mean by data? Any observations or measurements you make during the experiment are considered data. Thus, if you measure the length of an object, you need to write that measurement down. It is often helpful to make an illustration of the experiment setup so you can better remember what you did. If you collect a large amount of data, you might want to organize it into a table. You will learn how to do that in module 1. The *Student Notebook* will help guide you in this process.

- For this Physical Science course, when you have finished the experiments for a module, choose only one of them and write a short report in your notebook. It should be a brief discussion of what was done and what was learned. You should not write a step-by-step procedure. Instead, write a brief summary that will allow someone who has never read the text to understand what you did and what you learned. For the rest of the experiments in a module, make sure you write a short paragraph to explain the major concept learned in the conclusions section. This is all explained in your *Student Notebook*.

- PLEASE OBSERVE COMMON SENSE AND FOLLOW SAFETY PRECAUTIONS! The experiments in this course are no more dangerous than most normal, household activities. Remember, however, that the vast majority of accidents do happen in the home. Chemicals used in the experiments should never be ingested, and hot containers and flames should be regarded with care; and all experiments should be performed while wearing eye protection such as safety glasses or goggles.

You Do Science

The You Do Science activities provide a hands-on way to further explore a concept introduced in the module. They utilize simple household materials so you can quickly and easily complete them. If you do them, make a few notes in your *Student Notebook*, telling what you did and what you learned. There is space provided to do this.

LABORATORY EQUIPMENT

All of the experiments for *Exploring Creation with Physical Science* utilize household equipment. Any materials you might need to purchase should readily be available from a grocery, hardware store, or pharmacy.

LEARNING AIDS
Student Notebook

The *Student Notebook* is highly recommended. It was designed to go with this course and will aid your studies greatly. This notebook contains a daily student schedule and space for your personal notes. It has the questions and space for your answers to the On Your Own and Study Guide questions. It also has additional exercises for you to do to help you dig deeper into a subject. The notebook also has lab report pages for each experiment found in the text and space for your module lab write-ups.

Book Extras

Extra material is available to help you in your studies. There is a special website for this course that you can visit. The website contains links to web-based materials related to the course. These links are arranged by module, so if you are having trouble with a particular subject in the course, you can go to the website and look at the links for that module. Most likely, you will find help there. Also, if you are enjoying a particular module in the course and would like to learn more about it, there are links that will lead you to advanced material related to that module.

To visit the website, go to the following address:

apologia.com/bookextras

Once there, create an account or use an existing Book Extras account. Once you log in, use the Add Course button to add the following password to your account:

Awestruckbycreation

Be sure that you do not put spaces between any of the letters and that the capitalization is correct. When you click on the button labeled "Submit," you will be sent to the course website.

Back Matter

There is information at the end of the book that you will find useful in your studies. An index will tell you where topics can be found in the course. In addition, we have included a complete list of all the supplies you need to perform the experiments and each You Do Science activity in this course.

TABLE OF CONTENTS

WELCOME

You are about to start an amazing journey of discovering a lot about the world around you. That's what science is—a way to learn about our physical world. Science is a systematic way to actively investigate, apply, and make connections to the world around you. And that is just what you will do this year. And in your study of science, you will see order, precision, and the creative hand of God. The more you learn about creation, and the way our world works, the more you can know the Creator and recognize how great He is.

> Great are the works of the Lord, studied by all who delight in them.
> —Psalm 111:2

Why should you learn *physical* science? Well, physical scientists study the Earth and all the processes and nonliving things on it. God designed the Earth specifically to be our home. Since we live on this amazing planet, it is a good thing to understand as much as we can about it. Also (and more importantly), by investigating Earth and the fundamental laws God set in place when He created it, you will begin to see God's fingerprints and learn more about His nature and power.

Natural Notes

Have you ever marveled at a rainbow or wondered how the sky turns such vibrant shades of orange and pink at sunset? Have you enjoyed seeing the changing colors of leaves in the fall, or the majesty of snow-covered mountain peaks in the distance? If you're curious about how rockets launch into space, or why blowing on a spark makes a fire start, then you are already a physical scientist. We'll look at these topics and so many more as we learn about our physical world this year.

> For his invisible attributes, that is, his eternal power and divine nature, have been clearly seen since the creation of the world, being understood through what he has made…
> —Romans 1:20

This year, you will learn about atoms that make up everything you see (and even things you don't see), the depths of the Earth, the atmosphere above the highest mountains, the waters that cover our planet, and the forces that govern our world. Through this study, you will marvel at how great God is.

For the Lord is a great God, a great King above all gods.
The depths of the earth are in his hand, and the mountain peaks are his.
The sea is his; he made it. His hands formed the dry land.
—Psalm 95:3–6

We at Apologia hope and pray that you will be fascinated and inspired by God's handiwork as you learn more about His creation through your study of physical science.

Proclaim the Lord's greatness with me; let us exalt his name together.
—Psalm 34:3

DEAR PHYSICAL SCIENCE STUDENT,

I'm so glad you're joining me this year as we learn more about our physical world. If you are like me, then science is already your favorite subject. But if that is not true for you, I want to take a moment to encourage you. Many people think science is only a book full of stuff you have to memorize, but that is not the case at all. Sure there are vocabulary words and concepts that you will need to know in your study of science, but there is so much more. Think about science like a journey of exploration—discovering how things you see (observations) work. This is what has always appealed to me in my science courses. God has given us all a natural curiosity and a desire to seek Him in creation. Science is one way to discover God's creative hand in our physical world.

> You will seek me and find me when you search for me with all your heart.
> —Jeremiah 29:13 (NIV)

Physical science is also a good course to begin a formal study of any science. You will find that what you learn this year will prepare you for all the sciences you may take in high school. From biology through chemistry and physics, this course will provide you with a solid foundation to build on. You still have a little way to go before you need to decide what God wants you to do with your life. But who knows, maybe something that you learn this year will spark an interest that God will use to direct you. Even if science is not a subject you will pursue after high school, science can help you understand and appreciate the beautiful and complex world around us.

The physical world we live in is amazing. Simply look at a sunset, a waterfall, or mountains in the distance to see and appreciate the splendor of creation. But do you also realize that God has brought detailed and exact order to the universe? From the structure of unseen atoms to the movements of planets in our solar system, we can observe the logical, orderly way our universe functions. Through our study of physical science this year, we will discover patterns in creation, observe God's goodness and wisdom and witness His invisible hand at work in our world and your life. It is my prayer that as we journey together through this course and you examine how precise and ordered our physical world really is, you will begin to see God's greatness and stand in awe of His works.

> The whole earth is filled with awe at your wonders; where morning dawns,
> where evening fades, you call forth songs of joy.
> —Psalm 65:8 (NIV)

Let's begin our adventure through physical science!

Your guide and fellow journeyer,

Vicki Dincher

SCIENCE— THE BASICS

Before we get started on our adventure in physical science, we should review some basics. It is quite possible that you have learned some of what you'll read in this module before, but it is necessary that we review before we add new, more in depth concepts. Thus, even if some of the topics we cover sound familiar, please read this module thoroughly so that you will not get lost in a later module. After all, most students your age know something about atoms, air, the construction of our planet, and weather. Just like every day of your life is familiar and yet different, so too is science. We build on the knowledge that comes before us.

Natural Notes

In this course, you are going to learn a lot about the non-living natural world around you and the universe it is in. You will study things as familiar as the air around you and others as mysterious as gravity, radioactivity, and quarks. You will learn about the structure of the Earth as well how weather affects the Earth. These topics and many others like them are all a part of what we call physical science. We promise that as you work to learn the material in this course, you will gain a grand appreciation for the wonder of God's creation!

FIGURE 1.1
Lightning Strikes the Rock Formations in Monument Valley, Utah

We will try to illustrate as many concepts as possible with experiments. Hopefully, the "hands on" experience will help you understand the concepts better than any discussion could. In some cases, of course, this will not be possible, so we will use as many illustrations to accompany the words as possible.

IN THIS MODULE YOU WILL READ ABOUT THE FOLLOWING MAIN IDEAS:
- What is Science
- The Scientific Process
- Measuring and Manipulating Data
- Organizing, Analyzing, and Presenting Data

WHAT IS SCIENCE

Have you ever flipped over a rock to see if anything was living under it? Or added a new ingredient to the cookies you baked to see if they tasted better? Or mixed two different paint colors (or food coloring) together to see what new color you could make? If you have, then you have exercised your God given gift of curiosity *and* you've engaged in science! You see curiosity is the basis of science. When you're curious about something you ask questions and hopefully try to figure out ways to find the answers to your questions—that is science.

You may have thought of science as textbooks full of facts. Or maybe you think science is what chemists, astronauts, marine biologists, and geologists do (Figure 1.2). And you would be right—in a way. Science is a body of knowledge and provides wonderful careers for many people, but science is also so much more. It is a way of investigating and discovering the natural world around us—God's creation. Science is also a system of organizing the knowledge discovered and forming explanations and predictions about different natural phenomena and sharing that knowledge with others. So, science is both a system of knowledge and a process used to find that knowledge, as well as a sharing of that knowledge. Science is exciting because you never know what you might discover!

FIGURE 1.2
Some Aspects of Science

Science and Technology

As scientific knowledge is discovered, it can be applied to help people. This is called technology—using scientific knowledge to solve practical problems and improve people's lives. Take telephones, for example. It may be hard to believe, but your parents will remember a time when there were no cell phones. And your grandparents may even remember a time when not every home had a phone! Every time you make or receive a phone call on a cell phone, you're making use of technology. Figure 1.3 illustrates how telephones have changed over the years as technology improved.

FIGURE 1.3
Telephone Technology Timeline

Science and technology are embedded in every aspect of life. From growing the food you eat to the jet skis you ride on vacation, from electric blankets that keep you warm to satellites that measure global temperatures, science and technology improve human life at every level. As you can see with the telephone, the more science we understand, the better our technologies become. Often, the better our technologies become, the more science we're able to understand!

What is Physical Science

If you studied *Exploring Creation with General Science, 3rd Edition* last year, you got a taste for all the different branches of science. Natural science is generally divided into three categories, life science, physical science, and Earth and space science. Each of these 3 branches of science can be further subdivided into more specialized topics (Figure 1.4).

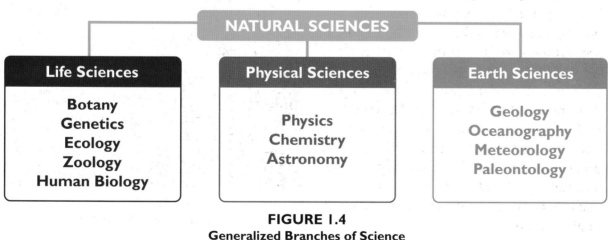

FIGURE 1.4
Generalized Branches of Science

This is a nice way of dividing science into groups, however it really isn't as simple as this.

You see, there is often a great deal of overlap between these subdivisions. For instance biology, the study of living things, incorporates botany, zoology, ecology, oceanography, chemistry, and even some physics. So the boundaries separating each science is often not always very clear.

So what is physical science? Physical science deals with the study of non-living things. In this course we will be discussing two of the three main areas: chemistry and physics. Chemistry is the study of matter—its composition, structure, properties, and interactions or reactions. Physics is the study of matter and energy and how they interact through forces and motion. We'll then use the information we learn in our study of physical science to briefly study the Earth (Earth science). Since so much of what you'll study in other science courses depends on an understanding of matter and energy, physical science is a good background course for all further science courses.

There is one thing that is important to keep in mind. Remember that science is both a process and a body of knowledge. The information you will read in this text represents the best, most up-to-date scientific knowledge and models we have of how God created the universe to work. But like all scientific knowledge, it can be rejected or replaced in the future as new information becomes available with better technologies. So as you read, think, ask questions, and be aware that the scientific facts today may change tomorrow. The scientific process, though, is the best process we have to make new scientific discoveries, so you'll want to practice it as you study this year. Just think, you may be the one who makes a discovery that will change what we know about how Creation works in the future! Before reading about the scientific process, complete On Your Own questions 1.1–1.3.

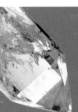

ON YOUR OWN

1.1 What is science?

1.2 How are science and technology related?

1.3 What is physical science and why is it an important course?

THE SCIENTIFIC PROCESS

In the last section I mentioned that the scientific process is the best method we have for making new scientific discoveries, so in this section we will review that process. You have probably heard of this process referred to as the scientific method. The scientific method is a systematic process that scientists use to help them solve problems, answer questions, or better understand observed events. Figure 1.5 outlines the steps to the scientific method as described in this section. Keep in mind that scientific methods can vary depending on what is being studied. The steps shown in Figure 1.5 are important and the skills required for each step should be practiced as you work through this course. However sometimes in everyday science, the steps may be completed in a different order or the specific steps may not be as clear as shown. But one activity always occurs: making observations.

Making Observations

Gaining new scientific knowledge through the scientific process is based on observations of the natural world. You make observations when you gather information using your five senses or with the help of instruments.

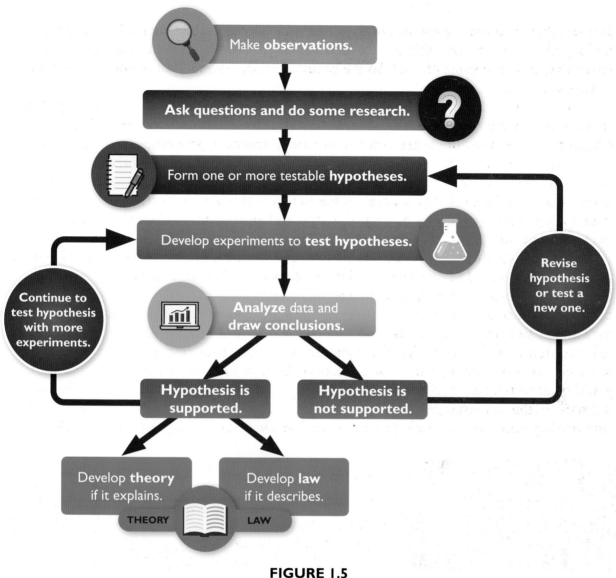

FIGURE 1.5
The Scientific Method

Observation—Gathering information using senses or with the aid of instruments

Notice in the definition of observation that there are two ways to make observations. These are called qualitative and quantitative observations.

Qualitative observation—Observations made using one of the five senses: sight, smell, touch, taste, or hearing

Quantitative observations—Observations made with instruments such as rulers, balances, graduated cylinders, beakers, thermometers, etc.

When you observe the natural world with any of your senses, that is called making qualitative observations. You use your senses all the time to make observations. You notice the changing shape of the moon over several weeks. You smell ammonia gas as you clean windows. You feel the heat radiating from a bonfire. You hear thunder shortly after seeing a lightning flash. All of these are qualitative observations.

Sometimes qualitative observations can be made specific or more detailed by using instruments. You measure the heat radiating from the bonfire with a thermometer. You use a watch to time how long it takes to hear the thunder after seeing the lightning flash. You use a telescope with a ruler to see the moon better and measure the changes over the weeks. These observations use instruments to make numerical measurements, so they are quantitative observations. All quantitative observations will have a number in them. The number may be a counting number, but is most often a measurement that includes a unit. We'll discuss units in much more detail in a later section.

Look at the photo in Figure 1.6. Make two qualitative and two quantitative observations about the photo before reading the paragraph below.

FIGURE 1.6
African Animals Near a Water Hole
What quantitative and qualitative observations can you make about what is happening in this photo?

Hopefully you were able to make several observations of each kind even though you can only use your sight for this exercise. Some qualitative observations may include:
- the ground looks dry, the air looks hazy or hot,
- there is more space between the animals and the lion than between the animals and each other,
- the animals seem to be watching the lion,
- the antelope stay together.

Some quantitative observations may include:
- there are 4 giraffes,
- there is only 1 lion,
- there is only 1 ostrich.

Making observations is the basis of science. Experiments begin with observing. After you observe something that you are curious about, you ask questions which can lead to more observations. As you experiment and make more observations you may find you have more questions that lead to new experiments. So you can see making observations is important for making advancements in science. Complete Experiment 1.1 (use the lab report form in your student notebook) to gain experience in making observations.

EXPERIMENT 1.1
MAKING OBSERVATIONS

PURPOSE:
To explore qualitative and quantitative observations as they relate to the properties of solids.

MATERIALS:
- Alka Seltzer tablet
- A small solid object (such as a pebble or eraser)
- Magnifying glass
- Centimeter ruler
- Kitchen balance
- Beaker of water
- Stirring rod or spoon to stir

PROCEDURE:
1. Examine the small solid object using your senses. In the data table in your student notebook, make a list of your observations. CAUTION: Never taste anything in a science experiment. Unknown substances may be hazardous.
2. Observe the object with a magnifying glass. Record what you see.
3. Use the kitchen balance to determine the weight of the object. Add the weight (be sure to include units) to your list of observations.
4. Use a centimeter ruler to measure two dimensions (length, width, height, or diameter). Record these observations and be sure to include units.
5. Place the object in the beaker of water and stir. Record any observations.
6. Remove the object from the beaker.
7. Repeat steps 1 through 5 for the Alka Seltzer tablet. Record all observations in the data table of your student notebook.
8. Empty the beaker down the drain, rinse the beaker and return all materials to their proper place.

CONCLUSION: Answer the following questions in a paragraph as you sum up what you learned.
1. How did the appearance of each object differ under the magnifying glass?
2. Which data were obtained by qualitative observations?
3. Which data were obtained by quantitative observations?
4. How did the instruments extend the observations you made with your senses?
5. How did the objects change when placed in the beaker of water?

What did you learn in this experiment? You should have gained some experience in measuring and weighing solids. But you should also have noticed that the properties of some solids can change when they are in water. Hopefully you recorded in your observations seeing bubbles when the Alka Seltzer was dropped into water. I hope you were asking questions, such as "What caused the bubbles?" or "Where did the solid Alka Seltzer tablet go?" Part of the reason we make detailed observations is to spark good questions. Always include any questions that come to mind while your observing something so that later you can think about these or decide if you want to investigate further. This is an important step in the scientific process. You will learn more about what the bubbles meant and what happened to the Alka Seltzer tablet in a later module, so make sure your observations are written well enough that when asked to review them you will remember what happened!

One thing I should mention before we move on, is that scientists are always conducting background research. Research helps them make sense of their observations and helps them develop questions to answer. The best way to know how to design an experiment or understand your results is to research a bit. Now complete On Your Own 1.4 before reading on.

ON YOUR OWN

1.4 Label each of the following observations as qualitative or quantitative.

a. It is light blue in color. _____

b. It makes a loud popping sound. ____

c. It is 8.3 centimeters long. _____

d. It smells sweet. _____

e. The temperature increases by 6 degrees C. _____

FIGURE 1.7
Wood Burning
The phlogiston hypothesis states the wood burns because it contains phlogiston that escapes as it burns. The oxygen hypothesis says that wood combined with oxygen will burn.

Forming Hypotheses

A hypothesis (hi poth' uh sis) is a tentative explanation for one or more observations or a proposed answer to a question. For a hypothesis to be a good one, it must be able to be tested.

Hypothesis—A possible, testable explanation for one or more observations or a suggested, testable answer to a question

For example, scientists in the late 1600's observed that some substances burned very easily while others did not. They questioned how that could be. In 1697, one German scientist by the name of Georg Ernst Stahl hypothesized that easily combustible materials must contain a special substance he called *phlogiston*. Materials that did not burn easily were thought to not contain phlogiston. According to Stahl's hypothesis, wood was made up of ash and a lot of phlogiston. As wood burned, the phlogiston was given off into the air and only the ash remained. This seemed to explain why combustible substances such as charcoal lost weight when burned.

Years later, around 1772, Antoine Lavoisier (a 29-year-old French chemist) observed some things about materials burning that caused him to develop an alternate hypothesis. Lavoisier hypothesized that burning was the result of a combustible material combining with a component of air—oxygen, not phlogiston.

For a decade or so, both hypotheses were used. Both hypotheses about how things burned could explain why candles burn down completely. According to the phlogiston hypothesis, candles contain a lot of the substance phlogiston and so will burn until all the phlogiston is burned off. According to the oxygen hypothesis, there is enough oxygen in the air around the candle to allow it to burn down completely. Both hypotheses are good ones, because you can predict what might happen based on each hypothesis and then you can test your predictions.

Testing Hypotheses

What led Lavoisier to think of an alternate hypothesis for why things burn? Observations, of course. As a chemist, he was studying metals. According to the phlogiston hypothesis if a metal burned it would lose all its phlogiston and then it should weigh less after it burned than before. So with that prediction in mind, he tested the hypothesis. Lavoisier conducted experiments where he weighed the metals phosphorus, sulfur, and lead and recorded their weights. He then burned the metals and reweighed them. What he found was that the metals gained weight after burning and that combustion re-quired air. What did that do to the phlogis-ton hypothesis?

If you said, it disproved the hypoth-esis, you're right. Since the prediction that the metals would weigh less after burning was based on the phlogiston hypothesis and that is not what happened, then the phlogiston hypothesis must be changed or discarded. As it turns out, the phlogiston hypothesis was ultimately discarded. It took about five more years of experiment-ing for Lavoisier (with the help of Joseph Priestley) to propose his new theory of combustion that excluded phlogiston.

In 1774, Joseph Priestley conduct-ed an experiment in which he discovered

FIGURE I.8
Burning Magnesium
A scientist burns magnesium at extremely high temperatures.

that one of the components of air was very combustible. (At the time scientists called all gases air because they had not yet identified what a gas was.) Priestley called this "dephlo-gisticated air" because a candle would burn five or six times longer in this "air" than in "common air." He told Lavoisier about his discovery and this provided the spark Lavoisier needed to flesh out his new hypothesis. Lavoisier named the "dephlogisticated air" oxygen in 1779 and cast doubt on the substance phlogiston.

So how would you test the oxygen hypothesis? First what would you predict would happen to a burning candle when placed under a jar that cuts of the air supply? For the oxygen hypothesis to be supported, you should predict that if a jar is placed over a burning candle then the flame will go out when the oxygen inside the jar is used up. To test your prediction based on the oxygen hypothesis, you would conduct an experiment in which you place a jar over a burning candle (this seals out the air) and record observations. This experiment is shown in Figure 1.9.

FIGURE 1.9
Flame Extinguishes Under Glass
When a jar is placed over a burning candle, the flame is extinguished. What hypothesis explains this observation?

Experiments

Experiments, like the ones shown in Figures 1.8 and 1.9, are how scientists methodically test their hypotheses and the predictions based on their hypotheses. There are a few very important things to remember when developing experiments. First, it is crucial to make sure you are testing only one thing at a time. This is called a controlled experiment.

Controlled experiment—An investigation in which the factors that influence the outcome are kept the same except for one, the factor being studied

The factors that influence the outcome of an experiment are called variables (vayr' ee uh bulz).

Variables—A factor that changes in an experiment

All variables in a controlled experiment should be kept the same throughout the experiment except the one variable whose effect you are studying. This variable, which you intentionally change or manipulate, is called the independent variable or the manipulated variable. The variable that responds to the changing variable is called the dependent variable or the responding variable.

For example, suppose your hypothesis is that the number of swings per second of a pendulum is determined by the mass of the pendulum. Based on this hypothesis your

FIGURE 1.10
Physics Pendulum Experiment
As a controlled experiment, what variables (other than mass) should be kept the same?

prediction would be that the number of swings per second will change as you change the mass of the ball at the end of the pendulum string.

You can easily set up an experiment to test the prediction based on your hypothesis. Look at Figure 1.10. The pink, green, and tan pendulum balls are all of different masses. You can see that the pink and green are attached to pendulum strings. If both balls are pulled back and released from the same height, the number of swings in a given time interval of each pendulum can be counted. The number of swings and the mass of each pendulum is recorded.

Think about the other variables that could affect the number of swings in a certain time interval in this experiment. If you thought of the length of the string, the position of the pendulum ball before release, and the shape of the pendulum ball, then you are thinking like a scientist. For this to be a controlled experiment, all the factors except the mass of the ball must not change during the experiment. We are intentionally changing the mass of the ball, so mass is the independent variable (the manipulated variable). The number of swings per second would be our dependent variable (the one responding to the variable we changed).

You could change the experiment to test a different independent variable—length for example. If you tested the length of a pendulum to determine if that affects the number of swings per second, then you would need to keep the mass constant (as well as the other variables) and only change the length of the pendulum string. How would you test whether the initial position of the pendulum ball influenced the number of swings per second? Well you would need to keep both the mass and the length constant and only change the starting height from which you release the pendulum ball.

It is often difficult to be sure that all variables are really being controlled. For this reason, and to be sure that the results found are only because of the independent variable, good science requires that an experiment be repeatable. What that means is that someone else must be able to conduct the experiment the exact same way and get the exact same results. This is why it is so important to record exactly what materials you use in an experiment and detail the steps you follow in the procedure. Many scientists will include sketches in their notes to show how they set up an experiment like this one. Any time you repeat an experiment and your results contradict a hypothesis that has survived many previous experiments, look for variables that may not have been controlled properly.

Before we move on, you should be aware that there are different types of experiments. Look back at Experiment 1.1 and notice that there was no hypothesis. That is because some experiments are simply observational experiments where the object is to investigate something and simply make observations. Studying things under the microscope or dissections are good examples of this type of experiment. However, this type of experiment often provides the observations that will spark questions that lead to the type of experiment where you make hypotheses and predictions, develop ways to test them, and then make more observations. Review what you've read so far in this section by completing On Your Own questions 1.5–1.7.

ON YOUR OWN

1.5 For a hypothesis to be considered useful, it should be

    a. in mathematical terms.

    b. a creative guess made without observations.

    c. capable of being tested.

    d. general and broad in scope.

1.6 What are variables? How are they important in controlled experiments?

1.7 What is the difference between independent and dependent variables?

Analyzing Data

Any time you collect and record observations you're gathering data. To use data to make conclusions your data should be organized, and data tables will help you do that. You can also visually show the data using graphs and charts (Figure 1.11). We will go over measuring data and creating data tables, graphs, and charts in more detail in the next two sections.

Analyzing your data is important. A big part of what goes on in science involves thinking about the data that have been collected. The key thing for you to remember is to try to look at your data results with a critical eye. Ask yourself if you followed all the instructions or did you forget something? Did you make any mistakes? Did you record units with all your data measurements and record thorough qualitative observations? Do you have enough data to see any patterns or do you need to collect more data? Did you calculate an average for the different trials of your experiment (if needed)?

FIGURE 1.11
Graphs and Charts
Graphs and charts help scientist visualize and analyze data.

Drawing Conclusions

The reason scientists think about and analyze data for patterns is so they can try to draw conclusions about their hypotheses. Conclusions summarize whether your results support or contradict your original hypothesis. Your conclusion summary could take a few sentences, but most often it will require a paragraph or more.

If your experiment results support that your hypothesis is true, you should summarize how you could tell that by comparing the relationship between the independent and dependent variables. In other words, explain in words how the responding variable changed when you manipulated the independent variable. If your experiment results do not support the hypothesis, then you know your hypothesis is false. What happens if you find your hypothesis is false? It doesn't mean that your experiment was a failure! It is important, however, to never change the results to fit the original hypothesis. Simply explain why things did not go as expected. If you think you need additional experimentation or parts of the experiment should be altered, you should include a description of what you think should happen next in your conclusion summary.

Scientists often find that results do not support their hypothesis. In fact, science works by making mistakes *and* learning from them. Many times scientists use their unexpected results as the first step to revising their original hypothesis or proposing a new one. They must then design a new experiment to test the revised or new hypothesis and the process of science continues.

Scientific Theories and Laws

You've probably heard the word theory used in detective stories before. The everyday, ordinary meaning of a theory is like a hypothesis—a tentative explanation of observations that may or may not be correct. But the word theory in science means something different. To a scientist a scientific theory is one or (more often) a set of hypotheses that explain some aspect of the natural world. Theories have been well-tested by many experiments and have a *large* amount of supporting data.

> **Scientific theory**—An in-depth explanation of a range of phenomena in the natural world that has been thoroughly tested and is supported by a significant amount of evidence

For example, you will learn about the theory of the atom in a later module. The atomic theory is a scientific theory that explains the nature of matter which is composed of atoms. Through many experiments in the field of chemistry, a large amount of evidence was collected that supported the theory that the smallest "unit" of matter were atoms. Once something has become a theory, it is well accepted by scientists because it agrees with many observations and experiments.

Even so, a scientific theory is not permanent. If evidence is ever gathered that contradicts a theory, the theory is changed to explain the new evidence. For example, the atomic theory has changed greatly in the last hundred years as scientists have discovered more about how atoms behave. If enough evidence is gathered that contradicts a theory, the theory may be completely discarded.

Unlike a scientific theory which explains, a scientific law accurately describes some phenomenon or relationship in the natural world without explaining what causes it or why it exists.

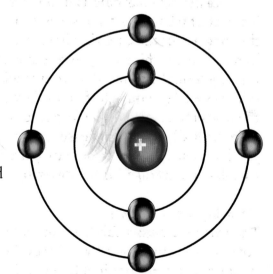

FIGURE 1.12
Carbon Atom
This 1913 model of a carbon atom is based on the atomic theory.

Scientific law—A description of a natural phenomenon or relationship that is supported by a significant amount of evidence and often include mathematical terms

Just like a theory, a law is supported by many, many experiments and observations. And also like a theory, a law is well accepted by scientists. Remember, the difference is that theories explain while laws describe.

For example, you will learn about Newton's laws of motion in a later module. Newton made many observations and performed many experiments to understand how forces affect the motion of objects. Newton's third law states, "every action has an equal and opposite reaction." This is a statement that describes what we observe to be true and it has been verified over and over. But scientists have not yet been able to explain, with hard evidence, how Newton's third law happens or why it works that way. A law can provide predictions of an observed pattern in nature without necessarily explaining the pattern.

Like scientific theories, scientific laws must be consistent with observations and provide accurate predictions. If a law is determined to not be true under all conditions, then it must be changed or discarded.

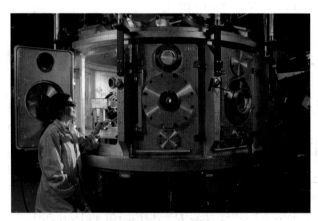

FIGURE 1.13
Chamber for Subatomic
Particle Experimentation
Experiments on positrons collect evidence to support their existence but cannot prove their existence.

There is one last thing we want to point out about scientific theories and laws (and hypotheses for that matter). Some people think that if scientists find enough evidence that supports a hypothesis, the hypothesis is then raised to a theory. Then if the theory is found to be true through more testing, it is raised to a law. That is not how it works! One cannot grow into another. Scientific hypotheses, theories, and laws all have data to support them (or they would be changed), but they differ in scope. Hypotheses are possible explanations about a single or limited idea. Scientific laws describe (but don't explain) a broad range of phenomena or observations. Theories are more developed explanations than hypotheses and they apply to a broad range of observations. Theories usually include explanations for many hypotheses and laws.

Science Does Not Prove

You may have heard a statement that starts out something like, "this is scientific proof that…" Finish the sentence however you like but know that the statement will always be false. Why? Because science is not about proving things. Science is about collecting evidence. Even if all the evidence ever collected supports the atomic theory or Newton's law of gravity, there's always the chance that some evidence collected in the future (maybe when we have better instruments) will contradict what we think we know. Science is *continually* changing based on new information—nothing in science is ever final.

All the scientific knowledge, theories, and laws we have today are just the currently accepted, best explanations and descriptions we have so far. Science is a process and so any hypothesis, theory, or law—no matter how widely accepted today—can be overturned tomorrow if the evidence warrants it. In other words, scientific hypotheses, laws, and theories are only valid if they can explain all the available data. Science accepts or rejects ideas based on the evidence. Science does not prove or disprove ideas. This is what makes science so much fun! You might be the next scientist to shed light on something we don't yet know.

When the Scientific Method Isn't Possible

It's not always possible to directly observe some things studied in science. For example, scientists cannot directly observe atoms and molecules, black holes, or the bottom of the deepest part of the ocean. Yet, scientists want to know more about these things, so they gather information in other ways.

Inferences

Besides the conclusions made at the end of an experiment to summarize their results, scientists often make another type of conclusion. An inference (in' fer uns) is a logical conclusion drawn from observations and information that is available.

Inference—Logical conclusion drawn from observations, previous knowledge, and available information

Scientists usually make many inferences when trying to put together an overall picture of what is taking place.

Scientists also make inferences when they investigate things that they cannot directly observe. For example, paleontologists (scientists who study fossils) have never observed living dinosaurs, but they gather evidence about them in other ways. Paleontologists have been able to study fossilized dinosaur droppings and so have gathered evidence about what the dinosaur ate while it was alive. They haven't observed the dinosaur eating but used the evidence they gathered from the fossilized dropping to make an inference. An inference is an educated guess that explains evidence or observations.

It's important not to mix up observations and inferences. Look at Figure 1.14. In this photo we can observe a meadow, some clouds, and a very vivid rainbow. These are all qualitative observations we can make because we can see them in the photograph. If we take those observations and combine them with knowledge we already have, we can make some inferences. We can infer that it must have been (or perhaps still is) raining. We can also infer that the sun must be shining. Although we can't observe the rain or the sun in the photo we know that rainbows occur when

FIGURE 1.14
Observations and Inferences
What observations and inferences can you make about this picture?

the sun hits water particles in the air. So in order to see that vivid rainbow, we infer that the sun must be shining on water droplets left in the air after a rain shower.

Models

Another way that scientists try to make it easier to understand things that are unfamiliar or to visualize things they cannot see is to use models.

> **Scientific model**—Useful simplification used to make it easier to understand things that might be too difficult to directly observe

Look back at Figure 1.12. That drawing is a Bohr model of the carbon atom. Niels Bohr used the data he collected (as well as data collected from scientists before him) to infer how an atom looks. He then constructed the Bohr model of the atom based on his inferences. Notice how it looks different than the Bohr model shown in Figure 1.15. Bohr used Rutherford's model but added the new information that the nucleus was composed of subatomic units. A model's job is to help you mentally picture objects too large or small to see, or to identify what is going on in a process you can't observe.

Scientific models need to change if they don't accurately represent all the evidence available. So when new data is collected that is not explained by the current model, the model is changed to reflect the new information. For example, models of the atom changed quite a bit from 1803 until our current model designed in 1926. Study Figure 1.15 to see how the model of the atom changed as new information came to light.

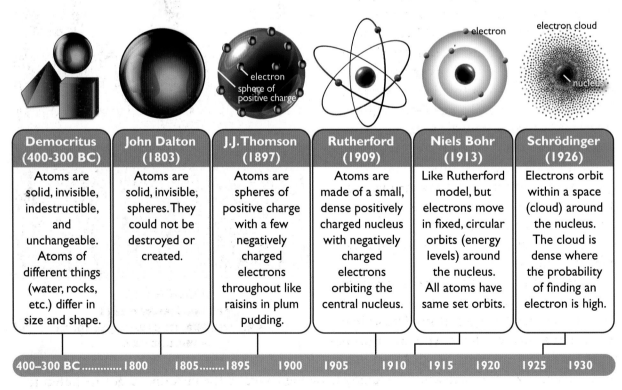

Democritus (400–300 BC)	John Dalton (1803)	J.J. Thomson (1897)	Rutherford (1909)	Niels Bohr (1913)	Schrödinger (1926)
Atoms are solid, invisible, indestructible, and unchangeable. Atoms of different things (water, rocks, etc.) differ in size and shape.	Atoms are solid, invisible, spheres. They could not be destroyed or created.	Atoms are spheres of positive charge with a few negatively charged electrons throughout like raisins in plum pudding.	Atoms are made of a small, dense positively charged nucleus with negatively charged electrons orbiting the central nucleus.	Like Rutherford model, but electrons move in fixed, circular orbits (energy levels) around the nucleus. All atoms have same set orbits.	Electrons orbit within a space (cloud) around the nucleus. The cloud is dense where the probability of finding an electron is high.

400–300 BC 1800   1805 1895   1900   1905   1910   1915   1920   1925   1930

FIGURE 1.15
Atomic Models Timeline

Review what you learned in this section by completing On Your Own questions 1.8–1.10.

ON YOUR OWN

1.8   Match the term with the definition.

    a.   hypothesis   A well supported description of a natural phenomenon

    b.   scientific theory   A possible, testable explanation for an observation

    c.   scientific law   A well supported explanation of a range of phenomena

1.9   Why do we say science cannot prove anything?

1.10   What is meant by a model in science?

MEASURING AND MANIPULATING DATA

As you saw in the last section, when you make an observation that you describe with numbers, you are making a quantitative observation. Quantitative observations involve taking measurements. Measurements always have two parts—a number followed by a unit.

Let's suppose I'm making curtains for a friend's windows. I ask the person to measure his windows and give me their dimensions, so I can make the curtains the right size. My friend tells me that his windows are 50 × 60, so that's how big I make the curtains. When I go over to his house, it turns out that my curtains are more than twice as big as his windows! My friend tells me that he's certain he measured the windows right, and I tell my friend that I'm certain I measured the curtains correctly. How can this be? The answer is quite simple. My friend measured the windows with a metric ruler. His measurements were in *centimeters*. I, on the other hand, used a yardstick and measured my curtains in *inches*. Our problem was not caused by one of us measuring incorrectly. Instead, our problem was the result of measuring with different units.

When we are making measurements, the units we use are just as important as the numbers that we get. If my friend had told me that his windows were 50 centimeters (cm) by 60 cm, there would have been no problem. I would have known exactly how big to make the curtains. Since he failed to do this, the numbers that he gave me (50 × 60) were essentially useless.

FIGURE 1.16
Making Measurements
Making measurements is one way to collect quantitative data.

think about this

It's important to note that a failure to indicate the units involved in measurements can lead to serious problems. For example, on July 23, 1983, the pilot of an Air Canada Boeing 767 passenger airplane had to make an emergency landing because his plane *ran out of fuel*. In the investigation that followed, it was determined that the fuel gauges on the aircraft were not functional, so the ground crew had measured the fuel level manually. However, the fuel gauges were metric, so those were the units with which the pilot worked. The ground crew, however, ended up using English units to report the amount of fuel. The number they reported was the correct *number*, but since the units were wrong, the airplane ran out of fuel. Thankfully, the pilot was skilled and was able to make the emergency landing with no casualties.

FIGURE 1.17
A Boeing 767

In the end, then, scientists never simply report numbers; they always include units with those numbers so that everyone knows exactly what those numbers mean. That will be the rule in this course. If you answer a question or a problem and do not list units with the numbers, your answer will be considered incomplete. In science, numbers mean nothing unless there are units attached to them. Since scientists use units in all their measurements, it is convenient to define a standard set of units that will be used by everyone. This system of standard units is called the metric system. The modern metric system, known as the International System of Units or SI (from the French *Système International d'Unitès*) contains the units that scientists all over the world have agreed to use—from very large to very small.

Unfortunately, there are many other unit systems in use today besides the metric system. In fact, the metric system is probably not the system with which you are most familiar. You are probably most familiar with the English system. We will discuss the English system as you learn about the metric system for comparison, but in this course you will be using SI units.

The Metric System

The metric system is a system of measuring. SI units have only 3 base units (although we will learn about more); the *meter* for length, the *kilogram* for mass, and the *second* for time. Believe it or not, with just these 3 simple measurements we can measure just about everything in creation!

TABLE 1.1 Physical Quantities and Their Base SI and English Units				
Physical Quality	**Base SI Unit**	**SI Unit Symbol**	**Corresponding English Unit**	**English Unit Symbol**
length	meter	m	foot	ft
mass	kilogram	kg	slug	sl
time	second	s	second	s

Time

The SI unit for time is the second (s), a very familiar unit to you. For very short time intervals, time is measured in milliseconds (ms). A millisecond is 1/1000 of a second and is also an SI. Other everyday units for measuring time include the minute (abbreviated min) and the hour (abbreviated h). You have probably used a stopwatch to measure time at some point. Stopwatches (Figure 1.23) are the most commonly used instruments for measuring time because they are quite accurate, inexpensive, and easy to use. Now days all smart phones come with a stopwatch app, so making time measurements has never been easier.

FIGURE 1.23
Stopwatch
Stopwatches are the most common instrument of time measurement.

Temperature

In science, temperature is a measurement of how much heat energy a substance has. In chemistry and physics courses, you will do quite a few experiments requiring you to measure the transfer of heat energy with a thermometer.

The unit for temperature measurements that is used in scientific research is degrees Celsius (°C). The Celsius scale (then called the centigrade scale) was developed in 1742 by the Swedish astronomer, Anders Celsius. Celsius developed this scale using the melting point of ice and the boiling point of water as reference points. Using the Celsius scale, ice melts (or water freezes) at 0 °C and water boils at 100 °C.

You may be more familiar with temperature measurements in Fahrenheit (°F) since this is what is used in the United States. However, the scientific community (and most other countries of the world)

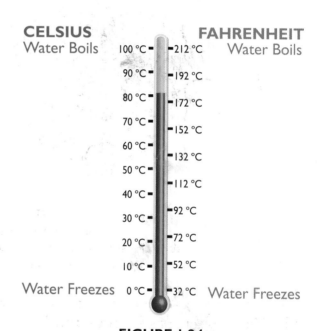

FIGURE 1.24
Thermometer Scale
The Celsius scale is used more commonly in science than the Fahrenheit scale. Can you see why?

has adopted the Celsius scale for temperature measurement because it is more compatible with the other base ten units of the metric system of measurements (Figure 1.24).

The SI base unit for thermal energy (heat energy) is the Kelvin (K), named after Lord William Kelvin, who developed the scale in 1854. The Kelvin scale uses the same unit of division as the Celsius scale, and you will learn much more about it in future chemistry and physics courses. In this course we will be using the Celsius scale for heat measurements. You can use Table 1.3 to familiarize yourself with the common SI units, their symbols, and prefixes.

TABLE 1.3 Common SI Units and Prefixes		
Used for	**Name**	**Symbol/Abbreviation**
Prefix meaning: 1000 Prefix meaning: 1/100 Prefix meaning: 1/1000	kilo- centi- milli-	k- c- m-
mass	kilogram gram milligram	kg g mg
length	meter kilometer centimeter millimeter	m km cm mm
time	second millisecond *minute *hour	s ms min h
volume	cubic meter cubic centimeter *liter *milliliter	m^3 cm^3 L mL
temperature	*degrees Celsius	°C

*Not an SI unit, but may be used along with SI units

Converting Units

Now that you understand what prefix units are and how they are used in the metric system, you must become familiar with converting between units within the metric system. In other words, if you measure the length of an object in centimeters, you should also be able to convert your answer to any other distance unit. For example, if I measure the length of a pencil in centimeters, I should be able to convert that length to millimeters, decimeters, meters, etc. Accomplishing this task is relatively simple if you remember a trick you can use when multiplying fractions. Study Example 1.1.

EXAMPLE 1.1

Suppose I asked you to complete the following problem:

$$\frac{7}{64} \times \frac{64}{13} =$$

There are two ways to figure out the answer.

Option One: Multiply the numerators together and then multiply the denominators together. Simplify the fraction.

$$\frac{7}{64} \times \frac{64}{13} = \frac{448}{832} = \frac{7}{13}$$

Option Two: Cancel out common factors in the numerator and the denominator. Thus, the 64 in the numerator cancels with the 64 in the denominator and gives you a value of 1. Now the only factors left are the 7 × 1 in the numerators and the 13 × 1 in the denominators.

$$\frac{7}{{}_1 64} \times \frac{64^1}{13} = \frac{7}{13}$$

Notice how you could arrive at the answer much more quickly using the second approach. In this way the problem takes one less step.

We will use the same idea in converting between units. Suppose I measure the length of a pencil to be 15.1 centimeters, but the person who wants to know the length of the pencil would like me to tell him the measurement in meters. How would I convert between centimeters and meters? Study the steps below in Example 1.2.

EXAMPLE 1.2

Convert 15.1 centimeters to meters.

1. First you need to know the relationship between centimeters and meters. According to Table 1.2 *centi-* means 0.01. So 1 centimeter is the same thing as 0.01 meter. This is called a conversion factor and should be written in mathematical form:

$$1 \text{ cm} = 0.01 \text{ m}$$

2. Now that we know the relationship between cm and m (the conversion factor), we can convert from one to the other. Always start a problem by writing down what you know (or are given in the problem):

$$15.1 \text{ cm}$$

3. Remember that any number can be expressed as a fraction by putting the number over the number 1 (any number divided by 1 is the same number). Rewrite the measurement as a fraction:

$$\frac{15.1 \text{ cm}}{1}$$

4. Now you can take that measurement and convert it into meters by multiplying it with the conversion factor from step 1. Pay attention to which way the conversion factor should be written as a fraction so that you can cancel the units properly:

$$\underset{\substack{\text{Given} \\ \text{Unit}}}{\frac{15.1 \text{ cm}}{1}} \times \underset{\substack{\text{Conversion} \\ \text{Factor}}}{\frac{0.01 \text{ m}}{1 \text{ cm}}} = \underset{\substack{\text{Wanted} \\ \text{Unit}}}{0.151 \text{ m}}$$

This tells us that 15.1 centimeters is the same as 0.151 meters. There are two reasons this conversion method, called the factor-label method, works.

1. Since 0.01 m is the same as 1 cm, multiplying our measurement by (0.01 m)/(1 cm) is the same as multiplying by 1. Since nothing changes when we multiply by 1, we haven't altered the value of our measurement at all. *All conversion factors are equal to 1.*

2. By putting the 1 cm in the denominator of the conversion factor ((0.01 m)/(1 cm)), we allow the centimeters unit to cancel. Once the centimeter units are canceled, the only unit left is meters, so we know that our measurement is now in meters.

This is how we will do all our unit conversions. In your high school chemistry and physics classes you will learn about significant figures and how to round your answers properly, but for now learning how to use conversion factors in the factor-label method will give you a good start for future science classes. You will see many examples of the factor-label method through this course, so you will have plenty of practice. But since the factor-label method is so important in our studies of physical science, let's see how it works in another example now.

EXAMPLE 1.3

A student measures the mass of a rock to be 14,351 grams. What is the rock's mass in kilograms?

1. First you need to find the conversion factor which is the relationship between kilograms and grams. According to Table 1.2, the prefix *kilo-* means 1000. So 1 kilogram is equal to 1000 grams. (Always put the 1 in front of the prefix unit, and then the base unit gets the number that corresponds to the definition of the prefix.) Write as:

$$1 \text{ kg} = 1,000 \text{ g}$$

2. Now that we know the conversion factor for kg and g, we can convert from one to the other. Now you can start the problem. Always start a problem by writing down what you know (or are given in the problem) and write it in fraction form:

$$\frac{14,351 \text{ g}}{1}$$

3. Take the given measurement and convert it into kilograms by multiplying it with the conversion factor from step 1. Pay attention to which way the conversion factor should be written as a fraction so that you can cancel the units properly (in this case place 1,000 g in the denominator):

$$\frac{14,351 \cancel{\text{ g}}}{1} \times \frac{1 \text{ kg}}{1,000 \cancel{\text{ g}}} = 14.351 \text{ kg}$$

Given Unit	Conversion Factor	Wanted Unit

Thus, 14,351 g = **14.351 kg**

26

You can use the factor-label method and conversion factors to convert between systems of units as well as within the metric system of units. Thus, if a measurement is done in the English system, the factor-label method can be used to convert that measurement to the metric system, or vice versa. Remember, a conversion factor is the relationship between 2 units and will always equal 1. So you can always convert from one unit (no matter what system of measurement) to another with the factor-label method. Any time you will be asked to convert between systems in this course, you will be given the conversion factor you need. Review what you've learned by completing On Your Own problems 1.11–1.12.

ON YOUR OWN

1.11   Give the name and symbols for the following base SI units (Hint: look back at Table 1.1):
a. time   b. mass   c. length

1.12   If a glass contains 0.121 L of milk, what is the volume of milk in mL? What is the volume of milk in gallons (gal)? (1 gal = 3.78 L)

think about this

Conversion factors aren't just mathematical facts you find in science. There are examples everywhere you look in life. Money is traded widely on global financial markets and conversion rates, often called foreign exchange rates, represent the ratio between two currencies. Stock markets, interest rates, and even economic activity worldwide depends on the rate of exchange. Farmers use a variety conversion factors. They convert crops on the ground into estimated bushels of product which then convert to truckloads and eventually to storage bin size. Businesses use conversion rates to estimate how many website visitors will turn into actual customers. Can you think of other conversion factors? Perhaps you will find some in your kitchen the next time you are baking.

ORGANIZING AND PRESENTING SCIENTIFIC DATA

Now that you're familiar with taking scientific measurements and converting between them, we need to spend some time discussing how to record your data. Data must be collected and then organized and presented so that it can be analyzed. Remember that the goal of experimentation is to draw conclusions about your hypothesis by analyzing your data and looking for relationships between the independent and dependent variables. We'll start with data tables.

Data Tables

If you plan your data tables before you conduct your experiment, recording your data becomes easy and orderly. A good data table will have the following elements:

- A short, concise title that explains what the information in the table contains
- Column labels that explain what data is in each column
- Row labels that explain what data is in each row

An orderly data table will help you find any patterns in your data. Look at Figure 1.25 as an example. These are two data tables of a pendulum experiment similar to the one shown in Figure 1.10.

TABLE 1.4
Testing Length of a Pendulum Released from the Same Spot

Length (m)	Mass (g)	Trial 1 Time for 10 Full Swings (s)	Trial 2 Time for 10 Full Swings (s)	Trial 3 Time for 10 Full Swings (s)	Average Time for 10 Full Swings (s)
1.0	45	19.7	20.1	20.3	**20.0**
0.8	45	17.0	16.9	17.0	**17.0**
0.6	45	14.7	14.8	14.7	**14.7**
0.4	45	11.8	12.1	12.0	**12.0**
0.2	45	8.5	8.4	8.2	**8.4**

TABLE 1.5
Testing Mass of a Pendulum Released from the Same Spot

Mass (g)	Length (m)	Trial 1 Time for 10 Full Swings (s)	Trial 2 Time for 10 Full Swings (s)	Trial 3 Time for 10 Full Swings (s)	Average Time for 10 Full Swings (s)
30	1.0	20.0	20.9	20.3	**20.4**
45	1.0	19.7	20.1	20.3	**20.0**
60	1.0	19.9	19.7	20.1	**19.9**
75	1.0	20.4	19.5	20.1	**20.0**
90	1.0	19.2	20.0	19.9	**19.7**

FIGURE 1.25
Data Tables of a Pendulum Experiment
Good data tables show all the trials conducted, have titles, and clearly show what data is collected including units.

Notice how each data table has a title that explains the data contained in the table. You can also clearly identify what data is contained in each row and column by their titles. Look over the titles and the data listed. Can you tell which variables where kept constant in each experiment? Well the table titles tell us that the pendulum balls were released from the same spot, so we know that the height of release was held constant. In Table 1.4, notice that the mass of the pendulum doesn't change, so that was held constant in that experiment while the length was the independent variable because it was intentionally manipulated. In the second experiment shown in Table 1.5, notice that the variable of length is held constant while the mass becomes the independent or manipulated variable. In both experiments the average time for 10 full swings is the responding or dependent variable.

Are you wondering why we took the average of 3 trials for each length or mass? That's a good question and an important point of science experiments. Whenever we do experiments it's always a good idea to do multiple trials. In other words, make the same measurement in your experiment many times (at least 3 times, but more is better). When we do multiple trials of the same experiment, we look to see if our data are consistent. If they are consistent, then we can be more confident that our data is reliable and resulted from our manipulated variable and not by some random event or measurement errors.

Now look at the data in Table 1.4—what do you notice? Hopefully you can see a pattern. As the length of the pendulum decreases, the average time it takes the pendulum to make 10 full swings also decreases. Check the data in Table 1.5. You should notice that as the pendulum mass increases, the average time for 10 full swings stays about the same. Seeing the data presented in an organized data table helps you to see patterns that you might miss otherwise.

Analyzing Data with Graphs

Another way that scientists look for patterns in data is to plot the data on a graph. In fact, plotting data on graphs helps scientists see the patterns in a visual way which helps them to analyze their data and make conclusions. There are several types of graphs that can be used depending on how you want to visualize your data. There are bar graphs, line graphs, and circle graphs to name a few. Let's look at these types of graphs and when to use them.

Bar Graphs

Bar graphs are one of the most common type of graphs. Bar graphs are used when you want to compare the differences between two or more groups or to show changes over time. For example, you can use a bar graph to show the temperature data collected over a given time period in two or more different cities as shown in Figure 1.26.

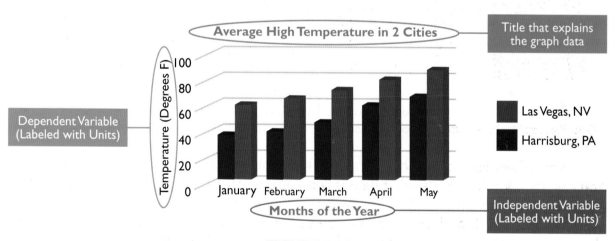

FIGURE 1.26
Bar Graph Comparing High Temperatures for Harrisburg, PA and Las Vegas, NV
Bar graphs compare two or more groups over time.

When you look at the bar graph in Figure 1.26, notice how easy it is to see which city has the highest temperatures. Bar graphs make visualizing the differences in data easy if the differences are large enough. Also notice that the bar graph has a title. The graph also shows the independent variable (in this case, time) on the horizontal axis of the graph while the average temperature (the dependent variable) is shown on the vertical axis of the graph.

Circle Graphs

Circle graphs (also called pie charts) are useful for showing how a part of something relates to the whole. In other words, they are good graphs to use when your data can be expressed as percentages of the total. For example, if you are trying to determine the composition of an unknown mixture of gases, you might show your results using a pie chart, such as the one shown in Figure 1.27.

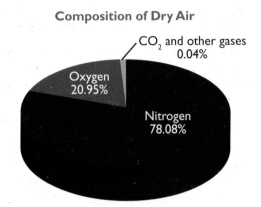

FIGURE 1.27
Pie Chart of the Composition of Dry Air
Circle graphs show how different parts of something relate to the whole.

In Figure 1.27, notice that the gases that make up the air we breathe are shown as a percentage. You can easily see that dry air is made up of more nitrogen than anything else. Isn't it interesting to realize that when you take a breath, only 20.95% of what you're breathing is oxygen! It was this percentage of air that Joseph Priestley identified as combustible in his candle burning experiments.

Line Graphs

If you conduct an experiment in which you hypothesize that when you change the independent variable the dependent variable will also change, then a line graph (also called a scatter plot graph) is the best graph to show your data. Line graphs are the most commonly used graphs in science experiments because they can show even the smallest patterns or trends.

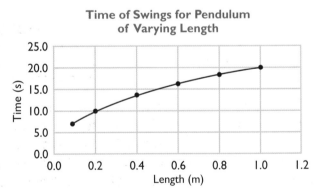

FIGURE 1.28
Line Graph of Swing Time for Pendulum of Varying Length
Line graphs can show even the smallest patterns or trends, so they are most common in science.

It is important to create the line graph correctly, though, so that the data can be properly analyzed. You should only use line graphs if your independent variable is quantitative data (data with numbers) just like the data shown in Figure 1.28. So how do you make good line graphs? Let's make one using the data shown in Table 1.4.

YOU DO SCIENCE

GRAPHING ACTIVITY

The key to correctly creating line graphs is to always graph the independent variable—the variable the experimenter controls—on the x-axis, and the dependent variable—the variable that responds when the independent variable is changed—on the y-axis. Remember that line graphs have an x-axis (horizontal axis) and a y-axis (vertical axis) and the points on the graph are the data points. With the data in Table 1.4 Figure 1.25, then, we would make our x-axis be the length of the pendulum because that was the variable the investigator manipulated. The y-axis would then be the average time for 10 full swings because that is the responding variable. Remember to choose a scale that will show all the data without being too large or too small. And finally plot the individual points of data. You should have a graph that looks like the one below.

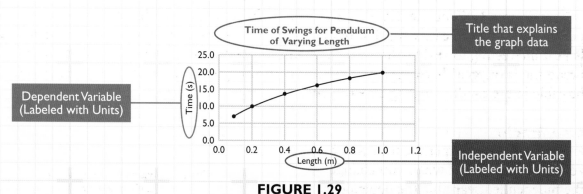

FIGURE 1.29
Important Parts of Line Graphs
Line graphs should have a title, labeled axes (with units), and scales that show all the data using as much of the space as possible.

   Notice that the data makes an almost straight line that rises to the right. This tells us that as the length of the pendulum increases, the time to complete 10 full swings also increases. This is called a direct relationship and relationships between variables in experiments are what scientists look for. When you take a physics course, you will be able to do more with this data and see even more detailed relationships than the one shown here. For now, look at Figure 1.29 to remind yourself of what to include in line graphs when you make them for this course. Then try the pendulum experiment yourself by completing Experiment 1.2. You should include making data tables and graphs to analyze your data. You will find more help for this in your student notebook.

think about this

RELATIONSHIPS IN GRAPHING. In science we look for relationships between variables, specifically between the independent and dependent variables. Graphing is a good way to visualize those relationships. There are three main relationships we look for: no relationship, direct, and inverse (or indirect) relationships.

No relationship occurs when you change the independent variable, but the depending variable does not change in response. Or the dependent variable changes even when the independent variable does not. Both situations tell us that the dependent variable does not depend on the independent variable. Graphs that show no relationship between the independent and dependent variables will look something like these:

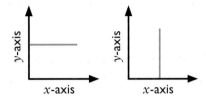

A direct relationship occurs when you increase the independent variable and the dependent variable also increases in response. Graphs that show a direct relationship between variables look like these:

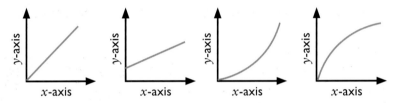

An inverse (also called indirect) relationship occurs when you increase the independent variable and the dependent variable decreases. Graphs that show an inverse relationship between variables look like these:

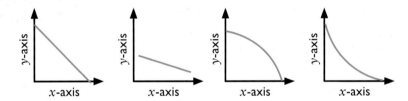

EXPERIMENT 1.2
PRACTICE COLLECTING AND ANALYZING DATA WITH PENDULUMS

PURPOSE:
To explore collecting and analyzing data using tables and graphs while investigating pendulums

MATERIALS:
- String
- Masking tape
- Stopwatch or other 30 second timer (If you have access to a timer you can set the timer for 30 s and do this experiment without a helper. Otherwise you will need a helper to track the stopwatch and tell you when 30 seconds has gone by while you count swings.)

1.12   0.121 L = _____ mL

1.   First find the conversion factor. According to Table 1.2 the prefix *milli-* means 0.001. So, we write the relationship, keeping the 1 with mL (since it is the prefix unit) and putting the definition of *milli-* with the base unit:

$$1 \text{ mL} = 0.001 \text{ L}$$

2.   Now you can start the problem. Always start a problem by writing down what you know (or are given in the problem) and write it in fraction form (place over 1):

$$\frac{0.121 \text{ L}}{1}$$

3.   Since we want to end up with mL, we must place L of our conversion factor on the bottom, so it cancels out. The problem looks like:

$$\frac{0.121 \text{ L}}{1} \times \frac{1 \text{ mL}}{0.001 \text{ L}} = 121 \text{ mL}$$

Given Unit	Conversion Factor	Wanted Unit

Thus, 0.121 L = 121 mL.

0.121 L = _____ gal

1.   In this case the conversion factor is given to you.

$$1 \text{ gal} = 3.78 \text{ L}$$

2.   Now you can start the problem. Always start a problem by writing down what you know (or are given in the problem) and write it in fraction form (place over 1):

$$\frac{0.121 \text{ L}}{1}$$

3.   Since we want to end up with mL, we must place L of our conversion factor on the bottom, so it cancels out. The problem looks like:

$$\frac{0.121 \text{ L}}{1} \times \frac{1 \text{ gal}}{3.78 \text{ L}} = 0.032 \text{ gal}$$

Given Unit	Conversion Factor	Wanted Unit

Thus, 0.121 L = 0.032 gal.

STUDY GUIDE FOR MODULE 1

1. Match the word with its definition.

   a. Quantitative observation   Tentative explanation for an observation

   b. Qualitative observation   A well-supported, in-depth explanation of a broad range of phenomena

   c. Hypothesis   Observations made using 5 senses

   d. Variable   Observations made using numbers or measurements

   e. Scientific Theory   Conclusions based on observations, previous knowledge, and available information

   f. Inference   Any factor that changes in an experiment

2. Which type of data can you graph, quantitative or qualitative data? Why?

3. Give the numerical meaning for the following prefixes:

   a. *centi-*

   b. *milli-*

   c. *kilo-*

4. If you wanted to make the following measurements, what metric unit would you use?

   a. mass

   b. length

   c. solid volume

   d. liquid volume

5. What is a conversion factor (give an example of one)? Why is it helpful in solving problems in physical science?

6. To convert 3.8 cm to m, you should multiply by which conversion factor?

   a. $\dfrac{1 \text{ km}}{1{,}000 \text{ m}}$ b. $\dfrac{1{,}000 \text{ m}}{1 \text{ km}}$ c. $\dfrac{0.01 \text{ m}}{1 \text{ cm}}$ d. $\dfrac{1 \text{ cm}}{0.01 \text{ m}}$

7.   In the SI symbol km, the "m" stands for ___?

    a. minute   b. meter   c. *milli-*   d. metric

8.   The SI unit for power is the watt (W). One kW must be equal to ___?

    a. 1,000 W   b. 1,000 m   c. 0.001 W   d. 0.001 m

9.   How many centimeters are in 1.3 meters?

10.   If a person has a mass of 75 kg, what is their mass in grams?

11.   A meterstick is 100.0 centimeters long. How long is it in inches (in)? (1 in = 2.54 cm)

12.   A small pool filled with water is being drained. Table 1.6 shows the volume of water remaining in the pool at different times.

    a. Make a graph showing how the volume of water changes as time passes. Include title, labeled axes, and units. (Hint: time is the independent variable.)

    b. What type of relationship between the independent and dependent variable does your graph show? (Hint: use the Think About This box to help you describe it.)

    c. Predict how long it will take for half the water to drain out. How long will it take to drain the pool?

TABLE 1.6	
Time (min)	Volume of Water Remaining in Pool (L)
0	1,000
5	950
10	900
15	850
20	800
25	750
30	700

CHEMISTRY— PROPERTIES AND STATES OF MATTER

We start our study of chemistry by discussing matter.

Matter—Anything that has mass and takes up space (has volume)

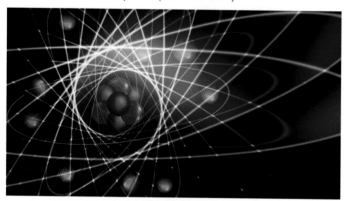

FIGURE 2.1
Matter Makes up Everything
We can't see what matter is made of, but we know it has mass and volume.

Natural Notes

When God created the world, He spoke everything into existence.

In the beginning God created the heavens and the earth.

Genesis 1:1

...all things were created through Him and for Him. He is before all things and in Him all things hold together.

Colossians 1:16b–17

So what is everything made of? In chemistry we call it matter, and that is what this module is about; the study of matter and how matter changes. We know from the scripture above that God holds everything together. Through your study of chemistry we hope you will catch a glimpse of the wisdom and power of the Creator as you learn more about what matter is and how matter behaves.

We classify types of matter according to how they behave. This allows us to group similar matter together. And if we know something about some members of a group, we can expect other members of the same group to be similar.

As we dig deeper into matter, an important fact for you to keep in mind is that matter can change. Sometimes the change does not cause one form of matter to transform into a different kind of matter. For example, cutting a sheet of paper in half changes the paper shape, but both halves are still paper. At other times, changes can form a different kind of matter altogether. An example would be what happened in Experiment 1.1 when you added the solid Alka Seltzer to water. The Alka Seltzer bubbled and disappeared as it combined with water. A new, different kind of matter was formed in this process. We'll investigate all this and more in this module.

IN THIS MODULE YOU WILL READ ABOUT THE FOLLOWING MAIN IDEAS:

- Classifying Matter
- Properties of Matter
- Changes in Matter

CLASSIFYING MATTER

Matter makes up everything, including everything you see in Figure 2.2. The plates are made of one kind of matter, the silverware out of another kind of matter, and the glasses still another kind of matter. How do we know this? Well, you can recognize the difference between the various types of matter shown in the figure based on their properties— characteristics that describe how one kind of matter is different from another.

Notice the glass in the figure. Glass is a kind of matter and has several properties that you can use to identify it. Glass is transparent, meaning you can see through it. Glass breaks easily, leaving sharp edges. The surface of glass is hard, and you shouldn't be able to detect any odor with glass. Now notice the white dishes in the photo. Like glass, these dishes are also hard, odorless, and can break leaving sharp edges. But unlike glass, the dishes are not transparent. They are opaque, meaning you

FIGURE 2.2
Matter Comes in Many Forms
How many different kinds of matter are pictured here?

cannot see through them. You can see that the glasses and dishes share some properties but differ in others.

What kind of matter do you think the silverware is made of? What properties helped you decide? What properties do the silverware share with the glasses and dishes? What properties are different? What about the napkins and the table cloth? How are they similar and different? One thing you can clearly see in the photo is that all the different kinds of matter share two properties. They all have mass and volume. Don't, however, confuse mass and volume.

Look at Figure 2.3. Both balloons are the same size, so they take up the same amount of space. In other words they have the same volume. However, the blue balloon is filled with water while the pink balloon is filled with air. Since air is lighter than water, the pink balloon has less mass than the blue balloon. Both balloons are made of the same kind of matter, but inside each balloon is different kinds of matter.

FIGURE 2.3
Matter Has Mass and Volume
The blue balloon is filled with water. The pink balloon is filled with air.
The balloons have the same volume but different masses.

In science, each kind of matter is called a substance. Think back to Figure 2.2. Each substance, whether glass, metal, or cloth, was composed of different parts in different combinations to make up the whole of the substance. This is called the substance's composition and it's what gives each substance its unique properties. Glass, metal, and cloth are all substances with different compositions and so different properties that you can use to identify them.

Scientists organize substances into groups based on their similar properties. The process of organizing information is called classification. You probably classify things into groups every day without even thinking about it. For example, you may classify foods by their taste—sweet, sour, bitter, or salty. You might group other things by their texture or colors. Dirty laundry for example, is often sorted by the washing instructions so that you only wash like colors together. Let's look at several ways matter is classified in science.

Pure Substances and Mixtures

One important way to classify matter is as either a pure substance or a mixture. Matter that cannot be separated into any other substance and always has exactly the same composition is classified as a pure substance. A mixture contains two or more substances. Sugar is an example of a pure substance and sweetened tea is an example of a mixture (Figure 2.4). Let's look at each of these 2 classifications in more scientific detail.

FIGURE 2.4
Pure Substances and Mixtures
How do you think you can tell the difference between a pure substance and a mixture?

Pure Elements and Compounds

A pure substance will always have exactly the same composition. Pure substances can be further classified into two categories. They can be either an element (el' uh ment), composed of only 1 type of atom, or a compound (kom' pownd), composed of 2 or more types of atoms.

Element—A pure substance that cannot be broken down into a simpler substance and contains only one type of atom

Atom—The smallest chemical unit of an element

Compound—A pure substance that contains two or more elements chemically joined in a fixed proportion

While millions of different substances exist, only 118 of these substances have been identified as elements. You can see many elements in common, everyday objects (Figure 2.5). For example, gold rings are made of the element gold. Soda cans are made from the element aluminum, and copper wire is made from the element copper.

FIGURE 2.5
Everyday Elements
Elements found in common objects

An element is a pure substance that cannot be broken down into a simpler substance. If you could cut the gold ring into smaller and smaller pieces, eventually you would end up with one teeny, tiny gold atom. An atom is the smallest unit of an element. Atoms are smaller than anyone can see with any microscope.

Sugar is another example of a pure substance; however it is composed of three elements: carbon, hydrogen, and oxygen. So how can you tell it's a pure substance? Well for one thing, each spoonful of sugar tastes equally sweet. Also no matter how small a granule of sugar you have, it will

FIGURE 2.6
Sugar
Every molecule of the compound sugar has the same composition.

always have the same composition (carbon, hydrogen, and oxygen) in the same ratio as every other granule of sugar. Sugar is an example of a compound. Remember, a compound is a pure substance containing two or more elements chemically bonded in a fixed proportion. So unlike an element, compounds can be broken down into their simpler substances (elements), but it is usually very difficult to do. Also once broken down, the elements will always be in the same ratio. Let's look at what I mean by that.

Water is another example of a compound. Water is composed of two elements, hydrogen and oxygen chemically bonded together. Each molecule of water will always have 2 atoms of hydrogen and 1 atom of oxygen in that fixed proportion.

Molecule—The smallest unit of a chemical compound, composed of two or more atoms bonded together

What is interesting about compounds is that they will have different properties than the elements that compose them. For example, both hydrogen and oxygen are gases at room temperature. Hydrogen is an explosive gas that can fuel a fire. Oxygen, although it is a gas we breathe to stay alive, it is also necessary for things to burn (combustion). The compound water, however, is an odorless, colorless, tasteless liquid at room temperature and doesn't burn at all. Liquid water has completely different properties than the two gases from which it is made.

Thinking back to our sugar example, one of the simplest sugar molecule (glucose) is composed of 6 carbon atoms, 12 hydrogen atoms, and 6 oxygen atoms (think of it like a glucose recipe). Some properties of the element, carbon, are that it is a solid at room temperature and looks a lot like charcoal (Figure 2.7). But once it is combined with the two gases, hydrogen and oxygen, in just the right proportions, it is a sweet treat! Because glucose always has the same recipe (or ratio of carbon, hydrogen, and oxygen atoms) we call that recipe glucose's chemical formula.

FIGURE 2.7
Carbon, Hydrogen, and Oxygen at Room Temperature
Combining these three elements in the right proportion produces sugar.

Mixtures

Like compounds, mixtures are composed of two or more substances. But unlike a compound, a mixture can vary in the proportions of its components because they are not chemically bonded together.

Mixture—Two or more substances mixed together but not chemically bonded

Mixtures may consist of elements, compounds, or both. Unlike a compound which has properties different from the properties of the substances that make it, mixtures will maintain the properties of the substances that make up the mixture. For example, sweetened tea is a mixture of tea, water, and sugar (Figure 2.8). The sweet tea is a liquid (a property of water), tastes like tea, and is sweet like sugar. Another point about mixtures is that the substances making up the mixture can be combined in many different ratios—they are not fixed. Some people like their tea sweeter than others, or with a stronger tea flavor than others. With mixtures you can change the ratio to whatever you want. This is not true about compounds.

We are surrounded by mixtures in everyday life. The air we breathe is a mixture of several invisible gases. It contains nitrogen, oxygen, carbon dioxide, water vapor (gaseous water) and several other gases. The amounts of some of the gases in air change when conditions change. For example, in areas where it is humid there is more water vapor in the air than in more arid regions of Earth, like desserts. Mixtures can contain varying amounts of substances.

FIGURE 2.8
Sweetened Tea is a Mixture
How strong or sweet do you like your tea?

Scientists classify mixtures by how well the substances making up the mixture are distributed throughout the mixture. Sometimes in a mixture of two (or more) substances, both substances remain visible. For example if you mix sand into a glass of water (Figure 2.9), both the sand and the water can be seen. When the parts of a mixture are noticeably different from one another, the mixture is classified as a heterogeneous (het uh roh gee' nee us) mixture. The term heterogeneous comes from two Greek words—*hetero*, meaning "different," and *genus*, meaning "kind." In Figure 2.9 you can clearly see that the sand and water are different substances in the mixture.

FIGURE 2.9
Sand in Water, a Heterogeneous Mixture
Can you see the different substances?

If you look again at Figure 2.8, notice how you can't see anything in the cup of tea except the caramel colored water. Since we're told that it's sweetened tea, we know it is a mixture of tea, water, and sugar. However, we can't see any of those individual substances. This type of mixture is classified as a homogeneous (hoh moh gee' nee us) mixture. *Homo* is the Greek word meaning "same." A homogeneous mixture appears to contain only type of substance because the substances are so evenly distributed that it is difficult to distinguish one substance in the mixture from another.

Homogeneous mixtures are most often made by dissolving one substance into another. When you place a spoonful of sugar into your hot tea and stir, the sugar dissolves producing a homogeneous mixture. The grains of sugar seem to disappear (see Figure

2.10). In reality they have spread out evenly throughout the whole mixture. You can tell this because each sip of the tea is equally sweet. When homogeneous mixtures are made this way, the resulting mixture is called a solution.

Solution—A homogeneous mixture made by dissolving one substance in another

The most common solutions are mixtures of water and something else. The substance that dissolves is the solute (sol' yoot). The substance which does the dissolving is the solvent (sol' vent).

FIGURE 2.10
Mixtures
Both beakers contain mixtures. Which mixture is a solution? How can you tell?

Solute—The substance in a solution that gets dissolved

Solvent—The substance in a solution in which the solute dissolves

In a sugar water solution, water is the solvent. Sugar is the solute. Review Figure 2.11 to see a visual representation of how a solution or mixture is different than compounds and elements.

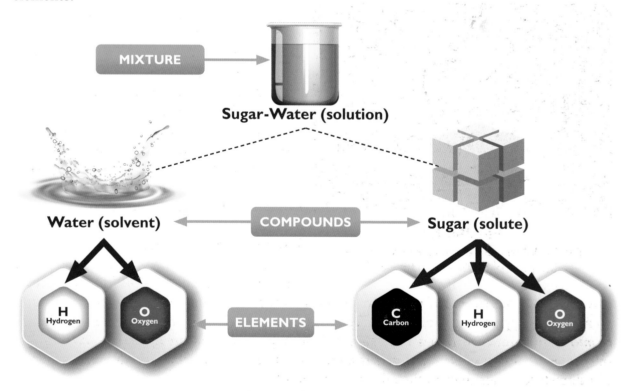

MIXTURE

Sugar-Water (solution)

Water (solvent) ⟷ COMPOUNDS ⟷ Sugar (solute)

H Hydrogen   O Oxygen   ELEMENTS   C Carbon   H Hydrogen   O Oxygen

FIGURE 2.11
Mixtures and Solutions
How are mixtures, compounds, and elements different?

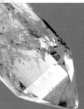

Before continuing on, review by completing On Your Own questions 2.1–2.3.

Solids, Liquids, and Gases

You learned about pure substances and mixtures in the last section. Another very useful classification scientists use is to order matter by the state or phase it is in at room temperature. For example, most of the substances you can see, smell, or feel around you exist as a solid, liquid, or gas—the most common states of matter on Earth. Look at the snow globe in Figure 2.12. The glass is a solid. The water inside is a liquid. And if you look at the top of the glass jar, you can see air bubbles—a gas. In this section we'll look at why the behavior and appearance of solids, liquids, and gases are so different.

Basically, matter can be classified as a solid, liquid, or gas depending on whether its shape and volume are definite or variable. Use the following definitions to help you remember how to classify matter into their appropriate states.

FIGURE 2.12
A Snow Globe
The solid jar contains both a liquid (water) and a gas (air). Why do you think the air bubble is at the top of the jar?

Solid—The state of matter in which a substance has a definite shape and a definite volume

Liquid—The state of matter in which a substance has a definite volume

Gas—The state of matter in which a substance has neither a definite shape nor a definite volume

Solid, liquid, and gas are known as the three states or phases of matter.

You might think this is a fairly simple way to organize matter, but can you explain how to categorize matter this way? You might notice, for example, that this book you are holding has a definite shape and takes up a certain amount of space or volume. The shape and volume of the book do not change. The jar in Figure 2.12 also has a definite shape and volume. Other materials, however, do not.

The water in the jar takes up space so it has a definite volume, however it has no definite shape. The water takes the shape of the jar. If the water was in a different container, its shape would change to that of the container. Therefore, liquids have a definite volume but do not have a definite shape, they conform to the shape of their container.

Now think about the air in the jar. Notice the bubbles of air at the top of the jar. Air is a mixture of several different gases. Like liquids, gases such as air, have no definite shape but take the shape of their container. In the snow globe the gas is shaped into bubbles, but the bubbles will change shape depending on the position of the globe. The air inside the globe does not take a definite shape. Unlike liquids, gases have no definite volume. What do we mean by that? Well, gases have volume, but their volume changes to match the volume of its container. If the volume of the snow globe was larger but the volume of the water and the solids inside the globe stayed the same, the volume of the air would change to take up the added space in the globe.

Let's look at another example of gases. Notice the balloons in Figure 2.13. The balloons are filled with the gas, helium. The helium inside each balloon takes the shape and volume of the balloon. No matter what shape balloon you have, the helium will take the shape of that balloon. If the volume of the balloon changes (sometimes happens if you leave a balloon in a very cold or very hot area), the volume of the helium also changes inside to match the volume of the balloon.

FIGURE 2.13
Helium Balloons
The helium gas inside the balloons takes the shape and the volume of their container. What shapes does the helium gas take in this picture?

Another interesting thing to note about gases is that they are less dense than liquids.

Density—The ratio of a substance's mass to its volume; defined by the equation:

$$\text{Density} = \frac{\text{Mass}}{\text{Volume}}$$

In the snow globe, the air bubbles will always be at the top because air is less dense than water. So when you shake the snow globe, the bubbles will always make their way back to the top of the globe. In Figure 2.13, the gas helium is less dense than air, so the helium-filled balloons will always rise.

Other States of Matter

Almost all matter on Earth exists in one of the three states of matter; solid, liquid, or gas. But most of the matter that we observe in the universe exists as a fourth state of matter called plasma (plaz' muh). This fourth phase of matter exists where temperatures reach millions of degrees Celsius—such as in stars or the sun.

In 1924 a physicist from India, Satyendra Bose, sent a paper about the behavior of light to Albert Einstein. Einstein thought Bose's work so important that he had it published and did more work on the topic himself. A year after reading Bose's paper, Einstein predicted that a fifth state of matter exists at extremely low temperatures—known as absolute zero or –273 degrees Celsius. In 1995 a group of scientists managed to make this state of matter in the laboratory and called it a Bose-Einstein Condensate (BEC). They won the Nobel Prize in Physics for the BEC in 2001. In July 2018, a BEC was created during an experiment aboard the International Space Station. This experiment holds the record for making the coldest object in space.

Kinetic Theory of Matter

Under normal everyday conditions, some things (like most metals) exist as solids, others (such as water) exist as liquids, and still others (such as helium) exist as gases. Scientists have studied why this is so and have developed a theory to explain it. This theory is called the kinetic (kih net' ik) theory of matter.

You might be wondering what the word *kinetic* means. Kinetic comes from the Greek word meaning "to move." Kinetic energy is the energy of an object in motion.

Kinetic energy—The energy an object has due to its motion

Think about what this means. Objects that move faster have more energy than objects that move slower. In other words, the faster an object moves, the more kinetic energy it has. You will learn a lot more about kinetic energy in a later physics module, but kinetic energy also explains the behavior of solids, liquids, and gases.

You see, the kinetic theory of matter states that all particles of matter are in constant motion, that particles move with greater energy as they become warmer, and that particles move with less energy as they become cooler. Examine Figure 2.14 which shows the particles that make up solid, liquids and gases. Notice how the particles in the solid are fixed but separated by a small amount of space. The forces of attraction keep the particles close to each other. The liquid particles are also attracted to each other, but they can move around each other making the space between them larger than in a solid. In a gas, the particles are really moving, so the attractions between molecules is very weak and the amount of space between the particles is relatively large.

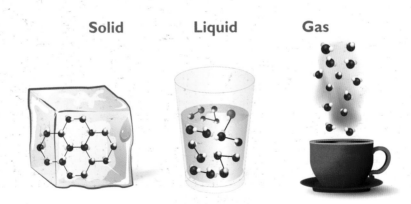

Solid   **Liquid**   **Gas**

FIGURE 2.14
Particles in the States of Matter
Solid particles vibrate around fixed positions but do not move within the substance. Liquid particles vibrate and are free to move around each other. Gas particles are in constant, random motion.

Solids

You may not think that the particles making up solids move at all, but they do! While the particles that make up a solid (whether molecules or atoms) are not free to move throughout the solid, they each vibrate back and forth or up and down around a fixed position. You can think about this like an auditorium full of people all sitting in their seats (Figure 2.15) watching a show. Each person is in a fixed seat and does not move from their seat during the performance. However, each person is free to shift positions within their seat. This is similar to how the particles of solids move (vibrate) without changing

FIGURE 2.15
Audience Members Are Like Solid Particles
Solid particles vibrate around fixed positions but do not move much just like audience members shift around on their seat, but do not move from their seats.

"seats." The particles of a solid have a small amount of kinetic energy because they vibrate back and forth, but their strong force of attraction keeps the particles in fixed positions within the solid. This explains why solids have a definite volume and a definite shape.

Liquids

The particles in liquids have even more kinetic energy than those of solids. The particles in liquids are not as closely packed together as the particles of solids (see Figure 2.14). Unlike solids where the attractions between molecules is very strong, the attraction between liquid particles is weaker and does not prevent the movement of the particles. You can think of this like a race (Figure 2.16). All of the runners are moving but a runner's path may be blocked by the positions of other runners around them and so they may group together for a time. After a bit, the group breaks apart.

FIGURE 2.16
Runners in a Race are like Liquid Particles
Liquid particles are always in motion but the attractions between particles does affect the movement of the particles.

This is similar to the behavior of liquids. There is a sort of tug of war in liquids between the constant motion of the particles and the forces of attraction between the particles. Generally, liquid particles have enough kinetic energy to keep from being held in a fixed position. Yet, they do not have enough energy to free themselves from the forces attracting the particles to each other. This tug of war explains the behavior of liquids. A liquid has a definite volume because forces of attraction keep the particles close together. However, a liquid does not have a definite shape because particles in a liquid have enough kinetic energy to flow to new locations around each other. Thus, it takes the shape of its container.

Gases

Gas particles have the most kinetic energy and are in constant, random motion. In fact, at room temperature, gas molecules can move, on average, at about 440 m/s—that's 990 miles per hour. But they rarely travel very far before they are colliding with each other or the walls of their container. After a collision the particles go off in other directions. Because the particles are moving so fast and moving apart after collisions, the attractions between the particles are too weak to have an effect. In fact, under ordinary conditions scientists ignore the forces of attraction between gas particles.

You can think about the movements of gas particles like the bouncers in a bounce house (Figure 2.17). Notice how there is a lot of room between the bouncers and they can bounce anywhere within the walls of the bounce house. If they bump into each other, they will each move away in another direction. This is similar to how gas particles behave. Even though there are many, many gas particles in a given space, (there are more than a million times a million times a million – or $10^6 \times 10^6 \times 10^6 = 10^{18}$ molecules – in 1 cubic centimeter of air) the particles are so tiny that over 99% of the volume is empty space! Because the particles of a gas are in constant motion, the gas is able to spread out and fill a container of any shape or size. So gases have no definite shape and no definite volume of their own.

One way you can understand how gas molecules move is to have someone

think about this

The term "average" is a math term that means it is a calculated central or middle value of a set of numbers. In the context of the speed of gases, it means that not all gas particles are moving at the same speed. Some gas particles will be moving faster than 440 m/s and some will be moving slower.

FIGURE 2.17
Bouncers in a Bounce House Are Like Gas Particles
Gas particles are in constant, random motion. Their speed, and collisions with each other and the walls of the container keep the forces of attraction from affecting them.

FIGURE 2.18
Diffusing Essential Oils
Gas particles, oil droplets, and water vapor diffuse throughout the room as this diffuser operates.

spray air freshener, perfume, or mist essential oils on the opposite side of the room from where you're standing (Figure 2.18). See how long it takes before you can smell the scent. What happens is that the gas particles of perfume move randomly through the air until they reach your nose. It often does not take very long for the scent to move across a rather large space so that everyone in the room can smell it. This is called diffusion (dih fyoo' zhun).

Diffusion—The natural (passive) movement within gases and liquids that spreads out particles from an area of higher concentration to an area of lower concentration

Diffusion occurs in both liquids and gas particles because both are constantly in motion. Diffusion, however, occurs faster in gases than in liquids. Can you think why that is? If you thought that it is because there is much more space between gas particles and that gas particles have more kinetic energy than liquid particles you are correct!

think about this

Diffusion, the movement of particles from an area of higher to lower concentration is an example of something called Brownian motion. Brownian motion simply means the random movements of particles in a fluid (liquid or gas) caused by the collisions with other atoms or molecules. This random movement of particles gets its name from the Scottish botanist Robert Brown. In 1827 Brown observed pollen grains moving randomly in water and described the motion even though he couldn't explain why it was happening. Have you ever seen dust motes randomly moving in the sunlight of a still room? That is Brownian motion.

Before you read on about another way to classify matter, conduct Experiment 2.1 to see how temperature affects kinetic energy. Remember we said that as temperature increases kinetic energy increases. That means that the molecules in solids, liquids, or gases will move even faster when they are warmer than they usually do. See how diffusion in a liquid is different at different temperatures. Then answer On Your Own problems 2.4–2.6.

EXPERIMENT 2.1
DIFFUSION AT DIFFERENT TEMPERATURES

PURPOSE:
To demonstrate the relationship between temperature, kinetic energy, and the rate of diffusion.

MATERIALS:
* 4 beakers (250 mL) or clear glass cups (The beakers or cups must be the same size.)
* Hot and cold water
* Ice
* Red, blue, green, and yellow food coloring
* Measuring cup
* Stopwatch (optional)
* A helper

QUESTION:
How does changing the temperature affect the rate of diffusion?

HYPOTHESIS:
Write your prediction of which beaker of water (steaming hot, hot, cold, or freezing) will have the faster rate of diffusion.

PROCEDURE:
1. Place a cup of ice cubes into a bowl and add a cup of water. Let sit for 10 minutes.
2. Add 2/3 cup of tepid (not too hot, not too cold) water to a beaker and let it sit to come to room temperature.
3. After 10 minutes remove the ice cubes and measure out 2/3 cup of the ice water and put into a beaker.
4. Fill another beaker with 2/3 cup very hot tap water.
5. Fill another beaker with 2/3 cup very cold tap water.
6. Place the beakers or cups side by side.
7. With your helper and at the same time, put three drops of yellow food coloring in the beaker of very hot tap water, three drops of red food coloring in the beaker of room temperature water, three drops of green food coloring in the beaker of very cold tap water, and three drops of blue food coloring in the beaker of ice water. It is important to add the food coloring to the beakers at the same time. Have your helper adds drops to 2 beakers at the same time that you add drops to the other 2 beakers. If you have a stopwatch start the timer as soon as the drops of food coloring enter the water.
8. Do not mix the water. Allow the drops of food coloring to spread on their own.
9. Observe which food coloring fills the water of the beaker first. (Diffusion is complete when the beakers are uniformly color.) Record your observations in your data table. If you have a stopwatch record the times that the food coloring spread throughout the beakers.
10. Pour the colored water down the drain and rinse and dry the beakers. Put everything away in its proper place.

CONCLUSIONS:
Explain your results by using the kinetic theory of matter and making connections to the text.

ON YOUR OWN

2.4 Explain how shape and volume are used to classify solids, liquids, and gases by matching the terms to their descriptions.

    solid   a substance that does not have a definite shape nor a definite volume but takes the shape and volume of its container

    liquid   a substance that has a definite shape and a definite volume

    gas   a substance that has a definite volume but takes the shape of its container

2.5 What is kinetic energy?

2.6 When a substance cools down, what happens to the speed of its particles?

Metals and Nonmetals

Another way that substances can be classified is into metal or nonmetal groupings. You are likely familiar with metals like copper, tin, iron, aluminum, silver, and gold. Can you think of some things each of these have in common?

Generally, metals are shiny. Metals are also good conductors of heat and electric current—especially copper and silver. And, except for mercury, metals are solids at room temperature. Most metals can be flattened into sheets or formed into thin wires.

Most nonmetals, on the other hand, are poor conductors of heat or electricity. They also can vary in appearance. For example, glass, some plastics, and polished wood can be shiny. But for the most part, nonmetals are dull in appearance.

FIGURE 2.19
Metal vs. Nonmetal
With which spoon would you rather stir a pot of hot soup? Why?

PROPERTIES OF MATTER

Being a good conductor of heat and electricity is a property of metals. All matter has certain properties that define how it is similar or different from other substances. For example you've already learned that all matter has mass and takes up space. These are two properties that all matter share. In science we can describe substances based on their physical properties and their chemical properties.

Physical Properties

We use physical properties to observe and describe matter. A physical property is any characteristic of a substance that can be observed or measured without changing the composition or the identity of the substance. Besides mass and volume, physical properties include appearance (color, texture, size), odor, conductivity, density, hardness, malleability (flexibility), viscosity (gooeyness), and melting and boiling points.

Appearance and Odor

These two properties are the easiest to understand. Picture three clear glasses on the counter. One contains orange juice, another contains tomato juice, and the third contains pomegranate juice (Figure 2.20). Even without the fruit in the picture to give you a hint, you probably could tell which juice is which just by the color of each juice. If you could smell each juice, that would be another way to tell them apart. Of course each juice also has a distinct taste that is unique. But in most cases in scientific investigations, tasting is not a way to test physical properties of substances.

FIGURE 2.20
Three Different Juices
You can tell the difference between these three juices by their appearance—their color and texture—and their distinguishing smell.

Conductivity

Look back at Figure 2.19. Which spoon would you choose to stir a pot of hot soup—a metal spoon or a wooden spoon? Since metal is a good conductor, it is easy to see that the part of the metal spoon handle that you are holding will eventually get as hot as the soup if you stir long enough. The ability of a substance to allow heat to flow through it is called conductivity. Metals are good conductors and so they have high conductivity. If a substance is a good conductor of heat it is usually also a good conductor of electricity.

Nonmetals, such as the wooden spoon, are not good conductors so they have very low conductivity. This is why you should choose wooden spoons to stir hot things on the stove. It will not conduct the heat from the pot to your hand.

Density

Density is another physical property unique to each substance. Remember that density is the ratio of the mass of a substance to its volume. It is usually measured in grams per cubic centimeters (g/cm³). For example, water has a density of 1.0 g/cm³. Aluminum has a density of 2.7 g/cm³. What can this tell us? Well, if you had one cubic centimeter each of water and aluminum, the water would have a mass of 1.0 g and the aluminum would have a mass of 2.7 g. If you doubled the volume of water to 2 cubic centimeters, the mass of the water would be 2.0 g. Likewise if you had 2 cubic centimeters of aluminum, the mass of aluminum would double to 5.4 g.

The density of a substance is constant—it never changes. If you cut a gold coin in half, both halves would have the same density as the whole coin—19.3 g/cm³, the density of gold. The density of a substance does not depend on the amount of the substance. The density of aluminum is always 2.7 g/cm³ whether the aluminum is in a 2 gram thin piece of foil or in a 250 g grill grate (Figure 2.21).

FIGURE 2.21
Aluminum Foil and Grill
Whether aluminum is in foil or a grill grate, it's density will always be 2.7 g/cm³.

Things that are less dense will float on top of things that are more dense. Likewise, denser substances will sink in less dense substances. Explore how densities of different substances affect each other by completing Experiment 2.2.

EXPERIMENT 2.2
EXPLORING DIFFERENT DENSITIES

PURPOSE:
To explore the different densities of several solids and liquids.

MATERIALS:
- Paper towels
- 4 beakers (250 mL size) or pint sized, large mouth glass jars
- 1 large quart jar
- 4 spoons
- Measuring cup
- Water
- Vegetable oil
- Corn syrup
- Rubbing alcohol (isopropyl alcohol)
- Red and blue food coloring
- 4 Small cork pieces
- 4 Pennies
- 4 Grapes (or raisins)
- 4 Small paper clips
- 4 Marbles
- 4 Washers
- 4 Ice cubes

QUESTIONS:
How do the densities of the solids compare to the densities of the liquids? Will the solid objects sink, float, or be suspended in each of the liquids? How do the densities of the liquids compare with each other?

HYPOTHESIS:
Write your prediction of what will happen when you place a grape (or raisin), paper clip, small cork, penny, marble, and washer into each of the four different liquids. Will they sink, float, or be suspended? Write your prediction of what will happen when you mix the four liquids together. Will they mix, or will they separate into layers? If they separate, what order will they be in?

PROCEDURE—PART 1, DENSITY COMPARISONS OF SOLIDS IN FOUR LIQUIDS:
1. This is a messy experiment. Place enough paper towels down on your work surface to cover the area under the 4 beakers to help with clean up. Set the four beakers on your paper towels.
2. Add 150 mL (or 2/3 cup) water to the first beaker.
3. Add 150 mL (or 2/3 cup) vegetable oil to the second beaker.
4. Add 150 mL (or 2/3 cup) corn syrup to the third beaker.
5. Add 150 mL (or 2/3 cup) alcohol to the fourth beaker.

6. Add the cork pieces to each beaker. Do they sink, float, or become suspended in each liquid. Record your observations in the data section of your student notebook.
7. Take the cork pieces out with a spoon.
8. Repeat steps 6 and 7 with the pennies.
9. Repeat steps 6 and 7 with the grapes.
10. Repeat steps 6 and 7 with the paper clips.
11. Repeat steps 6 and 7 with the marbles.
12. Repeat steps 6 and 7 with the washers.
13. Repeat steps 6 and 7 with the ice cubes.
14. Remove the ice cubes from the four beakers.

PROCEDURE—PART 2; DENSITY COMPARISONS OF FOUR LIQUIDS:

15. Place a few drops of blue food coloring in the water and stir. Place a few drops of red food coloring in the alcohol and stir.
16. Slowly and carefully pour each of the liquids into the quart jar in this order—corn syrup, water, vegetable oil, and alcohol. Let them settle. Record your observations.
17. Add one of each type of solid, one at a time, and record where the solid stays within the column of liquids. Is it where you expected from the first part of the experiment?
18. Remove all of the solids. Dispose of all the liquids down the sink. Clean up and put everything away in its proper place.

CONCLUSIONS:

Were your predictions correct? Did the solid objects sink, float, or become suspended as you thought? Why do you think the solid objects acted the way they did? Did the liquids arrange themselves in the order that you predicted? What does this tell you about the densities of the liquids and solids you tested? Place the substances in order of their densities from highest to lowest.

Because density is unique to each substance, it can be used to identify substances. Silver and stainless steel can look similar (Figure 2.22), both are shiny, silver metals. However, their densities are different and so can be used to tell them apart. Table 2.1 gives the densities of some common substances.

FIGURE 2.22
Silver and Stainless Jewelry
A silver ring (left) and stainless earrings (right) have similar qualities but distinctly different densities.

TABLE 2.1	
Densities of Common Substances at 25°C	
Substance	**Density (g/cm³)**
Gold	19.3
Mercury	13.6
Lead	11.3
Silver	10.5
Copper	8.9
Steel	7.9
Iron	7.86
Aluminum	2.7
Bone	1.80
Sugar	1.59
Sea water	1.03
Water at 4°C	1.00
Ice at 0°C	0.92
Pine wood	0.50
Balsa wood	0.12
Oxygen	0.0013
Hydrogen	0.00009

FIGURE 2.23
A Carved Silver Ring
Malleable metals can be carved and hammered into interesting shapes.

Hardness

Hardness is a physical property that helps determine how a substance might be used. For example, some elements such as silver and gold, are rather soft. Have you ever bent a silver spoon? Other elements, such as titanium and tungsten are very hard.

One way to compare the hardness of two substances is to perform a scratch test. A scratch test is done to see which substance can scratch another. The hardest material is a diamond which is made of carbon. What's interesting is that another form of carbon, graphite—the stuff in pencils that we write with—is one of the softest materials.

In 1812, a German geologist named Friedrich Mohs developed a scale of hardness by observing which minerals were able to scratch other minerals. This scale is named after him and is called the Mohs scale of mineral hardness. We'll look at this physical property a bit more in a later module.

Malleability

Malleability (mal ee uh bil' uh tee) is the ability of a solid to be hammered, pressed, or rolled into thin sheets without shattering. Most metals are very malleable. Aluminum can be formed into thin sheets of aluminum foil. Gold and silver can be pressed and hammered or chiseled into many different forms. Notice the ring in Figure 2.23. It is a ring carved and hammered from silver.

Other materials are not very malleable. Glass, for example, will shatter when hit with a hammer or any other hard object. Have you ever broken a glass window when a ball accidentally hit it? Solids that shatter when struck are brittle rather than malleable.

Viscosity

Have you ever heard the saying that something is "as slow as molasses in January?" If you have then you know they meant that the thing they were describing is very slow. Molasses is a liquid at room temperature but if you pour molasses, it flows *very* slowly. If your molasses is cold (as it would be sitting out in January in most northern states) it would pour even more slowly. The physical property of a liquid to resist flowing is called viscosity (vih' skah sih tee).

Thick liquids, such as molasses, honey, and corn syrup have high viscosity. Thin liquids such as water and vinegar have low viscosity. When liquids are heated their viscosity usually decreases. This is why many people heat their maple syrup before putting it on their pancakes. It makes the syrup flow more easily and keeps the pancakes warm.

FIGURE 2.24
Molasses
Molasses has high viscosity compared to water. It resists flow especially when cold.

Melting and Boiling Points

Every pure substance has a unique temperature at which it changes from a solid to a liquid. This temperature is called its melting point. Solid water, or ice, has a melting point at 0 °C (32 °F). Sometimes the melting point is also referred to as the freezing point because freezing and melting occur at the same temperature. Think about water. Water freezes into ice at 0 °C, but ice also melts back into water at 0 °C. We'll talk more about this phenomenon a bit later in the module.

Every pure substance also has a unique temperature at which its liquid form changes into its gaseous form. This is called its boiling point. Again think of water. At 100 °C (212 °F) liquid water begins to boil and is changed to steam. If you boil the water long enough all of the water will be converted to water vapor—the gaseous form of water. The whole time that the water is boiling and being changed to a gas, the temperature stays at 100 °C. Look at Table 2.2 to see the wide range of melting and boiling points of some common substances.

TABLE 2.2 Melting and Boiling Points of Common Substances		
Substance	Melting Point (°C)	Boiling Point (°C)
Oxygen	−218.8	−183.0
Alcohol (isopropyl)	−88.5	82.5
Octane (found in gasoline)	−56.8	125.6
Water	0.0	100.0
Acetic acid (found in vinegar)	16.6	117.9
Aluminum	660.0	2,467
Table salt	800.7	1,465
Gold	1,064.2	2,856

We've covered the main physical properties scientists use, however there may be a few others you'll discover as you complete this course. How are these physical properties used? Well, every day people use physical properties of substances to solve different types of problems. For example, when you make spaghetti by boiling the noodles, you have a mixture of noodles and water. Before adding the sauce you must remove the water from the noodles. To do this you can use a colander which allows the water to pass through separating the noodles. Thus physical properties (like particle size) are used to separate substances in a mixture. Physical properties are also used to help identify a substance. Crime scene technicians, for example, use the physical properties of unknown substances to identify the type of paint or lipstick found at a crime. Physical properties are also used to help people choose the right materials for a specific job. You wouldn't want to make a tool out of a metal that didn't have a high boiling point if you plan to use the tool to stoke a fire. You can see that classifying substances by their physical properties has some very helpful uses. Remember, physical properties are the characteristics of a material that we can use to observe or measure in a substance without changing its composition. Review what you've learned about physical properties by completing On Your Own problems 2.7 and 2.8.

ON YOUR OWN

2.7　Which has the greater density—200 grams of silver or 600 grams of aluminum? Hint: Use Table 2.1.

2.8　Why are the melting and boiling points of a pure substance considered a physical property?

Chemical Properties

What physical properties can you observe about the candles in Figure 2.25? Notice they are floating on water which tells us their density is less than the density of water. If you have seen candles before, then you know that they are hard, but are easily scratched by even harder materials.

Unlike the physical properties of matter that you read about in the last section, chemical properties are those properties that are measured or observed when matter undergoes a change and becomes an entirely different kind of matter. The candles in Figure 2.24 are mainly made of paraffin wax which is a mixture of compounds con-

FIGURE 2.25
Floating Candles
What physical properties do these candles possess?

taining the elements carbon and hydrogen. When the candles begin to burn, the carbon and hydrogen in the paraffin combine with oxygen in the air and are changed into carbon dioxide and water vapor—two new compounds. The ability to burn is a chemical property because new substances are formed. There are two main chemical properties that we will study, flammability and reactivity.

FIGURE 2.26
Burning Wood
What new substances are formed when wood burns?

Flammability

The ability of matter to burn in the presence of oxygen is called flammability. When substances burn, they combine with oxygen and new substances are formed. Some substances are more flammable than others.

Look at the wood burning in Figure 2.26. Notice how the wood appears white in places. This is one of the new substances formed (ash). When oxygen in the air combines with the carbon and hydrogen in the wood, ashes, carbon dioxide, water vapor, and other gases are formed. After all the wood has burned, all that will be left are these new substances.

Flammable materials usually require a spark or a source of heat to ignite it. This is a very good thing since our air contains about 21% oxygen. If flammable materials could ignite just by being in the presence of oxygen, then things would catch fire all the time! Flammable materials include wood, paper, gasoline, fabric, etc. Non-flammable substances are substances that do not easily burn in the presence of oxygen even with a spark to ignite them. Non-flammable materials include water, nitrogen, brick, glass, etc.

Reactivity

Reactivity is the ability of matter to combine chemically with other substances to form new substances. Some kinds of matter are extremely reactive. Other kinds of matter don't react at all.

You read about oxygen reacting with flammable substances in the presence of heat or a spark in the section above. Oxygen is a highly reactive element. Helium, on the other hand, almost never reacts with any other substance. You can see how oxygen reacts with iron metal and water in Figure 2.27. The iron chain shows signs of rust, a reddish-brown substance. Rust makes the chain brittle and weaker, so it is more likely to break.

When the air is humid, it contains more water vapor. Since there is water and oxygen in the air on humid days, anything made of iron or steel can rust just by sitting outside. Rust can destroy bicycles, cars, bridges, ships, etc. All of these must be treated and have signs of rust removed to keep them in working order.

FIGURE 2.27
A Rusty Chain
Rust forms when oxygen reacts with iron in the presence of water.

CHANGES IN MATTER

Substances change. Just as matter has physical properties and chemical properties, changes to matter can be physical changes or chemical changes. As you might expect, physical changes are the changes in the properties of a substance without changing the composition of the substance. Chemical changes occur when the composition of the substance is changed, and new substances are formed. This occurs because of chemical reactions.

Physical Changes

Physical changes involve changes in one or more of a substance's physical properties. For example, you can cut paper into small pieces or shred it into long ribbons (Figure 2.28) but it is still paper. You haven't changed the composition of the paper. Likewise, when you step on an empty can and crush it, you've caused a physical change. You've changed the shape of the can, but it is still a can. Physical changes can occur in several different ways.

FIGURE 2.28
Physical Change
Cutting paper is a physical change because the composition of paper stays the same.

Volume and Density Changes

In the can-crushing example above, you changed the volume of the solid can by crushing it. Changes in volume are physical changes. You can also change the volume of a substance by changing its temperature. Generally, when you increase the temperature of a substance its volume increases; and when you decrease the temperature of a substance its volume decreases.

Gases change volume and density with temperature. This may seem confusing since you just read that the density of a substance never changes. Well both statements are true. Let me explain. The density of a substance never changes for a given temperature. For example, water has a density of 1.0 g/cm³ at 4 °C . However, the density of water at room temperature (about 22 °C) is 0.998.2071 g/cm³. Now that is close enough to 1 that we don't need to worry about the difference. But solid water at 0 °C has a density of 0.9150 g/cm³. This is why ice floats on water. And steam, water in gas form at 100 °C , has a density of 0.000596 g/cm³, which is why you always see steam rise quickly into the air. So you see density is constant for each substance at a given temperature. That is why the title of Table 2.1 listed the temperature of 25°C for the substance. But water and ice listed the temperature associated with their densities separately.

Now let's look at how the volume and density changes of air in hot air balloons allow them to fly. Notice that the bottom of a hot air balloon is not tied off with a knot as a rubber balloon you might blow up would be. This means the air is free to move in and out of the balloon. As the air inside a hot air balloon is heated (Figure 2.29), the air molecules start moving faster (their kinetic energy increases). As the gas molecules speed up, the air inside the balloon expands and some of the molecules escape the balloon. Since the volume of the balloon doesn't change, the decrease in the mass of molecules inside the balloon causes the density to decrease because density = mass/volume. Since the density of the heated air inside the balloon is less than the density of the air outside the balloon the balloon rises. This is where we get the saying that hot air rises.

FIGURE 2.29
Volume and Density Changes
The way a hot air balloon works demonstrates how physical changes to volume and density occur.

If you had a little trouble following the reasoning for the density decreasing as the mass decreased, that's okay. It might help you to see it using numbers. So follow along in the example to see if it makes a little more sense. Then you can try some density science at home in the You Do Science activity that follows.

EXAMPLE 2.1

Let's use easy numbers to define the mass and volume of a hot air balloon. Now keep in mind that the true numbers would be very different, but this is just to show you how the relationship between mass, volume, and density works. So for our purposes we'll use the following data for a hot air balloon sitting on the ground before liftoff:

$$mass = 4.0 \text{ g}$$

$$volume = 4.0 \text{ cm}^3$$

With the mass and volume above what would the density be?

$$Density = \frac{mass}{volume} = \frac{4.0 \text{ g}}{4.0 \text{ cm}^3} = 1 \frac{g}{cm^3}$$

Now let's say when the air in the balloon is heated, the gas molecules speed up and the gas expands so that half of the air molecules leave from the bottom of the balloon. This means that the volume of the balloon is the same (the balloon is the same size as it was before, so it holds the same amount of air), but the new mass is 2.0 g.

What would the new density be?

$$Density = \frac{mass}{volume} = \frac{2.0 \text{ g}}{4.0 \text{ cm}^3} = \frac{1.0 \text{ g}}{2.0 \text{ cm}^3} = 0.5 \frac{g}{cm^3}$$

You can see the density is now ½ of what it was originally. Since the density of the heated air inside the balloon is now lower than the air surrounding the balloon on the outside, the balloon rises. This is similar to the objects that floated in Experiment 2.2.

YOU DO SCIENCE
Volume and Density Change Activity

Think about a balloon filled with air. In fact, if you have a balloon you can try this for yourself. Measure the circumference of a balloon that you've blown up with air. Place the balloon in a sink filled with about 3-4 inches of water and note how it sits on the water. Then place it in the freezer (or refrigerator but it will take longer) for an hour. When you take the balloon out of the freezer, remeasure the circumference. What you should find is that the balloon has shrunk. It may even look a bit shriveled. What happened? Well you know that there is the same amount of air in the balloon because the balloon was tied shut. This means the mass of air inside the balloon stayed the same. So as the temperature decreased, the air molecules inside the balloon slowed down (their kinetic energy decreased) and as a result the volume that the air occupied decreased. This is why you see the balloon shrivel a bit. If you put the balloon back in the sink of water, you should notice it sits a bit lower than it did before. This is because when the mass stays the same but the volume decreases, the density increases. Remember density equals mass divided by volume. As the balloon warms up again to room temperature, you should notice the balloon goes back to its original size.

Liquids and solids also increase in volume when temperature is increased, although they are not as easy to see. If you look at telephone or electric power lines on very hot days you will notice them sagging a bit. That is because the increased temperature causes the molecules to expand. These same power and phone lines will tighten up again in very cold weather. Concrete sidewalks are poured in sections with space in between to allow the molecules to expand on hot days and contract on cold days. Even with the spaces, you will often notice concrete sidewalks and pavement cracking and crumbling due to the changes in weather temps.

Phase Changes
What happens to a piece of chocolate when you leave it in your car on a warm day? The chocolate starts melting from a solid to a liquid (Figure 2.30). This is called a phase change. A phase change is a reversible physical change that occurs when a substance changes from

FIGURE 2.30
Melting Chocolate
Chocolate melts from a solid to liquid when heat is added.

one state of matter to another. In Figure 2.30 two states of the chocolate are present at the same time. There is still some solid chocolate and there is also liquid (although very viscous) chocolate.

Study Figure 2.31. A state of matter is shown at each corner of the triangle. We've already discussed how water freezes or melts at 0 °C and boils, changing to water vapor (a gas) at 100 °C. It should not surprise you to learn that the process of changing a solid into a liquid is called melting and that occurs when heat is added (temperatures rise). Likewise the process of changing a liquid to a solid is called freezing and that occurs when heat is removed (temperatures lower). This is shown on the bottom of Figure 2.31 where the blue arrow indicates heat being removed and the red arrow indicates added heat. It's important to remember that the temperature of a substance does not change during a phase change.

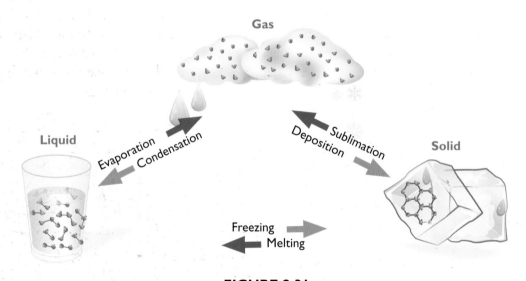

FIGURE 2.31
Phase Changes
Most substance on Earth exist in the 3 phases, solid, liquid, and gas.
Can you give examples of the six ways substances can change from one phase to another?

You should also be familiar with the left side of Figure 2.31. Have you noticed puddles after a rain shower on a warm day and several hours later the water was gone? The water disappeared due to the process of evaporation (ih vap' uh ray' shun). Evaporation is the change in phase from liquid to gas. Notice the red arrow on evaporation in Figure 2.31. Adding heat will speed up the phase change from liquid to gas.

Condensation (kon' den say' shun) is the reverse phase change from gas to liquid. Think about setting a glass of ice-cold juice outside on a warm day. In just a few minutes you will notice drops of water on the outside of the glass. Where did these droplets of water come from? Water vapor in the warm air comes in contact with the exterior surface of the cold glass. The cooling of the water vapor in the air leads to condensation.

Occasionally substances will go directly from the solid state to the gaseous state without becoming a liquid first. This process is called sublimation (sub' lih may' shun). Have you ever seen dry ice? Dry ice is the common name of solid carbon dioxide. Dry ice is used to ship food items across the country because it is very cold, and it doesn't melt to a liquid as it warms. Notice that sublimation required the addition of heat energy.

The opposite process is called deposition (dep' eh zih' shun). Deposition occurs when a gas changes directly into a solid without first changing into a liquid. You can see by the red arrow that heat energy must be removed for deposition to occur. If you've ever seen frost develop on a cold car window, you've seen deposition occur. When the water vapor in air comes in contact with the cold window it loses enough heat energy to go from gaseous water vapor to solid frost.

Solubility Changes

Temperature changes can cause changes in solubility (sol' yoo bil itee). Solubility is the ability of one substance to dissolve in another. Solubility is a physical change. Gases, such as carbon dioxide, are very soluble and can easily dissolve in water. You have experience with dissolved carbon dioxide if you've ever drank a carbonated soda. The colder the soda is the more dissolved gas it can hold. That is why you want to store carbonated beverages in the refrigerator if you want to keep them carbonated longer. If you leave a carbonated beverage open in a warm room, the beverage soon becomes flat because the warm liquid cannot hold as much of the carbon dioxide which escapes into the room.

Oxygen is another gas that is soluble in water. However, much smaller amounts of oxygen dissolve in water than does carbon dioxide. It is a good thing that the small amount of oxygen can dissolve in water because that is how fish and other aquatic life get the oxygen they need to survive (Figure 2.32). Fish depend on the oxygen dissolved in water the same way land animals depend on oxygen in the air.

In some streams or lakes the water becomes warmed by excess heat release by power companies or other industry manufacturing. What do you think happens to the amount of oxygen dissolved in the water when the temperature rises? Just like what happens when your soda warms, the

FIGURE 2.32
Dissolve Oxygen
Underwater plants and animals can survive because oxygen is dissolved in the water of rivers, lakes, and oceans.

water in the stream cannot hold as much oxygen. This is called thermal pollution and can have hazardous effects on the fish and other aquatic life. There are guidelines limiting the amount of thermal pollution permitted to protect aquatic ecosystems.

Some solids will also dissolve in water. But unlike gases, solubility of most solids increases with temperature. Maybe you have seen mineral deposits around hot springs. Look at the photo in Figure 2.33. This is a picture of Mammoth Hot Springs in Yellowstone National Park. Notice the rust colored and salt-like deposits on the rock formations. The hot water below the surface of the Earth dissolves large quantities of minerals—in this case a mineral called calcium carbonate. The hot solution cools as it reaches the surface of the Earth. The calcium carbonate (the salty-white looking substance) is not as soluble in the cooler water, so some of the dissolved minerals leave the solution. The calcium carbonate is deposited as the water evaporates and a limestone rock called travertine is formed. If you're wondering why some of the travertine is rust colored, the color comes from certain algae that live in the hot springs. The algae contain pigments that color the rocks.

FIGURE 2.33
Mineral Deposits
The rust colored and salt-like deposits on the rock formations are minerals deposited as the hot water cools.

Chemical Changes

All of the changes discussed in the last section were physical changes. Remember that in physical changes no new substances are formed. Chemical changes, however, are changes that produce new substances. Recognizing chemical changes can sometimes be tricky so let's start with some obvious ones.

When you bake a cake you add eggs, flour, oil, and other ingredients, then mix them together. At this point you have a mixture. But then you put it in the oven and the added heat causes the batter to start to change. The batter mixture becomes a new substance, a solid cake with totally different properties than those of the batter ingredients. Much of our food is prepared using chemical changes. Cooking meat, toasting bread, and frying eggs are all examples of chemical changes. Once we eat these foods, our bodies use chemicals to break them down and more chemical changes occur. Our bodies use the components from the food to make new cells and produce energy for activities. So what are some clues for recognizing chemical changes?

A Change in Color

Look at Figure 2.34. Notice how the roofs of some of the bird houses are shiny copper and some of them are blueish-green. This process of color change is because of a chemical reaction between the copper atoms and the carbon, hydrogen, and oxygen atoms in moist air. A new compound, called copper hydroxycarbonate, is formed and it has a blueish-green color.

You may have noticed other color changes that indicate a chemical change has occurred. A shiny silver necklace will become darker and dull when exposed to air for very long. The wood burning in Figure 2.25 show areas of black and gray which are changes in color indicating a chemical change. Rust forming on steel or iron changes the color and makes the substance more brittle. A change in color is often a clue that a chemical change has produced one or more new substances.

FIGURE 2.34
Colorful Chemical Change
When copper is exposed to water vapor and oxygen it forms a thin blueish-green coating called a patina.

think about this

One of the most famous examples of colorful chemical change is the Statue of Liberty (Figure 2.35). Over time the statue turned blueish-green because hydrogen, oxygen, and carbon atoms from various substances in the air combined with copper atoms to make copper hydroxycarbonate. When the Statue of Liberty was first given to the United States in 1885 by France it was shiny copper colored—like the copper roofs in Figure 2.34. It took about 30 years for the patina to form and for the statue to look like we see it today. It was decided to leave the Statue of Liberty with her patina rather than cleaning the copper because the blueish-green layer of patina actually protects the copper underneath. Plus we're all used to seeing her this color now.

You may wonder why the flame stays such a shiny gold color and hasn't turned blueish-green. Well the original torch was replaced in 1984 and now is on display in the Statue of Liberty Museum. In 1986 a new copper flame covered in 24 karat gold replaced the damaged original flame. The reflective gold does not react with moist air the same way that copper does and so will remain shiny.

FIGURE 2.35
The Statue of Liberty

Production of a Gas

Think back to Experiment 1.1 when you put Alka Seltzer in water. What observations did you record? You should have recorded that the tablet started bubbling. The bubbles (the production of a gas) resulted from a chemical reaction between the solid Alka Seltzer tablet and the water (Figure 2.36). The production of a gas is a clue that a chemical change has occurred.

Maybe you have made a volcano for one of your classes. You mix vinegar and baking soda together and immediately a reaction occurs in which lots of bubbles are formed. Just as in the Alka Seltzer experiment, bubbles of carbon dioxide form immediately when the two substances combine.

When you bake a cake with baking powder you can also see the formation of bubbles indicating a chemical change. Baking powder is a mixture of baking soda and one or more other substances that react when wet. The cake rises as it bakes because of the bubbles of carbon dioxide produced during the chemical change.

FIGURE 2.36
Bubbles Show Chemical Change
Production of a gas (bubbles) are a clue that a chemical change occurred.

Formation of a Solid

Another clue that a chemical change has occurred is the formation of a solid, called a precipitate (prih sip' uh tayt). You can try this in your kitchen! Make a cup of tea (a light herbal variety will show this best) and add a squeeze of lemon juice and some milk. What you should notice is the milk curdling and forming small bits of white solids that separate out of the tea (Figure 2.37).

When the acid of the lemon juice mixes with the milk, the proteins in the milk react with the acid and a chemical change occurs. The shape of the proteins is altered which causes them to clump together forming the precipitate.

Review this section by completing Experiment 2.3 and then complete On Your Own problems 2.9–2.12.

FIGURE 2.37
Precipitates Indicated a Chemical Change
When milk curdles in the presence of an acid, precipitate forms.

EXPERIMENT 2.3
CHANGES IN MATTER

PURPOSE:
To explore physical and chemical changes in matter.

MATERIALS:
- A beaker or a small, clear glass (like a juice glass)
- Baking soda
- Tap water
- A 9 volt battery (the kind that goes in a radio, smoke detector, or toy. DO NOT use an electrical outlet, as that would be quite dangerous! A 1.5 volt flashlight battery will not work.)
- Two 9 inch pieces of insulated wire. The wire itself must be copper.
- Scissors
- Some tape (preferably electrical tape, but cellophane or masking tape will work.)
- A spoon for stirring
- Eye protection such as goggles or safety glasses

QUESTION:
What types of clues indicate physical and chemical changes are occurring?

HYPOTHESIS:
Write what you predict will happen when you add electricity through a copper wire to a solution of baking soda and water.

PROCEDURE:
1. Fill the beaker or small glass ¾ full of tap water.
2. Add a teaspoon of baking soda and stir vigorously.
3. Use your scissors to strip about a quarter inch of insulation off both ends of each wire. The best way to do this is to put the wire in your scissors and squeeze the scissors gently. You should feel an increase in resistance as the scissors begin to touch the wire. Squeeze the scissors until you feel that resistance and then back off. Continue squeezing and backing off as you slowly turn the wire round and round, as shown below:

Be careful. You can cut yourself if you are not paying proper attention! You will eventually have a cut that goes through the insulation all the way around the wire. At that point, you can simply pull the insulation off. It will take some practice to get this right, but you can do it. Make sure there is at least ¼ inch of bare wire sticking out of both ends of the insulation.

4. Once you have stripped the insulation off both ends of each wire, connect the end of one wire to one of the two terminals on the battery. Do this by laying the wire over the terminal and then pressing it down. Secure it to the terminal with a piece of tape. It need not look pretty, but the bare wire needs to be solidly touching one terminal and not in contact with the other terminal.

5. Repeat step 4 with the other wire and the other battery terminal. Now you have two wires attached to the battery, one at each terminal. **Do not allow the bare ends of these wires to touch each other!**

6. Immerse the wires in the baking soda/water solution that is in the small glass so that the bare end of each wire is completely submerged. It doesn't really matter how much of the insulated portion of the wire is immersed; just make sure that the entire bare end of each wire is fully submerged. Once again, don't allow the ends to touch each other. In the end, your experiment should look something like this:

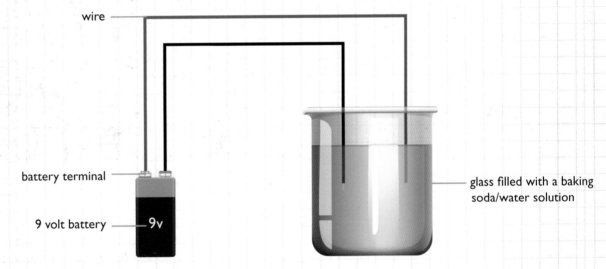

7. Look at the bare ends of the wires as they are submerged in the baking soda/water solution. What do you see? Well, if you set everything up right, you should see bubbles coming from both ends. If you don't see bubbles, most likely you do not have good contact between the wires and the battery terminals. Try pressing the ends of the wire hard against the terminals to which they are taped. If you then see bubbles coming from the submerged ends of the wire, then you know that electrical contact is your problem. If not, then your battery might be dead. Try another one.

8. Once you get things working, spend some time observing what's going on. Notice that bubbles are forming on *both* wires. Record your observations in the data section of your student notebook.

9. Allow the experiment to run for about 10 minutes. After that time, pull the wires out of the solution and look at the bare ends. What do you see? Well, one of the wires should not look very different from when you started. It might be darker than it was, but that should be it. What about the end of the other wire? It should now be a different color. What color is it? Write that color down in the data section.

10. If you let the experiment run for 10 minutes, it's very possible that your solution became slightly colored. Write in your data section whether or not that happened and what color, if any, the solution became.

11. Looking at the wire that changed color, trace it back to the battery and determine the terminal (positive or negative) to which it is attached. Write that in your laboratory notebook as well.

12. **Clean up:** Disconnect the wires from the battery, dump the solution down the sink, run tap water to flush it down the drain, and wash the glass thoroughly. Put everything away.

CONCLUSION:

Explain your observations in terms of the clues for chemical and physical changes you learned about. Can you say a chemical reaction occurred? Explain how you know.

ON YOUR OWN

2.9   What is an important difference between physical and chemical changes?

2.10 Explain why cutting your hair is a physical change.

2.11 When you put a tablespoon of butter in a frying pan and forget about it, it melts and then burns in the pan. Explain what is a physical change and what is a chemical change?

2.12 If you spill bleach on a red shirt a white spot appears where the bleach hit the shirt. Is this change chemical or physical? How can you tell?

SUMMING UP

You've learned a lot about how matter is classified and what properties different types of matter possess. You've also read about what types of changes matter can undergo and how to tell the difference. As we mentioned before, we will build on what you learn in one module in future modules. So, take some time to review the answers to the On Your Own problems and work through the Study Guide questions so you are sure you understand the main concepts. Then you'll be ready for the module test.

ANSWERS TO THE "ON YOUR OWN" QUESTIONS

2.1 Pure substances are substances that have a fixed composition. They can be either elements or compounds. A pure substance always has the same properties because its composition never changes.

2.2 Properties of mixtures can vary because the composition of a mixture is not fixed. Sweet tea is an example. The more sugar you add (to a point) will cause the tea to taste sweeter. Note: examples may vary.

2.3 If salt was added to tea instead of sugar, the tea would be salty rather than sweet. The salt-tea is a homogeneous mixture also known as a solution.

2.4 solid   a substance that does not have a definite shape nor a definite volume but takes the shape and volume of its container

liquid   a substance that has a definite shape and a definite volume

gas   a substance that has a definite volume but takes the shape of its container

2.5 Kinetic energy is the energy an object has due to its motion.

2.6 As a substance cools, the speed of movement of its particles slows down.

2.7 Since the density of a substance is not dependent on the amount of the substance, according to Table 2.1 silver has the greater density.

2.8 Melting and boiling points are unique for each pure substance and they can be measured or observed without changing the composition of the substance. That is the definition of a physical property.

2.9 Physical changes only affect physical properties of a substance and do not change the composition of the substance. Chemical changes create new substances with different physical properties than the original substances. Chemical changes produce new substances while physical changes do not produce new substances.

2.10 When you cut your hair you are not changing the composition of the hair, just the size of the hair. Because you are not changing the composition, it is a physical change.

2.11 Melting is a physical change. Burning is a chemical change.

2.12 Because the bleach caused the red shirt to change color, the change is most likely a chemical change.

STUDY GUIDE FOR MODULE 2

1.   Match the word with its definition.

a. Solution   The substance in a solution that does the dissolving

b. Solute   A homogeneous mixture made by dissolving one substance in another

c. Solvent

d. Solid   The state of matter with a definite volume but not a definite shape

e. Liquid   The substance in a solution that gets dissolved

f. Gas   The ratio of a substance's mass to its volume

     The state of matter with a definite shape and definite volume

g. Density   Movement in gases and liquids that spreads out particles

h. Diffusion   The state of matter with no definite shape nor definite volume

2.   Complete the following diagram.

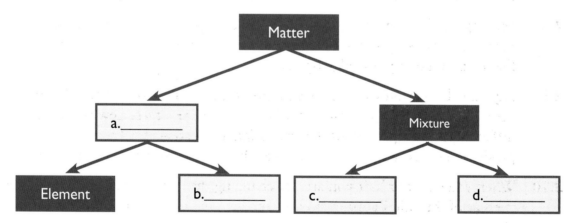

3.   All matter takes up space and

a. dissolves in water.

b. has mass.

c. has a definite shape.

d. is visible.

4. Which of these substances is not an element.

    a. water   b. hydrogen   c. aluminum   d. iron

5. All pure substances

    a. contain only one type of atom.

    b. can be broken down into simpler substances.

    c. have a variable composition.

    d. have a fixed composition.

6. The three common phases of matter used to group substances are

    a. solvents, solutes, and solutions.

    b. elements, compounds, and mixtures.

    c. solids, liquids, and gases.

    d. metals, plastics, and wood.

7. Salty water is best classified as a(n)

    a. element.   b. compound.   c. mixture.   d. plasma.

8. Which of the following is not an example of a physical property?

    a. melting point   b. reactivity   c. density   d. hardness

9. A property metals have in common is that they

    a. conduct electricity.

    b. take the shape of their container.

    c. dissolve in water.

    d. can be broken down into other substances.

10. Which action involves a chemical change?

    a. making sweet tea

    b. freezing water into ice cubes

    c. shredding paper

    d. baking a cake

11. Evaporation and condensation

    a. are chemical changes.

    b. both result in the production of a liquid from a gas.

    c. involve a change of phase.

    d. are identical processes.

12. What is the difference between an element and a compound?

13. Put a check mark in the correct column to indicate if the property is a physical property or a chemical property.

Property	Physical Property	Chemical Property
a. red color		
b. flammability		
c. density		
d. solubility		
e. melting point		
f. odor		
g. hardness		
h. reacts with water to form a gas		
i. malleability		

14. Put a check mark in the correct column to indicate if the change is a physical change or a chemical change.

Change	Physical Change	Chemical Change
a. salt dissolves in water		
b. a penny is cut in two		
c. an acid and a base react to form a salt, water, and heat		
d. water is heated and turns to steam		
e. copper reacts with moist air to form a patina		
f. iron rusts		
g. ice melts		
h. milk curdles		
i. volume of air decreases when the temperature decreases		

15. Would breaking down a compound into its elements be a physical or chemical change? Why?

16. Why is viscosity classified as a physical property?

CHEMISTRY—ATOMIC STRUCTURE AND THE PERIODIC TABLE

Look at the photograph of snowflakes in Figure 3.1. There are 12 different designs in that one photo and yet each one is perfectly ordered around a central point. Each snowflake is unique and yet each one is formed in an orderly pattern. The fact that there are observable patterns suggests purposeful direction in the process by which each snowflake is formed. In fact there is beauty and order all around us in creation. This is no surprise since God brought beauty and order to the universe, from the smallest unseen particles to the largest cosmos. Through our study of physical science we can discover the patterns of creation. In this module, you will

FIGURE 3.1
Snowflakes
Snowflakes show diversity and order at the same time.

Natural Notes

Studying atoms is a bit like studying air. We can't see air, but we know it exists when we feel the wind blow. When we see the branches moving on a tree, we can infer that the invisible wind is blowing in the same direction as the branches are moving.

Studying the structure of atoms poses a similar problem. Atoms are so small that we can't see them with even the strongest microscopes. But much like how we study air, scientists have been able to study atoms through indirect evidence. Perhaps you will feel called to make creation connections with your studies:

By faith we understand that the universe was formed at God's command, so that what is seen was not made out of what was visible.
Hebrews 11:3

As you progress in your scientific studies, you will learn that much of the universe is made up of things that are not visible with the naked eye. And even further, everything that you do see is composed of what is unseen – those tiny invisible atoms.

begin to see how everything we see (from plants to stars) as well as things we can't see (like air) is composed of just 90 naturally occurring building blocks known as atoms. We will also see that looking into the ordered nature of atoms will show us creation.

IN THIS MODULE YOU WILL READ ABOUT THE FOLLOWING MAIN IDEAS:

- A History of the Atom
- Modern Atomic Theory
- Organizing Elements: The Periodic Table
- Representative Groups

A HISTORY OF THE ATOM

As you learned in the last module, matter can be classified into one of the following groups—pure substances (elements and compounds) or mixtures. You also learned that atoms are the building blocks of matter. Atoms are the smallest particle of an element that has all the properties of the element.

Although no one has seen an atom, we have a lot of evidence of their existence and behavior. In fact, Figure 2.2 is a colored scanning transmission electron micrograph of silicon atoms (center, yellow) in a sheet of graphene (carbon-like atoms). New microscopes like the scanning transmission electron microscope (STEM) are making it easier to see atoms. What do I mean? Well the STEM passes electricity across a thinly sliced sample and measures the interactions between the electricity and the atoms of the sample. The microscope sends that data to a computer, which uses complicated mathematical equations from a theory called "quantum mechanics" (we'll learn a bit more about that later) to calculate what the atoms on the surface of the object should look like. The computer then creates a virtual image of the sample and adds color to enhance the quality of the image.

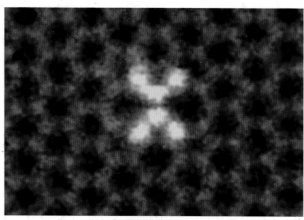

FIGURE 3.2
Silicon Atoms in Graphene Sheet
In 2013, researchers from Oak Ridge National Laboratory in TN, used a scanning transmission electron microscope to show the 'dancing' motions of 6 silicon atoms (center, yellow) in a sheet of graphene (an isomer of carbon).

So what you're really seeing in Figure 3.2 is the result of a *calculation* that comes from a *theory* about how electricity flows and interacts with parts of atoms under certain circumstances. Thus, *if* the theory is correct, and *if* the computer calculation is correct, *then* you are seeing *a representation* of atoms on the surface of the substance examined with the STEM. Now I personally think that both the theory and the calculations are correct, so I think that what you see in Figure 3.2 (excluding the color, which was added) is probably a good representation of how the silicon and graphene atoms are arranged. So even with such modern tools as the STEM, we have not seen atoms. However, if the computer calculations are correct, we can see the representation of atoms. Let's look now at how we got this far—and maybe you will begin dreaming of how a career in chemistry would help you advance our knowledge even further!

Ancient Atomic Models

The history of the atom begins almost 2,500 years ago—around 400 B.C. The Greek philosopher, Democritus, pondered what would happen if a piece of matter, such as a grape, was cut into smaller and smaller pieces. He reasoned that there would come a point at which the grape could not be cut any smaller. He called this smallest, uncuttable piece *atomos*. The word atomos roughly translates as uncuttable or indivisible and it where the term atom comes from.

Democritus's philosophy of matter being composed of atoms held until about 100 years later when Aristotle, another Greek philosopher, began debating the topic. Keep in mind that the idea of experimentation was not yet developed, so scholars of this time argued or debated their ideas. The philosopher who argued the best was considered right, even if his argument was wrong. As one of the most influential philosophers of the time, Aristotle rejected Democritus's idea of atoms, thinking it was ridiculous. Aristotle argued that a substance could be divided indefinitely and that there was not a limit to how small the resulting particle could be. Therefore there could be no such thing as an atom. Aristotle upheld the view of yet another Greek philosopher, Empedocles, who reasoned that everything we see is made up of four elements. These elements were earth, water, air, and fire (Figure 3.3). The four elements were further connected by four qualities—hot, cold, wet, and dry. He argued that everything on the Earth was made up of these four elements in varying proportions. He also suggested that one substance could become another through the quality that they had in common. For example, earth can become fire through the action of dryness or fire could become air through the action of heat.

Aristotle also argued that there was no limit to the number of times a substance could be divided. So unlike Democritus, his view was that there was no fundamental, indivisible particle of matter. Unfortunately, Aristotle's powers of persuasion were great and most people accepted Aristotle's view on the structure of matter for about 2,000 years. This is why alchemists of the Dark and Middle Ages were continually trying to turn metals into gold. They reasoned, based on Aristotle's theory, that if all substances possess the same four elements in different proportions why couldn't one substance be transformed into another.

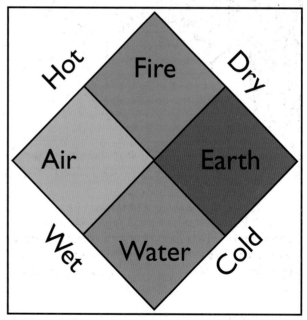

FIGURE 3.3
Aristotle's View of Matter
Aristotle argued that all substances were built from only 4 elements (air, fire, earth, and water) which were a combination of 4 qualities (hot, dry, cold, and wet).

think about this

You are holding a science textbook that has been thoroughly researched and methodically created to give you a solid course in Physical Science. While we can look back in history and think that the methods used to expand scientific knowledge were quite a bit different from how we now use the established scientific method, we must keep in mind that 2,000 years from now, students may think the same about us! Science advances as we build on the knowledge of those who came before us and use technology to give us tools to investigate our ideas. In the times of Democritus and Aristotle all they had available to use were their abilities to observe nature. Don't discount the value of such powers of observation. It is the beginning of the scientific method. Because of the technology available today, we sometimes reject the knowledge that others considered correct, but that is all part of the rigorous process of testing and expanding our understanding of creation. Science isn't just knowing what is true; it is also knowing what isn't true, as well as acknowledging that we don't have the capabilities (yet) to answer some questions.

Dalton's Atomic Theory

Aristotle's erroneous ideas persisted into the late 1700s. How could a wrong scientific idea last that long? Good question. The most likely explanation is that the language of science was Greek—because that was the language of the Ancient Greek philosophers. As the world became more Latin under the Roman Empire and then entered the Middle Ages (AD 476–1500), much of the scientific and philosophical knowledge of the Greeks was lost. The Greek texts were rediscovered during the Renaissance (AD 1500–1700) and began to be translated. It was during the late 1700s when scientists such as Lavoisier began to suggest that Aristotle had been seriously wrong.

So, it's not until 1808 that science fully revives Democritus's ideas and returns to the atom. John Dalton (Figure 3.4), an English chemist and teacher, began experimenting and making observations on the behavior of gases in physical and chemical changes. After making many observations and gathering evidence for the existence of atoms, Dalton developed a theory to explain why elements in a compound always join in the same proportion. Dalton proposed the following points in his theory.

- All matter is made of particles called atoms, which cannot be divided into smaller particles. Atoms cannot be created or destroyed.

- All atoms of the same element are identical in mass and properties, and the atoms of different elements have different masses and properties.

- Atoms from two or more different elements join together to form compounds in chemical reactions.

- Chemical reactions rearrange atoms, but in specific compounds the atoms of the different elements always combine in the same way.

FIGURE 3.4
John Dalton
John Dalton developed the first atomic theory.

Dalton's atomic theory was the first complete attempt to describe matter in terms of atoms. Dalton based his theory on the law of conservation of mass and the law of constant composition.

Law of conservation of mass—Matter cannot be created or destroyed, but it can change forms

Law of constant composition—Samples of a pure compound always have the same elements in the same mass proportion

Evidence for the law of conservation of mass was meticulously documented by Antoine Lavoisier in the 1770s as he experimented on gases. Remember him from module 1 and his work on debunking the phlogiston hypothesis? Well he also conducted experiments to see if total mass would change or stay the same when two substances were combined. He found that when he combined two gases, or broke down water into hydrogen and oxygen, the total mass before always equaled the total mass after the experiment. In fact Lavoisier gathered so much evidence to support this law that it is often called Lavoisier's Law.

Look at Figure 3.5. This is a modern experiment providing evidence for the law of conservation of mass. Notice in the beakers on the left that there is a clear, liquid substance in each of the 2 beakers. Now look at the two beakers on the right which are the beakers after the one clear liquid was poured into the beaker of the other. Notice that one is empty and the other contains a cloudy, milky liquid. We learned in module 2 that a color change like that shown in the figure indicates a chemical change. But look at the mass shown on the mass scale that the beakers are sitting on. Both before and after the chemical reaction, the scale indicates the exact same mass providing more evidence to support the law of conservation of mass.

FIGURE 3.5
Conservation of Mass Experiment
The mass before the two liquids are combined equals the mass after they are combined.

Discovery of the law of constant composition is credited to Joseph Proust, a French chemist, who lived around the same time as Dalton was conducting experiments. Proust conducted experiments in which he found evidence that chemical compounds always have a specific composition. In other words if you chemically mix hydrogen and oxygen gases together (and add energy) you will always get water with the elements in a ratio of 2 hydrogen atoms to 1 oxygen atom. This is exactly what Dalton was finding in his own experiments.

Take a moment to think about how the process of science occurred here. Lavoisier uses a scientific law to make predictions on how matter will behave. The law describes the behavior but doesn't explain it. He then conducts experiments and records his observations providing more evidence that supports the scientific law. Likewise, Proust conducts experiments and they provide evidence for the law of constant composition. Neither man can explain why mass is conserved or composition is constant in his experiments, but he can see that every time he conducts an experiment his predictions are validated. Then 30 years after Lavoisier, and independent of Proust, Dalton does some research and starts experimenting knowing what each of these laws predicts. Through his experiments he starts to formulate some reasons for how mass can be conserved and how pure compounds have constant compositions. He does many more experiments based on his hypothesis of how the atoms behave in chemical reactions. After conducting many experiments that validate all of his predictions, he develops a theory. Remember that a theory must explain the data from many experiments by many scientists attempting to test the theory. Because Dalton's atomic theory met this goal, it became widely accepted.

FIGURE 3.6
Dalton's Atomic Model
Each type of atom is represented by a solid sphere with a different mass.

Now as it turns out, years later, some of Dalton's atomic theory was revised. Dalton's theory proposed that the atom is the smallest indivisible unit of an element. He used solid, wooden spheres of different sizes as models of atoms of elements (Figure 3.6) . We will see that evidence has accumulated that disproves that idea. But instead of discarding all of Dalton's atomic theory, that part of the theory was revised to account for the new discoveries you'll read about next. So most of Dalton's atomic theory is still accepted today. This is a great example of how science works!

Thomson's Atomic Model

In 1897 an English scientist, J. J. (Joseph John) Thomson conducted some experiments with gas tubes and electric currents to learn more about atoms. The diagram of the tube shown in Figure 3.7 is similar to the one Thomson used. During his experiments, Thomson observed that electricity consists of flowing, negatively charged particles. He further observed that all matter gives off small negatively charged particles.

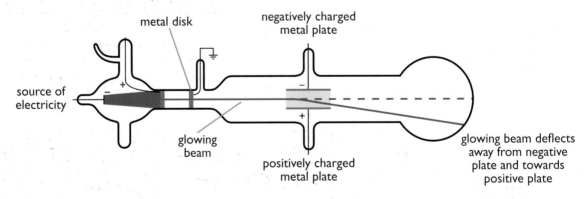

FIGURE 3.7
Thomson's Experiment
Thomson used a sealed tube of gas that allowed the glowing beam of electrons to be seen when the current was on. When the beam passed through 2 charged plates it would always bend toward the positive plate.

This discovery was important because many scientists during Thomson's time thought that electric current was positively charged and behaved like light rays rather than particles. Thomson's experiments showed that all matter has negatively charged particles which is why the beam was attracted to (or bent towards) the positive plate.

The results of Thomson's experiments also showed that negative particles from any substance are all alike but smaller than an atom. No matter what metal disk Thomson used, the negative particles were identical and always had the same mass. He determined that these negative particles could not be the smallest, fundamental unit of matter because they were all identical regardless of the element. Remember Dalton's theory states that different elements have different atoms with different properties which was still supported by all the data. But Thomson's experiments were the first ones that provided evidence that atoms are made of even smaller particles. Thomson concluded that the negative particles must be parts of the atom. The negatively charged particles were later called electrons.

Plum Pudding Model

Thomson knew that atoms are neutral in charge. This means that an atom is neither negatively nor positively charged. So he questioned how an atom could be neutral and yet contain negative particles. He reasoned that there must be an equal amount of positive charge in the atom. Thomson described the atom as similar to a traditional English desert—plum pudding—in which the plums are scattered throughout the pudding. If you're like me and have never seen plum pudding, you can think of it more like a blueberry muffin model in which the negatively charged blueberries are randomly spread throughout the positively charged muffin dough. Figure 3.8 is an illustration of Thomson's plum pudding model and a blueberry muffin. The red sphere (and the muffin) represent the positively charged mass of matter, and the smaller yellow spheres (and the blueberries) represent the negatively charged particles evenly scattered throughout.

Before reading on, review what you've learned so far by completing On Your Own questions 3.1–3.3.

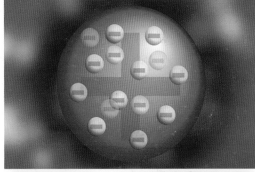

FIGURE 3.8
The Plum Pudding Model
Thomson's atomic model where the negatively charged particles are spread evenly throughout a positively charged mass of matter.

ON YOUR OWN

3.1   What is the difference between Democritus' and Aristotle's view of matter?

3.2   Why was Dalton's model of the atom changed after Thomson's experiments?

3.3   What evidence from Thomson's experiment led him to conclude that the glowing beam contained negatively charged particles?

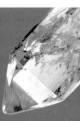

Rutherford's Atomic Model

Have you ever conducted an experiment only to have the results not turn out as you expected? Remember in module 1 that we talked about how in science unexpected results do not mean failure. In fact unexpected results are quite often the spark for new discoveries. That's just what happened to Ernest Rutherford, a physicist from New Zealand who had been a student of J. J. Thomson in England.

FIGURE 3.9
Ernest Rutherford
Rutherford received the Nobel Prize in Chemistry in 1908 for his work with radioactive substances.

It happens that in 1899 Rutherford, who was friends with Pierre and Marie Curie, was researching radioactive materials. He discovered that certain elements (such as uranium) emit fast-moving positively charged particles that he called *alpha (α) particles*. He found that alpha particles could penetrate just about anything. This sparked a lot of questions for more experiments, one of which was how could he use alpha particles to learn more about the structure of the atom.

By 1909 Rutherford was working with two assistants, Hans Geiger (he later developed the Geiger counter that measures radioactivity) and Ernest Marsden. They created a clever experiment to see what they could discover about the atom. Remember when developing an experiment, you want to be able to accurately test your predictions. In this case, Rutherford was working from Thomson's plum pudding model of the atom.

Rutherford predicted that if they sent a beam of alpha particles through a thin gold foil that the alpha particles would all go straight through (Figure 3.10). He reasoned that since the alpha particles were very fast moving and very positively charged they would not be affected (or only minimally affected) by the positively charged mass of the gold atom. This might seem counter to what you'd expect since the positive alpha particle and the positive mass of the gold atom should repel each other. But think about it the way Rutherford did. Because the positive charge of the gold atom was spread out over the whole area of the atom, the charge in any one spot of the atom would be very weak. So even though the gold atom had a positively charged mass, the charge was so weak that it would hardly deflect the speeding, highly concentrated positive charge of the alpha particles. Using our blueberry muffin example—it would be like shooting a bullet through the muffin. The muffin (atom) would hardly change the path of the bullet (the alpha particle).

Now Rutherford had to figure out how to observe where the alpha particles went after they hit the gold foil. This is where his clever creativity came into play. Rutherford knew that a substance called zinc sulfide

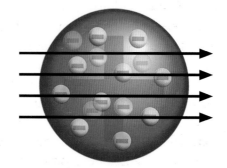

FIGURE 3.10
Rutherford's Prediction Using Thomson Model Atom
If the plum pudding model of the atom is correct then alpha particles should go straight through the gold atoms.

would show a small flash of light when hit by scattered alpha particles. So Rutherford, Geiger, and Marsden built an apparatus similar to the one shown in Figure 3.11.

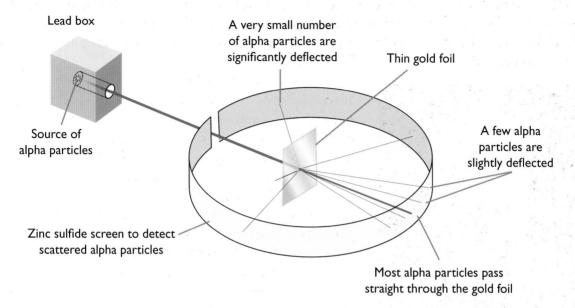

Lead box

A very small number of alpha particles are significantly deflected

Thin gold foil

Source of alpha particles

A few alpha particles are slightly deflected

Zinc sulfide screen to detect scattered alpha particles

Most alpha particles pass straight through the gold foil

FIGURE 3.11
Rutherford's Gold Foil Experiment
Rutherford expected the paths of the positively charged alpha particles to only be slightly affected by the gold foil they were aimed at. But more particles than expected were affected and some bounced back at angles larger than 90 degrees.

When Rutherford and his team began analyzing their data, they were surprised at the results. Remember they did not expect to see any alpha particles bending too far from a straight path through the gold foil. But that was not what they found. Although most of the alpha particles did go straight through the foil, more than expected were bent off course—and some were deflected back at greater than 90 degrees from the foil! It seemed Thomson's model of the atom no longer explained all of the evidence. Their results led to more questions. What could cause a small number of the alpha particles to deflect greatly from the straight path, a few to deflect slightly, and most to go straight through as expected?

Rutherford's analysis of the data from the gold foil experiment led him to formulate his own atomic model in 1911. He reasoned that the mass of the atom could not exist like the pudding in plum pudding if there were even a few very deflected alpha particles. Rather there must be a tiny but concentrated positively charged mass. A dense mass with a concentrated positive charge located in the center of the atom could account for the results he found (Figure 3.12). He called this center mass the nucleus and his model is often called the nuclear model of the atom.

Rutherford interpreted his results based on this new model. The alpha particles that passed straight through

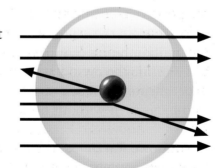

FIGURE 3.12
Rutherford's Interpretation of Results
The atom must be mostly empty space but have a concentrated positively charged center that greatly deflects alpha particles when hit straight on.

the gold foil did not come close to a nucleus of any of the gold atoms. Those alpha particles that were slightly bent away from the straight path came close enough but not too close to the nucleus of a gold atom so that it was slightly repelled. And those alpha particles that were bent more than 90 came very close to a nucleus and were greatly repelled. Rutherford's model is shown in Figure 3.13. He suggested that the smaller (less mass) electrons circle the positively charged nucleus (containing most of the atom's mass) in orbits much like the planets orbit the sun. For these reasons Rutherford's model is also called the nuclear model or the planetary model. In this model you can see how most of the atom is empty space.

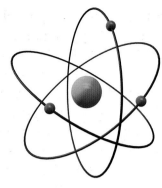

FIGURE 3.13
Rutherford's Model
Rutherford's nuclear model of the atom shows a tiny, heavy, positively charged nucleus with electrons orbiting.

Rutherford continued to research the atom and radioactivity and in 1919 he named the positive charge in the nucleus. He called it a proton. At that time Rutherford also suggested that the nucleus contained particles that had mass but no charge. However, it was Rutherford's student, James Chadwick, who in 1932 discovered this massive, neutral particle and called it a neutron.

think about this

Later in Rutherford's life he was interviewed and when asked about his reaction to the results of the gold foil experiment, Rutherford said, "It was quite the most incredible event that has ever happened to me in my life. It was almost as incredible as if you fired a 15 inch shell at a piece of tissue paper and it came back and hit you." Hopefully you will be like Rutherford in your scientific investigations. Always look for questions to ponder when you get unexpected results. You never know where they might lead.

The Structure of Atoms

You should have guessed by now that atoms are extremely small. So small, in fact, that the distance from the center of an atom to its outer edge is well under 1 nanometer, which is one-millionth of a centimeter. It may be hard to imagine just how small that is, so consider this—inside the period at the end of a sentence would fit trillions of atoms! Thanks to the experiments of the scientists we've talked about so far, the structure of atoms was coming into focus even without being able to see them.

Subatomic Particles

Thomson, Rutherford, and Chadwick all contributed to revising Dalton's atomic theory. The evidence they collected showed that the atom was not solid and indivisible, but rather composed of subatomic particles—protons, neutrons, and electrons. But how could these tiny particles be distinguished? Scientists can tell protons, neutrons, and electrons apart by their mass, charge, and location in the atom.

Protons, neutrons, and electrons all have different properties. Through experiments and indirect evidence it was determined that the nucleus contained protons and neutrons and that most of the mass of the atom exists in the nucleus. It was also determined that electrons are very tiny particles. Electrons have a mass of approximately 0.0000000 00000000000000000000911 grams. Now that is small! From Thomson's experiments it was clear that electrons have a negative electrical charge. In fact, the motion of electrons in a wire is what we call "electricity." When you flip a light switch to turn on a light, for example, electrons travel through the wire to the light. The energy the electrons have in their motion is converted to light energy, and as a result, the light glows.

FIGURE 3.14
Comparison: Proton & Electron
If a proton had the same mass as a 9,200 pound elephant, an electron would have the mass of a 5 pound bag of flour.

The mass of a proton is 0.00000000000000000000001674 grams which is 1,836 times more massive than that of an electron, but it's still pretty small. Again it may be hard to imagine how small this is. But to picture the comparison in size, think of it this way (Figure 3.14). If the mass of the proton was the same as a 4.6 ton elephant, then the mass of the electron would be the same as a 5 lb bag of flour. Protons have a positive charge that is equal in magnitude to the negative charge of the electron. Since we know that opposite charges attract one another, we can conclude that protons and electrons are attracted to one another. Atoms are neutral because they contain the same numbers of protons and electrons.

The neutron is roughly the same size as the proton. It is actually slightly heavier (0.14%) but the difference is so small that scientists consider them to be about equal in relative mass. Neutrons are considered electrically neutral, which is where it got the name neutron. Scientists recognized that protons and neutrons existed in the nucleus which accounted for the greatest part of the mass of the atom and the tiny electrons orbited around the nucleus. Look at Table 3.1 to see a comparison of the properties of the subatomic particles. Then answer On Your Own questions 3.4 and 3.5.

TABLE 3.1 Properties of Subatomic Particles				
Particle	Symbol	Relative Charge	Relative Mass (proton = 1)	Actual Mass (g)
electron	e−	1−	$\frac{1}{1836}$	0.00000000000000000000000000911
proton	p+	1+	1	0.0000000000000000000000001674
neutron	n	0	1	0.0000000000000000000000001675

ON YOUR OWN

3.4   In Rutherford's gold foil experiment, why weren't all the alpha particles deflected?

3.5   What 3 properties can be used to distinguish an electron from a proton?

think about this

Think about the atom for a moment. Although Figure 3.15 makes the atom look like a pretty simple structure, it is actually quite complex. For example, consider the electrical charge that exists on the proton and the electron. The mutual attraction between the proton and electron holds the electrons in orbit around the nucleus. Therefore, the opposite charges of the electron and proton are essential for atoms to exist. The overall electrical charge of an atom, however, is zero because an atom has equal numbers of protons and electrons. Thus, even though an atom has several positive charges in it, it has an equal number of negative charges, making the total charge on the atom equal to zero.

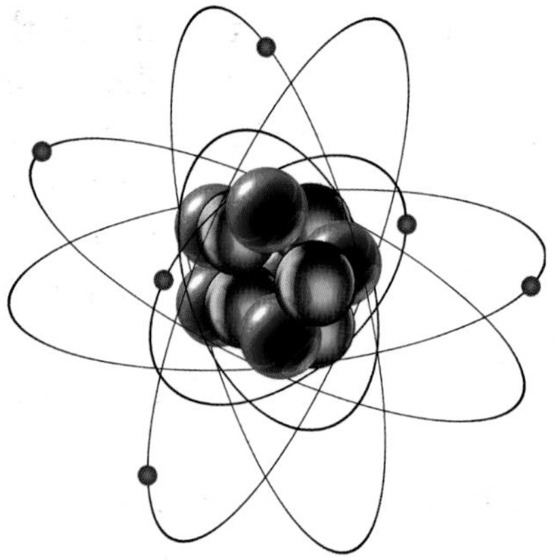

FIGURE 3.15
Model Showing Neutrons in the Nucleus
Rutherford's model of the atom was tweaked to show a nucleus with protons and neutrons.

In order for this to work, the electron must have just as much negative charge as the proton has positive charge. In fact, calculations indicate that if the electron's negative charge were even *one billionth of one percent* different from the proton's positive charge, the resulting electrical imbalance in the atom would cause any sizable amount of matter to *instantaneously explode!* Now remember, the proton and electron are wildly different. The proton is almost 2,000 times more massive than the electron. Nevertheless, the proton has just as much positive charge as the electron has negative charge, to specifications better than 1 billionth of 1 percent!

Think about all of this for a minute. Suppose we design something and ask a master machinist to build it. If we told him that the measurements had to be followed to within 1 billionth of 1 percent, the machinist would laugh. At *very* best, a machinist might be able to follow the specification to within 1 tenth of 1 percent. Nevertheless, two of the components of the atom fit together with a precision of 1 billionth of 1 percent! When we see something that is so delicately balanced, we believe, and perhaps instinctively know, that it is the result of *perfect design*, not chance. When you see how precisely the atom is put together, you should contemplate and appreciate that it was created by the most incredible of engineers—God.

Atomic Number and Mass Number

Dalton predicted that the atoms of one element would have different masses and properties from all other atoms. What makes the atoms of different elements different from each other? With the discovery of the subatomic particles, scientists were now able to describe the differences between atoms of one element and atoms of other elements just as Dalton had predicted.

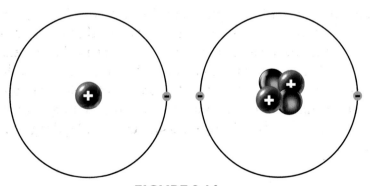

FIGURE 3.16
Hydrogen and Helium Atoms
Hydrogen (left) has 1 proton and 1 electron. Helium (right) has 2 protons, 2 electrons, and 2 neutrons.

It turns out that the all the atoms of any given element always have the same number of protons. For example, there is only 1 proton in every hydrogen atom. In every helium atom there are 2 protons. So, any atom that has only 1 proton is a hydrogen atom and any atom that has 2 protons is a helium atom (Figure 3.16). Since the number of protons in an atom is fundamental in determining what kind of atom it is, there is a special term for the number of protons in an atom. It is called the atomic number of the atom.

Atomic number—The number of protons in an atom

So hydrogen has an atomic number of 1 and helium has an atomic number of 2. If you look at the atom in Figure 3.15, you can count the protons (red balls). There are 6 protons which makes that atom a carbon atom since carbon has an atomic number of 6.

In the end then, the number of protons in an atom tells you what *kind* of atom it is, and since atoms are neutral and must have equal numbers of protons and electrons, it also tells you how many electrons the atom has. Because the electrons swirl around the outside of the atom, it is the electrons of one atom that affects the electrons of the atoms it comes near. If you think about it then, the number of electrons in an atom will be the most important factor in determining how one atom behaves relative to another atom. Thus, the number of electrons in an atom determines the vast majority of an atom's properties. And we can know the number of electrons in an atom by the number of protons it has which is the atomic number.

What about neutrons? How does the number of neutrons in an atom affect the nature of the atom? Well, the short answer to this question is, not much. We know that neutrons have a tiny bit more mass than protons, so each neutron will increase the mass of the atom. But because neutrons have no electrical charge, they do not affect how many electrons an atom has. As a result, the number of neutrons in an atom has only a small effect on the properties of that atom.

Even though the number of neutrons in an atom affects the properties of the atom only slightly, it is still important to keep track of them. Thus, scientists have defined the mass number of an atom to be the sum of the protons and neutrons that exist in the nucleus of an atom.

Mass number—The sum of the protons and neutrons in the nucleus of an atom

The atom illustrated on the right in Figure 3.16, for example, has 2 protons, 2 neutrons, and 2 electrons. The fact that it has 2 protons determines that it also has 2 electrons. It also tells us it is a helium atom. Since there are 2 neutrons in the nucleus as well, the mass number of the atom is 4 (2 neutrons + 2 protons). As a result, we call the atom helium-4.

The hydrogen atom in Figure 3.16 has 1 proton and 1 electron. So it has an atomic number of 1. But notice that there are no neutrons in the hydrogen atom. So that gives hydrogen a mass number of 1 also (1 proton + 0 neutrons). Hydrogen-1 is the only atom that has no neutrons.

Isotopes

There are actually three different kinds of hydrogen atoms in nature, shown in Figure 3.17. Notice that all three of the atoms illustrated in the figure have 1 proton and 1 electron. Thus, they are all hydrogen. Despite the fact that they all have the same number of protons and the same number of electrons, they have different numbers of neutrons. As a result, they all have different mass numbers. The atom with just 1 proton and no neutrons is hydrogen-1 and is sometimes referred to as protium (just a proton in the nucleus). The atom with 1 proton and 1 neutron in its nucleus is hydrogen-2 (deuterium), and the atom with 1 proton and 2 neutrons in its nucleus is hydrogen-3 (tritium). Scientists have a name for atoms like this. They are called isotopes (eye' suh tohps).

Isotopes—Atoms of an element with the same number of protons
but different numbers of neutrons

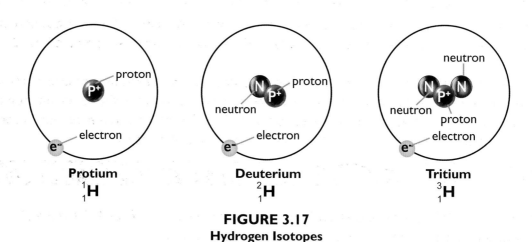

FIGURE 3.17
Hydrogen Isotopes
Hydrogen-1 (left) has 1 proton and 1 electron. Hydrogen-2 (middle) has 1 proton, 1 electron, and 1 neutron. Hydrogen-3 (right) has 1 proton, 1 electron, and 2 neutrons. Notice the abbreviations ^{1}H, ^{2}H, and ^{3}H. H is the chemical symbol for the element hydrogen and the superscripts before the symbols indicate the mass number. Sometimes (as shown above) there are also subscripts before the symbol indicating the atomic number.

Isotopes of an element have the same atomic number but different mass numbers because they have different numbers of neutrons. All isotopes are identified by the name of the element followed by the mass number (hydrogen-2). Only the element hydrogen has different common names for its isotopes.

Hydrogen isn't the only element that has isotopes. The helium-4 that is pictured in Figure 3.16 is one of three naturally occurring isotopes. The other two isotopes are helium-3 and helium-5. Can you figure out how many neutrons each helium isotope has? When you buy a helium-filled balloon, it contains a mixture of helium-3 and helium-4. The vast majority of the atoms (more than 99.99%) are helium-4 atoms. However, a few (less than 0.01%) of them are helium-3. Since the only difference between these types of helium atoms is the number of neutrons in their nuclei (the plural of nucleus), they all have essentially the same properties. Nevertheless, they are different from one another. Helium-3 is less massive than helium-4.

The element carbon also has three different isotopes—carbon-12, carbon-13, and carbon-14. A sample of carbon (like that which you find in coal) is a mixture of all of those isotopes. To make sure you really understand the structure of atoms, study the examples below and then answer the On Your Own problems 13.6–13.7.

think about this

Did you know there is such a thing as heavy water? Remember that a molecule of water is made up of 2 atoms of hydrogen and one atom of oxygen. Ordinary water is made up of hydrogen-1 atoms, but heavy water is made up of hydrogen-2 atoms. Hydrogen-2 atoms have twice the mass of hydrogen-1 atoms which is why the water is called heavy water. With most elements it's hard to notice any differences in the physical or chemical properties of their isotopes. That is not the case with hydrogen. Heavy water has slightly higher melting point, boiling point, and density than ordinary water.

EXAMPLE 3.1

All atoms that make up the element nitrogen have 7 protons. If a particular nitrogen atom has 8 neutrons, what is its name? How many electrons does it have?

Since we are talking about a nitrogen atom here, we know it has 7 protons because all atoms that make up the element nitrogen have 7 protons. Since all atoms have the same number of electrons and protons, **this atom has 7 electrons.** With 7 protons and 8 neutrons in the nucleus, the mass number is: 7 + 8 = 15, so we call this atom **nitrogen-15.**

EXAMPLE 3.2

Which of the following atoms is an isotope of nitrogen-15? What is its name?
a. an atom with 5 protons, 5 electrons, and ten neutrons
b. an atom with 8 protons, 8 electrons, and 7 neutrons
c. an atom with 8 protons, 8 electrons, and 8 neutrons
d. an atom with 7 protons, 7 electrons, and 7 neutrons

Two atoms are isotopes if they have the same number of protons but different numbers of neutrons. As we determined earlier, there are 7 protons, 7 electrons, and 8 neutrons in nitrogen-15. Thus, any isotope of nitrogen-15 will also have to have 7 protons. It must have something other than 8 neutrons as well. Thus, **the atom in choice (d) is an isotope of nitrogen-15. It's name is nitrogen-14, because its mass number is 7 + 7 = 14.**

ON YOUR OWN

3.6   The element sodium is made up of all atoms with 11 protons. How many protons, electrons and neutrons are in a sodium-23 atom?

3.7   Of the following atoms, two are isotopes. Which ones are they?

a.   An atom with 16 protons, 16 electrons, and 17 neutrons
b.   An atom with 17 protons, 17 electrons, and 16 neutrons
c.   An atom with 16 protons, 16 electrons, and 18 neutrons
d.   An atom with 18 protons, 18 electrons, and 17 neutrons

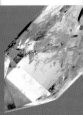

MODERN ATOMIC THEORY

The nuclear model explained Rutherford's experimental results, but like all good science, it also raised further questions. For example, scientists questioned what exactly the electrons were doing in the atom. And if opposites attract as we know they do; then how did the electrons keep from flying into the nucleus? Well, science was ready for the challenge! Scientists, such as Danish physicist Niels Bohr, continued to design experiments to test the nuclear model of the atom, which eventually evolved into the electron cloud model.

Bohr's Atomic Model

Niels Bohr worked in Rutherford's lab in England and supported Rutherford's nuclear model of the atom. Since Rutherford's model didn't detail how the electrons behaved, other than to suggest they orbited the nucleus like planets, Bohr decided to focus on electrons and how they are arranged in the atom.

Bohr was also interested in what caused different elements to emit certain colors of light when heated. Have you noticed the different colors of fireworks (Figure 3.18)? Fireworks are made by causing an explosion of substances containing various metal elements. It was discovered that when the element strontium is heated it produces a red light. When the element barium is heated it produces green light. When the element sodium is heated, yellow light is produced. And when the element copper is heated, blue light is produced. Bohr was interested in explaining why that happens and he thought it might have something to do with electrons.

FIGURE 3.18
Fireworks
Fireworks are the result of heating different elements that produce different colors of light.

Because of his work with the light emitting metals (as well as work done by other scientists such as Max Planck and Albert Einstein), Bohr hypothesized that electrons orbit around the nucleus at fixed distances, like planets around the sun. He reasoned that each electron had a certain amount of energy and that energy determined the fixed distance of the orbit. Bohr called these fixed distances energy levels, or electron shells.

These electron shells would circle around the nucleus one outside of the next, sort of like a sphere within a sphere (Figure 3.19). He further hypothesized that electrons with less energy would be found in lower energy levels closest to the nucleus. Electrons with more energy would be found in higher energy levels farther from the nucleus. So energy levels would increase in the energy they

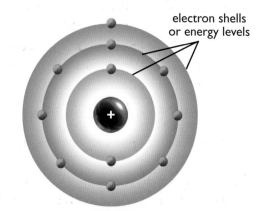

electron shells or energy levels

FIGURE 3.19
Bohr Model of Sodium
Sodium has an atomic number of 11 so it has 11 electrons occupying 3 energy levels.

contained from the nucleus outward.

Bohr also hypothesized that if an electron absorbed energy it could jump to a higher energy level. And if the electron lost energy, if would jump down to a lower energy level. The amount of energy gained or lost determined how many energy levels an electron could jump. Also, while electrons could exist in a specific energy level, they could never exist in between two energy levels. If you're having trouble picturing that, think of it like a ladder (Figure 3.20). You can stand on any rung on the ladder. The rungs lower to the ground require less energy for you to climb onto them. To climb to the higher rungs requires more energy. With enough energy you can go up more than one rung at a time. And while you can stand on any rung of the ladder, you can never stand in between two rungs. So Bohr's hypothesis was that electrons can orbit the nucleus only in shells at fixed distances from the nucleus and not in between them.

Energy Levels

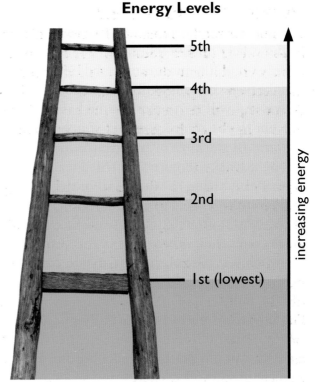

FIGURE 3.20
Ladder Model
The rungs of a ladder are like the energy levels in an atom.

Bohr's hypothesis explained the light he saw when metals were heated—the same colors seen in fireworks. When the explosions in the fireworks heats some of the electrons of the metal atoms, they gain energy. This added energy causes the electrons to move to higher energy levels. In order to move back to their original energy levels, the electrons must give off the added energy. Some of that energy is released as visible light. Because each element has a unique set of energy levels, different elements emit different colors of light.

Niels Bohr formulated his atomic model in 1913. He won a Nobel Prize in Physics in 1922 for his work. Bohr's model was the first model of the atom that could account for the known properties of atoms. As you will see in the next section and should expect by now, as science has become more advanced there have been some changes to his model. Even so, the Bohr model gives us a reasonably good picture of an atom and is the model you will see most often even today.

The Electron Cloud or the Quantum-Mechanical Model

Just as Rutherford improved upon Thomson's model and Bohr improved upon Rutherford's model, Bohr's model was improved as scientists discovered new things about atoms. The electron cloud model is the *currently* accepted model. Because of new discoveries, this model of the atom assumes that the movement of electrons is less predictable than those in Bohr's fixed energy levels. In the current model, an electron cloud is used to describe the likely locations for electrons in atoms.

Scientists call the electron cloud model the quantum-mechanical model. This model is very complex because it relies heavily on mathematical probabilities that require post-calculus skills to understand. However, I will try to explain the basic concept to you. Have you ever watched a swarm of starlings or other birds move through the sky (Figure 3.21)? It's really quite mesmerizing to watch. All of the birds seem to move as one unit, but parts of the swarm are moving and twisting much faster than other parts of the swarm. In the densest part of the swarm you can't pick out a single bird in any given moment because it is in constant motion. That's a lot like the motion of electrons.

FIGURE 3.21
A Cloud of Starlings
A flock of starlings acting as a swarm.

Electrons perform a sort of set dance—some are dancing fast, and others are dancing slowly—but each follows mathematical patterns described by an equation discovered by the Austrian physicist, Erwin Schrödinger in 1926. Electrons will stay in their patterned dance until they gain energy and speed up (dance faster and farther from the nucleus) or lose energy and slow down (dance slower and closer to the nucleus). No two electrons can occupy the same space at the same time. So comparing that to the swarm of starlings, the birds are moving so fast that what you see looks like a blur. You know there are birds in that blur, but at any specific moment in time you can't be exactly sure where a specific bird is. And no two birds occupy the same space in the swarm at the same time. The electron cloud is a bit like that.

Look at Figure 3.22—it is an electron cloud model of a helium atom. Since helium has an atomic number of 2, we know it has 2 protons and 2 electrons. Based on the quantum mechanical or electron cloud model, each electron is represented by a cloud in the space around the nucleus. We cannot say for certain where the electron is or how it is moving, but we know the electrons are more likely to be found where the cloud is denser.

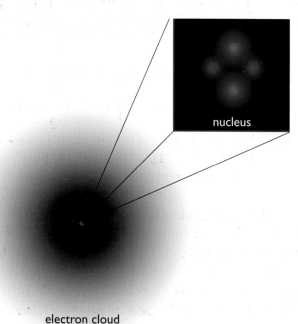

nucleus

electron cloud

FIGURE 3.22
Electron Cloud Model of a Helium Atom
The 2 electrons in helium are more likely to be found where the cloud is denser.

Electron Orbitals

According to the electron cloud model, rather than the electrons existing in fixed orbits, they have fixed amounts of energy that correspond to each energy level.

Because of this, physicists realized that electrons have wave-like properties (similar to light waves) as well as properties of particles of matter. It is these wave-like properties of electrons that keep them at certain distances from the nucleus. Even though the negative electrons are attracted to the positive protons, electrons bend around the nucleus rather than crashing into it, because they behave like waves. Think about how light waves bend around obstacles. When you're in a dark room with the door shut, you can still see light coming around the door frame. Sometimes it's enough to see things that are around the door quite clearly. This is because light waves bend, which is called diffraction.

Wave behavior also explains why electrons only exist where the wave is stable (the rung of the ladder) and not where the wave is not stable (between rungs). Scientists have a name for the stable areas in each energy level where electrons are most likely to be found. They call them orbitals.

Orbitals—A region of space around the nucleus where electrons are most likely to be found

It turns out that there is a limit to how many electrons can exist in each orbital and how many orbitals can exist in each energy level. An orbital can only hold 2 electrons. The first energy level—the one with the lowest amount of energy—only has 1 orbital so it can never hold more than 2 electrons. The second energy level has 4 orbitals so it can hold up to 8 electrons. The third energy level has 9 orbitals so it can hold up to 18 electrons. The fourth energy level has 16 orbitals so it can hold up to 32 electrons. This information is summarized in Table 3.2.

TABLE 3.2 First Four Energy Levels, Their Orbitals and Electrons		
Energy Level	Number of Orbitals	Maximum Number of Electrons
1	1	2
2	4	8
3	9	18
4	16	32

The way electrons are arranged in the orbitals in each energy level is called an atom's electron configuration. An atom has the most stable electron configuration when all of its electrons are in the lowest possible energy levels. Scientists call this stable state the atom's **ground state**. For example, look again at Figure 3.19. That is a representation of a sodium atom. It has 2 electrons in the first energy level, 8 electrons in the 2nd energy level, and 1 electron in the 3rd energy level. It has filled the first 2 energy levels since they each contain the maximum number of electrons for that level. Now the electron in the 3rd energy level could absorb enough energy (by heating for example) that it would move to an orbital with higher energy. When that happens the atom is said to be in an excited state. An excited state is very unstable and eventually the electron that has jumped to a higher energy level will lose that energy again to return to its ground state. When the electron in sodium returns to its ground state, the energy it releases is seen as yellow light. This is what happens in fireworks.

This completes our discussion on how we know what we do about atoms. Before moving on and to get some hands-on experience with the structure of atoms, complete Experiment 3.1. Then answer On Your Own questions 3.8–3.9.

think about this

The nucleus is like a blueberry placed in the center of a major-league baseball stadium. The electrons (about the size of tiny gnats) orbit this blueberry out at the edges of the stadium. What lies between the blueberry and the edge of the stadium? Nothing. Absolutely nothing. There is *nothing* between the nucleus and the electrons. What does this tell you about the atom? It tells you that the atom is made up mostly of empty space. Indeed, the atom is more than 99.99999% empty space! Since atoms make up all of matter, this tells us that *matter is mostly empty space.*

FIGURE 3.23
Baseball Stadium
Picture a tiny blueberry on the center of the field. The electrons the size of gnats swirl in orbitals of energy levels around the outside of the stadium.

Now wait a minute. If you lean your hands against the top of a table, the tabletop certainly doesn't feel like empty space, does it? Your hand doesn't just pass right through it. Instead, the tabletop stops your hand. How can it do that if it is mostly empty space? Well both your hand and the tabletop are made of molecules, which are made up of atoms. Look again at Figure 3.22 and notice how the electrons are swirling around the nucleus. So the positively charged portion of the atom is basically covered up by the negatively charged electrons. Since the electrons swarm in their orbital paths outside the nucleus, the electrons act like a negative blanket, covering the nucleus.

Think of what happens when your hand gets nearer and nearer to the table. The swarming blanket of electrons in the atoms of your hand gets closer to the swarming blanket of electrons in the atoms of the table. As they get closer the patterns of their swarms change. This is because the electrons in the atoms of your hand can't occupy any of the space taken by the electrons of the atoms of the table since that space is already taken. So just as heat supplied energy for an electron to jump to a more energetic orbital in fireworks, the force of your hand on the table provides energy to the electrons as they come in contact with the table's atom's electrons.

FIGURE 3.24
Solid Tabletop
The dance of electrons and their resistance to move to a less stable energy level makes solids feel solid.

But pushing the atoms close enough together so that electrons are pushed into unoccupied higher energy states takes *a lot* of energy. In fact it takes so much energy that your muscles simply can't supply enough no matter how hard you might hit the table. So what you feel as you rest your hand on the table is the resistance of the electrons to move to a higher energy state and that makes the table feel solid to your touch.

EXPERIMENT 3.1
CONSTRUCTING 3-D ATOMIC MODELS

PURPOSE:
To create models of isotopes of an element.

BACKGROUND
Scientists and engineers use models all the time. Remember from module 1 that a model is a useful simplification used to make it easier to understand things that might be too difficult to

directly observe. Good models also allow scientists to make and test predictions. As always in science, models are changed when they no longer explain the data. The globe is a model of the planet Earth. It wasn't until 2005 that the globe was made using actual satellite pictures from NASA. There are computer models, such as weather models, in which scientists use mathematical calculations to predict weather patterns. Engineers build models of bridges or buildings to determine what materials will best suit the parameters of the project. In this investigation, you will build a model of 2 atoms and use them to compare their structure.

MATERIALS:
- 2 small Styrofoam balls (Balls should be about 2 inches in diameter. Styrofoam balls from craft stores work well.)
- Pipe cleaners (white or gray)
- Plastic pony beads (These can be found at craft stores.)
- 2 bamboo skewers
- Fishing line
- 2 wire hangers
- Red and blue pushpins

QUESTION:
How can the materials listed be used to show the difference between isotopes of an element?

PROCEDURE:
1. Choose one of the elements from the table below. Use the information in the table to determine the number of protons, neutrons, and electrons in each of two isotopes of the element you chose. (Some elements have 3 isotopes and you can build all 3 if you like, but you only need to build 2 models.) In your data table, record this information and the names of your isotopes.

TABLE 3.3 Some Elements and Their Isotopes		
Element	**Atomic Number**	**Isotopes**
Nitrogen	7	nitrogen-14, nitrogen-15
Oxygen	8	oxygen-16, oxygen-17, oxygen-18
Magnesium	12	magnesium-24, magnesium-25, magnesium-26
Chlorine	17	chlorine-35, chlorine-37

2. Red pushpins will represent protons. Blue pushpins will represent neutrons. The plastic beads will represent electrons. Set aside the correct number of each item for your isotopes.
3. The Styrofoam ball will represent the area of the nucleus. You may need to ask for help on this part. Take the bamboo skewer and carefully insert it through the Styrofoam ball so that there is about 1 inch of skewer exposed on each side of the ball. Break or cut off any longer than 1 inch pieces.
4. Insert the correct number of red and blue pushpins for one isotope into a Styrofoam ball. Repeat using the other Styrofoam ball for the other isotope.

5. Use fishing line to attach the nucleus to the hanger. Tie the fishing line around each end of the bamboo skewers and then onto the hanger. Repeat for the second isotope.

6. Determine how many energy levels your isotopes have. Record this number in your data table. Remember that the first energy level can hold 2 electrons, the second energy level can hold 8 electrons, and the third energy level can hold 18 electrons.

7. Use pipe cleaners to construct the correct number of energy levels for one of your isotopes. Depending on the length of your pipe cleaners you may need more or fewer, but generally 2 to 3 pipe cleaners are needed to make the first energy level, 4 to 5 for the second energy level and 5 to 7 for the 3rd energy level. Twist the ends of the pipe cleaners together to make each energy level but do not yet close the circle so you can add the beads. Your model should look similar to the one shown in the photo.

8. Determine the number of electrons in each energy level of your isotopes. Record in your data table. Place the appropriate number of beads on each pipe-cleaner circle. Close each circle by twisting the pipe-cleaners together.

9. Use fishing line to attach the energy levels to the hanger. Make sure to hang the energy levels in the correct order at the same level as the nucleus.

10. Repeat steps 7–9 to complete the second isotope.

11. Clean up and put away all materials.

12. If you have parental permission, submit a photo of your isotopes for the Book Extras page. You can send your photo to customerservice@apologia.com. Be sure to include that you have parental permission, as well as your first name (not your last) which we can post with your photo.

CONCLUSIONS

In a conclusion paragraph, answer the following questions. How were the two models you constructed similar? How were they different? Why did both of your models contain the same number of protons and electrons? What are some ways your models were not accurate in depicting the nucleus and electrons of an atom?

ON YOUR OWN

3.8 When do atoms emit energy as light?
   a. protons move to a higher energy level
   b. electrons move to a higher energy level
   c. protons move to a lower energy level
   d. electrons move to a lower energy level

3.9 A beryllium atom has 2 electrons in the first energy level and 2 in the second energy level. How do the relative energies of these electrons compare to each other?

ORGANIZING ELEMENTS: THE PERIODIC TABLE

As scientists became more familiar with the elements, they began to look for similarities. They noticed that some groups of elements behaved similarly—they had similar properties. For example, fluorine, chlorine, bromine, and iodine all react very easily with metals such as sodium and magnesium. Because of these similarities, scientists tried many different arrangements to logically classify the elements, but none of their systems had an organizing principle that worked for all elements. That is until a Russian chemist and teacher, Dmitri (Duh mee' tree) Mendeleev (Men duh lay' uff), developed an ingenious method of organizing elements in 1869. Mendeleev's method of organizing elements worked so well that, with some revisions, it is still used today.

Mendeleev's Periodic Table

As a teacher of chemistry, Mendeleev was trying to find a way to organize the 63 known elements for a textbook he was writing. He wanted to make it easier for students to learn about the elements so he wanted to group them by their properties. He used the idea of a deck of cards where each suit (hearts, spades, clubs, diamonds) could be put in order by increasing number. He did the same thing with the known elements. He made a set of element cards on which he wrote the name, the atomic mass, and other known properties of each element. He continued to arrange and rearrange the element cards to see if he could find a pattern. When he arranged the cards in rows of 8 by increasing atomic mass (each column also had increasing masses), a pattern began to emerge. Mendeleev's table is called a periodic table because the pattern repeats. *Periodic* means repeating. The periodic table is an arrangement of elements in columns with properties that repeat from row to row. Figure 3.25 shows a copy of the periodic table Mendeleev published in 1872.

Reihen	Gruppe I. R^2O	Gruppe II. RO	Gruppe III. R^2O^3	Gruppe IV. RH^4 RO^2	Gruppe V. RH^3 R^2O^5	Gruppe VI. RH^2 RO^3	Gruppe VII. RH R^2O^7	Gruppe VIII. RO^4
1	H=1							
2	Li=7	Be=9.4	B=11	C=12	N=14	O=16	F=19	
3	Na=23	Mg=24	Al=27.3	Si=28	P=31	S=32	Cl=35.5	
4	K=39	Ca=40	—=44	Ti=48	V=51	Cr=52	Mn=55	Fe=56, Co=59, Ni=59, Cu=63.
5	(Cu=63)	Zn=65	—=68	—=72	As=75	Se=78	Br=80	
6	Rb=85	Sr=87	?Yt=88	Zr=90	Nb=94	Mo=96	—=100	Ru=104, Rh=104, Pd=106, Ag=108.
7	(Ag=108)	Cd=112	In=113	Sn=118	Sb=122	Te=125	J=127	
8	Cs=133	Ba=137	?Di=138	?Ce=140	—	—	—	— — — —
9	(—)	—	—	—	—			
10	—	—	?Er=178	?La=180	Ta=182	W=184	—	Os=195, Ir=197, Pt=198, Au=199.
11	(Au=199)	Hg=200	Tl=204	Pb=207	Bi=208	—	—	
12	—	—	—	Th=231	—	U=240	—	— — — —

FIGURE 3.25
Mendeleev's Periodic Table
Mendeleev placed elements in rows and columns based on their atomic mass and similar properties. He found a repeating pattern when 8 elements were placed in each row.

Notice the gaps (dashes) in Mendeleev's periodic table. The dashes represent elements that were unknown in Mendeleev's time. Because of the pattern Mendeleev found he was able to predict that there were missing elements yet to discover. He was even able to predict the masses and some of the unknown element's properties. Remember that a good scientific model must be able to be used to make accurate predictions. It turns out that Mendeleev's periodic table of elements was a very good and useful model as all of the missing elements he predicted have been discovered and their properties were a close match to his predictions. Try your hand at creating a periodic table of elements like Mendeleev did by using color cards in Experiment 3.2.

EXPERIMENT 3.2
CREATING A PERIODIC TABLE

PURPOSE:
To model Mendeleev's process by attempting to arrange color cards according to their observed properties of color and intensity.

MATERIALS:
- Color cards found in the student notebook (You can also find a copy to print on the Book Extra site.)
- Scissors
- Glue or tape

QUESTION:
Can you form a periodic table with rows and columns showing a repeating change in properties (color) and increasing atomic mass (shade or color intensity)?

BACKGROUND:
The color of a card represents its properties. For example, you can consider all green color cards to have similar properties. The green color cards will all have different properties from the orange cards (and all other color cards). The shade (intensity) of a color card represents its atomic mass. In other words, a light (lower intensity) green color card represents an element with a lower atomic mass than a dark (higher intensity) green color card.

PROCEDURE:
1. Remove the color cards page from your student notebook. Cut the color cards apart.
2. Arrange the color cards in 8 columns in the order of the rainbow (with the addition of a teal or green-blue): red, orange, yellow, green, teal, blue, indigo, violet. There should be one of each color in each row, except the first row in which there are only 2 color cards. There should be 5 rows.
3. Arrange each column by increasing intensity. So lighter shades of each color at the top of the column and darkest shades at the bottom.
4. You will have missing elements. Predict where they would be placed in the table by leaving a space for them. Describe the properties of the missing color cards in your data section.
5. Turn to the appendix in the back of your student notebook and remove the page with the missing elements. Cut them apart. Do they fit where you predicted?
6. Paste your color chips in your student notebook in the order of your periodic table.
7. Clean up.

CONCLUSION:
Were your predictions correct? Explain how the periodic table is a good model for predicting unknown elements and their properties.

Groups and Periods

Mendeleev placed the elements across the rows by increasing mass. He discovered that if he place 8 elements across each row, then down each column the elements shared similar properties. Mendeleev called the columns groups. Groups are sometimes also called families since like families, the members of a group share similar characteristics but are not identical.

The rows of a periodic table are called periods. Across each period of 8 elements in Mendeleev's table, the atomic masses increase and the properties of the atoms change. This same pattern repeats in each period. Mendeleev's periodic table of elements not only helped scientists discover new elements, but also helped them to understand the properties and behavior of atoms.

Modern Periodic Table

Mendeleev developed his periodic table in the 1870s. The proton was not discovered until Rutherford's experiments about 40 years later. After the discovery of protons and atomic number, scientists found that Mendeleev's table made even more sense when the elements were arranged by increasing atomic number rather than atomic mass. Now realize that using the atomic number did not change the order of Mendeleev's elements because protons contribute to the mass of the element. But knowing that each element is defined by the number of protons in its nucleus, it became the standard way to arrange the periodic table. Figure 3.26 shows a modern period table of elements. There are a lot more known elements now than there were in Mendeleev's time.

1A	2A	3B	4B	5B	6B	7B	8B	8B	8B	1B	2B	3A	4A	5A	6A	7A	8A
1 **H** 1.01																	2 **He** 4.00
3 **Li** 6.94	4 **Be** 9.01											5 **B** 10.8	6 **C** 12.0	7 **N** 14.0	8 **O** 16.0	9 **F** 19.0	10 **Ne** 20.2
11 **Na** 23.0	12 **Mg** 24.3											13 **Al** 27.0	14 **Si** 28.1	15 **P** 31.0	16 **S** 32.1	17 **Cl** 35.5	18 **Ar** 39.9
19 **K** 39.1	20 **Ca** 40.1	21 **Sc** 45.0	22 **Ti** 47.9	23 **V** 50.9	24 **Cr** 52.0	25 **Mn** 54.9	26 **Fe** 55.8	27 **Co** 58.9	28 **Ni** 58.7	29 **Cu** 63.5	30 **Zn** 65.4	31 **Ga** 69.7	32 **Ge** 72.6	33 **As** 74.9	34 **Se** 79.0	35 **Br** 79.9	36 **Kr** 83.8
37 **Rb** 85.5	38 **Sr** 87.6	39 **Y** 88.9	40 **Zr** 91.2	41 **Nb** 92.9	42 **Mo** 96.0	43 **Tc** (98)	44 **Ru** 101.1	45 **Rh** 102.9	46 **Pd** 106.4	47 **Ag** 107.9	48 **Cd** 112.4	49 **In** 114.8	50 **Sn** 118.7	51 **Sb** 121.8	52 **Te** 127.6	53 **I** 126.9	54 **Xe** 131.3
55 **Cs** 132.9	56 **Ba** 137.3	57 **La** 138.9	72 **Hf** 178.5	73 **Ta** 181.0	74 **W** 183.8	75 **Re** 186.2	76 **Os** 190.2	77 **Ir** 192.2	78 **Pt** 195.1	79 **Au** 197.0	80 **Hg** 200.6	81 **Tl** 204.4	82 **Pb** 207.2	83 **Bi** 209.0	84 **Po** (209)	85 **At** (210)	86 **Rn** (222)
87 **Fr** (223)	88 **Ra** (226.0)	89 **Ac** (227)	104 **Rf** (265)	105 **Db** (268)	106 **Sg** (271)	107 **Bh** (270)	108 **Hs** (277)	109 **Mt** (276)	110 **Ds** (281)	111 **Rg** (280)	112 **Cn** (285)	113 **Nh** (284)	114 **Fl** (289)	115 **Mc** (288)	116 **Lv** (293)	117 **Ts** (294)	118 **Og** (294)

58 **Ce** 140.1	59 **Pr** 140.9	60 **Nd** 144.2	61 **Pm** (145)	62 **Sm** 150.4	63 **Eu** 152.0	64 **Gd** 157.2	65 **Tb** 158.9	66 **Dy** 162.5	67 **Ho** 164.9	68 **Er** 167.3	69 **Tm** 168.9	70 **Yb** 173.0	71 **Lu** 175.0
90 **Th** 232.0	91 **Pa** 231.0	92 **U** 238.0	93 **Np** (237)	94 **Pu** (244)	95 **Am** (243)	96 **Cm** (247)	97 **Bk** (247)	98 **Cf** (251)	99 **Es** (252)	100 **Fm** (257)	101 **Md** (258)	102 **No** (259)	103 **Lr** (262)

Nonmetals
Standard metals
Transition metals
Inner transition metals

FIGURE 3.26
Modern Periodic Table

The modern periodic table has 118 elements instead of Mendeleev's 63. So far 24 synthetic elements have been created (those with atomic numbers 95–118). There are 7 periods and 18 groups (excluding the 2 bottom rows which are their own series).

The modern table works the same way as Mendeleev's table. The rows are called periods and the columns are called groups. Across each period each element has 1 more proton than the one before it. In other words, the elements increase by atomic number and down each group the elements share similar properties.

Notice that each block is one element. Each element is represented by its symbol—H is the symbol for hydrogen. Sometimes the symbols make sense with the English name of the element (like Al for aluminum). But other symbols refer to the Latin name for the element. For example look at the element with atomic number 79. That element is gold, but the symbol is Au. The Latin word for gold is *aurum*, so that is where the symbol Au comes from. Because of this some periodic tables show both the name and the symbol. Also notice the two numbers in each block. The top number is the atomic number and the bottom number is the atomic mass of the element.

REPRESENTATIVE GROUPS

Did you wonder why there are two numbering systems on the periodic table? In the United States, the letter A is used to designate the main group elements. Sometimes you will see periodic tables that designate these groups with Roman numerals and the letters A or B. Most recently periodic tables simply have the groups labeled 1 through 18 or will show both numbering systems together. The B groups of elements are called the transition elements, and you will spend time in chemistry learning more about them. In this course we will focus on the A groups of elements.

The 8-A columns also tell us about the electron configuration of the elements in each group. The number of the group matches the number of electrons in the outermost or highest energy level. As we will see, the electrons in the highest energy level of an atom play an important role in chemical reactions. They are so important that scientists have given them their own name—valence electrons.

> **Valence electrons**—Electrons that are in the highest energy level (the energy level farthest from the nucleus) of an atom of an element

Look at the periodic table in Figure 3.26. Notice how the number of valence electrons increases from left to right as you go across each period (row). Mendeleev placed elements across periods as their properties varied. It turns out that properties vary across a period because the number of valence electrons increases as you go from 1A to 8A. Notice that the first row (period 1) contains only 2 elements, hydrogen and helium. That is because there is only 1 orbital and so only 2 possible electrons in the first energy level.

Now look down each group of the periodic table in Figure 3.26. Each element in group 1A has only 1 valence electron in their outermost energy level. So even though each element down that group has a different number of energy levels, they all have similar properties because they each have only 1 valence electron. This is the reason that hydrogen is placed where it is on the periodic table—it only has 1 electron.

Elements in groups 1A through 8A are important for other reasons too. These groups contain the most important elements for life. They are the most naturally abundant elements and they comprise about 80% of the Earth's crust. These elements are considered the main group elements. Let's look at some of the properties of these groups.

The Alkali Metals

The elements in group 1A are called the alkali metals. Now you may be wondering why hydrogen gas is placed at the top of column 1A with metals. Well it is because hydrogen only has 1 electron. So it's important to remember that hydrogen has 1 valance electron like alkali metals and sits on top of the alkali metals in Group 1A, but it is *not* classified as an alkali metal.

So we will be discussing the rest of group 1A starting at the second row: lithium (Li), sodium (Na), potassium (K), rubidium (Rb), cesium (Cs), and francium (Fr). Because alkali metals have only 1 valence electron they are extremely reactive. Since they are so reactive, alkali metals only exist in nature in compounds. You are already familiar with one of these compounds—table salt. Table salt is a compound of sodium and chlorine called sodium chloride.

You can tell by their name that the members of the alkali metals family are metals. This means they are shiny and malleable, but since they are also the most reactive group on the periodic table, you would not want to use them for coins or jewelry. In fact sodium is such a soft metal that it can be cut with a sharp knife (Figure 3.27 top). Sodium is also less dense than water and so floats. But it is so reactive that it will soon react violently with the water (Figure 3.27 bottom).

Not all the elements in Group 1A are equally reactive. In fact, their reactivity increases as you go down the group. So sodium is more reactive than lithium but less reactive than potassium. Rubidium is more reactive than potassium but less reactive than cesium. Francium is a very heavy, very rare element that is highly radioactive so not as much is known of its properties. But it is predicted that francium's reaction with water would possibly be explosive. Because alkali metals are so highly reactive, they are stored under oil or in sealed glass tubes to keep them from reacting with water or oxygen! (See Figure 3.28.)

Group 1A

| 3 |
| Li |
| 6.94 |
| 11 |
| Na |
| 23.0 |
| 19 |
| K |
| 39.1 |
| 37 |
| Rb |
| 85.5 |
| 55 |
| Cs |
| 132.9 |
| 87 |
| Fr |
| (223) |

FIGURE 3.27
Alkali Metals
The alkali metals are relatively soft metals that are very reactive. Reactivity increases down the group.

FIGURE 3.28
Sodium Stored in Oil
Sodium is stored in oil to prevent reactions.

The Alkaline Earth Metals

Group 2A is where the alkaline earth metals are found. This group is the second most reactive family of elements in the periodic table. Have you wondered why they are called alkaline? The reason is that when mixed in solutions, alkaline metals usually form solutions with a pH greater than 7. Remember that a pH greater than 7 is referred to as basic or alkaline.

The members of this family of elements include the metals; beryllium (Be), magnesium (Mg), calcium (Ca), strontium (Sr), barium (Ba), and radium (Ra). All of these elements share certain properties. These metals are silver or gray, relatively soft (not as soft as alkali metals), and reactive. While not as reactive as the alkali metals, this family each have 2 valence electrons and so are still quite reactive. In fact, calcium, strontium, and barium will react with water (magnesium will react with hot water) but not as violently as the alkali metals. Beryllium doesn't react with water at all.

You are likely familiar with magnesium and calcium as both play a role in the biological functions of living things. Magnesium is central atom in chlorophyll which allows plants to make their own food and is why they look green. Calcium is needed to keep your bones and teeth strong. The other elements in this family are used in things such as sparklers, fireworks, and batteries. Radon, like francium, is a radioactive element.

The Boron Group

The Boron group is the family of elements in group 3A of the periodic table. Each member of this family has 3 valence electrons. Members include boron (B), aluminum (Al), gallium (Ga), indium (In), thallium (Tl), and nihonium (Nh).

Boron is not classified as a metal but as a metalloid. Metalloids are elements that have some characteristics of metals but not all. The rest of this family are classified as metals. These elements are solid at room temperature.

Boron is used in a compound that makes the glass used to make the beakers you use. This type of glass does not easily shatter and can withstand extreme changes in temperature which makes it great for labware and cookware. You are likely most familiar with the shiny, silver metal, aluminum. Aluminum is the 3rd most common element in the Earth's crust.

Gallium is used in laser diodes and LEDs. Indium is used as an anticorrosion agent when added to other metals. Thallium is toxic and has been used in rat poison. Nihonium is a radioactive element that was created in the lab by Japanese scientists in 2012 and officially named in 2016. Only a few atoms of nihonium have ever been made, so scientists know very little about it yet.

Group 2A

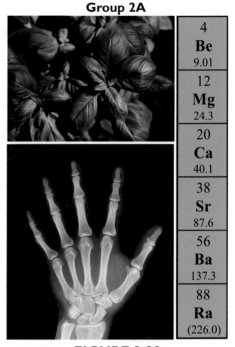

4	**Be** 9.01
12	**Mg** 24.3
20	**Ca** 40.1
38	**Sr** 87.6
56	**Ba** 137.3
88	**Ra** (226.0)

FIGURE 3.29
Alkaline Earth Metals
The alkaline earth metals are silvery gray metals that easily react. Magnesium in chlorophyll of plants and calcium in bones are examples.

Group 3A

5	**B** 10.8
13	**Al** 27.0
31	**Ga** 69.7
49	**In** 114.8
81	**Tl** 204.4
113	**Nh** (284)

FIGURE 3.30
Boron Group
The elements in group 3A have 3 valence electrons making them less reactive than alkaline earth metals.

The Carbon Group

Group 4A contains a mix of element types all with 4 valence electrons. Carbon (C) is a nonmetal. Silicon (Si) and germanium (Ge) are metalloids, and tin (Sn), lead (Pb), and flerovium (Fl) are metals. The metallic characteristics of the elements increases as you go down the group from top to bottom.

The element carbon is required for life. All the reactions that occur in your body are controlled by compounds containing carbon. All living things contain carbon. Silicon is the second most abundant element in the Earth's crust. Clay used in pottery making contains a compound with silicon. A compound of silicon and oxygen is the major component of glass. The computer industry uses germanium because of its important semiconductor properties. Before aluminum, tin was used to make cans. Lead is used to block radiation and many water pipes are made of lead components. Like nihonium, flerovium is highly radioactive and is not naturally occurring. It was first created by Russian scientists in 1998.

The Nitrogen Group

Group 5A contains elements each having 5 valence electrons. The group contains two nonmetals—nitrogen (N) and phosphorus (P). It also contains two metalloids—arsenic (As) and antimony (Sb). Finally it contains two metals—bismuth (Bi) and moscovium (Mc).

Like the carbon group, the nitrogen family has a wide range of physical properties. Nitrogen is a nonmetal gas, phosphorus is a nonmetal solid, arsenic and antimony are both silvery like metals but brittle like nonmetals. Bismuth is dense, soft pinkish-silver metal. Moscovium (you may be seeing the trend by now) is a man-made, radioactive element about which little is known.

Nitrogen is used in fertilizers and explosives. Phosphorus is also used in fertilizers and can be found in many detergents. Both nitrogen and phosphorus are essential elements used by molecules in our bodies to release energy from food. Arsenic and antimony are used in the production of batteries. You may have come in contact with bismuth if you've ever taken Pepto-Bismol for an upset stomach. Compounds containing bismuth is also a common ingredients in cosmetics.

Group 4A

6	**C** 12.0
14	**Si** 28.1
32	**Ge** 72.6
50	**Sn** 118.7
82	**Pb** 207.2
114	**Fl** (289)

FIGURE 3.31
Carbon Group
4A have 4 valence electrons. Glass and pottery contain the element silicon.

Group 5A

7	**N** 14.0
15	**P** 31.0
33	**As** 74.9
51	**Sb** 121.8
83	**Bi** 209.0
115	**Mc** (288)

FIGURE 3.32
The Nitrogen Group
The elements in group 5A have 5 valence electrons. Nitrogen and phosphorus are the most common.

The Oxygen Group

Group 6A is known as the oxygen group and they have 6 valence electrons. Oxygen (O), sulfur (S), and selenium (Se) are nonmetals. Tellurium (Te) and polonium (Po) are metalloids, and livermorium (Lv) is considered a metal. As you may have guessed, livermorium is an extremely radioactive, man-made element that has never been observed in nature.

Oxygen and sulfur are common elements. In fact, oxygen is the most common element in the Earth's crust. Oxygen reacts with just about everything to form new compounds. Most living things need oxygen to stay alive. Oxygen is a gas and can be stored in tanks. Because flammable materials burn in the presence of oxygen, the tanks must be kept away from sparks or fire. Sulfur, a yellow element is often found in nature alone—not combined with anything else—in large natural deposits. Selenium is used in solar cells and as a toner in photograph printing. Tellurium is used to improve stainless steel. Polonium is a rare radioactive element discovered by Marie Curie.

The Halogens

The elements in Group 7A are called halogens and each element has 7 valence electrons. The word halogen means salt-former and when a Group 7A element reacts with a metal, it forms a salt. All halogens are nonmetals, but (like the other groups) they do have differing physical properties. Fluorine (F) and chlorine (Cl) are gases, bromine (Br) is a fast evaporating liquid, and iodine (I) and astatine (At) are solids. By now it shouldn't be a surprise that tennessine (Ts) is a radioactive, artificially produced element of which little is known. It is expected to be a solid, but scientists are not sure of its classification.

The halogens are very reactive nonmetals. Remember that the alkali metals group increased in reactivity as you went down the column. Well with the halogens it is the opposite. The most reactive halogen is fluorine. Compounds containing fluorine are used to prevent tooth decay and can be found in many toothpastes. You have likely smelled chlorine when you were at a pool. Chlorine is added to pools to kill bacteria and algae. Your thyroid gland needs iodine to

Group 6A

8
O
16.0
16
S
32.1
34
Se
79.0
52
Te
127.6
84
Po
(209)
116
Lv
(293)

FIGURE 3.33
Oxygen Group
The elements in group 6A have 6 valence electrons. Oxygen and sulfur are the most common.

Group 7A

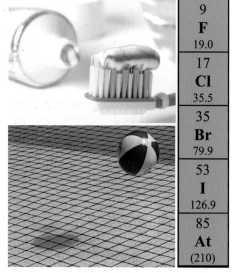

9
F
19.0
17
Cl
35.5
35
Br
79.9
53
I
126.9
85
At
(210)

FIGURE 3.34
The Halogens
The elements in group 7A have 7 valence electrons. Fluorine can be found in compounds in toothpaste and chlorine is added to pools.

work properly. You can find iodine in seafood and in iodized salt (salt that contains iodine compounds).

The Noble Gases

The elements in Group 8A are called noble gases and they each have 8 valence electrons, except for helium which can only hold 2 electrons. The noble gases are all odorless and colorless, rather rare, and extremely unreactive—which made them quite hard to discover. This group includes helium (He), neon (Ne), argon (Ar), krypton (Kr), xenon (Xe), radon (Rn), and—you guessed it—the radioactive, synthetic element oganesson (Og) which little is known about.

Noble gases are pretty useful for the reason that they do not react with other elements. For example, argon is used in light bulbs because it does not react with the metal at high temperatures. Helium is used to inflate blimps, tires of airplanes, and weather balloons because it is nonflammable. Neon is used in making signs because, when electricity is passes through it, neon glows bright red. Krypton and xenon generate very bright light when electricity passes through them, so they have been used as lighthouse lights and in photography flash units.

All of the noble gases except radon are used to make "neon" lights. When electricity passes through the noble gases they emit different colored light. Helium glows pink, neon glows red-orange, argon glows lavender, krypton glows white, and xenon glows blue (Figure 3.35 middle photo). Review what you've learned by answering On Your Own problems 3.10–3.12.

Group 8A

| 2 |
| He |
| 4.00 |

| 10 |
| Ne |
| 20.2 |

| 18 |
| Ar |
| 39.9 |

| 36 |
| Kr |
| 83.8 |

| 54 |
| Xe |
| 131.3 |

| 86 |
| Rn |
| (222) |

| 118 |
| Og |
| (294) |

FIGURE 3.35
The Noble Gases
The elements in group 8A have 8 valence electrons—except helium which has 2. Noble gases do not react with other elements.

ON YOUR OWN

3.10 Why do elements in a group have similar properties? Why do they not have identical properties?

3.11 How does the reactivity of alkali metals change as you go down the group from top to bottom?

3.12 Which group of elements is the least reactive?

SUMMING UP

Even the smallest unit of matter, the atom, shows us God's organization of the universe. Atoms are the fundamental building blocks that make up everything. Atoms are neutral—arranged with the same number of protons as electrons. The arrangement is so orderly, in fact, that we can organize the elements in the periodic table and predict the properties of unknown elements. It seems impossible that the structure of atoms, with the ordered way the electrons are arranged to produce the properties of each element, could be the product of chance. Instead the tiny atom can be contemplated as evidence of creation by a God of order.

ANSWERS TO THE "ON YOUR OWN" QUESTIONS

3.1 Democritus argued that the smallest, indivisible unit of matter is the atom. Aristotle argued that all matter is made up of four elements—fire, earth, water, and air—in varying proportions.

3.2 When Thomson's evidence supported the idea that the atom is made of smaller particles, Dalton's model was changed to reflect the new evidence.

3.3 The glowing beam of electricity was attracted to the positively charged plate and repelled by the negatively charged plate.

3.4 Not all of the alpha particles were deflected in the gold foil experiment because the nucleus is small compared to the space of the whole atom. Only a few of the alpha particles came close enough to a nucleus in a gold atom to be deflected.

3.5 Mass, charge, and location in an atom can be used to distinguish one subatomic particle from another.

3.6 Since all sodium atoms have 11 protons, this one has 11 protons. This tells us that it also has 11 electrons. Since the mass number is 23, we know that the sum of protons and neutrons in the nucleus must equal 23. So 23 – 11 = 12 neutrons.

3.7 Isotopes have the same number of protons in their nuclei, but different numbers of neutrons. Only (a) and (c) have the same number of protons. They each have 16. In addition, they have different numbers of neutrons. The atom in (a) has 17 neutrons and the atom in (c) has 18 neutrons. Thus, since they have equal numbers of protons but different numbers of neutrons, (a) and (c) are isotopes.

3.8 Atoms emit light energy when electrons go from an excited state (higher energy) to a lower energy state. So the answer is (d).

3.9 The 2 electrons in the 2nd energy level will have more energy than the 2 electrons in the 1st energy level.

3.10 Elements in a group have similar properties because they have the same number of valence electrons. They do not have identical properties because their valence electrons are in different energy levels.

3.11 The reactivity of alkali metals increases as you go down from the top of Group 1A to the bottom.

3.12 The noble gases, Group 8A, are the least reactive.

STUDY GUIDE FOR MODULE 3

1. Match the term to the correct definition.

    a. Law of Conservation of Mass   The sum of the protons and neutrons in the nucleus of a cell

    b. Law of Constant Composition   Atoms of an element with the same number of protons but different numbers of neutrons

    c. Atomic number   Matter cannot be created or destroyed, but it can change forms

    d. Mass number   Electrons that are in the highest energy level of an atom

    e. Isotopes   Samples of a pure compound always have the same elements in the same mass proportions

    f. Orbitals   The number of protons in an atom

    g. Valence electrons   A region of space around the nucleus where electrons are most likely to be found

2. Where is almost all of the mass of an atom found?

    a. protons   b. neutrons   c. electrons   d. nucleus

3. What type of particle is an electron?

    a. a negative charge, found in the nucleus

    b. a negative charge, found outside the nucleus

    c. a positive charge, found in the nucleus

    d. no charge, found outside the nucleus

4. All atoms of an element have the same

    a. number of isotopes.

    b. atomic number.

    c. mass number.

    d. number of neutrons.

5.   The atomic number of argon is 18. How many electrons are there in argon-38?
        a. 16   b. 18   c. 20   d. 56

6.   How many neutrons would be in argon-38?
        a. 16   b. 18   c. 20   d. 56

7.   If elements have the same number of valence electrons, they are
        a. called halogens.
        b. called noble gases.
        c. in the same group.
        d. in the same period.

8.   What are the most reactive metals?
        a. alkali metals
        b. alkaline earth metals
        c. transition metals
        d. metalloids

9.   Which elements are all gases?
        a. Group 1A   b. Group 2A   c. Group 7A   d. Group 8A

10.   J.J. Thomson's experiments provided what evidence about atoms?
        a. Atoms are the smallest particles of matter.
        b. Atoms contain negatively charged particles.
        c. Atoms have a negative charge.
        d. Atoms have a positive charge.

11.   Who provided evidence for the existence of a dense, positively charged nucleus in the center of an atom?
        a. John Dalton   b. J.J. Thomson   c. Democritus   d. Ernest Rutherford

12.   Which statement about oxygen-17 and oxygen-18 is true?
        a. They have identical mass.
        b. They are isotopes of oxygen.
        c. They have different numbers of protons.
        d. They have different numbers of electrons.

13. Which statement describes how electrons move in Niels Bohr's model of the atom?

    a. like planets orbiting the sun

    b. like balls tossed on waves

    c. like fan blades spinning

    d. like stones rolling down a hill

14. What must happen for an electron to move to a higher energy level?

    a. The atom must lose an electron.

    b. The atom must become more stable.

    c. The electron must gain energy.

    d. The electron must lose energy.

15. What does the electron cloud model describe?

    a. the number of electrons in an atom

    b. where in the atom the electrons will most likely be

    c. the mass of all the electrons in an atom

    d. the exact location of the electrons in an atom

16. What is the maximum number of electrons that an atomic orbital can contain?

    a. 2   b. 4   c. 8   d. 16

17. If an atom of an element has a mass number of 31 and 16 neutrons in its nucleus, what is the atomic number of the element?

18. If an atom of germanium has a mass number of 70 and an atomic number of 32, how many neutrons are in the nucleus?

19. How does the state of the atoms in a neon light change when the neon light glows?

20. A sample of sulfur contains sulfur-32, sulfur-33, sulfur-34, and sulfur-36 atoms. Explain why these atoms can have different mass numbers, but they must have the same atomic number.

---

[1] E. N. da C. Andrade, *Rutherford and the Nature of the Atom* (1964), p. 111

MOD 4

CHEMISTRY— CHEMICAL BONDS

When you combine a good theory and good model you are able to explain lots of observations. Dalton's atomic theory states that all matter is made of atoms and that different substances are made from different combinations of atoms. Bohr's model of the atom, with electrons in energy levels, can be used to explain how elements combine to form compounds and even how some compounds will "stick" together.

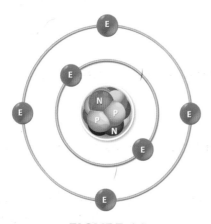

FIGURE 4.1
Model of a Carbon Atom
The valence electrons in the outer energy level determine an atom's chemical properties.

Natural Notes

We saw in the last module how the ordered nature of God is revealed in the structure of the atom and the organization of the elements in the periodic table. Yet the study of chemistry can show us so much more about the Creator. Looking at how atoms bond with each other will give us a glimpse at the diversity of creation. Just imagine— everything you see around you is made up of atoms from just 90 elements. It is in the way these atoms give, take, or share their valence electrons in chemical bonds that new substances are formed. Scripture tells us that God holds all things together.

> *He is before all things, and in him all things hold together.*
> Colossians 1:17

May you see how beautifully ordered and bountiful the diversity of creation is as you study this module.

IN THIS MODULE YOU WILL READ ABOUT THE FOLLOWING MAIN IDEAS:

- A Model for Chemical Changes
- Types of Chemical Bonding
- The Wonder of Water

A MODEL FOR CHEMICAL CHANGES

In any chemical change, old combinations of elements break up and new combinations form. This means that the bonds that link two or more atoms together must break so that new bonds can form. How these bonds form or break depends on the valence electrons of the atoms in each molecule. Chemical properties, such as reactivity, depend on the electron configuration of the element. Before we can get into the details of how this happens, however, we need to discuss how we represent molecules in chemistry.

Chemical Formulas

Have you ever made peanut butter cookies? There is a simple recipe using just 3 ingredients: 2 cups peanut butter, 1 cup sugar, and 2 eggs. This recipe makes about 48 cookies and the ratio of ingredients is 2:1:2. You can increase or decrease the number of cookies you make simply by increasing or decreasing the amount of the ingredients. But, to have your cookies taste the same, you must keep the ingredients in the same ratio. For example, to make 24 cookies you would need to divide all ingredients by 2—1 cup peanut butter, ½ cup sugar, and 1 egg.

Chemical compounds also have "ingredients" in a certain ratio. However, while you can tweak the peanut butter cookie recipe to your taste—add a little less sugar or a little more peanut butter—chemical compounds always have the exact same ratio of elements. This ratio is represented by a chemical formula.

FIGURE 4.2
Peanut Butter Cookies
A recipe can be used as an analogy for a chemical formula.

Chemical formula—A notation indicating the elements in a compound and the ratios of the atoms of each element

For example, the "recipe" or the chemical formula for water is H_2O. Notice that the elements in the compound, water, are represented by their chemical symbols. Also notice that the ratio of hydrogen atoms to oxygen atoms is represented by the subscript 2. The formula H_2O tells us that each water molecule contains two hydrogen atoms and one oxygen atom. Any time there is no subscript with the symbol (as with the oxygen in the water formula) it means there is 1 atom of that element. Figure 4.3 shows a model of a water molecule. The red sphere represents an oxygen atom and the 2 white spheres represent the 2 hydrogen atoms.

Using symbols and subscripts, chemical formulas can be written for any substance. Oxygen gas has a formula of O_2. This tells us each molecule of oxygen gas has 2 oxygen atoms. Sugar (glucose) has a chemical formula of $C_6H_{12}O_6$. How many atoms of each element is in a sugar molecule? The formula tells us there are 6 carbon atoms, 12 hydrogen atoms, and 6 oxygen atoms in every molecule of sugar. Chemical formulas make it possible to describe what happens in a chemical change (chemical reaction). We can do that using chemical equations.

FIGURE 4.3
Water Molecule Model
This model is called a space-filling model because it shows a 3D representation of the structure of a molecule.

FIGURE 4.4
Chemical Change
When carbon in charcoal combines with oxygen in the air, a chemical reaction occurs producing carbon dioxide and heat.

Chemical Equations

A common chemical change occurs when carbon combines with oxygen to form carbon dioxide. This change occurs any time charcoal is burned (Figure 4.4). A useful way of describing this change is to write what substances are present before the change and what substance(s) are present after the change. We can write that description out using a word equation as shown below.

$$\text{carbon + oxygen} \longrightarrow \text{carbon dioxide}$$

This is the word equation for the chemical reaction in which carbon dioxide is formed. The substances on the left are called reactants. The substance on the right is the product.

Reactants—Substances that undergo a chemical change

Products—New substances formed as a result of a chemical change

Reactants are substances that exist before a chemical change. Products are formed during the change. Keep in mind that more than one product can be formed in a chemical change. The arrow indicates the direction of the change.

$$\text{Reactants} \longrightarrow \text{Products}$$

Any word equation can be simplified by writing the reactants and products as chemical formulas.

$$C + O_2 \longrightarrow CO_2$$

This is a chemical equation and it is the way scientists summarize a chemical change. A chemical equation, then, is a representation of a chemical reaction using chemical formulas for the reactants and products. To "read" this chemical equation, you would say, "one carbon atom reacts with one oxygen gas molecule yielding one carbon dioxide molecule."

think about this

In nature oxygen only exists as a gas molecule composed of 2 oxygen atoms bonded together. There are 7 elements that exist in nature this way—hydrogen, oxygen, nitrogen, fluorine, chlorine, bromine, and iodine. Each of these elements are found as 2 identical atoms bonded together. Scientists call them **homonuclear diatomic molecules**. Homonuclear means having the same type of nucleus, so it means the same element. Diatomic means 2 atoms. So homonuclear diatomic means 2 atoms of the same element. Therefore, any time you see these elements in a chemical equation, you will see them written with the subscript 2.

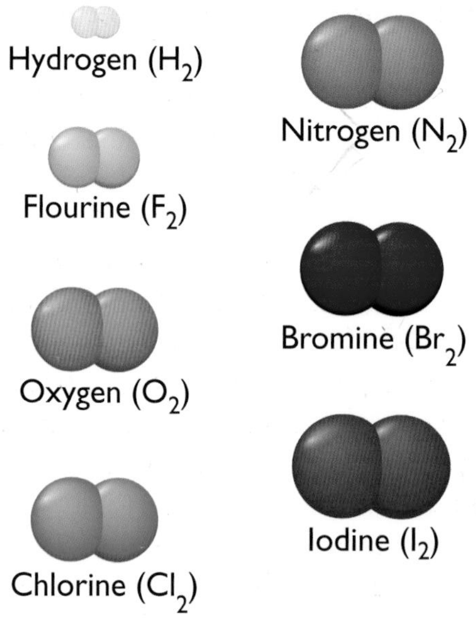

Balancing Equations

Look again at the chemical equation for carbon dioxide. Notice the number of atoms of the reactants and product. There is one carbon atom and 2 oxygen atoms in the reactants of the chemical equation. There is the same number of each atom on the products side of the reaction. This should make sense to you if you think back to the law of conservation of mass that you learned about in the last module. Remember that matter cannot be created or destroyed, it can only change form. That is exactly what is happening in a chemical reaction described by a chemical equation.

Now study the chemical equation for the formation of water shown below and in Figure 4.6.

Hydrogen (H_2)

Nitrogen (N_2)

Flourine (F_2)

Bromine (Br_2)

Oxygen (O_2)

Iodine (I_2)

Chlorine (Cl_2)

FIGURE 4.5
Diatomic Molecules
These are the space-filling models for the diatomic molecules H_2, F_2, O_2, Cl_2, N_2, Br_2, and I_2.

$$H_2 + O_2 \longrightarrow H_2O$$

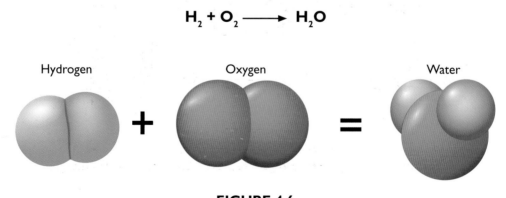

Hydrogen + Oxygen = Water

FIGURE 4.6
Unbalanced Chemical Equation
How many atoms of oxygen and hydrogen are present before and after the change?

Does the equation have the same number of atoms of hydrogen and oxygen on both sides? Well it does have the same number of hydrogens, but there are 2 oxygen atoms on the reactants' side and only 1 oxygen atom on the products' side. This reaction equation is unbalanced. In order to show that mass is conserved during a reaction, a chemical equation must be balanced (have the same number of atoms of each element on both sides of the equation). So how do we achieve that? By using coefficients.

Coefficients—Numbers that appear before a formula in a chemical equation to show how many atoms or molecules of each reactant or product are involved in the reaction

Let's walk through balancing the chemical equation for water to see what I mean. First, consider what we must do to balance the equation. In other words, what molecules can we add that will give us the same number of atoms of hydrogen and oxygen on both sides? At this point, the hydrogen atoms are balanced. But in order to balance the number of oxygen atoms on the reactant's side, we must add another water molecule to the product's side. Now why can't we add just one oxygen atom? Well, since oxygen only exists as a diatomic molecule we can't add only one atom. And since oxygen gas is a reactant, we don't want to produce it in the reaction. We want to produce water, so that's what we need to add.

Once we add a water molecule to the right side of the equation, the number of our oxygen atoms is balanced, but now we have 2 extra hydrogen atoms on the right side of the equation. To balance the hydrogen atoms, we must add one more hydrogen gas molecule to the left side of the equation. Our balanced equation is shown in Figure 4.7. Notice how we show the addition of the hydrogen molecule on the left and the water molecule on the right by placing the coefficient 2 in front of their chemical formulas. The number 2 indicates how many molecules of each substance is involved. When there is no coefficient (like with O_2) it is implied that there is 1 molecule or atom.

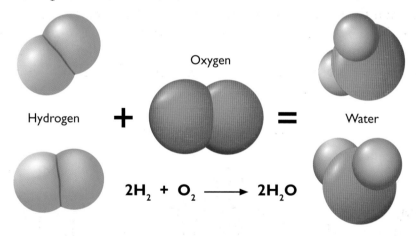

Oxygen

Hydrogen **+** **=** Water

$$2H_2 + O_2 \longrightarrow 2H_2O$$

FIGURE 4.7
Balanced Chemical Equation
How many atoms of oxygen and hydrogen are present before and after the change?

One very important thing to remember when balancing equations is that you must *never change a subscript in a formula*. Changing the subscript in a formula will change the identity of that reactant or product. So the only way to adjust the number of atoms or molecules is to use coefficients. Balancing a chemical equation takes a certain amount of trial and error, but you generally follow a few steps.

- Always start with the proper formulas for the reactants and the products (these will be given to you in this course). Count each type of atom on both sides of the equation. If the number of atoms of each element of reactants does not equal the number of atoms of each element of products, the equation is *not* balanced. Go to the next step.

- Write down the number of each atom on each side. Choose one of the atoms (it is generally best to leave oxygen and hydrogen until last) and place coefficients, as needed, in front of the atoms or molecules to increase their numbers. Use the smallest coefficients possible. (Remember, *never* change the subscripts in a formula.) Do this until that atom is balanced on both sides. If all atoms are not yet balanced, go to the next step.

- Repeat for each atom until the equation is balanced. You may need to go back and adjust atoms previously balanced—just keep at it.

Study Example 4.1 to review these steps and then complete On Your Own problems 4.1–4.2. With a little practice, you can become quite good at balancing equations!

EXAMPLE 4.1   Balancing Equations

Under pressure and heat, nitrogen gas (N_2) reacts with hydrogen gas (H_2) to produce ammonia (NH_3). Balance the equation for this reaction.

$$N_2 + H_2 \longrightarrow NH_3$$

Look carefully at the equation. Is it balanced? If not (as in this equation) write out how many atoms of each molecule are on each side like shown:

$$N_2 + H_2 \longrightarrow NH_3$$

$N = 2$	$N = 1$
$H = 2$	$H = 3$

Leaving hydrogen until last, add the coefficient of 2 in front of the ammonia molecule. Now you must adjust the numbers of both atoms in the ammonia molecule. To adjust the hydrogen atoms in ammonia, you must multiply the coefficient by the subscript. So 2 (coefficient) × 3 (subscript) = 6. There are now 6 hydrogen atoms on the right side of the equation. Mark as shown:

$$N_2 + H_2 \longrightarrow 2NH_3$$

$N = 2$	$N = \cancel{4}\ 2$
$H = 2$	$H = \cancel{3}\ 6$

Now the nitrogen atoms are balanced but the hydrogen atoms still need to be balanced. You must go back to the reactants' side of the equation and add a coefficient that will make the number of hydrogen atoms equal 6. A coefficient of 3 will achieve that because 3 (coefficient) × 2 (subscript) = 6.

$$N_2 + 3H_2 \longrightarrow 2NH_3$$

N = 2	N = ~~4~~ 2
H = ~~2~~ 6	H = ~~3~~ 6

Double check that the numbers of all atoms on the left side of the equation equals the numbers of all atoms on the right side of the equation. If so, then this is the balanced equation for the production of ammonia from nitrogen gas and hydrogen gas.

$$N_2 + 3H_2 \longrightarrow 2NH_3$$

ON YOUR OWN

4.1 How many atoms of each element are in the following molecules? (Use the Table of Atomic Numbers and Element Symbols in the Appendix to identify the elements.)

    a. CH_4 b. SF_6 c. Mg_2SiO_4

4.2 Balance the following equations.

    a. $C + O_2 \longrightarrow CO$ b. $NO_2 \longrightarrow NO + O_2$ c. $Zn + HCl \longrightarrow ZnCl_2 + H_2$

TYPES OF CHEMICAL BONDING

Remember that the arrow pointing from left to right in a chemical equation shows that the reactants change into the products during the reaction. How does a chemical change affect the number of protons and electrons in an atom? In a chemical change, the number of protons in an atom cannot change. If it did, the atom would become a different element. However the number of the valence electrons can change.

The most stable electron configuration for atoms is when their highest energy level has a full set of electrons. Remember that the first energy level has only 1 orbital so it can contain only 2 electrons. The first energy level is full when it contains 2 electrons. Helium has 2 electrons in its outermost energy level, so it has a stable electron configuration. This is the reason that helium is not reactive. All of the other energy levels are stable when they have a set of 8 electrons in them. So all of the rest of the noble gases found in Group 8A have a stable electron configuration with 8 valence electrons and therefore are not reactive.

Elements that do not have a stable electron configuration with complete sets of valence electrons tend to be reactive. By reacting, atoms form chemical bonds to achieve electron configurations similar to those of noble gases.

Chemical bond—A force of attraction between atoms or groups of atoms

In other words, in a reaction chemical bonds between the atoms in the reactant molecules break and new bonds form with different atoms to create the products. As a result, the products are different chemical substances than the reactants that started in the reaction, but the atoms in the substances will all have stable electron configurations. There are two main ways atoms achieve this—by transferring electrons or by sharing electrons.

Ionic Bonds

So far we've been talking about neutral atoms. After all, you know that atoms have the same number of electrons as they do protons, therefore they are neutral. But some atoms that do not have a stable electron configuration will achieve that by transferring electrons. You may have guessed that if an atom gives away or takes an extra electron then the atom will no longer be neutral. You are correct, so we first need to discuss what happens to the atom.

Ions

Atoms that are not neutral will have a positive or negative charge depending on whether they give away or take on an extra electron. Atoms with an electrical charge are called ions (i' unz).

Ion—An atom or a group of atoms that has a positive or negative charge

Remember that the alkali metals in Group 1A of the periodic table have only 1 valence electron. Look at the Bohr model of the sodium atom (Na) in Figure 4.8. Remember that sodium's atomic number is 11 so we know it has 11 protons in the nucleus. It also has 11 electrons. But look at what would happen if sodium lost that one valence electron. When sodium loses its valence electron, it has the same electron configuration as neon. Neon has a full valence shell with 8 electrons in it, which is a very stable electron configuration. So sodium and the other alkali metals easily give up their valence electron to achieve the more stable electron configuration of the noble gas in the row above them. This is why alkali metals are so reactive.

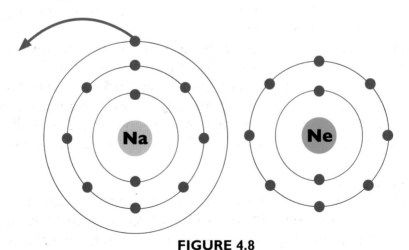

FIGURE 4.8
Electron Configurations of Sodium and Neon Atoms
If sodium loses its valence electron it has the same stable electron configuration as neon.

When sodium gives up that electron it now has one more proton than it does electrons. It is no longer a neutral atom. It is an atom with a positive charge. Atoms with a positive charge are called positive ions or cations (kat' eye unz). The charge on a cation is represented by a plus sign. So when a sodium atom (or any alkali metal atom) gives away its valence electron, it becomes a cation with a charge of 1+. The symbol for the sodium ion is Na+ (notice that the 1 is understood but not written). Naming cations is easy—it is simply the element name followed by the word ion, such as *sodium ion.*

Atoms in the alkaline earth metals (Group 2A) have 2 valence electrons. These elements are also reactive because they will lose their 2 valence electrons quite easily to achieve the stable electron configurations of a noble gas. They become ions with a charge of 2+. An example is the magnesium atom. The symbol for the magnesium ion is Mg^{2+}.

Now look at the Bohr model of a chlorine atom, shown in Figure 4.9. Remember that chlorine has an atomic number of 17 so it has 17 protons in its nucleus and 17 electrons. It has 7 valence electrons. If chlorine had one more electron in its valence shell it would have the same stable electron configuration as the noble gas argon (Ar). (Look back at the periodic table in the Appendix if you need to.) This is what makes chlorine so reactive. Chlorine easily accepts an electron to give it a more stable valence shell.

The ion that forms when a chlorine atom gains an electron has 17 protons and 18 electrons—one extra electron. Thus, chlorine forms a negative ion. The charge on negative ions is represented by a minus sign. So when chlorine takes on an extra electron, it becomes a negative ion with a charge of 1−. Negative ions are called anions (an' eye unz). The symbol for the negatively charged chlorine atom is Cl−.

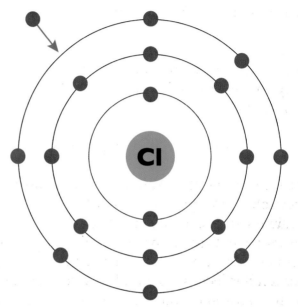

FIGURE 4.9
Electron Configuration of Chlorine
If chlorine gains a valence electron it has the same stable electron configuration as argon.

Anions, like the Cl− ion, are named in a special way. To name anions use the first part of the element name plus the suffix –*ide*. So, Cl− is called a *chloride ion.* Atoms of the elements in the halogen family all easily accept one extra electron. They will all have a 1− charge and will have names such as fluoride ion, bromide ion, and iodide ion.

Formation of Ions and Ionic Bonds

The formation of ions requires the transfer of electrons between atoms. Table salt is a common example. The formula for table salt, sodium chloride, is NaCl. As you should know by now, Na is the chemical symbol for sodium and Cl is the chemical symbol for chlorine. From the formula, NaCl, we can tell that there is one atom of sodium and one atom of chlorine. So what happens at the atomic level when sodium reacts with chlorine? Look at Figure 4.10.

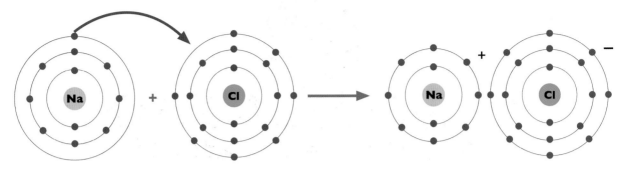

FIGURE 4.10
Reaction of Sodium and Chlorine
Chlorine readily accepts the valence electron that sodium easily gives up. Both ions that are formed have stable electron configurations and opposite charges.

The sodium atom gives up its valence electron to the chlorine atom. What do you notice about the ions produced in the reaction shown in Figure 4.10? Both the sodium ion and the chloride ion have a stable electron configuration and Na^+ has a positive charge while Cl^- has a negative charge. Cations and anions are attracted to each other and pull on each other because of their opposite charges. This force of attraction keeps the positive and negative ions together in a compound. Compounds held together in this way are called ionic (eye on' ik) compounds. Since the bond formed is between ions it is called an ionic bond.

Ionic bond—A chemical bond formed between oppositely charged ions

It's important to realize that since there is a positive ion and negative ion bonded together by their attraction, the ionic compound itself is neutral. That's why you don't see a charge on NaCl.

Elements of the alkali metals form ionic compounds with elements of the halogen family. *Ionic compounds are formed between cations (usually a metal) and anions (usually a nonmetal).* Other examples include, potassium bromide (KBr), magnesium chloride ($MgBr_2$), and lithium chloride (LiCl).

think about this

Have you ever noticed how salt particles look like crystals? The ionic bonds between the sodium ions and the chloride ions explains why. Look at Figure 4.11. In the diagram notice the way the sodium ions and chloride ions are positioned. Each positive Na^+ ion in the compound is surrounded by 6 negative Cl^- ions. And each Cl^- ion is surrounded by 6 Na^+ ions. The ions are arranged in an orderly, symmetrical, 3-dimensional pattern that repeats over the entire structure. There are strong ionic bonds between each ion and its neighbor. This forms the geometric crystalline lattice you see in salt particles. If you want to grow your own salt crystals, try the You Do Science activity.

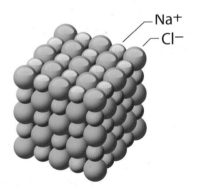

FIGURE 4.11
Sodium Chloride
A grain of salt gets its shape from the ionic bonds between Na^+ and Cl^- ions.

YOU DO SCIENCE

GROW A SALT CRYSTAL

You can grow your own sodium chloride crystals with a little help from a parent. It takes a few days, but you will get some experience in making a solution and seeing how the crystalline shape of salt is formed. To grow your own salt crystals you'll need: table salt (sodium chloride), distilled water, a clean, clear glass container (a beaker or jam jar), string, and a wooden spoon. Here's what to do:

- Cut a length of string that is long enough to tie around the spoon and be suspended to the bottom of the jar when the spoon is laid across the top of the jar.
- Place about 1/2 cup of distilled water in a pan on the stove and bring to a boil.
- Make a solution by stirring salt into the boiling hot water until no more salt will dissolve. You will know when no more salt can dissolve when you see crystals start to appear at the bottom of the pan. It may take as much as ½ cup of salt or more. Be careful around hot stoves and hot liquid.
- Carefully pour the solution into your beaker or jar. You may need parental help with this part.
- Tie one end of the string around the spoon and lay the spoon across the top of the jar suspending the string into the salt solution.
- Leave the jar somewhere it will not be disturbed and wait for your crystal to grow.

You can take this further by trying different types of salt, such as sea salt, Epsom salts, or un-iodized salt. You can also try using tap water instead of distilled water to see if there is any difference in the crystals that develop.

Electron Dot Diagrams

Before we move on to bonds formed by sharing valence electrons, I want to show you another useful model of the atom and an easier way to keep track of what happens to valence electrons. It is difficult and time consuming to draw out Bohr models every time you want to show what happens in a reaction (like the one shown in Figure 4.10). So, chemists use what is called the electron dot diagram.

The electron dot diagram is a model of an atom in which each dot represents a valence electron. The symbol of the element in the middle represents the nucleus and all other electrons in the atom. Since we've been discussing how the atoms achieve a stable electron configuration of their valence electrons, this model is very useful. Look at Figure 4.12. It shows the same reaction that Figure 4.10 shows but using electron dot diagrams.

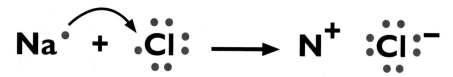

FIGURE 4.12
Electron Dot Diagram of the Sodium Chloride Reaction
Using electron dot diagrams makes it easier to keep track of valence electrons in chemical reactions.

The symbol Na represents the nucleus with 11 protons, all of the neutrons, and the 10 electrons in first 2 energy levels. The dot represents sodium's 1 valence electron. Likewise the symbol Cl represents the 17 protons and all the neutrons in the nucleus as well as the 10 electrons in the first 2 energy levels. The 7 dots represent the valence electrons.

Now look at the reaction for magnesium and chlorine. Remember magnesium is an alkaline earth metal in Group 2A so it has 2 valence electrons.

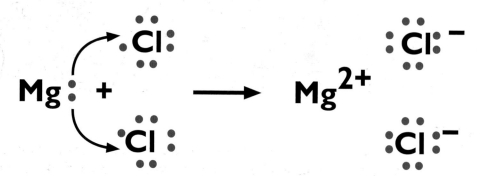

FIGURE 4.13
Electron Dot Diagram of the Magnesium Chloride Reaction
Magnesium gives away 2 electrons, one to each of two chlorine atoms to make magnesium chloride.

A magnesium atom cannot reach a stable electron configuration by reacting with only one chlorine atom. It has two electrons it must lose and so requires two chlorine atoms. Notice that after the electrons are transferred, the magnesium ion has a charge of 2^+ and is written as Mg^{2+}. The formula for the compound magnesium chloride is written as $MgCl_2$.

Table 4.1 shows you the electron dot diagrams for some Group A elements. Atoms with 1, 2, or 3 valence electrons (the metals) tend to give up their electrons easily. Atoms with 7 valence electrons (nonmetals) readily gain electrons. Review the table and then answer On Your Own questions 4.3–4.5.

TABLE 4.1
Electron Dot Diagrams of Some Group A Elements

1A	2A	3A	4A	5A	6A	7A	8A
H ·							He :
Li ·	· Be ·	· B ·	· C ·	· N ·	: O ·	: F ·	: Ne :
Na ·	· Mg ·	· Al ·	· Si ·	· P ·	: S ·	: Cl ·	: Ar :
K ·	· Ca ·	· Ga ·	· Ge ·	· As ·	: Se ·	: Br ·	: Kr :

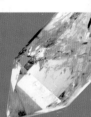

ON YOUR OWN

4.3   What causes an atom to become an anion?

4.4   When is an atom least likely to be reactive?

4.5   The elements hydrogen (H) and bromine (Br) react.

    a.   What ions are produced?

    b.   Write the electron dot diagrams for the reaction.

    c.   What is the chemical formula of the product?

    d.   Knowing that both hydrogen and bromine are diatomic molecules (H_2 and Br_2), how would you balance the equation?

COVALENT BONDS

We've discussed how atoms in Groups 1A, 2A, 3A, and 7A transfer electrons to form ionic bonds and make ionic compounds. I hope you're wondering what atoms with 4, 5, or 6 valence electrons do! Well atoms in these groups do not gain or lose electrons easily. Instead they tend to share electrons with other atoms. In fact the diatomic molecules (such as oxygen gas, O_2) that we've already talked about share electrons. Bonds that form because of shared electrons are called covalent bonds.

> **Covalent bond**—A chemical bond in which two atoms share one or more pairs of valence electrons

Covalent bonds form between atoms of nonmetals when they share valence electrons. Let's look at what this means using the hydrogen atom.

    Hydrogen atoms have 1 electron. It can give up that electron and then it would a hydrogen ion. Or it could share that electron with another atom. If hydrogen shares its electron with another hydrogen atom, together they would have 2 valence electrons.

Helium has 2 valence electrons and so has a stable electron configuration. When two hydrogen atoms each share their electron with the other in a covalent bond, they achieve the same stable electron configuration as helium. Figure 4.14 shows a model of hydrogen gas molecule. A molecule is a neutral group of atoms that are joined together by covalent bonds. In the case of H_2, both electrons travel around both nuclei.

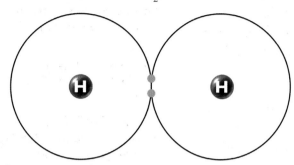

FIGURE 4.14
Hydrogen Gas Molecule
Each hydrogen atom shares its electron with the other forming a covalent bond. By sharing electrons each hydrogen has the stable electron configuration of helium.

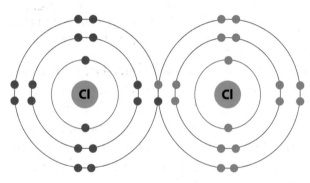

FIGURE 4.15
Chlorine Gas Molecule
Each chlorine atom shares one electron with the other forming a covalent bond. Now each chlorine atom has a stable electron configuration.

If you think back to the other diatomic molecules we talked about, you'll remember that most of the halogen gases (such as chlorine) are diatomic molecules. So that means that while chlorine will accept an electron from a metal and form an ion, it will also share a valence electron with another chlorine atom to form a covalent bond. Look at Figure 4.15. This figure shows a diagram of the molecule chlorine gas Cl_2. The electrons are shown positioned in pairs because each orbital of each energy level can hold 2 electrons. The electrons on the chlorine atom on the right are a different color so that you can see how the electrons are shared. You can see that each chlorine atom shares one of its valence electrons with the other atom. This gives both atoms 8 valence electrons. So what keeps the chlorine atoms together in the molecule? It is the attractions between the shared electrons and the protons in each nucleus that holds the atoms together in covalent bonds. The shared electrons travel around both nuclei because of this attraction.

Like with ionic bonds, it is easier to use electron dot diagrams to show covalent bonds. Figure 4.16 shows the electron dot diagrams for the reaction to make Cl_2.

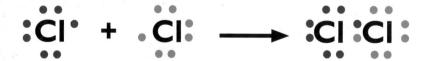

FIGURE 4.16
Electron Dot Diagram of Chlorine Gas Reaction Equation
This is an easier way of showing the valence electrons in a chlorine gas molecule.

It so happens that there is an even easier way to show co-valent bonds. It's called the structural formula model for a molecule or compound. In a structural formula the bonds and positions of the atoms are shown. Figure 4.17 shows the structural formula for Cl_2. In the structural formula the dot pairs of each covalent bond are replaced with a dash. The dots do not need to be added because it is implied that there is a stable electron configuration with the covalent bond.

Multiple Covalent Bonds

Now let's go back to the question about Groups 4A, 5A, or 6A elements—what do they do since they need more than one electron to have a stable electron configuration? Let's look at oxygen gas first. Oxygen has 6 valence electrons. If two oxygen atoms shared a pair of electrons, each one would have only 7 valence electrons, still not a stable electron con-figuration. But what if they each shared 2 electrons? Then they would each have a full outer energy level with 8 valence electrons. Each pair of shared electrons is represented by a long dash in the structural formula O=O. When two atoms share two pairs of electrons, the bond is called a double bond. Figure 4.18 shows the electron dot diagram for O_2.

Now think about nitrogen which is a Group 5A element. It has 5 electrons in its outer energy level. If two nitrogen atoms each shared one electron they would each only have 6 valence electrons. If they each shared 2 electrons, they would each still only have 7 valence electrons. But if they each shared 3 electrons, then they would each have the 8 valence electrons needed for a stable electron configuration. When two atoms share 3 pairs of electrons, the bond is called a triple bond and is represented by 3 long dashes in the structural formula—one for each covalent bond. The structural for-mula for N_2 is N≡N and its electron dot diagram is in Figure 4.19.

So what about group 4A? Group 4A elements have 4 valence electrons. Car-bon is an example of a Group 4A element. These elements can form 4 covalent bonds with other atoms. A good example is the compound methane, CH_4. Methane is a powerful greenhouse gas and consists of one carbon atom sharing an electron with 4 hydrogen atoms, each sharing their elec-tron. By sharing electrons, each hydrogen atom has 2 electrons and the carbon now has 8 electrons, so all atoms have a sta-ble electron configuration. The electron dot and structural formulas for CH_4 are shown in Figure 4.20.

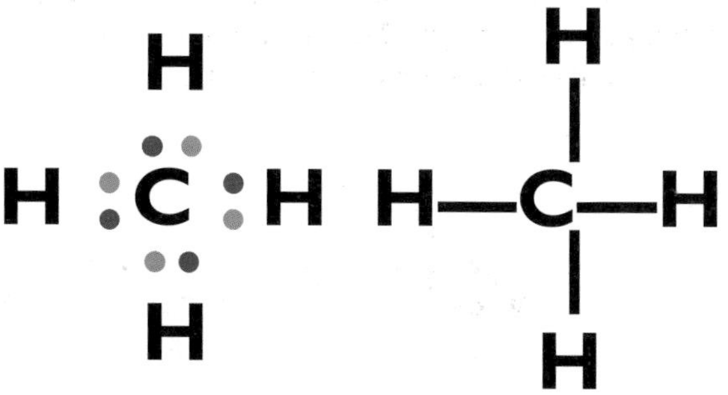

FIGURE 4.17
The Structural Formula for Cl_2
A dash represents a covalent bond. No dots are needed.

FIGURE 4.18
Electron Dot Diagram for O_2
Each oxygen atom shares 2 electrons to achieve a total of 8 valence electrons.

FIGURE 4.19
Electron Dot Diagram for N_2
Each nitrogen atom shares 3 electrons to achieve a total of 8 valence electrons.

FIGURE 4.20
Models of CH_4
The electron dot diagram (left) and the structural formula (right) both show shared electrons in covalent bonds.

think about this

The fact that carbon can form up to 4 covalent bonds makes it one amazing atom. In fact, carbon can be considered a designer element! Why? If carbon did not have the properties it does, there would not be life on Earth. Ask any chemist, biochemist, or biologist.

Living things are made up of billions of large, complex molecules. For example, proteins control everything that happens in your cells. Proteins are made up of tens of thousands of atoms all bonded together forming complex, three-dimensional molecules. The image on the left of Figure 4.21 shows you just one tiny part (called an amino acid) of a protein. To give you some perspective, the oxygen carrying protein in your blood (called hemoglobin, computer image shown on the right) has about 570 amino acids in it. Carbon is the atom that forms the backbone of proteins like hemoglobin. Why carbon? Of the 90 naturally occurring elements in creation, only carbon atoms have the ability to form long stable molecules made up of chains, ringed structures, 3D structures, single bonds, double bonds, or triple bonds with itself and other atoms. All of these properties are unique to carbon and are absolutely necessary for life to exist. Carbon is the only element with the necessary properties for life. Take a moment to consider how carbon is perfectly designed—just the right number of protons, neutrons, and electrons—to form stable bonds, build stable molecules, and sustain life.

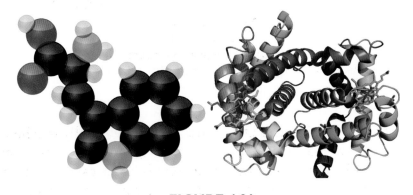

FIGURE 4.21
Models of Amino Acid and Protein
The amino acid, Tryptophan $C_{11}H_{12}N_2O_2$, is shown on the left. It has
11 carbon atoms (black balls) bonded in chains and rings. A comput-
er-generated model of hemoglobin is shown on the right.

Unequal Sharing of Electrons

So far, all of the bonds we've been talking about have been equal bonds. An equal bond means that the attraction for the shared electrons is equal between the nuclei of the atoms. But what happens if there is an unequal attraction?

Except for the noble gases, elements on the right side of the periodic table generally have a greater attraction for electrons than elements on the left side. Also, elements at the top of a group generally have a greater attraction for electrons than that of elements at the bottom of a group. So if you look back at the periodic table, which element do you think has the greatest attraction for electrons? Fluorine, on the top of Group 7A, has the strongest attractions for electrons which makes it the most reactive nonmetal.

When two atoms of the same element form a covalent bond, both nuclei have the same (equal) attraction for electrons. But in a compound where you have two or more atoms of different elements, the attraction for electrons may not be equal. Unequal attraction means unequal sharing of electrons.

For example, when hydrogen reacts with chlorine, each atom shares one electron and the compound hydrochloric acid is produced (Figure 4.22). It's easy to see why the chlorine nucleus will attract the shared electrons more. Chlorine has 17 protons in its nucleus and hydrogen has 1 proton. The greater positive charge pulls more strongly on the electrons. Since chlorine atoms have a greater attraction for electrons than hydrogen atoms do, the shared electrons spend more time near the chlorine atom than near the hydrogen atom.

Hydrochloric Acid (HCl)

FIGURE 4.22
Models of HCl
The 3D ball-and-stick model (left), the structural formula
(middle), and the 3D space-filling model (right) all represent HCl.

A covalent bond in which the electrons are not shared equally is called a polar covalent bond. In this context polar means opposite in charge (similar to how the 2 poles of a bar magnet are opposite in terms of their magnetic field). Because the electrons spend more time around the atom with the greater attraction for electrons when atoms form a polar covalent bond, that atom will have a partial negative charge. The atom with the lesser attraction for electrons will have a partial positive charge. To show which atom has which partial charge, scientist use the lowercase Greek letter delta (δ) followed by either a plus or minus sign. Using Figure 4.22, the symbol δ^- could be written next to the purple chlorine atom to show a partial negative charge on that side of the compound. The symbol δ^+ could be written next to the gray hydrogen atom to show a partial positive charge on that side.

Any time you have a compound made of only two different atoms held together by a polar covalent bond (like HCl), the molecule is considered to be a polar molecule.

> **Polar molecule**—A molecule that has slight positive and negative charges
> due to an imbalance in the way electrons are shared

But if you have a compound made up of more than two atoms it becomes a bit more difficult to determine if the molecule is polar. To help decide if a molecule is polar, chemists look at the types of atoms and the shape of the molecule.

For example, look at the two molecules in Figure 4.23. Both molecules are made of one central atom with two atoms on either side. In carbon dioxide (top molecule) there are double bonds between the carbon atom and each oxygen atom. Oxygen has a greater attraction for electrons than carbon does, so each double bond is a polar covalent bond. But look at the shape of the molecule. The three atoms form a straight line (called a linear shape). Because the carbon-oxygen double bonds are directly opposite each other, the pull on the electrons from each oxygen atom is equal. Because the pull on the electrons is equal from both sides, they cancel each other out and, even though CO_2 has polar bonds, it is a nonpolar molecule.

Now look at the water molecule. Again oxygen has a greater attraction for electrons than hydrogen so there is a single polar covalent bond between oxygen and each hydrogen. This time, however, the molecule has a bent shape, so the polar bonds do not cancel each other out. Water is a polar molecule. Since the two hydrogen atoms are located on the same side of the molecule (opposite the oxygen atom) the hydrogen side of the molecule has a partial positive charge. The oxygen side of the molecule has a partial negative charge because the two shared electrons spend more time around the oxygen atom than around the hydrogen atoms. It's important to remember that all polar compounds will contain polar bonds, but not all compounds that contain polar bonds are polar.

The polarity (poh lair' ih tee) of water gives it many important properties. Polarity simply means having opposite charges within the same substance Complete Experiment 4.1 to "see" the difference between polar and nonpolar molecules.

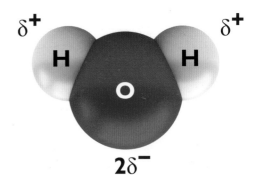

FIGURE 4.23
Polar and Nonpolar Molecules
CO_2 is a nonpolar molecule because the polar covalent bonds between carbon and oxygen cancel out. H_2O is a polar molecule because the polar covalent bonds do not cancel out.

EXPERIMENT 4.1
POLARITY OF WATER

PURPOSE:
To observe the attraction of polar and nonpolar molecules to a static electrical charge.

MATERIALS:
- A Styrofoam or paper cup
- Glass of water

- Vegetable oil
- Balloon
- Pen
- Eye protection such as goggles or safety glasses

QUESTION:

How will a stream of water (a polar substance) and a stream of vegetable oil (a nonpolar substance) react when a balloon with a static negative charge is brought near?

HYPOTHESIS:

Write your prediction of what a stream of water will do when a charged balloon is brought near. Write your prediction of what a stream of oil will do when a charged balloon is brought near.

PROCEDURE:

1. Use the pen to punch a small hole in the bottom of the cup. The smaller the hole, the better.
2. Blow up and tie off the balloon. Set near the sink in easy reach.
3. While holding the cup over the sink, fill the cup with water from the glass. Water should start running out of the hole in the bottom of the cup. Make sure that the water is pouring out of the hole in a steady stream, not dripping. If it is dripping, make your hole just a little bigger.
4. Once the water is pouring out of the cup in a steady stream, pick up the balloon with your other hand and rub it vigorously in your clean, dry hair. This is meant to make the balloon develop an electrical charge. If your hair is wet or oily, this may not work too well. You can also charge the balloon with different fabrics so try using your clothes if your hair isn't working.
5. Once you have rubbed the balloon in your hair (or clothes) for a few seconds, bring the balloon (the side you were rubbing) near the stream of water. Bring the balloon close but do not actually touch the water stream. Write your observations in your data table.
6. Repeat this same experiment using vegetable oil instead of water. You may have to make the hole a little bigger this time, because vegetable oil doesn't flow as easily as water does. You should also catch the oil in a jar to save for the next experiment. Record your observations in your data table.
7. Clean up and put everything away.

CONCLUSIONS:

Explain your observations and the difference between the way oil behaves and the way water behaves when both are exposed to an electrically charged balloon. Use the term polarity in your explanation and make connections to the text.

Other Types of Bonds

Before we leave the topic of types of bonds, I should mention two other types. The first type of bond involves metals. Most metals have a very low attraction for electrons which is why they give up their electrons so easily to become positive ions. Because of this the valence electrons of metals move more freely between atoms of the element than valence electrons of nonmetals. These freely moving valence electrons are what makes metals good conductors of electricity (moving electrons). The attraction of the positive metal ions to the valence electrons of neighboring metal ions is called a metallic bond. The metal ions and the constantly moving valence electrons form a lattice-like structure held together by the metallic bonds. This is also why metals are malleable (bend without breaking).

The second type of bond involves polar molecules. Remember polar compounds, such as water, are molecules that have a partial negative charge on one side and a partial positive on the other side of each molecule. Because of these partial charges, one water molecule is attracted to 4 other water molecules as shown in Figure 4.24. The positively charged hydrogen side of one water molecule is attracted to the negatively charged oxygen side of another water molecule. This force of attraction is called a hydrogen bond.

You should have seen this when you conducted Experiment 4.1. Because of the hydrogen bonds between the water molecules, the stream of water stayed together and bent towards the charged balloon.

Unlike the other bonds we've talked about, *hydrogen bonds are bonds that form between molecules, not between atoms.* They are weaker bonds than covalent or ionic bonds, but strong enough to make molecules "stick" together and they are very important. Hydrogen bonding occurs in any polar molecule in which positive hydrogen atoms are attracted to negative atoms of nearby molecules. But it is hydrogen bonds that allow water to have the many wonderful properties it exhibits. Before reading on, complete On Your Own questions 4.6–4.7.

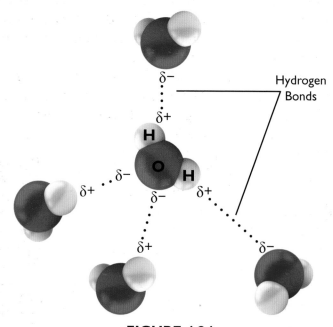

FIGURE 4.24
Hydrogen Bonds Between Water Molecules
Hydrogen bonds form between the partially positively charged hydrogen atoms of one water molecule and the partially negatively charged oxygen atoms of a nearby water molecule.

ON YOUR OWN

4.6 Which of these elements does not bond to form molecules?

    a. oxygen   c. neon

    b. chlorine   d. nitrogen

4.7 What attractions hold atoms together in covalent bonds?

THE WONDER OF WATER

Did you know that you can live for as many as two weeks without food, but if you were to go even a few days without water, it would surely be deadly. Water comprises almost two-thirds of our bodies and covers over two-thirds of the Earth's surface. Without water, life as we know it simply cannot exist. In addition to its necessity for life, water has many other properties that make it a truly remarkable substance. The polarity of water is actually responsible for a great many of its interesting properties.

Solubility

Water is able to dissolve many substances because of its polarity. Think about the types of substances a polar molecule like water can dissolve. Remember from module 2 that a solution is made when a solvent dissolves a solute. If the solute is an ionic compound, such as salt, then the partial charges in the water molecule can attract the charged ions in the ionic compound and easily dissolve it.

Figure 4.25 shows what happens when salt is dissolved in water. Notice what's happening in this figure. The positive sodium ions and the negative chloride ions are closely packed, because their opposite electrical charges attract one another. Water molecules, however, are attracted to the ions, so they move in close to the ions. The electrical charges in the water molecules attract the electrical charges of the ions, pulling the ions away from each other. Eventually, each ion in the solute molecule is pulled so far from the other ions that the substance is no longer visible in the solution. It is still there, but its ions are so far removed from each other that they exist on their own. Since the ions are too small to see, the substance seems to disappear.

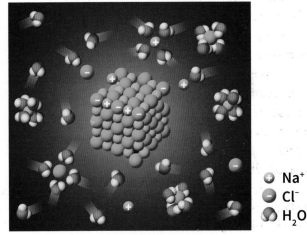

FIGURE 4.25
Water Dissolving NaCl
Water's polarity allows it to easily dissolve ionic compounds and other polar covalent compounds.

Notice how the water molecules are oriented in the figure. For the positively charged sodium ions, the water molecules orient themselves so that the small negative charge on the oxygen atom is close to the positive sodium ion. For the negatively charged chloride ion, however, the water molecules orient themselves so that the hydrogens, with their partial positive charge, are as close as possible. As time goes on, more water molecules will come in and pull more ions away from each other, eventually dissolving the table salt completely.

Although it's harder to picture, essentially the same thing happens when water dissolves any polar substance (sugar, for example). The electrical charges in the water molecules are attracted to the electrical charges in the polar solute molecules. The result is that the water molecules pull the solute molecules away from each other, dissolving the solute.

So, water tends to dissolve substances made up of either polar molecules or ions. If a molecule is nonpolar, however, water will not be attracted to it, since a nonpolar molecule has no net electrical charges in it. Olive oil and canola oil, for example, are made of nonpolar molecules. As a result, water will not dissolve them. In the end, then, water dissolves substances made of polar molecules or ions, and it will not dissolve substances made of nonpolar molecules. The reason that water seems to dissolve almost everything (it's called the universal solvent) is that the vast majority of compounds in creation are either polar or ionic. Thus, water dissolves a great many substances, but not everything. Something to keep in mind—as a general rule, ionic and polar substances can dissolve each other, non-polar substance can dissolve only other nonpolar substances.

Hydrogen Bonding and the Phases of Water

You've already read about how hydrogen bonding happens, but why is hydrogen bonding so special? Well, there are a couple of reasons. First, because water molecules are polar and hydrogen bond to each other, water molecules tend to stick much closer together than do other molecules. For example, consider the following molecules: H_2S, H_2Se, and H_2Te. Those chemical formulas look a lot like H_2O, don't they? In fact, the only real difference is that the other molecules have a different atom in place of the oxygen atom. From a chemistry point of view, those three molecules are very similar to water. In fact, they are the chemicals most like water in all of creation. Guess what, though? All three of those molecules are *gases at room temperature!*

Why is water a liquid at room temperature, when other chemicals similar to water are gases? The answer is hydrogen bonding. Remember from module 2 that the major difference between a liquid and a gas is how far apart the substance's molecules are and how quickly they move around. Well, hydrogen bonding keeps the water molecules close together and limits their movement somewhat. As a result, water is a liquid at room temperature when other chemically similar substances are gases. We are, in fact, very blessed this is the case. Water is one of the basic needs of life. All biochemists agree that if water were not liquid at room temperature, life as we know it could not exist. Despite the fact that all chemically similar molecules are gases at room temperature, water is a liquid, and so can sustain life. The chemical explanation for this is hydrogen bonding, but water's design should cause you to consider the Creator. He designed the world and its physical laws, and hydrogen bonding is just one more design element He used to make life possible!

FIGURE 4.26
Solid, Liquid, and Gaseous Water
Water's design gives it the properties that allow life to exist on Earth.

Hydrogen bonding actually gives water another interesting property. To learn about that property, perform Experiment 4.2.

EXPERIMENT 4.2
COMPARING SOLIDS

PURPOSE:
To observe the differences in solid water and solid butter.

BACKGROUND:
Typically as a substance is heated it expands. Because of the increase in kinetic energy supplied by the heat, the molecules of the substance speed up and move around more, increasing their volume (which decreases density). Likewise as most substances cool, they contract because their molecules slow down as their kinetic energy decreases. As they slow down their volume decreases because they take up less space (increasing density). Remember from Experiment 2.2 that less dense substance will float in more dense substances. In this experiment you will investigate if this phenomenon happens for both butter and water.

MATERIALS:
- Stick of butter or margarine (It must be fresh from the refrigerator so that it is solid.)
- Two beakers or microwave-safe glass bowls
- Water
- Ice cube
- Microwave (A saucepan and stove can be substituted for the microwave.)
- Knife (A serrated one works best. You will use it to cut the butter.)
- Spoon
- Eye protection such as goggles or safety glasses

QUESTIONS:
What happens when solid butter is placed in liquid butter? What happens when solid water is placed in liquid water?

HYPOTHESIS:
Predict what will happen when solid water and butter are placed in liquid water and butter respectively.

PROCEDURE:
1. Look at the tablespoon markings on the wrapper that covers the stick of butter. Using those markings as a guide, cut ½ tablespoon off the end of the stick with the knife so that you have a small square of butter.
2. Unwrap both the piece you cut off and the rest of the stick.
3. Put the ½ tablespoon of butter back in the refrigerator until it is needed in step 8.
4. Put the rest of the stick of butter into the beaker or microwave-safe glass bowl.
5. Melt the butter in the microwave for about 1 minute. (Check after 30 seconds to see if it is melted.) You can also melt the butter in a saucepan on the stove.
6. When the butter is completely melted, take it out of the microwave. If using the saucepan, carefully pour the melted butter into the beaker or glass bowl. You now have a beaker of liquid butter.

7.   Fill the other beaker with water. Set both beakers side by side.
8.   Go to the refrigerator and get the solid butter you put there. Also get an ice cube from the freezer.
9.   Drop the ice cube in the water.
10. Drop the ½ tablespoon of solid butter in the liquid butter.
11. Record your observations of what happened to the ice cube and the solid square of butter in your data table.
12. Clean up and put everything away.

CONCLUSION:

What was the difference in what happened to the ice cube and the solid butter square? Explain what happened (use density in your explanation) and make connections to the text (discuss hydrogen bonding).

When you dropped the ice cube into the water, it should have floated. When you dropped the square of solid butter into the liquid butter, it should have sunk. Why the difference? Well, we all know that ice floats; we take it for granted. However, for the vast majority of substances in creation, the solid form of a substance being less dense than the liquid form is extraordinary. For most substances the molecules get closer when the substance has a phase change from liquid to solid and farther apart during the phase change from solid to liquid. Butter is an example of such a substance. The molecules that made up the solid butter are closer together than the molecules that made up the liquid butter. As a result, the solid butter pushed its way through the liquid butter and sank.

Water was precisely the opposite. When water is a solid, its molecules stay in a rigid, geometric arrangement (Figure 4.27). That rigid arrangement requires the molecules to be a certain distance apart. When water is a liquid, however, its molecules are free to move around. As a result, hydrogen bonding can pull them closer together. *Water molecules are closer together when water is a liquid compared to when water is a solid.* Because of this, the ice cube could not push its way through the water molecules, and the ice cube stayed afloat.

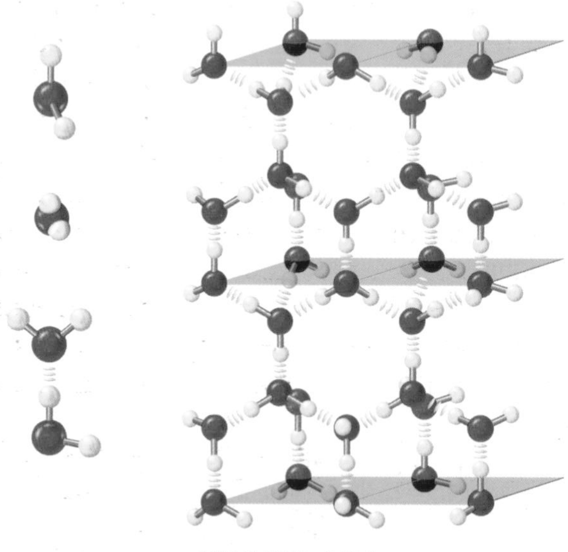

So, unlike most substances in creation, when water is a solid its molecules are actually farther apart than when it is a liquid. As a result, solid water (ice) floats in liquid

FIGURE 4.27
Structure of Ice
Water's design gives it the properties that allow life to exist on Earth.

water. Once again, we are quite "lucky" this is the case. After all, what happens to lakes in the winter? They freeze, don't they? Does all the water in the lake freeze? No. If that were the case, all living things in that lake would die. Instead, as the water freezes, *it floats to the top of the lake* because of this property (Figure 4.28). As a layer of ice builds on top of the lake, it insulates the water below, and at some point, no more water will freeze! Because of this, the living organisms in the lake survive the winter. Think about all the food we get from lakes or from other creatures that depend on the living organisms in a lake. If water didn't have this property, lakes in many regions of the world could not support life, and most likely would not be able to survive!

Because of water's hydrogen bonds, water has another interesting property. Changing from liquid to gas occurs when a substance gains energy. The energy causes individual molecules to speed up and move apart from each other. The hydrogen bonds of polar molecules (water) make it so that more energy is needed to break the bonds before the molecules can move apart. So, it takes higher temperatures for polar molecules to change from liquid state to gaseous state. This explains why polar compounds generally have higher melting and boiling points than nonpolar molecules.

FIGURE 4.28
Icebergs
Icebergs can float because the molecules in ice are farther apart than they are in liquid water.

So why is this important? Well, because of hydrogen bonds in polar water molecules, it takes a lot of heat to increase the temperature of water. This is because some of the heat must be used to break the hydrogen bonds between the water molecules. In other words, water has a high heat capacity, so water does not increase temperature easily. In fact the heat capacity of water is 5 times greater than that of sand. This means that when the sun is shining the beach absorbs the sun's energy 5 times faster (and gets much hotter) than the body of water near it. The land also cools down faster than the sea once the sun goes down. Since the water cools much more slowly, it releases heat to the nearby land during the night. This is why land near large bodies of water are more temperate than land without water. And just think of what this means for the creatures living in water! The design of water allows creatures to live in and near the water without freezing or overheating. Review what you've read so far by answering On Your Own questions 4.8–4.10.

ON YOUR OWN

4.8   Water does not dissolve gasoline. Is gasoline most likely made up of ionic, polar, or nonpolar molecules?

4.9   Water has a very high boiling point compared to most other substances that are liquid at room temperature. Use hydrogen bonding to explain why this is the case.

4.10   Butane is a gas at room temperature, but it is stored under pressure as a liquid in a butane lighter. The chemical formula is C_4H_{10}. Isopropyl alcohol (commonly called rubbing alcohol) is another liquid you might have around the house. Its chemical formula is C_3H_8O. One of these liquids participates in hydrogen bonding. Which one? How do you know?

Cohesion, Adhesion, and Surface Tension

Whether an object will sink or float has to do with its density, but also the tendency of the molecules to stick together. The polarity of water molecules, combined with hydrogen bonding, tends to keep water molecules close together when water is in the liquid state. Once they are close, they tend to want to stay close. Although the water molecules will move around, as all molecules do in liquid form, they still stay close together as they move. This phenomenon is called cohesion (cho he' shun).

> **Cohesion**—The force of attraction between molecules of the same substance so that they tend to stay together

Cohesion is much stronger for water than for most other liquids.

Cohesion makes a water drop spherical (Figure 4.29). Notice in the figure how the water droplets ball up pretty high. Water is "sticky" and the molecules clump together into drops because of water's cohesive property. The cohesive forces between water molecules occur because of the hydrogen bonds caused by the partial electrical charges of the oxygen and hydrogen atoms.

Because water molecules are polar, they are also attracted to other polar molecules besides water. The type of attraction that occurs between unlike molecules is called adhesion (add hee' shun).

FIGURE 4.29
Water Drops
Water forms droplets because of the cohesive attraction between water molecules.

> **Adhesion**—The force of attraction between molecules of different substances so that they tend to stick together

The next time you measure water in a measuring cup, notice how the water surface forms a U shape (Figure 4.30). This is because of adhesion between the polar water molecules and the polar molecules of the glass. The attraction between the partially charged molecules causes them to "stick" together. Notice how the water in the graduated cylinder shown in the figure rises up on the glass on each side. That is because of adhesion. The concave curve in the upper surface of the water in the graduated cylinder is called a **meniscus**.

The cohesion and adhesion properties of water are very important in creation. Have you ever wondered how water gets from the roots to the leaves of the tallest trees? Well, that happens because of the cohesive and adhesive properties of water. As you will learn in biology, water travels up from the roots of a plant to its leaves in

FIGURE 4.30
Meniscus
A meniscus forms because of adhesive forces between water molecules and the glass molecule on the wall of the glass container.

small tubes called xylem (zye' lum). Amazingly, there is no pump that causes the water to do this. You and I have blood running through our arteries and veins because our hearts pump the blood so that it can travel throughout our bodies. However, plants do not need any kind of pump to transport water. Water can travel from the roots all the way to the top of the tallest tree without any system that pushes it upward. The cohesion between water molecules and the adhesion between the water molecules and the cells of the xylem tubes make this water movement possible. This type of movement by cohesion and adhesion is called **capillary action** and you can see an example in Figure 4.31.

FIGURE 4.31
Capillary Action
Cohesion between water molecules and adhesion between water molecules and the glass cause water to move up in the capillary tube without help.

You are also likely familiar with another example of water's cohesion. Have you ever seen an insect "walking" across the surface of a pond (Figure 4.32)? Insects have a greater density than water and should sink, so how can this happen? Cohesion pulls the water molecules at the surface tightly together which forms a skin-like boundary that supports the insect. This phenomenon is known as **surface tension.** Notice how the surface of the water actually bends where the water striders' legs touch it. That shows you the water strider's weight is pushing down on the surface of the water. Nevertheless, water's surface tension is enough to keep the insects from sinking. Look back at Figure 4.29 and notice how the drops of water look almost like they have an invisible skin keeping them from falling apart. That is another example of surface tension.

Of all the liquids on Earth, water has one of the greatest tendencies towards cohesion, so it also has one of the largest surface tensions in all of creation. Investigate these properties of water by conducting Experiment 4.3 before beginning the Study Guide.

FIGURE 4.32
Surface Tension
A water strider can skate across the top of a pond because of the surface tension of water caused by cohesion.

EXPERIMENT 4.3
FORCES BETWEEN MOLECULES

PURPOSE:
To investigate cohesion and adhesion in water molecules.

MATERIALS:
- Water
- Bowl
- 4 beakers or clear glasses
- Paper towels
- Wax paper
- Pipette or eyedropper
- Straw
- 2 microscope slides
- Metal paper clip (Use a standard-sized paper clip. A big one will probably not work.)
- Toilet paper
- Dish soap
- Vegetable oil
- Toothpicks
- Scissors
- Blue and red food coloring
- Spoon
- Eye protection such as goggles or safety glasses

QUESTIONS:
Do drops of water look different than drops of oil or soapy water? Can drops of water be separated? Can water move against gravity? Can objects denser than water float? Can water act as glue?

HYPOTHESES:
Write your predictions by answering the questions listed above.

PROCEDURE—PART 1, MOVING WATER:
1. Fill one beaker ¾ full of hot tap water. Add a few drops of red food coloring and stir.
2. Fill one beaker ¾ full of cold tap water. Add a few drops of blue food coloring and stir
3. Place each beaker filled with water next to an empty beaker so they are side by side.
4. Roll two paper towel sheets into tight tubes.
5. Place one end of one paper towel tube in the beaker of hot water and the other end of the tube in the neighboring empty beaker. Make sure the paper towel roll extends at least half-way down in the water. You will need to bend the tube to a U-shape to have it go into the empty beaker. Repeat with the other two beakers. Draw your experimental set-up in the data table and describe what you observe.
6. Leave this set-up alone and complete the other parts of the experiment before coming back to observe again.

The trick is to work with the odd oxygen atom on the right. So if you put a coefficient of 2 in front of the NO in the products, you will then have an even number of oxygen atoms on the right side of the equation (even numbers are always easier to work with). Don't forget to adjust what happens to the nitrogen atoms when you add the coefficient.

$$NO_2 \longrightarrow 2\,NO + O_2$$

N = 1	N = ~~1~~ 2
O = 2	O = ~~3~~ 4

Now you simply need to balance the nitrogen atoms by placing a coefficient of 2 in front the compound on the left. You'll find that the oxygen atoms are balanced by this too!

$$2\,NO_2 \longrightarrow 2\,NO + O_2$$

N = ~~1~~ 2	N = ~~1~~ 2
O = ~~2~~ 4	O = ~~3~~ 4

Double check that all atoms are equal on both sides. If so, the equation is balanced.

Balanced equation is: $2\,NO_2 \longrightarrow 2\,NO + O_2$

4.2   c. $Zn + HCl \longrightarrow ZnCl_2 + H_2$

Zn = 1	Zn = 1
H = 1	H = 2
Cl = 1	Cl = 2

In this problem the zinc atoms are balanced. Let's leave the hydrogen atoms until last, so we'll focus on the chlorine atoms. There are 2 chlorine atoms on the right and only 1 on the left so we should put a coefficient of 2 in front of the HCl molecule on the reactants' side.

$$Zn + 2\,HCl \longrightarrow ZnCl_2 + H_2$$

Zn = 1	Zn = 1
H = ~~1~~ 2	H = 2
Cl = ~~1~~ 2	Cl = 2

Double check that all atoms are equal on both sides. If so, the equation is balanced.

Balanced equation is: $Zn + 2\,HCl \longrightarrow ZnCl_2 + H_2$

4.3 An atom becomes an anion which is an ion with a negative charge when it gains electrons and so has more electrons that it does protons.

4.4 An atom is least likely to be reactive when it has a stable electron configuration which means the highest occupied energy level of the atom is filled with electrons.

4.5 a. When hydrogen reacts with bromine, the hydrogen gives up its valence electron to become the cation H^+. Bromine receives the electron to become the anion Br^-. Each now have a stable electron configuration.

b. $H^{\bullet} + {\bullet}\ddot{Br}{\ddot{:}} \longrightarrow H^+ {\ddot{:}}\ddot{Br}{\ddot{:}}\ ^-$

c. Hydrogen bromide, HBr

d. $H_2 + Br_2 \longrightarrow 2HBr$

4.6 (c) Neon is a noble gas with a stable electron configuration so it does not bond.

4.7 The attractions between the shared electrons and the protons in each nucleus hold the atoms together in a covalent bond.

4.8 Gasoline is made up of nonpolar molecules. If water cannot dissolve a substance, it is likely that the substance is nonpolar.

4.9 Water has a high boiling point because the hydrogen bonds hold the molecules together. In order to turn into a gas, the water molecules need to get far apart from one another. When you heat something, you are giving it energy. Because the hydrogen bonds hold the molecules together, it takes a lot of energy (thus a high boiling temperature) to pull them apart.

4.10 Isopropyl alcohol participates in hydrogen bonding because it has an oxygen atom in its formula. Remember, hydrogen bonding in water takes place between the hydrogen and oxygen atoms. There are plenty of hydrogen atoms in butane, but no oxygen atoms. The other way you can tell is that butane is a gas at room temperature, thus the molecules are not held together tightly. Isopropyl alcohol is a liquid at room temperature, indicating that its molecules are held more tightly together. Between the two, then, the alcohol is the more likely one to have hydrogen bonds.

STUDY GUIDE FOR MODULE 4

1. Match the term to the correct definition.

a. Reactants

A chemical bond in which two atoms share one or more pairs of valence electrons

b. Products

A chemical bond formed between oppositely charged ions

c. Coefficients

A molecule that has slight positive and negative charges due to an imbalance in the way electrons are shared

Substances that undergo a chemical change

d. Ionic bond

The force of attraction between molecules of different substances so that they tend to stick together

e. Covalent bond

New substances formed as a result of a chemical change

f. Polar molecule

Numbers that appear *before* a formula in a chemical equation to show how many atoms or molecules of each reactant or product are involved in the reaction

g. Cohesion

The force of attraction between molecules of the same substance so that they tend to stay together

h. Adhesion

2. If a compound has 1 zinc (Zn) atom and 2 chlorine atoms (Cl) what is the compound's chemical formula?

3. How many atoms of each element are in the compound $AgNO_3$? (Hint: Ag is the symbol for silver, N is the symbol for nitrogen, and O is the symbol for oxygen.)

4. Calcium carbonate is an ionic substance commonly called "chalk." If this molecule has one calcium atom (Ca), one carbon atom (C), and three oxygen atoms (O), what is its chemical formula?

5. One of the most common household cleaners is ammonia, which has a chemical formula of NH_3. How many atoms are in a molecule of ammonia?

6. Balance the equation $CH_4 + O_2 \longrightarrow CO_2 + H_2O$.

7.   Why do ionic compounds include at least one metal and one nonmetal?

8.   Based on their chemical formulas, which of these compounds is not likely to be an ionic compound: KBr, SO_2, or $FeCl_3$? How can you tell?

9.   Describe two ways an element can achieve a stable electron configuration.

10.   What happens to the charge on atoms when they form a polar covalent bond?

11.   A certain molecule is composed of atoms that all pull on electrons with the same strength. Will the molecule be polar or nonpolar?

12.   Using Table 4.1 and the electron dot diagrams for phosphorus (P) and hydrogen (H), what is the formula for their covalently bonded formula?

13.   Suppose you were able to count the molecules in a substance. Which would have more molecules, 1 liter of liquid water or 1 liter of ice? Why?

14.   If the substance in question 13 were virtually any other substance, what would the answer be?

15.   What is responsible for water being a liquid at room temperature as well as for water's properties of cohesion and adhesion?

16.   What causes surface tension?

CHEMISTRY—REACTIONS AND ENERGY

You have already learned a bit about chemical reactions. From module 2, you now know what to look for to determine if a change is a physical change or a chemical change (Figure 5.1). Chemical changes always result from chemical reactions. There are several different kinds of chemical reactions that produce chemical changes in substances. These chemical reactions are accompanied by changes in energy. In this module you will learn about the different types of chemical reactions. You will also learn how energy may be needed to start a chemical reaction or may be released as a product of a reaction.

Natural Notes

Chemical reactions occur around us every day. Plants carry on photosynthesis, which requires many chemical reactions. Baking initiates chemical reactions between ingredients. Eating requires your body to break down food using chemical reactions. Even every breath you take triggers chemical reactions in your body that uses the oxygen in the air to produce energy molecules. Each of these chemical reactions help keep you alive.

As you read this module, think about how many reactions are going on in the world around you that you have never noticed.

FIGURE 5.1
Chemical Reactions Cause Chemical Changes
The production of a gas shows that a chemical change is occurring during the chemical reaction.

IN THIS MODULE YOU WILL READ ABOUT THE FOLLOWING MAIN IDEAS:

- Naming Compounds and Writing Formulas
- Types of Reactions
- Energy Changes in Reactions

NAMING COMPOUNDS AND WRITING FORMULAS

Before we delve into the different types of reactions we should first learn how to name compounds and write formulas. Why would we bother with learning this? Well learning the names of compounds will make it easier to discuss what happens to them in the various reactions. Plus, have you ever been talking about something, say a firefly, and the person you're talking to doesn't know what you mean. Then they mention a lightning bug and you realize that you're both talking about the same insect, but because you each called it by a different name it was confusing. In the same way, having two or more names for a chemical compound can be confusing. So chemists use a system for naming compounds and writing formulas that is based on rules established by the International Union of Pure and Applied Chemistry (IUPAC). And remember, formulas of compounds tell us the composition of the compound—the ratio and types of elements. In this way each chemical name refers to a single substance.

Describing Ionic Compounds

Look at Figure 5.2. Notice how the oval stone is coated in a green and a reddish-brown substance. Both substances are compounds composed of iron and oxygen, rust. Iron is a transition metal, so it will form cations. Oxygen will readily accept electrons to form an anion with a 2− charge. (Remember that the name of anions uses part of the name of the nonmetal with the suffix *–ide*.)

Based on the two colors of the coatings, iron and oxygen must form at least two compounds. If they were the same compound they would have the same physical properties and so would be the same color. Since iron and oxygen can form multiple compounds, one name will not be enough to describe all of them. There must be at least two names to distinguish green iron oxide from reddish-brown iron oxide. So the name of an ionic compound must distinguish one compound from others containing the same elements. In addition, the formula for ionic compounds must show the ratio of cations to anions in the compound.

FIGURE 5.2
Iron Oxide Compounds
With both green and reddish-brown colored iron oxides, one name is not enough to distinguish between them.

TABLE 5.1 Common Nonmetal Anions			
Element Name	**Ion Symbol and Charge**	**Base Name**	**Anion Name**
Hydrogen	H^-	*hyd-*	hydride
Fluorine	F^-	*fluor-*	fluoride
Chlorine	Cl^-	*chlor-*	chloride
Bromine	Br^-	*brom-*	bromide
Iodine	I^-	*iod-*	iodine
Oxygen	O^{2-}	*ox-*	oxide
Sulfur	S^{2-}	*sulf-*	sulfide
Nitrogen	N^{3-}	*nitr-*	nitride
Phosphorus	P^{3-}	*phosph-*	phosphide

Compounds that are made up of only two elements are relatively easy to name. These types of compounds are called binary compounds because *bi-* means two.

Binary compounds—Compounds made of only two elements

Think of the ionic compound formed between sodium and chlorine. The name is simply sodium chloride. All binary ionic compounds are named using the following predictable pattern.

1. Determine the name of the cation which is simply the name of the element.

2. Determine the name of the anion which is part of the element's name with the suffix *–ide*. Table 5.1 shows the names, symbols, and charges for nine common anions.

3. Write the name of the cation followed by the name of the anion.

This seems pretty straight forward, and it works beautifully for sodium chloride. It also works out that way for the alkali metals, the alkaline earth metals, and aluminum. Each of these metals form cations with positive charges equal to their group number. For example, the symbol for a lithium ion is Li^+, the symbol for a magnesium ion is Mg^{2+}, and the symbol for an aluminum ion is Al^{3+}.

TABLE 5.2
Some Metal Cations

Element Name	Ion Symbol and Charge	Cation Name
Copper	Cu^+	copper (I)
	Cu^{2+}	copper (II)
Iron	Fe^{2+}	iron (II)
	Fe^{3+}	iron (III)
Lead	Pb^{2+}	lead (II)
	Pb^{4+}	lead (IV)
Chromium	Cr^{2+}	chromium (II)
	Cr^{3+}	chromium (III)

But what do we do about metals that form more than one cation, like iron? Well, many transition metals in the B groups do form more than one type of ion. Table 5.2 shows some of these transition metal cations, but you will learn more about all of them when you take chemistry. Notice the two iron ions listed in Table 5.2. Iron (II) is an iron ion with a 2+ charge and iron (III) is an iron ion with a 3+ charge. When a metal forms more than one cation, *the name of the cation contains a Roman numeral to indicate the charge on the ion.* Now we can distinguish between the green iron (II) oxide and the reddish-brown iron (III) oxide shown in Figure 5.2. To read these names, you would say "iron two oxide" for iron (II) and "iron three oxide" for iron (III).

Polyatomic Ions

So far we've discussed ions in binary compounds where each ion is made up of only one element. But there are ions that are composed of two or more atoms covalently bonded together, yet chemically act as a single atom. These ions are called polyatomic ions. The prefix *poly-* means "many."

> **Polyatomic ions**—A covalently bonded group of atoms that has a positive or negative charge and acts as a unit

Figure 5.3 shows a group of atoms that includes one carbon and three oxygen atoms. The top image is the space-filling model and the bottom image is the electron dot diagram of a carbonate ion. The atoms are joined by covalent bonds, so why does the group have a 2⁻ charge? The carbon atom has 6 protons and each oxygen atom has 8 protons—a total of 30 protons.

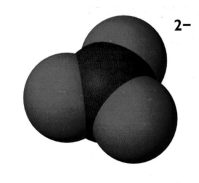

2–

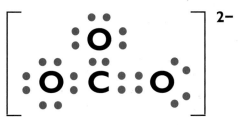

2–

FIGURE 5.3
Models of a Carbonate Ion
The carbon atom and 3 oxygen atoms are joined together by covalent bonds. The ion gains 2 electrons as it forms giving the ion 32 electrons to balance 30 protons.

Now look at the electron dot diagram and count up the valence electrons. Each atom in the carbonate ion has 8 valence electrons, so they all have stable electron configurations. There is a total of 24 valence electrons shown by the electron dots, but don't forget the electrons in the other energy shells represented by the symbol. Each atom has 2 electrons in their first energy level. How do I know that? Well, remember that the atomic number tells us the number of protons and electrons and the group number of each element tells us the number of valence electrons. So carbon is in Group 4A with an atomic number of 6, that tells me carbon has 2 electrons in its first energy level and 4 electrons in its valence energy level. Oxygen is in Group 6A with an atomic number of 8, so each oxygen atom also has 2 electrons in their first energy level and 6 electrons in their valence energy level. Finally, counting electrons: 4 atoms times 2 electrons in their first energy level equals 8 electrons. Eight electrons plus 24 valence electrons equal 32 total electrons. That's 2 more electrons than protons, so the entire group carries a charge of 2–.

Polyatomic ions have their own naming system. You will learn a lot more about polyatomic ions when you take chemistry. For now just look at Table 5.3 which lists the names and formulas for some common polyatomic ions. Notice how there is only one cation on the list, the ammonium ion. Also notice that all of the ions that have the suffix –*ite* have one fewer oxygen atom than those of the same name, but with the suffix –*ate*. You will not be expected to memorize any of the transitional metals or polyatomic ions. You will be allowed to use these tables to answer any questions.

TABLE 5.3 Some Polyatomic Ions			
Ion Name	**Formula and Charge**	**Ion Name**	**Formula and Charge**
Ammonium	NH_4^+	Carbonate	CO_3^{2-}
Hydroxide	OH^-	Peroxide	O_2^{2-}
Nitrite	NO_2^-	Nitrate	NO_3^-
Sulfite	SO_3^{2-}	Sulfate	SO_4^{2-}
Chlorite	ClO_2^-	Chlorate	ClO_3^-
Hypochlorite	ClO^-	Phosphate	PO_4^{3-}

Writing Formulas for Ionic Compounds

If you know the name of the ionic compound, you can write its formula. You simply need to know the symbols of the elements in the compound and the charges of their ions. You may use your periodic table and the Table of Atomic Numbers and Element Symbols to look up the symbols of the elements and the charges on their ions if you don't remember them. (You will not need to memorize them. You will be able to use the tables for Study Guide and test questions.) To write a formula for an ionic compound, follow these steps.

1. Place the symbol of the cation first, followed by the symbol of the anion.

2. Using the periodic table determine the charge of the cation and anion by finding what group the element is in. (If there is more than one possible cation, it will be given to you in this course.) Write the correct formula with the charges for the ions.

3. Use subscripts to show the ratio of the ions in the compound. Remember that all compounds are neutral, so the total charges on the cations and anions must add up to zero. To do this, use the following rules.

   a. If the charges on the cation and anion are equal in magnitude (1+ and 1-, 2+ and 2-, or 3+ and 3-) combine the them in a 1:1 ratio.

   b. If the charges on the cation and anion are not equal in magnitude, use the charge on the cation as the subscript for the anion (you won't use the + sign). Use the charge on the anion (without the – sign) as the subscript for the cation.

   c. If a polyatomic ion is used, place parentheses around the polyatomic ion if you need more than one of them in the formula.

Study the examples to see how to write chemical formulas. Then try it yourself by completing On Your Own problems 5.1–5.3.

EXAMPLE 5.1

Determine the formula for the ionic compound formed from sodium and sulfur.

1. First write out the symbols of the cation followed by the anion. If you don't know the symbols for the ions, look up the atoms on the Table of Atomic Numbers and Element Symbols in the Appendix.

$$NaS$$

2. Next use the periodic table to determine the charges on the ions. Sodium is in Group 1A, so it has a 1^+ charge. Sulfur is in Group 6A, so the sulfide ion has a charge of 2^-.

$$Na^{\oplus} S^{2\ominus}$$

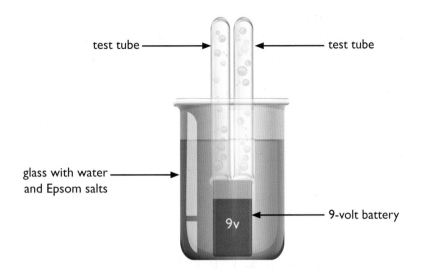

test tube   test tube

glass with water
and Epsom salts

9-volt battery

9v

8. With a little effort, you can make the test tubes balance on the battery so that you do not have to hold them there. If you have trouble doing that, you can tape the test tubes together and then lay two knives across the glass, sandwiching the test tubes between the knives.

9. Once you have gotten the test tubes to stand on the battery on their own, watch what's happening. The gases forming at each terminal travel up the test tube until they reach the top. At that point, they fill the top of the test tube, pushing away the water that was there. As time goes on, then, the gases produced at the terminals will be collected at the top of the test tubes. Draw your apparatus and record your initial observations in your student notebook.

10. Let the experiment sit for a while. Go back periodically and check, and you will see that the water level in the test tubes is decreasing. This is happening because as the gases are produced, they exert pressure on the water in the tubes. This pushes down on the water in the tubes, forcing water out of the tubes and into the glass. Add any observations to your data table in your student notebook.

11. The solution will probably turn a nasty color after a while, because substances in the battery will eventually leak into the solution. That's okay, though. It looks ugly, but it does not affect the results of the experiment. Be sure not to get any of the solution in your mouth! The chemicals coming from the battery can be toxic at high concentrations.

12. When one of the test tubes is filled halfway with gas, draw what the experiment looks like in your student notebook. Be sure to note which terminal is the positive one and which is the negative one. If it is not marked on the battery, the larger terminal is negative, and the smaller terminal is positive.

13. Clean up: Throw the battery away, pour the contents of the glass into the sink, rinse the glass thoroughly, and flush all the liquid down the drain with plenty of water. Put everything away.

CONCLUSION:

Were you able to collect gases in the test tubes on the positive and negative terminals of the battery? How much gas was in each test tube relative to each other? Knowing the composition of water (H_2O) can you tell which terminal produced oxygen gas and which terminal produced hydrogen gas? Write a conclusion paragraph answering these questions and making connections to the text.

think about this

Decomposition reactions like the one you observed in the experiment happen around you all the time. Every time you eat, your digestion process involves many decomposition reactions. When you open a can of soda, the fizzing reaction that occurs is the result of a decomposition reaction. Cement factories use heat to decompose the calcium carbonate ($CaCO_3$) in limestone into calcium oxide (CaO)—a component of cement—and carbon dioxide.

Even air bags in many automobiles use a decomposition reaction. When a car is involved in a crash, the impact triggers the crash sensors to send a small electric current to the air bag igniter. The air bag is filled with sodium azide pellets (NaN_3), a colorless salt. When the spark from the igniter adds energy, the sodium azide pellets decompose into sodium and nitrogen gas. It is a very fast reaction and the nitrogen gas quickly inflates the air bag. The equation for this decomposition reaction is $2NaN_3 \longrightarrow 2Na + 3N_2$. After inflating the bag, the nitrogen gas escapes through tiny holes in the bag allowing the bag to deflate slowly, protecting the driver's head.

FIGURE 5.9
Air Bags
Air bags use a decomposition reaction to fill the bag with nitrogen gas.

Single Replacement

When an element in a compound is replaced by another element, the reaction is called a single replacement reaction.

Single replacement reaction—A chemical reaction in which one element takes the place of another element in a compound

FIGURE 5.10
Single Replacement
General equation for single replacement reactions.

Basically a more reactive element switches places with a less reactive element in a compound. The general equation for single replacement reactions is shown in Figure 5.10.

In the general equation in Figure 5.10, the A represents a more reactive element and BC represents the original compound. During the reaction, A replaces B to form the compound AC and releasing the less reactive element B. These reactions usually involve ions and ionic compounds. Remember how reactive the alkali metals are? These metals readily replace less reactive elements in compounds.

Look at Figure 5.11. A drop of water is placed on the metal potassium. The violent reaction that you see in the figure is a single replacement reaction. The metal potassium replaces hydrogen in water to form a colorless solid named potassium hydroxide, KOH. Hydrogen gas and heat is produced. The heat produced by this chemical reaction is enough to cause the hydrogen gas to explosively ignite. The chemical equation for this reaction is shown below.

$$2K \quad + \quad 2H_2O \longrightarrow H_2 \quad + \quad 2KOH$$
potassium   water   hydrogen   potassium
                              gas   hydroxide

FIGURE 5.11
Potassium and Water
Potassium reacts with water in a violent single replacement reaction.

Another example of a single replacement reaction is when copper replaces silver in the compound silver nitrate as shown in Figure 5.12. In the flask on the left a copper wire is placed in liquid silver nitrate. A vivid reaction takes place. How can you tell chemical changes are occurring? Notice the change in color and the formation of a precipitate. As the more reactive copper replaces the silver in the compound, the solution turns blue which is the color of copper nitrate. The replaced silver metal builds up on the wire (see the flask on the right). The chemical equation for this single replacement reaction is shown below.

FIGURE 5.12
Copper and Silver Nitrate
A single replacement reaction occurs between copper and silver nitrate producing blue copper(II) nitrate and silver metal.

$$Cu \quad + \quad 2AgNO_3 \longrightarrow 2Ag \quad + \quad Cu(NO_3)_2$$
copper   silver   silver   copper(II)
              nitrate   nitrate

Double Replacement

Two ionic compounds may react and exchange ions in a double replacement reaction. This reaction produces two new ionic compounds.

Double replacement reaction—A chemical reaction in which two compounds exchange positive ions and form new compounds

Figure 5.13 shows the general equation for double replacement reactions. First, notice how the ions represented by B and D exchange places to form the new compounds. This means there are two replacements occurring in these reactions. Second, notice that A and C represent the cations and B and D represent the anions in the ionic compounds. Remember that when we name ionic compounds, we always write the cation first. Let's see how double replacement reactions work.

FIGURE 5.13
Double Replacement
General equation for double replacement reactions.

Look at Figure 5.14. In the first photo (the photo on the left), two colorless liquids are about to be mixed. The beaker that is held contains the ionic compound potassium iodide, KI. The beaker on the table contains lead(II) nitrate, $Pb(NO_3)_2$. Notice what happens as the potassium iodide is poured into the beaker containing lead(II) nitrate. A chemical reaction producing a chemical change occurs because we can see the formation of a precipitate. The yellow precipitate is lead(II) iodide which forms when the lead ions in

FIGURE 5.14
Lead(II) Nitrate and Potassium Iodide
When potassium iodide solution is poured into a lead (II) nitrate solution, a double replacement reaction takes place.

$Pb(NO_3)_2$ trade places with the potassium ions in KI. The remaining liquid is potassium nitrate. The equation for this reaction is shown below.

$$Pb(NO_3)_2 \quad + \quad 2KI \longrightarrow PbI_2 \quad + \quad 2KNO_3$$

<table>
<tr><td>lead(II)
nitrate</td><td></td><td>potassium
iodide</td><td>lead(II)
iodide</td><td></td><td>potassium
nitrate</td></tr>
</table>

Combustion

Have you ever caught a marshmallow on fire while trying to roast it to a perfect golden brown over a campfire? If you have then you've witnessed a combustion reaction firsthand.

Combustion reaction—A chemical reaction in which a substance reacts rapidly with oxygen, often producing heat and light

A combustion reaction is a reaction in which a substance reacts rapidly with oxygen gas, releasing energy in the form of light and heat.

All combustion reactions will have oxygen gas as one of the reactants. We've talked a bit about how hydrogen explosively combusts when we discussed the reaction in Figure 5.11. This very thing happened on May 6, 1937 when the Hindenburg airship exploded and burned (Figure 5.16). The Hindenburg was a hydrogen airship similar to the blimps you see at sporting events today. (Blimps today are filled with helium gas.) Hydrogen gas is less dense than air, so it allowed the large airship carrying many passengers to fly long distances. Unfortunately hydrogen is combustible when energy, such as a spark, is added in the presence of oxygen.

FIGURE 5.15
Burning Marshmallows
Burning marshmallows over a campfire is an example of a combustion reaction.

FIGURE 5.16
Hindenburg Explosion
The hydrogen gas reacted with oxygen gas in an explosive combustion reaction.

On its first trip to the U.S. from Germany, the Hindenburg had to travel through some stormy weather to reach its landing destination. The cause of the energy is unknown. Some say static electricity build up and others say lightning was the cause. Either way the energy added to the hydrogen and oxygen gases caused an explosive combustion reaction. The chemical equation for this reaction is shown below. Notice how this reaction is also a synthesis reaction for water. Sometimes the classification for chemical reactions can overlap.

$$2H_2 \quad + \quad O_2 \longrightarrow \quad 2H_2O$$
hydrogen $\qquad$ oxygen $\qquad$ water
gas $\qquad\qquad$ gas

In the chemical equation above, hydrogen gas is the fuel needed for the combustion reaction to occur. When you burn your marshmallow, the marshmallow contains many carbon and hydrogen atoms which are a common fuel for combustion reactions. Fossil fuels, such as natural gas, are composed of only carbon and hydrogen atoms, and so are referred to as hydrocarbons. Hydrocarbons are often used as fuel in combustion reactions. If you use a lighter (like the one shown in Figure 5.17) to light your grill or fireplace, it is most likely filled with the hydrocarbon butane, C_4H_{10}. The main component of natural gas is the hydrocarbon called methane, CH_4. When methane has an unlimited supply of oxygen, the following reaction occurs.

FIGURE 5.17
Butane Lighter
The lighter is filled with the hydrocarbon butane. A spark provides the energy to start the combustion reaction.

$$CH_4 + 2O_2 \longrightarrow CO_2 + 2H_2O$$

methane   oxygen gas   carbon dioxide   water

Notice how carbon dioxide and water are produced in a combustion reaction of a hydrocarbon. If a hydrocarbon and oxygen are reactants and CO_2 and H_2O are products you will know the reaction is a combustion reaction. You might be wondering how water can be a product of a reaction in which fire is involved. Well, because there is enough heat for fire, the temperature will be above water's boiling point. So, the water will be in its gaseous phase and will be water vapor. Review what you've read by completing the On Your Own questions.

ON YOUR OWN

5.6   Name the type of reaction for the following reaction equations.

a. $Ca + 2HCl \longrightarrow CaCl_2 + H_2$
b. $C + 2H_2 \longrightarrow CH_4$
c. $C_3H_8 + 5O_2 \longrightarrow 3CO_2 + 4H_2O$
d. $HCl + KOH \longrightarrow KCl + H_2O$
e. $2NaCl \longrightarrow 2Na + Cl_2$

5.7   The synthesis of water is described by the equation $2H_2 + O_2 \longrightarrow 2H_2O$. How is the decomposition of water related to this reaction? Use a chemical equation in your explanation.

5.8   Explain the difference between a single-replacement reaction and a double-replacement reaction.

ENERGY CHANGES IN REACTIONS
As you think back over the last section, I hope you realize that we talked a lot about energy. Some of the reactions, such as the decomposition of water, required energy to start them. Other reactions, such as the single replacement reaction shown in Figure 5.11, gave off energy in the form of heat and light. The fact is, all chemical reactions involve energy.

It's easy to think about combustion reactions giving off energy. In fact that is often the reason we start combustion reactions. If you've ever grilled your food on a gas or charcoal grill, you started a combustion reaction specifically for the heat it produced. Just as we classified chemical reactions by the types of reactants and products, chemical reactions can also be recognized by the energy changes that occur.

Energy in Chemical Bonds

So how is energy used in chemical reactions? The answer is in breaking and forming ionic or covalent bonds. Energy is used to break bonds, and energy is released when new bonds form. If you look at the chemical equation for the combustion reaction of propane (the fuel used in gas grills), you can write "heat" as one of the products on the right side of the equation.

FIGURE 5.18
Heat Producing Reaction
We start combustion reactions to cook food over a grill because the reactions produce heat.

$$C_3H_8 \; + \; 5O_2 \longrightarrow 3CO_2 \; + \; 4H_2O \; + \; \text{Heat}$$

propane   oxygen gas   carbon dioxide   water

Since the products are formed when the bonds of the reactants are broken, the equation tells us that the heat came from the reactants. Where was the heat energy when it was part of the reactants? Before the energy was transformed into heat energy, it was chemical energy stored in the chemical bonds of the propane and oxygen gas molecules.

Chemical energy—The energy stored in chemical bonds

Look at the bonds of propane in Figure 5.19.

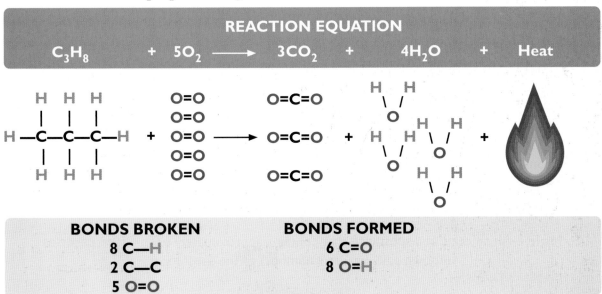

REACTION EQUATION
C_3H_8 + $5O_2$ $\longrightarrow$ $3CO_2$ + $4H_2O$ +   **Heat**

BONDS BROKEN	BONDS FORMED
8 C—H	6 C=O
2 C—C	8 O=H
5 O=O	

FIGURE 5.19
Propane Combustion
In order for propane to take part in a combustion reaction, all the chemical bonds in the reactants (propane and oxygen) must be broken. When the bonds in the products (carbon dioxide and water) form, the reaction is complete.

There are ten single covalent bonds in a propane molecule—eight C–H bonds and two C–C bonds. Each molecule of oxygen has one O=O bond and there are five oxygen molecules. The chemical energy of the propane and oxygen molecules are stored in these bonds. The chemical bonds of the products also store chemical energy. It is the changes that occur in the chemical bonds that causes the energy changes in reactions. In the combustion reaction shown in Figure 5.19, the bonds of propane and oxygen molecules are broken, while the bonds in carbon dioxide and water are formed.

Breaking bonds requires energy. Think about your grill for a moment. In order to start the combustion reaction you had to provide a spark. If your grill is a propane grill, they have built in ignitors that provide a spark. The spark provides enough energy to start the reaction by breaking the bonds of the reactants. All reactions require some amount of energy to get going. The energy required to start a reaction is called activation energy.

Look again at Figure 5.19. For each molecule of propane that reacts, three molecules of carbon dioxide and four molecules of water are produced. Look at the bonds formed in the reaction—six C=O bonds and 8 O–H bonds. When chemical bonds form, energy is released. So the heat and light you see when you start up your grill come from the formation of new chemical bonds. Once all the bonds in the propane and oxygen molecules are broken, the carbon, hydrogen, and oxygen atoms rearrange to form molecules of carbon dioxide and water.

Counting with Moles

Before we can talk about how much chemical energy is held in the bonds between atoms, we need to discuss how chemists count things. You see atoms and molecules are so small that to talk about the energy of just one atom is not at all practical. Also chemical reactions often involve large numbers of atoms, ions, or molecules so having a way to talk about them makes sense.

You can think about it as just another way to count things. For example, people usually count eggs by the dozen and gloves in pairs. But how would you count grains of salt from your saltshaker? That's a bit how it seems to count atoms or molecules. To give you a frame of reference, one drop of water contains about 10^{22} molecules of water, and each molecule has three atoms. It's impossible to count that many molecules! Yet chemists need a way to talk about large numbers of molecules or atoms.

Well in 1811, an Italian chemist named Amedeo Avogadro provided the number chemists could use to describe large amounts of very small particles. Chemists use **moles** to count atoms, ions, or molecules. These are not the moles that live in the forest or one you get on your skin. In chemistry, a mole (mol) is a unit of amount. One mole of any substance contains 6.02×10^{23} particles, and that number is now known as Avogadro's number.

Mole—An amount of a substance that contains approximately 6.02×10^{23} particles (known as Avogadro's number) of the substance

The mole is the SI unit for the amount of substance. In chemistry, one mole of a substance contains exactly $6.02214076 \times 10^{23}$ atoms, ions, or molecules of that substance. (Since that is such a long number, we round it to 6.02×10^{23}.) For example one mole of water contains 6.02×10^{23} molecules of water. One mole of silver contains 6.02×10^{23} atoms of silver.

The important thing to remember here is that a mole is always the same number of particles. So just as a dozen is always 12 and a pair is always 2, a mole is always 6.02×10^{23} particles. This is helpful so that we don't have to write out such long numbers! For example, we can say 1 mole of water instead of 6.02×10^{23} molecules of water are reacting or produced. And since reactions usually never involve just single atoms or molecules, we can compare the numbers of moles of reactants and products in balanced chemical equations.

In the equation for propane combustion, $C_3H_8 + 5O_2 \longrightarrow 3CO_2 + 4H_2O$, we've been reading that as one molecule of propane reacts with five molecules of oxygen to give three molecules of carbon dioxide and four molecules of water. But you can also read it as one mole of propane reacts with five moles of oxygen to give three moles of carbon dioxide and four moles of water. Notice how I used the coefficients to tell me how many molecules or moles of each substance is used or made in the reaction.

FIGURE 5.20
One Mole of Various Solids
Each beaker contains one mole of a different solid. One mole of any sample contains the same number of particles, but the weight and volume are different. The substances left to right are: sucrose, nickel(II) chloride, copper(II) sulphate, potassium manganate(VII), copper turnings, and iron filings.

Bond Energy

Now let's talk a bit about how energy is measured. Energy is measured in units called joules (J), named after James Joule, a nineteenth century English physicist. Larger amounts of energy can be described using the unit kJ for kilojoules. You will learn more about joules and energy in a later physics module. For now it's important to remember that energy is measured in joules.

Each kind of chemical bond has a specific amount of energy associated with it. Bonds with a high bond energy require more energy to break them apart than bonds with a low bond energy. For example, more energy is required to break an O–H bond than to break a C–H bond. The bond energy is a measure of how strong the bond is. Look at Table 5.5 to see the bond energies for different bonds. Notice how the energy is measure in kilojoules per mole of the substance.

How does the energy needed to break a hydrogen-nitrogen bond compare with the energy needed to break a hydrogen oxygen bond? A hydrogen-carbon bond? A hydrogen-chlorine bond? During chemical reactions, energy is either released or absorbed depending on the bonds that are broken and formed.

TABLE 5.5 Bond Energies	
Bond	**kJ/mole**
H–H	436
H–C	410
H–N	390
H–Cl	432
H–O	460
C–C	350
C=O	732
C≡O	1072
C–Cl	330
N≡N	945
N=O	607
O=O	498

Exothermic Reactions

Many chemical reactions release energy. Some reactions give off a little energy while others release a lot of energy. Fireworks or the combustion reaction of a wood fire release a lot of energy quickly. A compost heap (Figure 5.21), on the other hand, releases a little energy slowly as the grass clippings, vegetable scraps, and soil warm when decomposition reactions take place over time. A chemical reaction that releases energy to its surroundings is called an exothermic reaction.

Exothermic reaction—A chemical reaction that releases energy to its surroundings

FIGURE 5.21
Compost Heap
The decomposition reactions occurring in a compost heap are exothermic. The heap moderately warms up as the plant materials break down.

The combustion reaction of propane shown in Figure 5.19 is an exothermic reaction. When 1 mole of propane reacts with 5 moles of oxygen, about 2100 kilojoules (kJ) of heat is released. The chemical equation for the combustion reaction of propane can be rewritten replacing the word "Heat" with this value.

$$C_3H_8 + 5O_2 \longrightarrow 3CO_2 + 4H_2O + 2100 \text{ kJ}$$

Look at Figure 5.22. It is a graph showing how chemical energy changes during an exothermic reaction. Notice the chemical energy of the reactants (top dotted line) and the chemical energy of the products (bottom dotted line). The reactants have more chemical energy than the products in exothermic reactions. The difference in their chemical energies is equal to the amount of heat released during the reaction.

Notice the hump above the dotted line showing the reactant's chemical energy. That hump represents the activation energy, or the energy required to break the chemical bonds of the reactants. To understand this better, think about what has to happen at the atomic level in order for one atom to change places in a compound with another atom. The molecules must run into each other or collide. And they must collide with enough energy to break the bonds or the reaction will not happen. Consider the propane combustion reaction as an example of what I mean. Thankfully, propane can sit in the presence of oxygen at room temperature (or even outside on a hot day) and no reaction

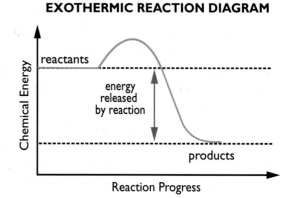

EXOTHERMIC REACTION DIAGRAM

reactants

energy released by reaction

products

Chemical Energy

Reaction Progress

FIGURE 5.22
Reaction Energy—Exothermic
In exothermic reactions, energy is released to the surroundings.

will occur. The heat energy of the surrounding air is not enough to result in combustion. But if you add a spark, you increase the heat energy sufficiently so that some of the molecules around the spark move faster. As they move faster, the molecules begin to collide with enough energy to start the reaction. Once the reaction is started, it will continue until one of the reactants is gone (or the reaction is extinguished by outside means).

Endothermic Reactions

In some chemical reactions, energy must be continually added, or the reaction will stop. This was the case in Experiment 5.1. As long as the battery was supplying electricity, the decomposition of water into hydrogen and oxygen would continue. (Or until all of the water was decomposed, whichever occurred first.) Another example is cooking vegetables. As long as the vegetables are in hot water or steam, they will continue to cook. But as soon as you remove the vegetables from the heat and place them under cold running water, they stop cooking immediately. Any chemical reaction that absorbs energy is called an endothermic reaction.

FIGURE 5.23
Cooking Vegetables
To stop vegetables from cooking, run under cold water. This stops the chemical reactions.

Endothermic reaction—A chemical reaction that absorbs energy from its surroundings

In endothermic reactions, the energy needed to break the bonds of the reactants is greater than the energy released when the bonds of the products are formed.

Look at Figure 5.24. This figure shows the energy graph for an endothermic reaction. Notice that in these reactions the chemical energy of the products is greater than the chemical energy of the reactants. The difference between the two is equal to the amount of energy that must be absorbed from the surroundings.

In water electrolysis, energy must be added to keep the reaction going. So when we write the chemical equation for the decomposition of water, the energy term appears on the side of the reactants.

$$2H_2O \ + \ 572 \ kJ \longrightarrow \ 2H_2 \ + \ O_2$$

According to this chemical equation, 572 kJ of energy must be added to separate 2 moles of water into 2 moles of hydrogen and 1 mole of oxygen.

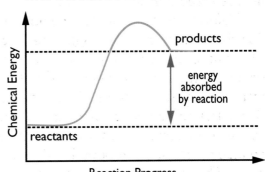

ENDOTHERMIC REACTION DIAGRAM

products

energy absorbed by reaction

Chemical Energy

reactants

Reaction Progress

FIGURE 5.24
Reaction Energy—Endothermic
In endothermic reactions, energy is absorbed from the surroundings.

One important thing to keep in mind when looking at the energy in reactions is that the total amount of energy before and after a reaction is always the same. In exothermic reactions, the chemical energy stored in the bonds of the reactants is converted into the chemical energy in the bonds of the products plus heat energy (sometimes also light and sound energy). Think of it like this: *reactants = products + energy*. In endothermic reactions, heat energy plus the chemical energy stored in the bonds of the reactants is converted into the chemical energy stored in the bonds of the products. Think of it like this: *reactants + energy = products*. Either type of reaction, though, will have the total energy of one side equal to the total energy of the other side of the equation. This is because, like matter, energy cannot be created or destroyed, it can only be transformed from one type to another. This principle is known as the law of conservation of energy. You will read more about how energy is conserved in later physics modules. Conduct Experiment 5.2 to observe endothermic and exothermic reactions.

EXPERIMENT 5.2
REACTION ENERGY

PURPOSE:
To observe endothermic or exothermic reactions and determine which absorb or release the most energy.

MATERIALS:
- Beaker or a clear glass
- Water
- White vinegar
- Baking soda (A fresh box will work best.)
- Salt substitute (Morton Salt Substitute, Nu-Salt, or NoSalt are brands you can find at your grocery store.)
- Epsom salts
- Hydrogen peroxide
- Steel wool
- Quick rising dry yeast (A new packet—check the expiration date—that has been kept refrigerated will work best.)
- Thermometer
- Tablespoon
- Timer
- Eye protection such as goggles or safety glasses
- Optional—Acetone (Some fingernail polish removers contain acetone. You may be able to find it at a drug or grocery store, read the labels for ingredients.)
- Optional—Styrofoam packing peanut

BACKGROUND INFORMATION:
A way to measure heat energy of a reaction is to measure the temperature change with a thermometer. An endothermic reaction will show a decrease in temperature as the

reactants absorb energy from the surrounding area. An exothermic reaction will show an increase in temperature as the products give off energy into the surrounding area. In this experiment you will make solutions in which chemical reactions occur and measure the temperature change.

QUESTIONS:

Which reactions will be endothermic? Which reactions will be exothermic? Why?

HYPOTHESES:

Write your prediction of which combinations of reactants from Table 5.6 will be endothermic reactions and which will be exothermic reactions.

PROCEDURE:

1. Table 5.6 has a list of solvents to combine with solid solutes. Starting with the first combination, fill the beaker or glass with ½ cup room temperature liquid.
2. Insert the thermometer in the solvent and record the initial temperature in your data table. Leave the thermometer in the beaker.
3. Add the solid solute and mix. Record your observations.
4. Wait 3 minutes and record the final temperature of the solution. It's important to measure the temperature of each solution at three minutes. Taking the temperature measurements at the same time for each trial allows you to compare the combinations.
5. Discard the solution, rinse and dry the beaker, thermometer, and tablespoon.
6. Repeat steps 1–5 for each of the combinations 2–4 (and combination 6 if you're doing it) in Table 5.6. (If you are doing combination 6, make sure to do it outside or near an open window as the acetone fumes can be strong.) Record your temperatures and observations.

TABLE 5.6	
Liquid Solvent	**Solid Solute**
1. Water	Salt substitute (1 Tablespoon)
2. Water	Epsom salt (1 Tablespoon)
3. Hydrogen Peroxide	Dry yeast (1 Tablespoon)
4. Vinegar	Baking soda (1 Tablespoon)
5. Vinegar	Steel wool pad
6. **Optional**-Acetone *Do this one outside!*	Half a Styrofoam packing peanut

7. For combination 5, place the steel wool pad in the beaker and cover it with vinegar. Let it set for 2 minutes.
8. After 2 minutes take the steel wool pad out of the vinegar and squeeze out any excess liquid. Drain the vinegar and dry the beaker.
9. Wrap the steel wool pad securely around the base of the thermometer and place the steel wool wrapped thermometer back into the empty beaker. Cover the beaker with a paper towel. Record the initial temperature as soon as you set them in the beaker. Wait 3 minutes.
10. After 3 minutes record the temperature of the steel wool.

11. Clean up and put everything away. Throw away the steel wool and rinse and dry the beaker, tablespoon, and thermometer.
12. For each trial, calculate the change in temperature of the reaction by subtracting the initial temperature from the final temperature. Record this change in your data table. (Note that some of your answers will be negative numbers. That just means the temperature dropped.)
13. Clean up and put everything away.
14. Graph your results. Make a bar graph for each reaction. Temperature change should be the y-axis with 0 at the origin. Since you will have negative temperature changes and positive temperature changes you will have numbers above and below the x-axis. Remember to label each bar with the reactants. There will be more help for graphing this in the student notebook.

CONCLUSIONS:

Were your predictions correct? Which reactions were endothermic and which reactions were exothermic? How were you able to tell? Write a conclusion paragraph explaining your results and graph in terms of exothermic and endothermic reactions. Make connections to the text.

What happened in your experiments? If they worked out correctly you should have seen that the water–salt substitute, the water–Epsom salt, and the vinegar–baking soda solutions were endothermic reactions. The other combinations should have been exothermic reactions. Why did it work out that way? Well salt substitute is made of potassium chloride (KCl) and Epsom salt is made of magnesium sulfate ($MgSO_4$). Because both KCl and $MgSO_4$ are ionic compounds, both of them will split into their ions (called dissociation) when placed in water. Remember that water is polar and so can dissolve ionic or other polar compounds. However, in order for the ionic bonds to be broken, the compounds must absorb energy from the water and so the water temperature goes down indicating an endothermic reaction.

When you poured out the hydrogen peroxide you started a decomposition reaction. Remember that we said hydrogen peroxide slowly decomposes into hydrogen and oxygen when it is in the presence of light energy. Well adding the yeast caused the normally slow reaction to speed up. Whenever you add a substance that speeds up a reaction, that substance is called a catalyst. Catalysts speed up reactions but are not changed in the process, which means they really aren't part of the chemical reaction. The addition of the yeast allowed the hydrogen peroxide to decompose much more rapidly. This is why you saw bubbles and maybe even foam which is caused by the rapid production of oxygen gas. The rapid formation of the covalent bonds in hydrogen and oxygen gases causes a release of heat which you should have measured as an increase in temperature. Therefore this was an exothermic reaction.

When baking soda reacts with vinegar it produces carbon dioxide, water, and sodium acetate as shown in the following equation. The bubbling you saw was the production of carbon dioxide.

$$CH_3COOH \quad + \quad NaHCO_3 \longrightarrow CO_2 \quad + \quad H_2O \quad + \quad NaC_2H_3O_2$$

| vinegar | baking soda | carbon dioxide | water | acetate |

Because it takes more energy to break the bonds in the baking soda and vinegar apart, the reaction absorbs energy and the temperature of the solution went down. Another endo-thermic reaction.

When you added vinegar to the steel wool, the acid in the vinegar was removing the protective coating on the steel wool. Steel wool contains iron. Remember from module 2 that when iron is exposed to oxygen, rust forms. Rust is a product of a chemical reaction between iron and oxygen. Once the protective coating was removed, the iron in the steel wool was able to come in contact with the oxygen in the air. This type of chemical reaction is called oxidation. When oxidation occurs, heat is released which should have been measured as an increase in temperature. The increase in temperature indicates an exother-mic reaction.

YOU DO SCIENCE
Elephant Toothpaste

While you have the hydrogen peroxide and yeast out, you might want to make some "Elephant Toothpaste." This is a fun but very messy experiment, so make sure to do it in the sink or outside where it's okay to make a mess. To make Elephant Toothpaste rinse out a 1 or 2 liter soda bottle and add ½ cup hydrogen peroxide, ¼ cup dishwashing soap, and a few drops of your favorite color of food coloring. Shake this well to mix it. In a measuring cup, mix a packet of active yeast with a little warm water. Let the yeast sit in the water for about 5 minutes so that the yeast is activated. Set the bottle with the hydrogen peroxide mixture in the sink or take everything outside for the next step. After 5 minutes, pour the yeast mixture into the bottle. The reaction occurs immediately after adding the yeast catalyst. Why does this reaction foam more than the one in Experiment 5.2? Well in this reaction you added the dishwashing soap which traps the oxygen gas that is produced in the reaction and makes more foam. Adding the food coloring just makes it more fun! Feel the bottle after the reaction slows down. It should feel warm as this is an exothermic reaction.

FIGURE 5.24
Elephant Toothpaste
A fun exothermic reaction.

Finish up this module by completing the On Your Own problems.

ON YOUR OWN

5.9   What happens to chemical bonds as a chemical reaction occurs?

5.10 Explain how chemical reactions involve energy.

5.11 Is energy created during an exothermic reaction? Explain.

5.12 Methane reacts with oxygen to form carbon dioxide and water as shown in the following reaction. What bonds are broken when one molecule of methane reacts with two molecules of oxygen? What bonds are formed? (Hint: refer to Figure 5.19.)

$$CH_4 \quad + \quad 2O_2 \longrightarrow CO_2 \quad + \quad 2H_2O$$

SUMMING UP

Well you've learned a lot about chemical reactions in this module! But would you believe me if I told you we've only scratched the surface? There is so much more to experiment with—things like solutions, gases, and acids and bases to name a few—that you'll want to take a whole course on chemistry in high school. There is an almost endless list of chemicals and chemical reactions that you come in contact with everyday. Continue to look for new examples. Your awareness of chemical reactions can increase your interest in and understanding of the world around you as well as your appreciation of our Creator.

ANSWERS TO THE "ON YOUR OWN" QUESTIONS

5.1   The formula of an ionic compound describes the ratio of the ions in the compound.

5.2   a.   This is a simply binary ionic compound. Find the elements on the Table of Atomic Numbers and Symbols in the Appendix to determine their symbols if you don't know them. Then use the periodic table to determine their charges. Start by writing the ions with charges (the cation followed by anion): $Ca^{2+}Cl^{-}$.

Since the charges do not equal 0 and they are different in magnitude, use the charge of the calcium ion as the subscript of the chloride ion. Use the charge of the chloride ion as the subscript of the calcium ion. Remember not to use signs and that the number one is implied (not written). The formula for calcium chloride is $CaCl^{2}$.

b.   Using the table you can find that Cu is the symbol for copper and S is the symbol for sulfur. You know that copper has a 1^{+} charge because of the Roman numeral. You can look sulfur up on the periodic table to determine its charge. It is in Group 6A so it has a 2^{-} charge. The ions with charges is: $Cu^{+}S^{2-}$.

Since the charges do not equal 0 and they are different in magnitude, use the charge of the copper ion as the subscript of the sulfide ion. Use the charge of the sulfide ion as the subscript of the copper ion. Remember not to use signs and that the number one is implied (not written). The formula for calcium chloride is Cu_2S.

c.   Two elements mean it is a binary compound. Looking up the symbol, Mg, the Table of Atomic Numbers and Element Symbols, we find that the name of the element is magnesium. Since it is first in the compound, it is the cation with the same name as the element. Cl is the symbol for chlorine. Since it is the anion, we change the name to chloride. So the name of this compound is magnesium chloride.

d.   Since there are three atoms in this compound, we know that this is not binary but must include a polyatomic ion. Use Table 5.3 to identify the polyatomic ion. Using the Table of Atomic Numbers and Element Symbols, find that Na is the symbol for sodium and since it is first we know it is the cation. Therefore, we just use the element's name. OH is the symbol for the polyatomic ion, hydroxide. So the name of this compound is sodium hydroxide.

5.3   A polyatomic ion is a covalently bonded group of atoms that has a positive or negative charge and acts as a unit.

5.4   The name and the formula of a molecular compound describe the type of element and the number of atoms of each element in the compound.

5.5   a. The name of N_2O_4 is dinitrogen tetroxide. Remember to drop the "a" of *tetra*-.

        b. The name of PCl_3 is phosphorus trichloride.

        c. The formula for diphosphorus pentoxide is P_2O_5. *Di*- tells us there are 2 phosphorus atoms and *penta*- tell us there are 5 oxygen atoms in the compound.

        d. The formula for selenium hexafluoride is SeF_6. There is no prefix in front of selenium, so we know there is only 1 selenium atom. *Hexa*- tells us there are 6 fluorine atoms.

5.6   a. **Single replacement reaction**

        b. Synthesis reaction

        c. Combustion reaction

        d. Double replacement reaction

        e. Decomposition reaction

5.7   In the reaction $2H_2 + O_2 \longrightarrow 2H_2O$, water is formed from its elements. During the decomposition of water, water is broken down into its elements, according to the equation $2H_2O \longrightarrow 2H_2 + O_2$.

5.8   In a single replacement reaction, an element replaces another element in one compound. In a double replacement reaction, two elements replace each other in two different compounds.

5.9   The chemical bonds in reactants are broken and the chemical bonds in products form during chemical reactions.

5.10   During chemical reactions, energy is either absorbed or released.

5.11 No, energy is not created during an exothermic reaction. The energy released by an exothermic reaction came from the chemical energy stored in the bonds of the reactants.

5.12 4 C–H bonds and 2 O=O bonds are broken. 2 C=O bonds and 4 O–H bond are formed.

STUDY GUIDE FOR MODULE 5

1. Match the terms to their definition.

    a. Binary compounds

    b. Polyatomic ions

    c. Mole

    d. Exothermic reaction

    e. Endothermic reaction

    An amount of a substance that contains approximately 6.02×10^{23} particles of the substance

    A chemical reaction that releases energy to its surroundings

    A chemical reaction that absorbs energy from its surroundings

    Compounds made of only two elements

    A covalently bonded group of atoms that has a positive or negative charge and acts as a unit

2. What is the name of the compound with the formula $CaCl_2$?

    a. calcium chlorine

    b. calcium dichloride

    c. calcium chloride

    d. monocalcium dichloride

3. What is the chemical formula for magnesium bromide (use the periodic table and the Table of Atomic Numbers and Element Symbols to help you)?

    a. $MgBr$ b. $MgBr_2$ c. $Mg(I)Br_2$ d. Mg_2Br

4. What is the name of the compound with the formula $SiCl_4$?

    a. silicon chloride

    b. silicon(I) chloride

    c. silicon chlorine

    d. silicon tetrachloride

5. What is the name of the binary compound formed from potassium and iodine?

Vector quantity—A physical measurement that contains both magnitude (number) and directional information

Scalar quantity—A physical measurement that contains only magnitude (number) and does not contain directional information

We use arrows on a graph to represent vectors. The length of the arrow shows the magnitude of the vector. We can add vectors by combining the vector magnitudes and directions. Look at Figure 6.6 to see what I mean. In situation A, the person walks 4 kilometers, stops for a while and then walks another 2 kilometers. Since the person walked in the same direction both times we add the vectors to find the displacement. The total magnitude of the displacement is 6 kilometers: 4 km + 2 km = 6 km. The direction is the positive direction (we can call it east). This makes their displacement 6 km east.

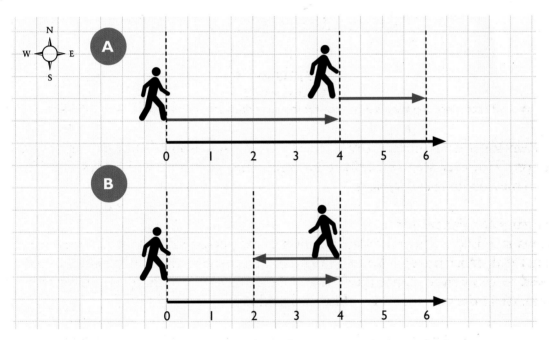

FIGURE 6.6
Displacement in a Straight Line
To add vectors you must account for direction.

Now look at situation B of Figure 6.6. In this instance the person walks 4 kilometers and then realizes they dropped their key. They then turn around and walk back in the direction from which they came 2 km until they find their key. Again they walked a distance of 6 km, but this time, their displacement was in opposite directions. So to find their total displacement we add them, but we must remember that the second vector is in the opposite or negative direction (we can call it west, but we need to show it is opposite of east by adding a negative sign). The total magnitude of the displacement is 2 kilometers: 4 km + (–2 km) = 2 km. Since the final position is still east of the starting position, the displacement is 2 km east. In both cases, the person walks a total distance of 6 kilometers, but their displacements are different.

Displacement Not Along a Straight Line

When two or more displacement vectors have different directions, we use graphing to combine them. Look at Figure 6.7. Suppose the person shown needed to walk from the picnic area through the park to the restroom. The blue arrows (called vectors) show the route the person walked to stay on the paved path. Let's call the area between the dashed lines a block. The person walked 1 block east (A), then turned and walked 1 block north (B). They turned again and walked 2 blocks east (C), and finally 3 blocks north (D). The length of the vectors representing this path are 1 block, 1 block, 2 blocks, and 3 blocks. To find the total distance you add the magnitudes of each vector. Thus, the person walked a total distance of 7 blocks to reach their destination.

To find the displacement of the person walking to the restroom, you need to find the distance and direction from the starting point to the ending point. In other words, you add all of the vectors. The red vector (E) shows the vector sum of vectors A + B + C + D, which is the displacement. Vector E is called the resultant vector and it points directly from the starting point to the ending point. The resultant vector is the displacement. If you measure the resultant vector (E), you will find that it measures the length of 5 blocks. Remember that displacement needs to have directional information too. So, the displacement of this person is 5 blocks northeast, while the distance they walked is 7 blocks.

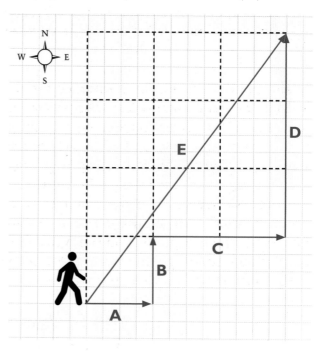

FIGURE 6.7
Displacement Not in a Straight Line
The magnitude of the resultant vector (E) shows that the displacement from the picnic area to the rest room is 2 blocks less than the distanced actually traveled.

ON YOUR OWN

6.1 Suppose you are standing still on an escalator (a moving stairway) in a mall going from the first floor to the second floor. Three friends are going to meet you. One is on the escalator with you, also standing still. The second friend is standing still on the first floor near the escalator but not on the escalator. The third is standing still on the other escalator that is moving down. In which friend's frame of reference are you in motion? In which friend's frame of reference are you not in motion?

6.2 How are distance and displacement similar? How are they different?

SPEED AND VELOCITY

If an object is in motion, its position is changing. *Over time,* that will result in a certain distance over which the object travels. This is called the object's speed. You've likely heard the term velocity used in this way too. In everyday conversation you probably use the terms speed and velocity interchangeably. In physics, however, there is a big difference between *speed* and *velocity*. Just like displacement contains more information than distance, velocity contains more information than speed does. Speed tells you how quickly an object moves in relation to a reference point. Velocity tells you how quickly *and in what direction* the object is moving in relation to a reference point. By now you should appreciate how including directional information can make a big difference when giving someone directions. Directional information is also important in talking about velocity. You will learn much more about the difference between speed and velocity when you take physics in high school, but we'll get a good foundation now. So let's talk about speed first.

Speed

Speed is described in units of distance and time. The SI unit of speed is meters per second (m/s). But other common units of speed are kilometers/hour (km/h), or in the English system of units (of which you are likely much more familiar) feet per second (ft/s) and miles per hour (mi/h). Just as with distances, you need to choose units that makes the most sense for the motion you are describing. And as is true with all measurements, you must keep the units with the number, or the measurement will not make sense.

You can measure the speed of a moving object by measuring the time it takes for the object to travel a certain distance. For example, you can measure how long it takes someone to bike 50 meters. Or, you can measure how far the person can bike in a certain time, such as 10 seconds. In either case, the speed will be the ratio of the distance traveled to the amount of time it takes to travel that distance. I can write that mathematically as:

Equation 6.1

$$\text{speed} = \frac{\text{distance}}{\text{time}} \quad \text{or} \quad v = \frac{d}{t}$$

Remember the word *per* means divided by so when we say the speed is 10 meters per second it means 10 meters divided by 1 second, or 10 m/s. You should also know that many physicists use the letter v as the symbol for both speed and velocity. In this course we will use v to symbolize velocity too, but remember that velocity requires direction while speed does not.

FIGURE 6.8
Speed
The speed of skaters is usually described in meters per second (or feet per second). The speed of cars is usually described in kilometers per hour (or miles per hour).

There are two ways to express the speed of an object, average speed and instantaneous speed.

Average speed—The ratio of the total distance traveled to the total time of the trip

Instantaneous speed—The rate at which an object is moving at a given moment in time

When you ride your bike, do you travel the same speed all the time? It's not very likely that you do. You may go slower when you bike up a hill and faster as you travel down the hill. This means that your speed is not constant. Because speed is not usually constant, we find how fast something moves for an entire trip. This is called the average speed (v) and it is the total distance traveled (d), divided by the time (t) it takes to travel that distance.

Sometimes, though, you need to know exactly how fast you are going in a particular instant. For example, when you're driving on the highway and the speed limit changes. It's important to know how fast you're going in that moment so you can adjust your speed accordingly. The speedometer in cars gives the instantaneous speed. During the time an object is moving, its instantaneous speed may change, but you can find the average speed over the entire trip using equation 6.1. Study the following example problems to see how this is done. Pay particular attention to the steps to solving physics problems as you will need to do this in the following modules as well. Then practice what you learn by completing the On Your Own problems that follow.

EXAMPLE 6.1

A. **A car travels 78 miles down the highway. It takes the car 1.2 hours to travel that far. What is the average speed of the car?**

Step 1   List the information that is given to you in the problem. Then list the unknown or what the question is asking you to find.

total distance (d) = 78 miles

total time (t) = 1.2 hours

average speed (v) = ?

Step 2   Write out the equation you will use.

$$v = \frac{d}{t}$$

Step 3   Write out the equation substituting the numbers from the list in step 1.

$$v = \frac{78 \text{ mi}}{1.2 \text{ h}}$$

Step 4   Solve the problem.

$$v = \frac{78 \text{ mi}}{1.2 \text{ h}} = 65 \frac{\text{mi}}{\text{h}}$$

Notice what I did here. When I put the values for speed and time in the equation, I kept their units with them. This is very important. *When working with physical quantities in equations, keep the units with the numbers.*

   Once I put the numbers in there, look at what I did. Since 78 over 1.2 means 78 divided by 1.2, I used a calculator and divided 78 by 1.2 and got 65. Look at what I then did with the units. I left the units in the same way they appeared in the equation. That's how I got **65 mi/h** or 65 miles per hour. Note that the question asked for speed not velocity so our answer does not need directional information.

B.   What is the speed of the car from the previous problem in meters per second? (1 mile = 1,609 meters, 1 hour = 3,600 seconds)

In this problem, you are asked to report the answer in metric units rather than English units. How can you do that? Well, think back to module 1 where you learned how to convert from one unit to another. That is added right after the first step in solving the problem. You need to convert 78 miles to meters and 1 hour to seconds. Then the rest of the steps stay the same.

Step 1A   List the information that is given to you in the problem. Then list the unknown or what the question is asking you to find.

d = 78 miles
t = 1.2 hours
v = ?

Step 1B   Convert any quantities using the given conversion factors. (Review module 1 if you need to.)

$$\frac{78 \text{ mi}}{1} \times \frac{1609 \text{ m}}{1 \text{ mi}} = 125{,}502 \text{ m}$$

$$\frac{1.2 \text{ h}}{1} \times \frac{3600 \text{ s}}{1 \text{ h}} = 4{,}320 \text{ s}$$

Step 2   Write out the equation you will use.

$$v = \frac{d}{t}$$

Step 3   Write out the equation substituting the numbers from the list in step 1B.

$$v = \frac{125{,}502 \text{ m}}{4{,}320 \text{ s}}$$

Step 4   Solve the problem.

$$v = \frac{125,502 \text{ m}}{4,320 \text{ s}} = 29.1 \text{ m/s}$$

If you do the calculation with a calculator (as you should), you will notice that the answer is 29.05138889. I rounded that to 29.1. When you take high school chemistry and physics, you will learn about significant figures, which will tell you when and where to round a number off. For this course, don't worry too much about rounding a number. Your answers will be right even if you round off at a different place than I do.

Now realize that 29.1 m/s and 65 mi/h *are both the same speed*. They simply express that speed in different units. That is why it is so important to put the units in any equation you use.

ON YOUR OWN

6.3   What is the average speed of an aircraft that travels 115 miles in 30 minutes? Put your answer in units of miles per hour.

6.4   When measuring the speed of a snail, a good unit to use is millimeters per minute. A snail takes all day (12 hours) to travel 5 meters. What is its average speed in millimeters per minute?

6.5   While traveling on vacation, you measure the times and distance between stops. You travel 45 kilometers in 0.5 hour, followed by 64 kilometers in 0.7 hour. What is your average speed in mi/h? Hint: Remember that average speed is the total distance divided by the total time.

Graphing Speed

I said that when you bike you likely do not travel at a constant speed. But think about a car on cruise control that is set at 55 mi/h. The car travels the same distances in the same time frames because the cruise control determines that the car will travel 55 miles every hour it is moving. That is constant speed. Constant speed means equal distances are covered in equal times.

Suppose you decide to jog around a marked track at a constant speed for a half hour. How could you check that your speed is constant? You could use a stopwatch to time how long it takes you to jog a lap of the track. If you jog each lap in the same amount of time, then you are jogging at a constant speed.

Let's say that you jogged 3 laps and each lap (400 m) took you 2 minutes. The next day you want to go back to the track, but you only have a half hour before you need to head home. You'd like to jog 14 laps. Can you jog 14 laps in a half hour? How can you figure that out? You can calculate the answer using equation 6.1 and rearranging the equation for time ($t = d/v$). But another way to find out the answer is to make a distance-time graph. A distance-time graph is a good way to describe motion.

Look at the graph in Figure 6.9. This is a graph showing the three laps you jogged. Notice that the distance is marked off on the vertical (y-axis) in units of laps. We could also use units of 400 m, but we'll use laps since the numbers are smaller. Time is marked off along the horizontal (x-axis) in units of minutes.

Notice the four points on the graph. There is a point at zero time and zero distance. At zero time you had not yet jogged any distance. The point at the time 2 minutes is placed at 1 lap to show that it took 2 minutes to jog the first lap. There is another point 2 minutes later showing another lap was jogged. Again, a point is placed 2 minutes later at 3 laps. So, you can see on the graph that after a total time of 6 minutes, 3 laps were jogged.

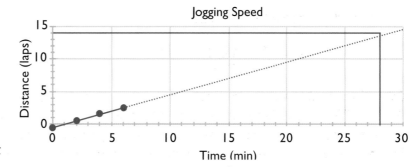

FIGURE 6.9
Graph of Jogging Speed
Each dot represents the number of laps covered (y-axis) after the total time (x-axis). How long does it take to jog 14 laps? Trace the red line over from 14 laps on the y-axis to the dotted line and then down to the time on the x-axis.

You can draw a straight line through all four points and then extend the straight line to 30 minutes. The solid line indicates the actual times and distances you ran. The dashed line is called an extrapolation (like you did in Experiment 1.2). Remember, an extrapolation is used to estimate values that are either higher or lower than the actual data collected. Now that you have the extrapolated line, you can see how long it will take you to jog 14 laps. Follow the red line to the right from 14 laps on the y-axis to the blue extrapolated line. Then follow the red line down to the time axis. It will take 28 minutes to jog 14 laps.

Now that was a pretty easy example. But I wanted you to see how to use graphing to describe motion. Let's consider another example. Suppose you're jogging with a couple of friends. One friend can't keep up with you. You find that they take 2.5 minutes to jog each lap. Your other friend is faster than you and can jog a lap in 1.5 minutes. The graph in Figure 6.10 shows distance-time graphs describing the motion of all three joggers. The blue line indicates your faster friend. The red line is you, and the gold line indicates your slower friend. What can you say about the steepness of each line? The fastest jogger has the steepest line. They covered more distance in the same amount of time as you. The line describing the motion of your slower friend is not as steep as yours. They covered less distance in the same time. Their speed was slower.

You can compare constant speeds on a distance-time graph. The greater the speed the steeper the line. The steepness of

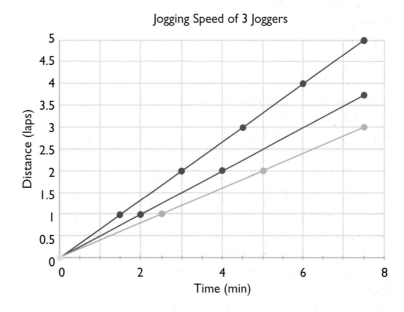

FIGURE 6.10
Distance-Time Graph of 3 Joggers
You can tell which jogger was faster by the steepness of the slope of the line. The steeper the slope, the faster the jogger.

a graph line is called the slope. *The slope of a line on a distance-time graph is speed.* A steeper line has a steeper slope. Thus, the greater the slope is on a distance-time graph, the greater the speed.

What if the average speed isn't constant? How will that look on a distance-time graph? Well constant speed is shown by a straight line, changing speed is shown by a curved line. Look at the graph in Figure 6.11 showing the speed of a car.

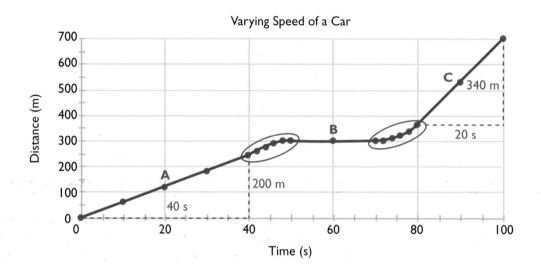

FIGURE 6.11
Distance-Time Graph of a Car
The car moves at a constant speed when you see straight lines. At the curves (red circles), the car is changing speed. What is the car doing between 50 and 70 seconds?

The slope shows straight lines from 0–40 s (A), 50–70 s (B), and 80–100 s (C). These are the times that the car displays constant average speed. From the graph we can see that the car travels 200 meters in 40 seconds (A). Using equation 6.1, we can find the speed of section A.

$$v = \frac{d}{t} = \frac{200 \text{ m}}{40 \text{ s}} = 5 \frac{\text{m}}{\text{s}}$$

What is the car doing during section B of the graph? From 50 to 70 seconds the car stays at 300 meters. This means the car is not moving, so we can say it has a constant speed of 0 m/s. A flat, horizontal line on a distance-time graph means the object is at rest with a constant speed of zero. At 70 seconds, the car starts back up and moves again until we reach section C (80 to 100 seconds). Let's figure out the speed of the car during time interval C using equation 6.1.

$$v = \frac{d}{t} = \frac{340 \text{ m}}{20 \text{ s}} = 17 \frac{\text{m}}{\text{s}}$$

The car is moving faster during the last 20 seconds of the graph (section C) than it was during section A. If you look carefully, you can see that the slope of the line at C is steeper than the slope of the line at A.

The sections of the graph that are circled are the areas where the car is changing speed. The circle between A and B (40 s to 50 s) shows the car gradually slowing to a stop (decreasing speed), so the line has a slight overhand curve (⌢). The circle between B and C (70 s to 80 s) shows a slight underhand curve (⌣) which indicates the car is gradually increasing in speed.

YOU DO SCIENCE

MEASURING AVERAGE SPEED ACTIVITY

You can practice measuring average speeds and have fun while you do it with this activity. You'll need a parent, sibling, or friend to help you. You'll also need a yard stick, meter stick, or tape measure, some masking tape, and a stopwatch.

First decide on an "event" to measure constant speed. Your event could be walking heel to toe, walking backwards, hopping, skipping, crawling—whatever you think you can do to move at a consistent and safe speed. (There are no prizes for the fastest!) Next, you'll need to measure out several lengths so go to a room with a lot of floor space or take your experiment outside if the weather is nice. Measure out the following distances: 1 yard (0.91 m), 2 yards (1.83 m), and 3 yards (2.74 m). Use masking tape to mark the starting point and the three different distances. Create a data table (there's one in the student notebook) with columns for time and distance.

Give your partner the stopwatch. Now using the "event" you decided on, start at the starting line and continue to the first 1-yard marking. Try to maintain a constant speed. Your partner should time how long it takes you to travel the first distance. Repeat this for 3 trials so you can average your time. Now do the same thing only time from the starting point to the 2-yard marking. Again, repeat for three trials. Finally have your partner time three trials from the starting point to the 3-yard marker.

Using your three trials for each distance, find your average time by adding the times together and dividing by 3. Then using equation 6.1 find your average speed for each distance. Hopefully your speeds are pretty close. You can also make a graph of the distance on the y-axis (0 yd, 1 yd, 2 yd, 3 yd) and time on the x-axis. You can then find your speed as the slope of the line.

While you are calculating your average speed, have your partner measure out a different distance than the ones tested (don't watch). They should remove the masking tape (except for the starting line) from the original trials and place new masking tape at the new distance. Your partner should not tell you what the new, unknown distance is. Once you know your average speed, have your partner time you while you are traveling from the starting tape to the tape marking the unknown distance. Again, time three trials and find your average time. Use this time and your average speed to calculate the unknown distance with equation 6.1. (You'll need to rearrange the equation to $d = v \times t$, or you can use your graph.) How close did you get?

Velocity

To review—speed, like distance, is a scalar quantity and so does not contain directional information. Velocity, like displacement, is a vector quantity and does contain directional information. Why is the distinction between speed and velocity so important? Perform Experiment 6.1 to find out.

EXPERIMENT 6.1
THE IMPORTANCE OF DIRECTION IN VELOCITY

PURPOSE:
To observe how direction plays a role when objects are moving at different speeds.

MATERIALS:
- At least 4 eggs
- Two pieces of reasonably strong cardboard (like the cardboard found on the back of writing tablets)
- Several books
- A pair of scissors
- Ruler
- A large tray or cookie sheet
- Paper towels
- Kitchen table
- Eye protection such as goggles or safety glasses

BACKGROUND:
The difference between speed and velocity is very important in physics. This experiment demonstrates that fact.

QUESTION:
How does direction affect two objects relative to each other when they are moving in the

same direction with the same speed? What about when they are moving with the same speed in opposite directions, towards each other?

HYPOTHESIS:

Write what you predict will happen to 2 eggs that roll down a ramp in the same direction. Write what you predict will happen to 2 eggs that roll down ramps in opposite directions, towards each other.

PROCEDURE:

1. This is a potentially messy experiment, so put some paper towels on the table for easier clean-up.
2. Make a pile of books about 8 inches high on the tabletop. (You will need to make a second pile 8 inches high for step 7, so gather all books now.)
3. Take the cardboard pieces and measure 2 inches in from each side and 1 inch from the top. Cut the 2 in × 1 in rectangles out (see Figure 6.12). Fold the long edges up to form "railings" on each side. Fold the short edge back.
4. Next, tuck the short edge between the top 2 books so that the cardboard leans against the pile of books, making what looks like a slide going from the top of the books to the tray. Your set-up should look like Figure 6.13.
5. Trial 1—Hold two eggs together on top of the slide. Hold them so that one egg is behind the other. Release them together, allowing them to roll down the slide one behind the other. Use your other hand to stop them when they roll off the slide and onto the tray. Note whether the eggs have been damaged or not. Record your observations in your data table. If the eggs were damaged, get new ones. If not, you can reuse them.
6. Trial 2—Lay one egg on the tray at the bottom of the slide. Allow the other egg to roll down the slide and hit the egg at the bottom of the slide. Record your observations, noting any damage caused. Once again reuse any undamaged eggs.
7. Build another slide like the one you've been using. It needs to be close to the same height as the first slide.
8. Place the two slides so that they are on opposite sides of the tray and so that they meet in the center of the tray.
9. Trial 3—Place one egg at the top of one slide and the second egg at the top of the other slide.
10. Simultaneously let both eggs go, allowing them to roll down the slides and crash into each other. Record your observations, noting the damage to the eggs.
11. Clean up and put everything away.

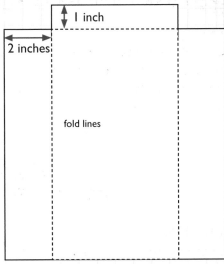

FIGURE 6.12
Cardboard Setup

FIGURE 6.13
Experimental Setup

CONCLUSION:
Were your predictions correct? What happened to the eggs when they were traveling at the same speed in the same direction? What happened when one egg was at rest, but the other egg was traveling towards it? What happened when both eggs were traveling at the same speed but in opposite directions? Answer these questions in a paragraph and make connections to the text.

What did you learn in this experiment? Well, it demonstrated the importance of direction in velocity. In trial 1 of the experiment, the eggs traveled down the slide together. When they reached the bottom, they had essentially the same speed. Nevertheless, since they were traveling in the same direction, they did not damage each other. In trial 3 of the experiment, the eggs were still traveling at roughly the same speed when they got to the bottom of their respective slides, since the slides were of essentially the same height. How did the eggs fare this time? Since the eggs collided with each other, at least one of them was likely strongly damaged if not broken. What made the difference? The direction made the difference. Even though the eggs had the same speed in trial 3, they had different *velocities*, and the result was devastating to the eggs.

Why did I have you do trial 2, where the eggs collided while one was sitting still? Well, compare the damage done to the eggs in trial 2 with the damage done to the eggs in trial 3. In which case was more damage done? The eggs in trial 3 suffered more damage. Why? Since the eggs were traveling at the same speed but in opposite directions, they were actually approaching each other much faster than one egg traveling at that speed and the other sitting still. As a result, more damage occurred from the collision in trial 3. Study Figure 6.14 as you read the next paragraphs.

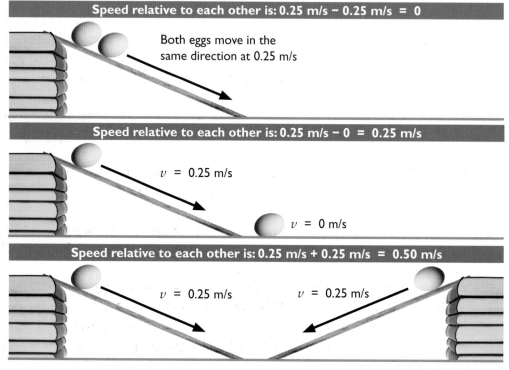

Speed relative to each other is: 0.25 m/s − 0.25 m/s = 0

Both eggs move in the same direction at 0.25 m/s

Speed relative to each other is: 0.25 m/s − 0 = 0.25 m/s

v = 0.25 m/s

v = 0 m/s

Speed relative to each other is: 0.25 m/s + 0.25 m/s = 0.50 m/s

v = 0.25 m/s

v = 0.25 m/s

FIGURE 6.14
Trials 1–3 of Experiment 6.1

up and over to the right a certain distance. Over the next 0.2 second time interval, the ball traveled up and over to the right, but not nearly as far. What does that tell us about the difference in the velocities between the first- and second-time intervals? In the first-time interval, a larger distance was traveled than in the second time interval, despite the fact that each interval was 0.2 seconds. If the ball travels less distance in the second time interval, we know that the ball's velocity is lower in the second time interval than in the first. Using that same reasoning, all the way up to the sixth image of the ball, the ball's velocity *decreased*.

What happened after the sixth image of the ball? Well, by the eighth image, it is clear that the distance between the images of the ball begins to increase. This tells us that during that time, the ball's velocity *increased*. Thus, the ball started out with a certain velocity given to it when it was thrown or bounced. That velocity decreased until it reached the very top of its path, and then the velocity started increasing again. What do we call this phenomenon? We call it acceleration.

Acceleration—The time rate of change of an object's velocity

When an object is in motion and its velocity changes, we say that the object has experienced acceleration. You most likely have felt the effects of changing speed or acceleration. You lurch forward against your seatbelt if the car your riding in must come to a sudden stop. If you've flown on an airplane, you get pushed back against your seat when the airplane is taking off down the runway. The acceleration of an object describes how fast the velocity is changing.

Equation 6.2

$$\text{acceleration } (a) = \frac{\text{final velocity} - \text{initial velocity}}{\text{time}} = \frac{v_f - v_i}{t}$$

Like speed we can express acceleration as a mathematical equation. Thus, the acceleration of an object can be calculated if you take the difference in its velocities over a certain time interval and divide by the number of seconds in that time interval. Let's think about the units that go along with acceleration. The units of acceleration are the units of velocity (m/s, km/h, mi/h) divided by a time unit. For example:

$$\frac{\text{speed units}}{\text{time units}} = \frac{\left(\frac{m}{s}\right)}{s}$$

What kind of units are these? Well, we could say that it is "meters per second per second," but there is a better way to express it. Remember that a fraction merely represents a situation in which you divide the numerator by the denominator. The denominator of our unit is just seconds, but we can write that as the fraction: s/1. An easy way to remember all of this is to memorize the saying; "*When dividing fractions don't ask why, just flip the bottom and multiply*". See what I mean below.

$$\frac{\left(\frac{m}{s}\right)}{\left(\frac{s}{1}\right)} = \left(\frac{m}{s} \times \frac{1}{s}\right) = \frac{m}{s^2}$$

Acceleration units are read "meters per second squared." Let's look at a quick example.

EXAMPLE 6.3

Suppose a ball is falling. A person with a radar gun measures its velocity to be 2.0 ft/s straight down. Just 0.30 seconds later, he measures the velocity again and finds that it is 11.6 ft/s straight down. What is the ball's acceleration?

Step 1   List the information that is given to you in the problem. Then list the unknown or what the question is asking you to find.

initial velocity (v_i) = 2.0 ft/s down

final velocity (v_f) = 11.6 ft/s down

time (t) = 0.30 s

acceleration (a) = ?

Step 2   Write out the equation you will use. Use equation 6.2.

$$a = \frac{(v_f - v_i)}{t}$$

Step 3   Write out the equation substituting the numbers from the list in step 1.

$$a = \frac{(11.6\frac{ft}{s} - 2.0\frac{ft}{s})}{0.30\ s}$$

Step 4   Solve the problem. (I will show you the flip for the units this time, but you don't have to do that each time. If you remember that acceleration units are distance units divided by time squared, then you can just divide the numbers as long as your units agree.)

$$a = \frac{(11.6\frac{ft}{s} - 2.0\frac{ft}{s})}{0.30\ s} = \frac{(9.6\frac{ft}{s})}{0.30\ s} = \left(\frac{9.6\ ft}{1\ s} \times \frac{1}{0.30\ s}\right) = \left(\frac{9.6\ ft}{0.30\ s^2}\right) = 32\frac{ft}{s^2}$$

The acceleration can be expressed as **32 ft/s² downward.**

The units on acceleration then, are a distance unit divided by a time unit squared. Thus, units like ft/s^2, m/s^2, mi/h^2, and km/min^2 are all valid acceleration units.

Did you notice that directional information was included in the answer to Example 6.3? That's because, like velocity, acceleration is a vector quantity. How do you attach directional information to acceleration? In order to determine the direction of acceleration, you need to know the direction of the velocity, and you need to know whether velocity is increasing or decreasing. Remember, acceleration is the change in velocity, and velocity can change in one of three ways.

1. If an object speeds up, the velocity obviously changes.

2. If an object slows down, the velocity changes as well.

3. Finally, if an object changes direction, the velocity changes.

Also remember that velocity is a vector quantity. Thus, direction is a part of velocity. Even if an object's speed does not change, if its direction changes, its velocity changes. In all three of these cases, then, there is an acceleration, because there is a change in the velocity.

We can determine the direction of the acceleration if we examine how the velocity is changing. For example, suppose a car is heading west and begins to increase its speed. The car is accelerating, but in what direction? Well, since the westward velocity is getting larger, the change in velocity results in *more* westward movement. Thus, the acceleration must have a direction of west. Suppose that the car began slowing down. What's the direction of the acceleration then? Well, if the westward velocity decreases, that means the acceleration is going against the velocity. Thus, the acceleration's direction is east. If an object is speeding up, then, its acceleration is in the same direction as its velocity. If it is slowing down, its acceleration is in the opposite direction as its velocity. See how that works in the following example problems.

EXAMPLE 6.4

A. **A rock is dropped from a bridge into a river. It starts out with zero initial velocity and it hits the river 2 seconds later, traveling with a velocity of 19.6 meters per second downward. What is the acceleration?**

Step 1   List the information that is given to you in the problem. Then list the unknown or what the question is asking you to find.

v_i = 0 m/s

v_f = 19.6 m/s down

t = 2 s

a = ?

Step 2   Write out the equation you will use. Use equation 6.2.

$$a = \frac{(v_f - v_i)}{t}$$

Step 3　Write out the equation substituting the numbers from the list in step 1.

$$a = \frac{(19.6\frac{m}{s} - 0\frac{m}{s})}{2\ s}$$

Step 4　Solve the problem.

$$a = \frac{(19.6\frac{m}{s} - 0\frac{m}{s})}{2\ s} = \frac{19.6\frac{ft}{s}}{2\ s} = 9.8\frac{m}{s^2}$$

The rock sped up because it started at zero and ended traveling 19.6 m/s downward. Thus, the acceleration must be in the same direction as the velocity. Therefore, the acceleration is **9.8 m/s² downward.**

B.　A bicyclist is traveling down a road at 18 ft/s to the east. The cyclist sees an obstacle in the road ahead, so he hits the brakes. In 1.8 s, the cyclist has come to a complete stop. What is the cyclist's acceleration?

Step 1　List the information that is given to you in the problem. Then list the unknown or what the question is asking you to find.

v_i = 18 ft/s east

v_f = 0 ft/s (A complete stop means a final velocity of 0 ft/s.)

t = 1.8 s

a = ?

Step 2　Write out the equation you will use. Use equation 6.2.

$$a = \frac{(v_f - v_i)}{t}$$

Step 3　Write out the equation substituting the numbers from the list in step 1.

$$a = \frac{(0\frac{ft}{s} - 18\frac{ft}{s})}{1.8\ s}$$

Step 4　Solve the problem.

$$a = \frac{(0\frac{ft}{s} - 18\frac{ft}{s})}{1.8\ s} = \frac{-18\frac{ft}{s}}{1.8\ s} = -10\frac{ft}{s^2}$$

What does the answer mean? When we subtracted 18 from 0, we got −18. When we divided that number by 1.8, the negative sign stayed around. What does a negative acceleration mean? Well, it tells you about the direction of the acceleration. The bicyclist slowed down. That means the acceleration is in the *opposite direction* as the velocity. That's what the negative sign means. It is reminding you that the cyclist slowed down, making the acceleration opposite of the velocity. Since the velocity's direction is east, the direction of the acceleration must be to the west. Therefore, the acceleration is **10 ft/s² west**. <u>Now, notice that I dropped the negative sign.</u> Why? Well, the negative sign helped me determine the direction of the acceleration. Thus, I didn't really drop the negative, I just turned it into a direction. That's what you should do as well. If you come across a negative acceleration, you should use that negative to help you determine the direction, but only the direction should show up in your answer.

Before we move on, there are a few more points about acceleration I want to make. We saw in the second problem of Example 6.4 that acceleration can be negative. This happens when velocity decreases (the object is slowing down) which makes the numerator of equation 6.2 negative. Some people use the term "deceleration" to describe acceleration that slows the speed of an object. Although that is an accepted term in everyday English, it is not an acceptable term in physics. When we talk about acceleration that slows an object down, we do not say deceleration. Instead, we give the direction of the acceleration. When compared to the direction of the velocity, the acceleration's direction tells a physicist whether an object slows down or speeds up. In the end then, when you read "acceleration," don't assume it means that an object is speeding up! **Acceleration can either speed up or slow down an object, depending on its direction.**

That brings me to my second point. You know that acceleration means a change in an object's velocity over time. But did you know an object can have constant speed and still have acceleration. How is that possible? Look at the carousel in Figure 6.16. Riders on the carousel experience a constant speed, but since the carousel is continually changing direction, the riders also experience acceleration. Remember that acceleration and velocity are both vector quantities. Thus, if an object moving at constant speed changes its direction of travel (such as going around in a carousel), there is still acceleration.

FIGURE 6.16
Carousel
When you ride a carousel you experience acceleration because of the changing direction, even if the speed is constant.

Of course, you can have changes in both speed and direction. You experience this type of motion if you ride on roller coasters. A roller coaster car whips you backward, forward, and sideways as its velocity increases, decreases, and changes direction. The thrill you experience riding a roller coaster comes from the constantly changing acceleration (changes in both speed and direction).

FIGURE 6.17
Roller Coaster
Roller coasters produce acceleration because both speed and direction change.

My last point is a reminder about units when solving acceleration problems. In order to properly do the math using equation 6.2, you must make sure that all of your units agree with each other. What do I mean? You should not have hours and seconds in the same equation. Nor should you have feet and miles in the same equation; you shouldn't even have millimeters and centimeters in the same equation. Every unit for length should be the same, and every unit of time should be the same. You must always remember to convert one of the two different quantities. Study the next example to fix this in your memory.

EXAMPLE 6.5

A sports car travels from 0 to 60 mi/h north in 6.1 s. What is its acceleration?

Step 1A List the information that is given to you in the problem. Then list the unknown or what the question is asking you to find.

v_i = 0 m/s

v_f = 60 mi/h north

t = 6.1 s

a = ?

Step 1B Convert any quantities using the given conversion factors. (In most cases you should convert whichever is easiest. For this problem convert 6.1 s to hours. 1 h = 3,600 s)

$$\frac{6.1 \text{ s}}{1} \times \frac{1 \text{ h}}{3600 \text{ s}} = 0.00169 \text{ h}$$

Step 2 Write out the equation you will use. Use equation 6.2.

$$a = \frac{(v_f - v_i)}{t}$$

Step 3 Write out the equation substituting the numbers from the list in step 1.

$$a = \frac{(60\frac{mi}{h} - 0\frac{mi}{h})}{0.00169\ h}$$

Step 4 Solve the problem.

$$a = \frac{(60\frac{mi}{h} - 0\frac{mi}{h})}{0.00169\ h} = \frac{60\frac{mi}{h}}{0.00169\ h} = 35{,}503\ \frac{mi}{h^2}$$

That's a big number! Since the car's speed increased, the acceleration and velocity have the same direction. Therefore, the acceleration is **35,503 mi/h² north.**

When looking at a physics problem, you must follow the steps for solving problems.

1. First write down your knowns (the values given in the problem) and the unknown (what the question is asking you to find). Remember to include units.

2. Check to make sure all of the units agree. If they don't, you'll need to convert some units into the other for agreement.

3. Next you need to figure out the equation you need to use. If you are looking for velocity or speed, use equation 6.1. If you are solving for acceleration, use equation 6.2.

4. Then determine where the values you listed in step 1 fit into the equation and write the equation with the listed values.

5. Finally, solve the problem.

Practice following the steps by solving On Your Own problems 6.9–6.11.

ON YOUR OWN

6.9 A child is sledding. He starts at the top of the hill with a velocity of zero, and 3 seconds later he is speeding down the hill at 12 meters per second. What is the child's acceleration?

6.10 Once that same child reaches the bottom of the hill, the sled coasts over a long, flat section of snow. If the child's velocity when the sled starts coasting is 12 meters per second east, and the child coasts for 6 seconds before coming to a halt, what is the child's acceleration?

6.11 A good runner can keep up a pace of 0.15 miles per minute for quite some time. If a runner starts from rest and settles into a velocity of 0.15 miles per minute south after 3 seconds of running, what is the runner's acceleration over that 3-second interval?

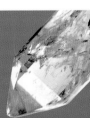

Graphing Acceleration

Just as we were able to graph velocity, we are able to graph acceleration. Suppose a biker is biking downhill in a straight line and the bike's speed increases 2 m/s every second. That means the biker's acceleration is 2 m/s^2. Figure 6.18 is a graph of the biker's speed over time. This is a speed-time graph and *the slope of a speed-time graph is acceleration.* Remember that the mathematical definition for acceleration is change in velocity (speed if it's a straight line) divided by the change in time. That is what the graph describes.

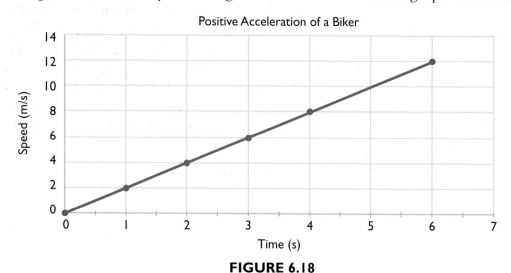

FIGURE 6.18
Positive Acceleration

The slope of a speed-time graph indicates acceleration. An upward slope indicates positive acceleration.

Let's say our biker, after increasing speed at 2 m/s for 6 seconds, starts to coast at a constant speed for 3 seconds. Then realizes he's going too fast, so he begins to slow down at 3 m/s until he stops. What would the graph of that acceleration look like? Well examine Figure 6.19.

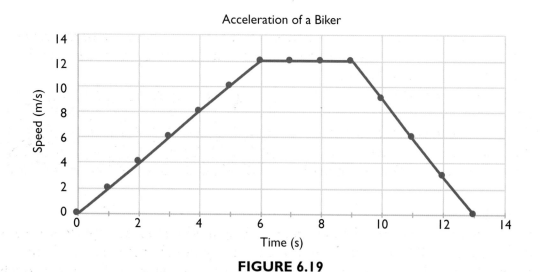

FIGURE 6.19
Acceleration of A Biker Over Time

Positive slope shows positive acceleration. The horizontal part of the graph shows constant speed.
The part of the graph with a negative slope shows negative acceleration.

Notice the positive acceleration indicated by the slope of the line from 0 seconds to 6 seconds. Then when the biker was coasting at a constant speed of 12 m/s, the line is a straight, horizontal line. That indicates there was no acceleration during those 3 seconds because neither the speed nor the direction was changing (the biker was still going down the hill). Now look at the slope of the line from 9 seconds to 13 seconds. That line segment is sloping downward which represents the bicycle slowing down. The change in speed is negative so the slope of the line is negative.

What does acceleration look like on a distance-time graph? Remember that the slope of a distance-time graph indicates velocity. When an object is accelerating, the object's velocity is constantly changing so you wouldn't expect a straight line. Remember that a straight line on a distance-time graph means the velocity is constant. It turns out that accelerated motion shown on a distance-time graph is represented by a curved line. This means it is a nonlinear graph in which a curve is used to connect the data points. Look at Figure 6.20 which shows the distance-time graph for a car starting from rest and accelerating for 8 seconds.

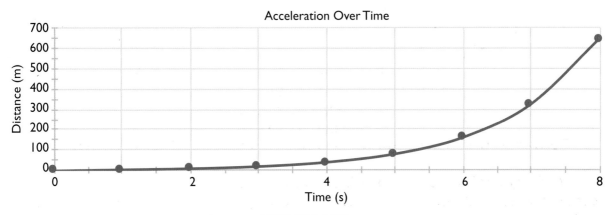

FIGURE 6.20
Distance Traveled Over Time During Acceleration
A distance-time graph of accelerated motion is a curve.

Compare the slope of the curve during the first second to the slope of the curve during the seventh second. Notice that the slope is much greater during the seventh second than during the first. Because the slope represents the speed of the car, an increasing slope means that the speed is increasing. An increasing speed means that the car is accelerating. Review this section by answering On Your Own 6.12.

ON YOUR OWN

6.12 What shows acceleration on a speed-time graph?

SUMMING UP

By now you should have a good handle on describing motion. This is important because most of physics (and all of science) is concerned with motion. In the next couple of modules you'll learn about what causes motion (forces) and the scientific answer to why motion occurs (energy). When you take physics in high school, you will go into more depth in your understanding.

ANSWERS TO THE "ON YOUR OWN" QUESTIONS

6.1 In the frame of reference of your friend on the escalator with you, you are not in motion. Your other two friends (the one on the first floor and the one on the down escalator) will see you moving from their frame of reference. Since you and the friend on the escalator are standing still, the escalator determines your motion. You are, therefore, both moving at the same speed, and the distance between you is not changing. Thus, relative to each other, you are not moving. The distance between you and each of your other friends is changing, so relative to those two, you are in motion.

6.2 Distance and displacement are similar in that they both refer to the length between two points. They differ because while distance is the length of an object's actual path from a starting point to an ending point, displacement is the length of a straight line from the starting point to the ending point that an object has moved. Displacement also includes directional information while distance does not.

6.3 Step 1A List what is given and what is needed.

$$d = 115 \text{ mi}$$

$$t = 30 \text{ min}$$

$$v = ? \text{ in mi/h}$$

Step 1B Convert any necessary units.

$$\frac{30 \text{ min}}{1} \times \frac{1 \text{ h}}{60 \text{ min}} = 0.5 \text{ h}$$

Step 2 Write the equation (use 6.1).

$$v = \frac{d}{t}$$

Step 3 Plug in the quantities from 1A and 1B into the equation.

$$v = \frac{115 \text{ mi}}{0.5 \text{ h}}$$

Step 4 Solve

$$v = \frac{115 \text{ mi}}{0.5 \text{ h}} = 230 \frac{\text{mi}}{\text{h}}$$

6.4 Step 1A List what is given and what is needed.

$$d = 5 \text{ m}$$

$$t = 12 \text{ h}$$

$$v = ? \text{ in mm/min}$$

Step 1B   Convert any necessary units.

$$\frac{12 \text{ h}}{1} \times \frac{60 \text{ min}}{1 \text{ h}} = 720 \text{ min}$$

$$\frac{5 \text{ m}}{1} \times \frac{1000 \text{ mm}}{1 \text{ m}} = 5000 \text{ mm}$$

Step 2   Write the equation (use 6.1).

$$v = \frac{d}{t}$$

Step 3   Plug in the quantities from 1A and 1B into the equation.

$$v = \frac{5000 \text{ mm}}{720 \text{ min}}$$

Step 4   Solve

$$v = \frac{5000 \text{ mm}}{720 \text{ min}} = 6.94 \frac{\text{mm}}{\text{min}}$$

6.5   Step 1A   List what is given and what is needed.

$$d = 45 \text{ km} + 64 \text{ km} = 109 \text{ km}$$

$$t = 0.5 \text{ h} + 0.7 \text{ h} = 1.2 \text{ h}$$

$$v = ? \text{ in mi/h}$$

Step 1B   Convert any necessary units.

$$\frac{109 \text{ km}}{1} \times \frac{1 \text{ mi}}{1.61 \text{ km}} = 67.7 \text{ mi}$$

Step 2   Write the equation (use 6.1).

$$v = \frac{d}{t}$$

Step 3   Plug in the quantities from 1A and 1B into the equation.

$$v = \frac{67.7 \text{ mi}}{1.2 \text{ h}}$$

Step 4   Solve

$$v = \frac{67.7 \text{ mi}}{1.2 \text{ h}} = 56.4 \frac{\text{mi}}{\text{h}}$$

6.6   The slope of a line on a distance-time graph is equal to the speed.

6.7   Velocity is speed with direction. So in order for a number to represent velocity, it needs a speed unit (a distance unit divided by a time unit) and a direction. Answer (d) does not have a speed unit. Answers (a–c) all have speed units, but only answer (b) also has a direction. Thus, the only velocity is answer (b).

6.8   Step 1   List the information that is given to you in the problem. Then list the unknown or what the question is asking you to find.

velocity (v) of plane 1 = 520 mi/h east

velocity (v) of plane 2 = 650 mi/h west

relative velocity = ? in mi/h

Step 2   Write out the equation you will use. Since the planes are flying towards each other we must add their speeds:

relative speed = speed of plane 1 + speed of plane 2

Step 3   Write out the equation substituting the numbers from the list in step 1.

relative speed = 520 mi/h + 650 mi/h

Step 4   Solve the problem.

relative speed = 520 mi/h + 650 mi/h = 1,170 mi/h

Since they are approaching each other, their relative velocity is 1,170 mi/h toward each other.

6.9   Step 1   List the information that is given to you in the problem. Then list the unknown or what the question is asking you to find.

v_i = 0 m/s

v_f = 12 m/s down the hill

t = 3 s

a = ?

Step 2   Write out the equation you will use. Use equation 6.2.

$$a = \frac{(v_f - v_i)}{t}$$

Step 3   Write out the equation substituting the numbers from the list in step 1.

$$a = \frac{(12\frac{m}{s} - 0\frac{m}{s})}{3\ s}$$

Step 4   Solve the problem.

$$a = \frac{(12\frac{m}{s} - 0\frac{m}{s})}{3\ s} = \frac{12\frac{m}{s}}{3\ s} = 4\frac{m}{s^2}$$

The sled's velocity increased, so the acceleration has the same direction as the velocity. Thus the acceleration is 4 m/s² down the hill.

6.10   Step 1   List the information that is given to you in the problem. Then list the unknown or what the question is asking you to find.

v_i = 12 m/s east

v_f = 0 m/s

t = 6 s

a = ?

Step 2   Write out the equation you will use. Use equation 6.2.

$$a = \frac{(v_f - v_i)}{t}$$

Step 3   Write out the equation substituting the numbers from the list in step 1.

$$a = \frac{(0\frac{m}{s} - 12\frac{m}{s})}{6\ s}$$

Step 4   Solve the problem.

$$a = \frac{(0\frac{m}{s} - 12\frac{m}{s})}{6\ s} = \frac{-12\frac{m}{s}}{6\ s} = -2\frac{m}{s^2}$$

The negative sign tells us that the acceleration is in the opposite direction as the velocity. This makes sense, since the sled slowed down. Since the negative sign tells us about direction, we drop it from the answer and replace it with the actual direction. Therefore the acceleration is 2 m/s² west.

6.11 Step 1A List the information that is given to you in the problem. Then list the unknown or what the question is asking you to find.

$v_1 = 0$ mi/min

$v_2 = 0.15$ mi/min south

$t = 3$ s

$a = ?$

Step 1B Convert any quantities using the given conversion factors. (In most cases you should convert whichever is easiest. For this problem convert 3 s to min. 1 min = 60 s)

$$\frac{3 \text{ s}}{1} \times \frac{1 \text{ min}}{60 \text{ s}} = 0.05 \text{ min}$$

Step 2 Write out the equation you will use. Use equation 6.2.

$$a = \frac{(v_f - v_i)}{t}$$

Step 3 Write out the equation substituting the numbers from the list in steps 1A and 1B.

$$a = \frac{(0.15 \frac{\text{mi}}{\text{min}} - 0 \frac{\text{mi}}{\text{min}})}{0.05 \text{ min}}$$

Step 4 Solve the problem.

$$a = \frac{(0.15 \frac{\text{mi}}{\text{min}} - 0 \frac{\text{mi}}{\text{min}})}{0.05 \text{ min}} = \frac{0.15 \frac{\text{mi}}{\text{min}}}{6 \text{ s}} = 3 \frac{\text{mi}}{\text{min}^2}$$

Since the runner sped up, the acceleration and velocity are in the same direction. Thus the acceleration is 3 mi/min^2 south.

6.12 The slope of the line on a speed-time graph shows the acceleration.

STUDY GUIDE FOR MODULE 6

1. Match the following terms to their definitions.

   a. Reference point

   A physical measurement that contains only magnitude (number) and does not contain directional information

   b. Displacement

   The time rate of change of an object's velocity

   c. Vector quantity

   A point against which direction is measured

   d. Scalar quantity

   The rate at which an object is moving at a given moment in time

   e. Average speed

   The distance an object travels plus the direction from the starting point

   f. Instantaneous speed

   A physical measurement that contains both magnitude (number) and directional information

   g. Acceleration

   The ratio of the total distance traveled to the total time of the trip

2. Motion is described with respect to a

   a. graph.   b. slope.   c. displacement.   d. frame of reference.

3. Two or more displacements can be combined by what method?

   a. graphing the slope   c. calculating the acceleration

   b. using vector addition   d. determining the velocity

4. What is acceleration equal to?

   a. distance divided by time   c. the slope of a distance-time graph

   b. change in speed divided by time   d. change in speed multiplied by time

5. If an object's position does not change relative to a reference point, it is in motion relative to that reference point?

6.   A child is floating in an inner tube on a still lake. His position does not change relative to a tree on the shore. He watches two girls jog along the shore of the lake. The girls are keeping perfect pace with each other. Neither is pulling ahead of nor falling behind the other.

    a. Relative to whom is the child moving?

    b. Relative to whom is the first girl in motion?

    c. Relative to whom is the second girl NOT in motion?

7.   Label each of the following quantities as speed, distance, velocity, acceleration, or none of these. Also, identify each as a vector or scalar quantity.

    a. 10 m   d. 56 L

    b. $1.2\ m/s^2$ east   e. 2.2 mi/min west

    c. 3.4 ft/h and slowing   f. 2.2 mm/year

8.   What is the speed of a boat that travels 10 miles in 30 minutes? Please give your answer in mi/h.

9.   What is the speed of a jogger who jogs 6 km in 45 min? Please give your answer in m/s.

10.   If a river current is 8.0 m/s downstream, and a boat is traveling 10.0 m/s upstream, what is the boat's speed relative to the riverbank?

11.   If two displacement vectors add to give a total displacement of zero, what do you know about the two displacements?

12.   A fly is walking on a wall. First it crawls 1 meter up, then 1 meter to the left, and then 1 meter down. What is its total displacement?

13.   A car and a truck are traveling north on a highway. The truck has a speed of 45 mi/h and the car has a speed of 57 mi/h. If the truck is ahead of the car, what is the relative velocity?

57 miles per hour north

45 miles per hour north

14. If an object travels for 15 minutes with a constant velocity of 12 mi/h west, what is the acceleration?

15. A sports car goes from a velocity of zero to a velocity of 12 meters per second east in 2 seconds. What is the car's acceleration?

16. A train takes a long time to stop. That's what makes trains so dangerous to people who cross the tracks when one is near. If a train is traveling at 30 miles per hour south and takes 12 minutes to come to a stop, what is the train's acceleration?

17. Describe a situation in which you can accelerate even though your speed doesn't change.

18. If an object is moving with a constant velocity, what do you know about its acceleration?

Use the graph in Figure 6.21 that shows the motion for a person walking through the park to answer questions 19 and 20.

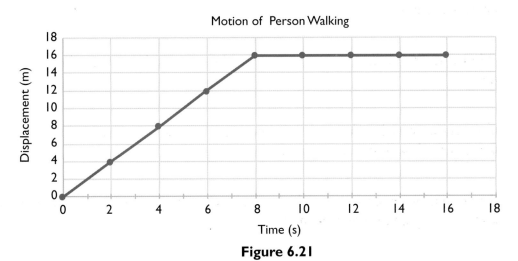

Figure 6.21

19. What was the person doing between 0 seconds and 8 seconds? What were they doing between 8 seconds and 16 seconds?

20. How fast is the person walking during the first 8 seconds?

PHYSICS—FORCES

In the previous module you learned a lot about analyzing motion. You now understand and can calculate speed, velocity, and acceleration. This knowledge and those skills are very valuable in trying to understand the physical creation around you. However in all of what you have learned so far, you have not discovered what causes objects in motion to behave the way they do. It all has to do with forces. Forces and motion are connected. Gravity is just one of the forces we'll consider in this module.

Natural Notes

When you think of forces you probably think of gravity. When you drop something you always know it will fall. Even helium-filled balloons that disappear up into the clouds will fall to Earth once the helium escapes out. Gravity pulls the oceans in high and low tides. Gravity keeps the Earth circling the sun and keeps your feet firmly on the ground. We can't see gravity, yet we know it is there because we see and feel the effects of it. Even with all the current scientific knowledge we have today, the force of gravity is still one of the universe's great mysteries.

FIGURE 7.1
Skydivers
Skydivers feel the effects of gravity as they fall to Earth.

225

IN THIS MODULE YOU WILL READ ABOUT THE FOLLOWING MAIN IDEAS:

- Forces
- Newton's Laws of Motion
- Fundamental Forces

FORCES

You experience forces every day. What exactly is a force? Well, have you ever had an umbrella lifted from your hands by a strong wind? Or started riding a skateboard by pushing off with one foot? Or pulled on a rope in a tug-of-war game? All of these are examples of forces. The wind lifts the umbrella away from you. You push against the ground to start the skateboard. Your team pulls the other team to your side to win the tug-of-war. A force is a push or a pull that acts on an object.

FIGURE 7.2
Everyday Forces
What forces do you experience in your daily life?

Force—A push or pull that acts on an object

Forces are what cause motion. A force can cause a resting object to move. A force can cause a moving object to slow or stop. And a force can accelerate moving objects by changing the speed or direction (or both) of the object.

It's usually not difficult to measure forces. In fact every time you step on a scale, you are measuring the force of gravity on you. In grocery stores, you buy produce by weight—meaning it costs so much per pound. If you look, you can usually find scales available (Figure 7.3) to help you figure out how much your produce weighs (a force), so you know how much it will cost.

The SI unit for force is the newton, abbreviated as **N**. One newton is the force required to make an object with a mass of 1 kilogram accelerate at 1 meter per second

FIGURE 7.3
Produce Scale
Scales measure the force of gravity on objects such as apples.

squared. In fact, 1 newton is equal to 1 kilogram-meter per second squared ($1 \text{ N} = 1 \text{ kg·m/s}^2$). The unit, newton, is named for Sir Isaac Newton (1642–1727), the English physicist who explained the relationship between force, mass, and acceleration. You will learn more about him and his laws later in this module.

Combining Forces

Like acceleration and velocity, force is a vector quantity. You can use vectors (arrows) to represent forces. The length of the arrow represents the strength of the force and the direction of the arrow represents the direction of the force. Like other vector quantities, forces can be combined. In the tug-of-war photo in Figure 7.2, all of the kids are combining their forces to try to pull the other team to their side. To show the result of how forces combine, we combine force arrows (Figure 7.4). Forces in the same direction add together and forces in opposite directions are subtracted from one another. The total overall force acting on an object (after all the forces are combined) is called the net force.

Have you ever been in a tug-of-war game where the forces on both sides were equal? What happened? Nothing! If each group pulled on the rope with equal force and they're pulling in opposite directions, then the rope doesn't move and neither group wins. When forces on an object combine to produce a net force of zero we say that the forces are balanced. When an object has balanced forces acting on it (net force = 0), there is no change in the object's motion.

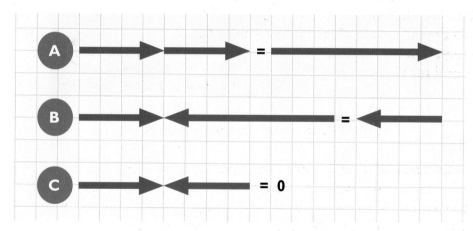

FIGURE 7.4
Combining Forces
You can add forces (A). You can subtract forces (B). Forces that are equal in magnitude but opposite in direction result in no net force (C).

It makes sense then, that when forces on an object are unbalanced, there will be a change in motion. If you can, set this book down on a nearby table (open to this page of course). Now with your hand push the bottom of the book away from you. What happened? The book moved away from you. That is because you provided an unbalanced force on the book when you moved it. (Okay now you can pick the book up again.) An unbalanced force occurs when there is a non-zero net force acting on an object. When an unbalanced force (net force ≠ 0) acts on an object, the object accelerates.

This is true whether your adding forces or subtracting forces—as long as the net force is not zero. Unbalanced forces are how you win a tug-of-war game (Figure 7.5). Your team needs to pull on the rope with a greater combined force than the opposing team does. When two forces are acting on an object in opposite directions, the net force equals the size of the larger force minus the size of the smaller force in the direction of the larger force.

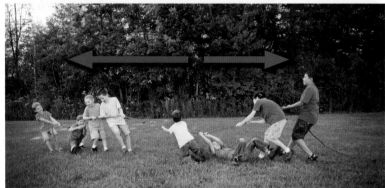

FIGURE 7.5
Forces and Motion
When forces are balanced, and net force equals zero (top image) there is no change in motion. When forces are unbalanced, acceleration occurs in the direction of the larger force (bottom). Which team wins?

Friction

Have you ever applied brakes while riding your bike? Or stopped a skateboard by stepping down on the back of the skateboard so it scrapes the pavement? If you have, then you were applying a force that opposed your motion. Stepping back on the skateboard (Figure 7.6) creates friction as the surface of the skateboard rubs against the ground.

FIGURE 7.6
Friction Opposes Motion
Whenever two surfaces are in contact, friction will oppose motion.

Friction—A force that results when surfaces of objects rub against each other and opposes motion

QUESTION:
What happens when you drop two different objects at the same time? Do they hit the ground simultaneously?

HYPOTHESIS:
Write what you predict will happen to the paper and the book when dropped from the same height at the same time. Will they hit the ground together, or will one hit before the other?

PROCEDURE:
1. Hold the book in one hand and the paper in the other. Hold both of them out at arm's length, and make sure that they are at exactly the same height. Make sure that there are no obstructions beneath the two objects so that they can fall to the floor without running into something.
2. Now, release them both at precisely the same instant. Note what happens. Specifically, note which object (the book or the paper) hits the ground first. If they hit simultaneously, note that.
3. Next, repeat the experiment in a slightly different way. This time place the piece of paper on top of the book and hold the book out at arm's length with both hands. Now release the book and paper. Note what happens this time.

CONCLUSION:
Write a paragraph about what happened in the two trials you performed. Make connections to the text (specifically the paragraphs that follow).

What happened in this quick experiment? In the first part, the book hit the ground first. That is what you would expect from your everyday experience. After all, the book is heavier than the paper. Thus, it should fall faster than the paper, right? This leads most people to believe that gravity accelerates heavy things faster than it accelerates light things. After all, both the book and the paper were being accelerated by gravity as they fell. The book fell faster, so it must have experienced more acceleration, right?

If that's the case, how can we explain the second part of the experiment? In that situation, the piece of paper stayed on top of the book, falling just as fast as the book fell! Why did this happen? The paper was not stuck to the book; therefore, it did not have to stay on the book. If it were really experiencing a smaller acceleration due to gravity than the book, the book should have started traveling faster than the piece of paper, eventually pulling away from it. Instead, they both fell at the same rate. Why? They both fell at the same rate because they both experienced the same acceleration. Thus, the conclusion I just stated from the first part of the experiment is wrong. How, then, do we explain the first part of the experiment?

The answer is fluid friction or air resistance. Remember air is made up of gases and as an object falls, the molecules and atoms of gas must get out of its way. Well, the molecules and atoms resist this movement, and the object must force its way through them. A heavy object is much better at doing this than a light object. Therefore, heavy objects fall faster than light objects not because their acceleration due to gravity is larger, but because they are not as strongly affected by air resistance as light objects are.

When we neglect air resistance, all objects falling near the surface of the Earth accelerate equally. In fact when we eliminate air resistance and drop an apple and a feather, they fall at exactly the same rate of acceleration (Figure 7.12). So, when dealing with objects falling near the surface of the Earth, we will always neglect air resistance. For most relatively heavy objects, this is a reasonable thing to do, because air resistance does not affect heavy objects very much.

Well, now that we know all objects accelerate equally under the influence of gravity, we need to know *what* that acceleration is. Near the surface of the Earth, the acceleration due to gravity is 9.8 meters per second^2. In English units, that turns out to be 32 feet per second^2. These are numbers that you must memorize.

> The acceleration due to gravity for any object is 9.8 m/s^2 in metric units and 32 ft/s^2 in English units.

FIGURE 7.12
All Objects Fall at the Same Rate of Acceleration
When air resistance is eliminated as shown by the feather in a vacuum tube, all objects experience the same acceleration due to gravity.

Whenever you do problems involving free fall, you will use one of those values for acceleration. Which one will you use? Well, that depends on the problem. If the problem deals with metric units, you will use 9.8 meters per second squared. If the problem deals with English units, you will use 32 feet per second squared. You will see what I mean in a moment.

It turns out that because the acceleration an object experiences in free fall is constant, there is one neat thing we can do. If an object is dropped without being given any initial push, we can determine how far it falls given just the time it is in the air. In other words, if we time an object as it falls, we can use the acceleration due to gravity to determine the distance it fell. We can do this by multiplying ½ × the acceleration due to gravity × the time squared, shown in equation 7.1.

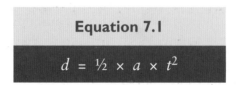

Equation 7.1

$$d = \tfrac{1}{2} \times a \times t^2$$

Don't worry about where this equation comes from, you will learn that when you take high school physics. For now, you just need to practice how to use the equation. Study example 7.1 to see how we do this.

EXAMPLE 7.1

A young woman is standing on a bridge overlooking a river. If she drops a rock from the bridge, and it takes 1.2 seconds for it to hit the river, how many meters did the rock fall?

Step 1   Write the list of knowns and the unknown. Since the rock is in free fall, we know it experiences acceleration due to gravity. And since the question asks for the distance in meters you'll want to use the acceleration due to gravity that has meters in it. Check that all units agree. If they don't, you must convert one to another for agreement.

$$t = 1.2 \text{ s}$$

$$a = 9.8 \text{ m/s}^2$$

$$d = ? \text{ in m}$$

Step 2   Write out the equation (use 7.1).

$$d = ½ \times a \times t^2$$

Step 3   Write out the equation substituting the numbers from step 1. You might find that using 0.5 (which is the decimal value for ½) is easier.

$$d = 0.5 \times (9.8 \tfrac{m}{s^2}) \times (1.2 \text{ s})^2$$

Step 4   Solve the problem. Remember that when something is squared, you take it times itself. I show that below for you to see what I mean.

$$d = 0.5 \times (9.8 \tfrac{m}{s^2}) \times (1.2 \text{ s})^2 = 0.5 \times (9.8 \tfrac{m}{s^2}) \times (1.2 \text{ s}) \times (1.2 \text{ s}) = 7.056 \text{ m}$$

Notice what happened here. When you put the numbers into the calculator, you type: 0.5 × 9.8 × 1.2 × 1.2 = 7.056. Now look at the units. A second × a second is a second squared, so the s^2 in the denominator of the acceleration cancels each of the units of time. This leaves just the meters unit. Since distance is measured in meters, we know the equation worked out the way it should.

    It turns out that this will always happen in physics and chemistry. When you use physical quantities in equations, the units will always work out like they did here. That's the reason the units in an equation must agree with one another before you can solve the equation. If they do not, units that are supposed to cancel will not be able to, and the answer will not make sense. This answer, however, is not nonsense. **The rock fell 7.056 m.**

    If you think about it, this little fact of physics can be incredibly useful. You can use time to determine the height of something too tall to measure. Do On Your Own problem 7.4 and try the You Do Science Activity to see what I mean.

ON YOUR OWN

7.4   A stone is dropped from the roof of a house. A person standing on the ground watches and times the fall of the stone with a stopwatch. If the stone takes 1.1 seconds to fall, how tall is the house using feet as your measurement?

YOU DO SCIENCE

Measuring HEIGHT WITH A STOPWATCH

Sometimes it is hard to measure the height of something because you do not have a ruler long enough. In this activity, you will use a stopwatch and a rock to measure the height of the ceiling in a room. For this activity you will need a stopwatch that reads hundredths of a second (many smartphones have this feature), a chair or stepladder, a rock or other heavy object to reduce air resistance (make sure your choice will not damage your floor), and a tape measure. Stand on the chair or stepladder and hold your rock so that it touches the ceiling of the room. With the stopwatch in your other hand, simultaneously drop the rock and start the stopwatch. If you have a friend, they can help you with this activity. When the rock hits the ground, stop the stopwatch. Record the time from the stopwatch (there is a place to record it in your student notebook). Repeat timing the drop of the rock 10

FIGURE 7.13
Stopwatch
Make sure your stopwatch shows the time to the hundredths of a second.

times. It is important to repeat this 10 times to reduce experimental error in timing because the time is so small. (Unless you live in a very tall house, the time on the stopwatch should be less than 1 second.) Once you have timed the rock drop 10 times, average the results by adding them all together and dividing by 10. Use the time you just calculated and equation 7.1 to determine the distance over which the rock fell. If the tape measure you have is marked off in feet, use 32 ft/s^2 for the acceleration. If it is marked off in meters, use 9.8 m/s^2 as the acceleration. Once you calculate the height of the room, measure it with the tape measure. How close are your numbers? They should be within 15% of each other.

NEWTON'S LAWS OF MOTION

Now that you have a pretty good understanding of what a force is, let's look at how force and motion are related. Suppose you and two friends are ice skating. You haven't yet put your ice skates on, but your friends have. Both of your friends stand side-by-side on the edge of the ice and you push each one with the same force. You notice that one friend moves farther on the ice than the other. Why does that happen? Why does one car accelerate faster than another? The answers to these questions have to do with the relationship between forces, mass, and a concept called inertia (ih ner' shuh).

Inertia—The tendency of an object to resist changes in its velocity

Sir Isaac Newton developed an explanation for these relationships. But before we dig deeper into them, let's look at how our modern scientific understanding developed.

A Brief History

Just as we started with the Greeks for a history of the atom, we'll start with the Greeks again for a history of the physical nature of motion. It's taken about 2,000 years for us to understand forces and motion the way we do today. Remember the Greek philosopher, Aristotle (384–322 BC) from module 2? Well, Aristotle spent an enormous amount of time observing and thinking logically about the world around him. He wrote many works covering such diverse subjects as physics, biology, morals, and even politics. Of course, we know that he was not always correct (as with his incorrect theory of matter).

FIGURE 7.14
Statue of Aristotle
Aristotle thought all objects required force to maintain constant speed.

Remember, the ancient Greek philosophers only used their skills of observation and logic to try to explain things. They didn't really conduct scientific experiments as we do today. Aristotle reasoned that there were two sets of laws governing motion—one for the heavens and one for objects on Earth. So by observation, Aristotle reasoned that the normal state of all objects in the heavens was to move in circles. In the same way that the Moon circles the Earth, for example. He also reasoned that the normal state of all objects on Earth was to be at rest. After all, if you put a rock on the sidewalk it will just sit there until you kick it. Then once you kick it, the rock will tumble a distance, but it will eventually stop. It does make logical sense of our observations. Aristotle believed that objects on Earth stopped because there was no force present to keep them moving. And at that time, he had no concept of friction and how frictional force always opposes motion. So, Aristotle incorrectly proposed that a continual unbalanced force is required to keep an object moving at a constant speed. (He did, however, have a difficult time explaining how an arrow shot from a bow continued to fly through the air once the string was no longer applying a force.) Even though they were incorrect, Aristotle was very influential, and his theories were accepted for over 1,500 years.

During and following the time of the Renaissance, however, scientists began to notice many discrepancies between the theories of Aristotle and their observations of the world around them. Aristotle's teachings had become so ingrained in the minds of the scientific (and religious) community, that most scientist were quite resistant to giving them up. It took many years of careful experiments by several scientists to turn the tide and dispose of Aristotle's mistakes. Italian scientist Galileo Galilei (1564–1642) was one of them.

Galileo promoted conducting experiments to develop scientific arguments. He used inclined planes to study motion because his methods of time keeping were not sufficiently accurate to measure free fall. Galileo did not have a stopwatch like you did for the You Do Science activity. With his rolling balls down inclined plane experiments Galileo began to develop the concept of inertia. He proposed that, if no forces acted on them, objects at rest would stay at rest and objects in motion would stay in motion. This was definitely contrary to what

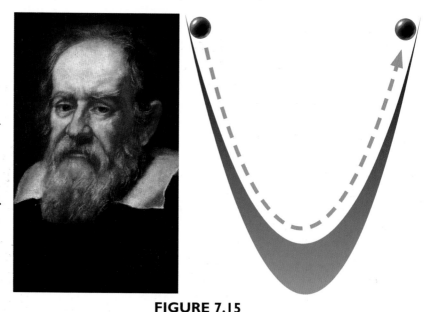

FIGURE 7.15
Galileo Galilei
Galileo noticed that if he dropped a ball on a smooth curved u-shaped ramp, it would nearly reach the same height on the other side. By reducing friction, he showed objects keep moving.

Aristotle thought. While Aristotle argued that it required a force to keep an object moving at a constant speed, Galileo argued that an object would continue moving at a constant speed forever, unless it was stopped by a force. We now know this stopping force is friction. Think about this for a second, though. All of Galileo's experiments would have had to deal with friction because friction exists in our world. Nevertheless, Galileo was able to imagine a frictionless world in which objects would continue moving forever if not changed or stopped by a force. This shows you what a genius Galileo was.

think about this

It may seem odd to you that the scientific world would accept wrong ideas for so long, but the truth was they just didn't have the tools they needed to conduct proper experiments. You see technology and science go hand in hand. You used a stopwatch in the You Do Science activity, but Galileo didn't have a stopwatch. That didn't stop him though! He created a water clock to time the travel of a ball down an inclined plane. How can water tell time? Well, when Galileo released a ball, he started his water clock by allowing water to flow into a container. When the ball reached the bottom of the inclined plane, he stopped the flow of water. He then weighed the amount of water in the container. This allowed him to compare the weights of the water in the container of different trials. If the weight of water from one trial was twice as much as that of another trial, Galileo knew it took the ball twice as long to travel the ramp. If it took that much ingenuity to develop a means of timing your experiment, it's no wonder science stalled for a long time. Galileo was a determined genius! (And I bet you'll never take your watch for granted again.) The advancement of science depends to some degree on the advancement of technology.

Though the groundwork was laid by Galileo (and to a different extent by others like Kepler and Copernicus), it was Isaac Newton who tied all of the threads together and developed laws of motion that governed objects in both the heavens and on Earth.

salt and light

Sir Isaac Newton (Figure 7.16) is an incredibly important figure in the history of science. He was born in England the year Galileo died, 1642. He was always interested in learning about how the world worked, and he devoted his life to performing experiments designed to help him understand creation. He is credited with many, many discoveries, including the three laws of motion you'll read about in this module. He also developed a law describing gravity, conducted a famous prism experiment showing white light is composed of many colors, and developed a new form of mathematics we now call calculus. Amazingly, Newton completed these three accomplishments in less than 18 months! He also built the first reflecting telescope. Newton was knighted for his accomplishments by Queen Anne in 1705. He died in 1727.

FIGURE 7.16
Sir Isaac Newton
Newton was a scientific genius and a man of faith.

Clearly, Sir Isaac Newton was a genius. He was also a devoutly religious man who spent as much time studying the Bible as he did studying science. As *The Columbia History of the World* says, "…at the end of his days he spent more time studying and writing about the prophecies in the Book of Daniel than he did in charting the heaven." Although not an orthodox Christian (he rejected the Trinity and the divinity of Christ), he held to many standard Christian beliefs. Here is a good quote the sums up Newton's theological views: "There is one God, the Father, ever living, omnipresent, omniscient, almighty, the maker of heaven and earth, and one mediator between God and man, the man Christ Jesus." As you can see, he clearly saw God as the almighty Creator, and he saw Christ as the mediator between man and God. However, he did not see Christ as divine. Instead, he refers to Christ as a man throughout his theological works. This is part of what made his religious views unorthodox.

Newton believed that in studying science, he was actually learning about God. In fact, it was his strong belief in God that made him study science. After all, he reasoned, studying science was a way of learning about creation, and learning about creation was a way of learning about God. Of course, Newton also realized that studying creation cannot be the sole means of learning about God. That's why he spent so much time studying the Bible as well. Newton applied his strong mind to interpreting Scripture and is responsible for many commentaries on passages in the Bible. Clearly, Newton had a great sense of priorities. He recognized the importance of science, but he also realized that learning about God is even more important.

During his life, Sir Isaac Newton established the scientific laws that govern 99% of what we see and feel every day. From how the planets orbit the sun and how the moon revolves around the Earth, to the sliding of a hockey puck hit on ice, to the launch of a rocket into space, Newton's laws accurately describe motion and the forces involved. Isaac Newton built on the work of Galileo and Aristotle (and others) which he readily acknowledged, "If I have seen further it is by standing on the shoulders of Giants."

Many consider Newton's laws to be the most important laws of all physical science. It's important, then, that you understand them too.

Newton's First Law of Motion

Newton's first law explains the connection between force and motion. He suggested that as long as the forces on an object are balanced, the object does not change its motion. He stated that an object at rest remains at rest, and an object in motion continues moving in a straight line at constant speed, unless acted upon by an unbalanced force. This has been found to be true in many, many experiments and is known as Newton's first law of motion.

Newton's first law—An object in motion (or at rest) will stay in motion (or at rest) until it is acted upon by an outside force

In other words, if an object is at rest, it will stay at rest until an unbalanced force causes it to move. In the same way, an object in motion will continue in motion at its current velocity until a force causes its velocity to change.

Remember what the definition of inertia was? Inertia is the tendency of an object to resist a change in its velocity. Basically, that is exactly what Newton was saying. For that reason, Newton's first law is also referred to as the law of inertia. Let's look at a couple examples. A soccer ball will set motionless of the field (all forces acting on the ball are balanced) until an unbalanced force such as a kick is applied. After the kick, the ball rolls down the field, but because the friction (an unbalanced force) between the grass and the ball is acting on the ball, it slows and eventually stops. The ball remained at rest until an unbalanced force acted on it. If it were not for the outside force of friction, the ball would have continued rolling down the field indefinitely.

Have you ever been riding down the road in a car when the driver suddenly slammed on the brakes? What happened? You were thrown forward in your seat until your seatbelt stopped you. Actually, you weren't *thrown* forward at all. What happened was the law of inertia at work. You see you were traveling with the same velocity as the car while you were riding down the road. When the driver hit the

FIGURE 7.17
Inertia of a Soccer Ball
The soccer ball has inertia. It will remain at rest until acted upon by an unbalanced force.

FIGURE 7.18
Fast Stop
In a moving car, your inertia is the same as the car's inertia. If the brakes apply a force to the car, you continue moving forward at your initial velocity until the seat belt provides an outside force to slow you. Please always wear your seatbelt!

brakes, the brakes applied a force to the car, and it began to stop. However since the brakes did not apply a force to you, you continued to move with the same velocity as before. Thus, the car slowed a lot and you continued moving forward quickly, which felt like you were lurching forward. Once your seat belt applied a force on you, however, you slowed down too.

This is a good example of how an object stays in motion until acted on by an outside force. As you were riding in the car, you had a certain amount of inertia. When the car began to stop, your inertia kept you moving at the same velocity until your seat belt exerted a force that overcame your inertia. Once the force was able to overcome your inertia, you stopped along with the car. Conduct Experiment 7.2 to see the law of inertia in action.

EXPERIMENT 7.2
NEWTON'S FIRST LAW

PURPOSE:
To observe Newton's first law of motion.

MATERIALS:
- A coin (nickels work well)
- A 3 inch by 5 inch index card (note the units listed)
- A small beaker or glass (like a juice glass)
- A raw egg
- A hard-boiled egg
- An aluminum pie pan
- A pair of scissors
- A marble or other small ball
- Eye protection such as goggles or safety glasses

BACKGROUND:
Sometimes it's hard to understand Newton's first law because it goes against our everyday experience (how can an object keep moving unless acted on by a force, for example). Experiments such as these help you visualize that this law of motion is really true.

QUESTIONS:
How can Newton's laws be observed?

HYPOTHESES:
1. Write your prediction of what will happen to a coin when a card is quickly removed from under it. Write your prediction of what will happen when the card is removed slowly.
2. Write your prediction of what will happen when you stop a spinning hard-boiled egg. Write your prediction of what will happen when you stop a spinning raw egg.

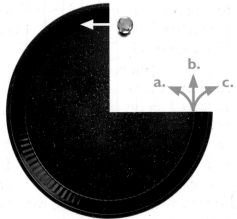

FIGURE 7.19

3. Write your prediction of what path (a, b, or c) the circling marble will take when it exits the pie pan in Figure 7.19.

PROCEDURE—PART 1:

1. Place the small beaker or glass on the table, right side up.
2. Place the index card on top of the glass so that it covers the opening. Center the index card so that the center of the card is over the center of the glass.
3. Place the coin on the center of the index card.
4. Flick the card quickly with your fingers so that it moves forward, uncovering the glass. You want to flick the edge of the card from the side. Don't flick upwards or downwards. Record what happens to the coin.
5. Set up the experiment again. This time, instead of flicking the card, grasp the card with your fingers and slowly pull it away from the glass. Keep the card level as you pull it away. Record what happens to the coin this time.

PROCEDURE—PART 2:

6. Place the hard-boiled egg on the table. Make sure it is on its side and not an end.
7. Spin the egg and watch how it spins. Be sure it spins on its side. Record your observations.
8. Do the same thing with the raw egg. Record your observations, noting the difference in the way the eggs spin, if any.
9. Spin the hard-boiled egg again. Once it is spinning, reach down and stop it for an instant, then immediately let it go. Record what happens.
10. Do the same thing with the raw egg. Record what happens in this case.

PROCEDURE—PART 3:

11. Use the scissors to cut a quarter of the pie pan away. Examine the diagram in Figure 7.19.
12. In this experiment, you are going to roll the marble into the pie pan as shown in Figure 7.19. The marble will roll around the pan, guided by the pan's walls. When it hits the edge where the quarter was cut out, it will begin to roll on its own.
13. Before you actually do this, make sure you have written your hypothesis or your prediction of which path the ball will roll once it begins to roll on its own. There are three possible choices.
14. Now you should actually perform the experiment. Hold the pie pan in place with one of your hands so that it doesn't move.
15. Using your other hand, propel the marble straight into the pan so that it rolls around the side of the pan as shown in the figure. Watch which way it ends up moving. Record your observations.

CONCLUSIONS:

Explain what happened to the coin, the eggs, and the marble in terms of Newton's first law of motion. Use the terms, inertia, force, and friction in your paragraph. Make connections to what you've read in the text.

What happened in your experiments? If everything worked well, you should have seen the coin fall directly into the glass when you flicked the index card away. But when

In the top scenario of Figure 7.23, the man is pushing his car with a force of F_m (I used the subscript m to stand for man). Friction is a force in the opposite direction of the man's motion with a force of F_f. That makes the net force (the sum of all the forces acting on the car in the horizontal direction) the difference of the two forces or $F_m - F_f$.

In the bottom scenario, the man's (very well trained) dog helps him. We need to apply the third force (F_d) to the sum of the forces. Since the dog is pulling the car in the same direction that the man is pushing, their forces add together. The force of friction opposes those forces, so it is still subtracted.

In the end, then, friction simply subtracts from the force being applied in an attempt to move the car. If the man applies 300 newtons (N) of force to the car in an easterly direction, and the frictional force is 290 N, the total force will be 10 N to the east. If the dog helps the man by pulling with another 150 N to the east, the net force will be 160 N to the east. Remember, too, that it takes more force to overcome static friction and get an object moving than it does to keep things moving as that involves kinetic friction. And static friction is always more than kinetic friction. Make sure you understand this by studying the example problems. Then try the On Your Own questions that follow.

EXAMPLE 7.2

A. **A man's car (m = 1,500 kg) has broken down, and he is pushing it to a gas station. Ignoring friction, with what net force (in newtons) must the man push in order to make the car accelerate 0.03 m/s² to the east?**

Step 1   List knowns and unknown and check units.

m = 1,500 kg

a = 0.03 m/s²

F = ? in N (Since a N = kg·m/s², no conversions needed.)

Step 2   Write the equation (7.2) and rearrange so the unknown is on the left side of the equals sign, if needed.

$F = m \times a$

Step 3   Add knowns from step 1 to equation. Double check units.

$F = (1500 \text{ kg}) \times (0.03 \frac{\text{m}}{\text{s}^2})$

Step 4   Solve

$F = (1500 \text{ kg}) \times (0.03 \frac{\text{m}}{\text{s}^2}) = 45 \frac{\text{kg·m}}{\text{s}^2} = 45 \text{ N}$

Notice that we could just substitute a newton for the unit kg·m/s² since they are the same thing. Remember force is a vector so it must include direction. Since the acceleration is always in the same direction as the force, we know that the man must push with a force of **45 N to the east.**

B. **A car with a mass of 1,000 kilograms accelerates when the traffic light turns green. If the net force acting on the car is 4,000 newtons in the forward direction, what is the car's acceleration?**

Step 1   List knowns and unknown and check units.

m = 1,000 kg

F = 4,000 N

a = ? in m/s^2

Step 2   Write the equation (7.2) and rearrange so the unknown is on the left side of the equals sign, if needed.

$$F = m \times a \quad \text{so} \quad a = F/m$$

Step 3   Add knowns from step 1 to equation. Double check units.

$$a = \frac{(4000 \text{ N})}{(1000 \text{ kg})} = \frac{4000 \frac{\text{kg}\cdot\text{m}}{\text{s}^2}}{1000 \text{ kg}}$$

Step 4   Solve (study how the units work out)

$$a = \frac{4000 \frac{\text{kg}\cdot\text{m}}{\text{s}^2}}{1000 \text{ kg}} = \frac{\left(4 \frac{\text{kg}\cdot\text{m}}{1 \text{ s}^2}\right)}{\left(\frac{1 \text{ kg}}{1}\right)} = \left(\frac{4 \text{ kg}\cdot\text{m}}{1 \text{ s}^2}\right) \times \left(\frac{1}{1 \text{ kg}}\right) = 4 \frac{\text{m}}{\text{s}^2}$$

I showed you how the units work out in this example, but you need only remember that when the force is in units of newtons and the mass is in units of kilograms, then you can find the acceleration in units of meters per second squared simply by dividing the force by the mass. Remember, though that acceleration is a vector quantity so you must include direction. Direction of acceleration is always the same as the force applied. So the answer is **4 m/s^2 forward.**

C. **In order to clear an area, a construction worker (F_w) pushes on a large rock (m = 300 kg) that is in the way (Figure 7.24). Once he gets the rock moving, it begins to accelerate at 0.12 m/s^2 to the north. If the construction worker is able to apply 400 newtons of force, what is the frictional force between the rock and the ground?**

FIGURE 7.24
Forces on a Rock

Step 1   List knowns and unknown and check units.

Notice in this problem we have two unknowns. We don't know the net force (F) that the rock experiences, but since we know the mass and acceleration of the rock, we can figure it out. But the question asks for the frictional force (F_f) between the rock and ground too. This will be a 2 part question.

m = 300 kg F = ? in N

a = 0.12 m/s² north F_f = ? in N

F_w = 400 N

Step 2   First we need to solve for the net force acting on the rock. This is equation 7.2.

$F = m \times a$

Step 3   Add knowns from step 1 to equation. Double check units.

$F = (300 \text{ kg}) \times (0.12 \frac{m}{s^2})$

Step 4   Solve

$F = (300 \text{ kg}) \times (0.12 \frac{m}{s^2}) = 36 \frac{kg \cdot m}{s^2} = 36 \text{ N}$

Okay so now we know the net force acting on the rock. Remember that the net force is the sum of all the forces on an object. We know that the force the worker applied (400 N) is opposite the force of friction, so those will need to be subtracted to equal the total net force We'll do this in the second part of the problem below.

Step 5   List of knowns and unknowns. (You can just add the total net force to the same list from step 1 of the first part of the problem - no need to rewrite them all as I did here.)

m = 300 kg F = 36 in N

a = 0.12 m/s² F_f = ? in N

F_w = 400 N

Step 6   Write the equation for the total forces acting on the rock and rearrange for the unknown force (F_f).

$F = F_w - F_f$ so $F_f = F_w - F$

Steps 7 & 8 Add knowns from steps 1 and 5 and solve.

$F_f = F_w - F = 400 \text{ N} - 36 \text{ N} = 364 \text{ N}$

We need a direction since forces are vector quantities. The direction of the motion is north, and friction always opposes motion, so the direction of the frictional force must be south. Thus, the answer is **364 N south.**

D. A man needs to push a desk (m = 100 kg) across the floor. The static frictional force (F_{sf}) can resist motion with as much as 196 newtons of force, while the kinetic frictional force (F_{kf}) is only 110 newtons. How much force is necessary to get the desk moving? If the desk accelerates at 1.0 m/s² to the west when the force is applied, how much force did the man use (F_m)?

FIGURE 7.25
Forces on a Desk

Step 1   List knowns and unknown and check units.

m = 100 kg F_{sf} = 196 N

a = 1.0 m/s² west F_{kf} = 110 N

F_m = ? in N

Again, this question asks for two different things, the force required to get the desk moving and how much force the man used. For the first part, we just need to remember our definition of static frictional force. In order to get the desk moving, the man must apply more force than what static frictional force is capable of supplying. Thus, **the man must apply a little more than 196 N of force to get the desk moving.**

The second part of the problem asks you to calculate the force the man used so you'll need to find the total net force on the desk.

Step 2   You will use equation 7.2.

$F = m \times a$

Steps 3 & 4   Add knowns from step 1 to your equation. Double check units and solve.

$F =$ (100 kg) $\times$ (1.0 m) = 100 N

So the *total* net force acting on the desk is 100 newtons. But remember that the net force is made up of two components: the force the man applies (F_m) and, since the desk is moving, the kinetic frictional force (F_{kf}). Since friction opposes motion, these two forces are subtracted.

Step 5   Write the equation for the total forces (F) acting on the desk and rearrange for the unknown force (F_m).

$F = F_m - F_{kf}$ so $F_m = F + F_{kf}$

Notice, when I rearranged the equation for the unknown, I had to add F_{kf} to both sides.

Step 6   Add knowns from step 1 and solve.

$$F_m = F + F_{kf} = 100\text{ N} + 110\text{ N} = 210\text{ N}$$

We know, then, that the man used a force that had a strength of 210 newtons. What is its direction? Well, the desk is accelerating west, so that must be the direction of the man's force. In the end then, **the man applied a force of 210 N to the west.**

ON YOUR OWN

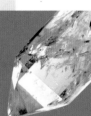

7.8   A box (mass = 15 kg) is given an initial shove and allowed to slide across the floor with no person pushing it. If the box slides north and experiences an acceleration of 1.1 m/s² to the south, what is the kinetic frictional force between the box and the floor?

7.9   Suppose someone wanted to keep the box in problem 7.8 moving at a constant velocity. What force must be applied in order to accomplish this feat?

7.10   A child wants to slide a block (m = 10 kg) to the east. Static friction between the block and the floor is capable of resisting motion with a force of 30 N west, while the kinetic frictional force is 20 N west. What force must the child exert in order to get the block moving? If the block accelerates at 1.5 m/s² east as a result of the child's force, what was the actual force used?

MOD 7

Weight and Mass

I mentioned in module 1 that in science there is a big difference between mass and weight. I want to talk a little more about that here. Mass and weight are related, but they are not the same. Remember that mass is the amount of an object. We can also say that mass is the measure of an object's inertia. Think about that for a moment. The more mass an object has the more it will resist a change in its motion (or rest). Weight is the force of gravity acting on an object. Just like any force, we can find weight using Newton's second law. Look at equation 7.3 and compare it to equation 7.2.

Equation 7.2
weight = mass × acceleration due to gravity,   or $W = mg$

Notice that weight (W) is substituted for force (F) and acceleration due to gravity (g) is substituted for acceleration (a). We always use either 9.8 m/s² or 32 ft/s² for acceleration due to gravity on Earth. Gravity always points down to the center of the Earth, so weight is also in the downward direction. But since everyone knows that gravity is downward, weight often does not include the written direction because it is implied. Study Example 7.3.

EXAMPLE 7.3

A.   An astronaut has a mass of 121 kg. What is his weight on Earth?

Step 1   List knowns and unknown and check units.

$$m = 121\text{ kg}$$

$g = 9.8$ m/s^2

$W = ?$ in N

Step 2   Write the equation (7.3) and rearrange so the unknown is on the left side of the equals sign, if needed.

$W = m \times g$

Steps 3 & 4 Add knowns from step 1 to equation. Double check units and solve.

$W = (121 \text{ kg}) \times (9.8 \frac{m}{s^2}) = \textbf{1185.8 N}$

FIGURE 7.26
Weight of an Astronaut

B.   **What is the astronaut's weight on the moon where the acceleration due to gravity is 1.625 m/s^2?**

Step 1   List knowns and unknown and check units.

$m = 121$ kg

$g = 1.625$ m/s^2

$W = ?$ in N

Step 2   Write the equation (7.3) and rearrange so the unknown is on the left side of the equals sign, if needed.

$W = m \times g$

Steps 3 & 4 Add knowns from step 1 to equation. Double check units and solve.

$W = (121 \text{ kg}) \times (1.625 \frac{m}{s^2}) = \textbf{196.6 N}$

Notice how in both locations the astronaut's mass is the same. But his weight on the moon is only about 1/6th of his weight on Earth.

Newton's Third Law
Well, we only have one more of Newton's laws of motion to go—Newton's third law.

> **Newton's third law**—For every action, there is an equal and opposite reaction

You've probably heard this one before. But what does it actually mean? Well, a force cannot exist alone. Forces always exist in pairs. In other words, whenever one object exerts a force on a second object, the second object exerts and equal and opposite force on the first object. These forces are called action and reaction forces.

Consider Figure 7.27. When you use a hammer to drive a nail, the hammer applies a force to the nail when you strike it. This is the action force and it drives the nail into the piece of wood. What is the reaction force? According to Newton's third law there must be an equal and opposite reaction force. The force that the nail applies to the hammer is the equal and opposite reaction force. It is this reaction force that stops the motion of the hammer.

Look at another example. Why does the trampoline in Figure 7.28 allow the boy to travel upward against the pull of gravity? Well, when he jumps on the trampoline, he exerts a force on it—the action force. If you were watching what happens, you would see the trampoline's surface bend in response to the force. What does Newton's third law say will happen as a result? It says that the trampoline will exert an equal but opposite force on him. You know this happens, because once he hits the trampoline, he slows down, stops, and then starts moving up into the air. Thus, his velocity changes. According to Newton's first law of motion, that cannot happen unless a force acts on him. What force was that? It was the equal and opposite reaction force. In other words, the boy exerted an action force on the trampoline (causing the surface to bow), and the trampoline exerted a reaction force right back on him (causing him to accelerate in a different direction). The force the trampoline exerted on him was equal in strength to the force he exerted on the trampoline.

It is very important to realize that the equal and opposite forces talked about in Newton's third law do not act on the *same* object. If that were the case, there would never be any acceleration. After all, if equal and opposite forces act on the same object, they cancel each other out, and the net force is zero. Instead, the equal and opposite forces discussed in Newton's third law affect *different* objects. Conduct Experiment 7.3 to get a better understanding of this law.

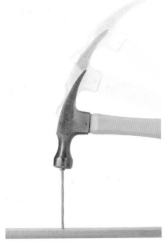

FIGURE 7.27
Equal and Opposite Forces
The hammer exerts a force on the nail. The nail exerts an equal and opposite force on the hammer.

FIGURE 7.28
Action Reaction Forces
The boy exerts an action force on the trampoline. The trampoline exerts a reaction force causing the boy to soar.

EXPERIMENT 7.3
NEWTON'S THIRD LAW

PURPOSE:
To investigate action and reaction forces and observe Newton's third law of motion.

MATERIALS:

- A plastic, 2 liter bottle
- A stopper that fits the bottle (It could be rubber or cork, but you cannot use the screw-on cap. It has to be something that plugs up the opening of the bottle but can be pushed out by a pressure buildup inside the bottle. Modeling clay can work as well. You could also try a large wad of gum, as long as the gum has dried out and has the texture of firm rubber.)
- A cup of vinegar
- Two teaspoons of baking soda
- Aluminum foil
- Four pencils
- Eye protection such as safety goggles or safety glasses

BACKGROUND:

You will want to do this experiment outside, because it is loud and messy!

QUESTION:

What happens when a chemical reaction produces a lot of pressure inside a closed container? How can Newton's third law explain this?

HYPOTHESIS:

Write your prediction for what will happens a chemical reaction causes a pressure buildup in a closed container.

PROCEDURE:

1. Pour about a cup of vinegar into the 2 L bottle.
2. Put the four pencils on the ground parallel to each other and about 2 inches apart. Lay the bottle on its side on top of the pencils. Do this carefully so that none of the vinegar spills out.
3. Take the aluminum foil and make a long, thin trough. The trough should be thin enough to fit inside the mouth of the bottle.
4. Once you have made the trough, fill it with 2 teaspoons of baking soda.
5. Gently push the trough into the bottle, so that it floats on top of the vinegar. Try to spill as little baking soda as possible.
6. Be careful to stay on the side of the bottle. You should not be in front of or behind it! Carefully use the stopper to plug up the mouth of the bottle.
7. Staying to one side of the bottle, roll the bottle to the side, allowing the baking soda to mix with the vinegar. For best results, make sure the bottle stays on the pencils.
8. Stand away to one side of the bottle. BE SURE TO STAY TO ONE SIDE OF THE BOTTLE. DO NOT GET IN FRONT OF OR BEHIND IT! Record what happens.
9. Clean up and put everything away.

CONCLUSION:

What happened in the experiment? Write a paragraph explaining what happened in terms of Newton's third law of motion. Make connections to the text.

You should have seen Newton's third law in action in Experiment 7.3. When the baking soda mixed with the vinegar, a chemical reaction took place. The sodium bicarbonate in the baking soda reacted with the acetic acid in the vinegar. One of the products of that reaction is carbon dioxide gas. As the CO_2 formed, it filled up the bottle. Eventually, so much gas was formed that the bottle became pressurized. This exerted an enormous force on the stopper. Eventually, that action force was great enough to push the stopper right out of the bottle. What happened as a result? The stopper pushed the gas with a force equal in strength and opposite in direction, so the bottle started moving in the opposite direction. The gas pushed the stopper in one direction and the stopper pushed the gas (which was inside the bottle) in the opposite direction.

YOU DO SCIENCE
BALLOON ROCKETS

Investigate Newton's laws with this activity. You can even have races if you like. For this activity you will need a balloon, some string or fishing line, a plastic drinking straw, and some scotch tape. Ask a parent, sibling, or friend to help you. Cut a piece of string or fishing line about 10 ft long. Tape one end of the string or fishing line to a door jam or have a helper hold that end. Thread the string or fishing line through the straw. Blow up the balloon but do not tie it shut. With help and while holding the blown-up balloon closed, tape the balloon to the straw as shown in the diagram in Figure 7.29. With the string taut, and the balloon rocket at one end of the string, release your hold on the balloon. What happens? Record your observations. What made your rocket move? How was Newton's third law of motion demonstrated? Draw pictures and use labeled arrows to indicate the action and reaction forces acting on the inside of the balloon before and after it was released.

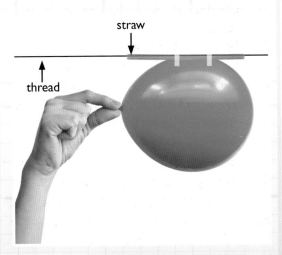

FIGURE 7.29
Balloon Rocket Setup

The You Do Science activity and Experiment 7.3 show how Newton's third law can explain how rockets fly. When a rocket or missile is launched (Figure 7.30), its fuel begins burning. As the fuel burns, it produces hot gas in great volumes. The pressure caused by the gas being formed pushes the gas out of the rocket. In response, the gas being pushed out pushes back on the rocket, causing the rocket to move in the opposite direction. This force is often called the thrust of the rocket. Thus, a rocket flies because gases are constantly being shoved out of the nozzles at its bottom (the action force). The equal and opposite reaction force pushes the rocket in the opposite direction. Practice what you've learned about Newton's third law by completing On Your Own problems 7.1–7.12.

FIGURE 7.30
Launching a Rocket
The gases pushed out of the rocket (action force) push back on the rocket (reaction force), causing lift-off.

ON YOUR OWN

7.11   A tennis player hits a ball with her racket. The ball was traveling towards the player but, once she hits it with the racket, the ball begins traveling in the opposite direction. During the hit, the strings on the racket bow. What evidence do you have that the racket exerted a force on the ball? What applied the equal and opposite reaction force, and where was the force applied? What evidence do you have for this force?

7.12   An ice skater stands on the ice in his skates. He is holding a ball. Assuming that friction is so small it can be ignored, what will happen to the ice skater if he suddenly throws the ball hard to the west?

FUNDAMENTAL FORCES

Believe it or not, physicists think that there are only four different kinds of force in creation: the electromagnetic force, the strong nuclear force, the weak nuclear force, and gravitational force. These forces are called the fundamental or universal forces, because all forces in creation can be traced back to one of them. I will give you a brief overview of these forces. You will learn more about them in your high school chemistry and physics courses.

Electromagnetic Forces

The electromagnetic force exists between particles with electric charge. Electric force and magnetic force are two different aspects of the electromagnetic force. The electromagnetic force is the only force that can be either attractive or repulsive.

Electric forces act between charged objects or particles whether or not they're moving. Remember from module 2 that protons and electrons are charged particles. You know that two positively charged objects (like two protons) repel each other, as do two negatively charged objects (like two electrons). You also know that two objects with opposite charges will attract one another. Have you ever taken clothes out of the dryer that were stuck together and when you pulled them apart you heard and felt the static charge? That's because some clothes lose electrons easily in the dry heat of the dryer and become positively charged. Others gain electrons easily and become negatively charged. Then the oppositely charged clothes cling together because of their electric attraction.

The magnetic force acts between moving charged particles and on the poles of magnets. Every magnet has two poles—a north pole and a south pole. Opposite poles attract one another and like poles repel. Look at Figure 7.31. The north pole of the bar magnet is attracting the iron filings attached to one of the poles of the red horseshoe magnet. That is your clue! If the poles are attracting each other, the pole on the red magnet must be a south pole. If you moved the bar magnet over to the other side of the red horseshoe magnet, the iron filings would be repelling each other.

FIGURE 7.31
Magnets
The magnetic force of attraction occurs between opposite poles. Can you tell which pole is on the bottom right of the red horseshoe magnet?

Have you ever played with magnetic toys like the train shown in Figure 7.32? If you have you've likely noticed what happens when you try to put two like poles near each other. Each car in the train set has a north pole on one end and a south pole on the other. If, when you try to connect two cars, you feel them pushing apart, you know you have two like poles. To connect them, just turn one car around and they'll quickly pull together.

FIGURE 7.32
Magnetic Toy
Opposite poles attach the wooden train cars. Same poles push them apart.

Electromagnetic force shows itself in many ways in your day to day life. This force is responsible for holding atoms together because of the electromagnetic attraction between protons and electrons. Light is an electromagnetic wave. The electricity powering the appliances in your house occur because of electromagnetism. And these examples just scratch the surface! The electromagnetic force is a fairly strong force. There is only one fundamental force stronger than it. You will learn much more about the electromagnetic force in the next module.

Nuclear Forces

Remember when we discussed the nucleus of the atom? It's composed of protons and neutrons. Did you wonder why the repulsive electromagnetic force of the positively charged protons didn't cause the nucleus to fly apart? Well, that's where the nuclear forces come into play. There are two nuclear forces, the strong force and the weak force.

The Strong Force

As its name implies, the strong nuclear force is the strongest of the four fundamental forces. However it only acts over a very short distance—approximately the diameter of a proton (10^{-15} m). Although the strong force only acts over a very small distance, it is about 100 times stronger than the repulsive electromagnetic force. This is the reason that protons do not repel each other. The strong nuclear force overcomes the force of repulsion at distances inside the nucleus and holds the protons and neutrons together.

Once the proton, neutron, and electron were discovered, scientists conducted many experiments to try to figure out how the nucleus could stay together. According to the current model of the atom (called the Standard Model of particle physics), protons and neutrons are made up of even smaller particles called quarks (Figure 7.33) that are held together by force-carrying particles called gluons. A quark is a subatomic particle scientists theorize to be among the basic units of matter—one that cannot be split into smaller parts—but of course they're still looking for smaller ones. You will learn much more about this in high school and college chemistry and physics, but I will tell you that the predictions made by this theory have (to date) been experimentally confirmed with good precision.

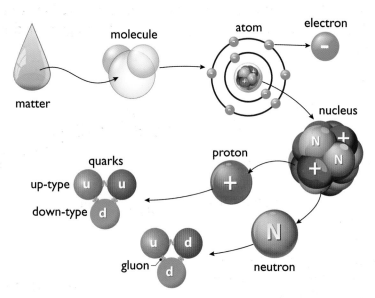

FIGURE 7.33
From Molecule to Quark
According to the Standard Model, protons and neutrons are each made up of three quarks.

The Weak Force

The other powerful force in the nucleus is the weak nuclear force. As you can tell by its name, the weak force is weaker in strength than the strong force. Like the strong force, the weak force acts over a very small range, about 10^{-18} m, and is explained by the Standard Model of particle physics. But unlike the attractive electromagnetic and strong forces, the weak force plays a bigger role in particles breaking down or decaying. As a result, the weak force governs certain radioactive processes in atoms in which one type of quark changes into another type of quark. Changing a quark in this way can cause a proton to change into a neutron, or vice versa. Remember if a proton is changed into a neutron, then you have changed an atom of one element into an atom of a whole different element. The weak force plays an important role in nuclear fusion, the reaction that powers the sun and hydrogen bombs.

Gravitational Forces

We've already talked a bit about the force of gravity. Gravity is the force that causes objects to have weight. It is probably the easiest one to recognize—so much so that you likely take it for granted. But did you know that gravitational force is the weakest of the four fundamental forces, and it is surprisingly hard to understand. Even today, scientists are not sure exactly what causes the gravitational force. We have two major theories that try to explain what gravity is, but we really do not know which (if either) is correct. We still have a *lot* to learn about this force!

Even though we still have a lot to learn about gravity, we have come a long way in understanding this perplexing force. At one time, scientists did not even know that the gravitational force that causes a ball to fall to Earth is the same as the force that holds the planets in orbit around the sun. It took the brilliance of Sir Isaac Newton (surprise!) to show that gravity is a universal force that applies to small things near the Earth's surface as well as large thing such as planets.

In fact Newton developed an equation (which we call the universal law of gravitation) that allows physicists to calculate the strength of the gravitational force between two objects. The equation is shown in Figure 7.34. Don't worry, you will not need to know how to use this equation in this course, but we will discuss the concepts of this law.

Basically Newton's law of universal gravitation states that every object in the universe attracts every other object. What does that mean exactly? Well, when you place two wooden blocks on the table, they are actually attracted to one another by the gravitation force between them. So why don't they just move toward each other? Remember I said the gravitational force is the weakest of the fundamental forces? Well, the gravitational force is so weak that it cannot even overcome the friction that exists between the blocks and the table. As a result, the blocks stay stationary, not because there is not gravitational force of attraction between them, but because the attraction is so weak that it cannot overcome static friction.

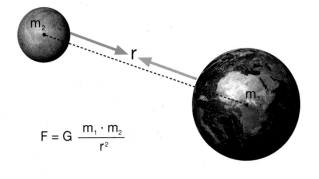

$$F = G \frac{m_1 \cdot m_2}{r^2}$$

FIGURE 7.34
The Universal Law of Gravitation
The Earth pulls on the Moon with the same gravitational force that the Moon pulls on the Earth.

Now when we talk about huge masses, like that of the Earth and Moon shown in Figure 7.34, that is when we see gravitational force exerted. Look at Newton's equation. You see that the masses of the two objects (m_1 and m_2) are in the numerator indicating that the gravitational force between two objects is directly proportional to their masses. This means that the strength of the gravitational force increases as the mass of either object increases. The greater the mass of the objects, the greater the gravitational force between them. Notice A and B in Figure 7.35. When the mass of the orange ball is doubled, the gravitational force of attraction that each mass applies to the other also doubles.

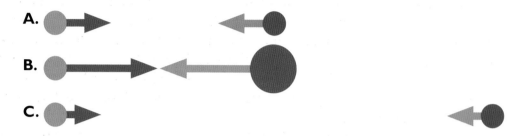

FIGURE 7.35
Gravitational Force
Gravitational force is directly proportional to mass and inversely proportional to the square of the distance.

Now look at the distance (r) in the equation in 7.34—it is squared and in the denominator. This means, gravitational force is *inversely proportional* to the *square* of the distance between the objects. Look again at Figure 7.35, only this time take notice of A and C. When the distance between the blue and orange ball doubles, the gravitational force between them decreases by 2^2 or 4. In other words the gravitational force is ¼th as strong when two objects are moved apart twice the original distance.

Even though gravity is the weakest fundamental force, it is the most effective force over long distances, especially for massive objects. Think about that for a moment. Even though the force of gravity decreases with distance, the planets stay in their orbits around the sun because of this force. The mass of the sun is about 300,000 times the mass of Earth, so the sun's gravitational force is strong enough to keep Pluto in orbit! Gravity holds you on Earth. It keeps the Moon in orbit around Earth and causes the oceans to bulge at high tides twice a day—yet it is the weakest fundamental force.

think about this

We often don't realize that when we drop a ball, Newton's law of universal gravitation states that the Earth exerts a force of attraction on the ball and the ball exerts an equal force on the Earth. What? That may be hard to grasp. We know that the Earth attracts the ball because we see the ball fall when we drop it. But the ball exerts an equal and opposite reactive force on the Earth (Newton's third law), so the Earth *rises toward the ball!* Why don't you feel the Earth accelerating toward ball? Well Newton's second law says that the force applied to an object equals the object's mass times its acceleration. Since the forces of the ball on the Earth and the Earth on the ball are equal, and because the mass of the Earth is so large, the resulting acceleration of the Earth is really tiny. So since the mass of the ball is so small compared to the Earth, we definitely notice the balls acceleration towards Earth, but we can't even detect the Earth's acceleration towards the ball.

What Causes Gravitational Force

At the beginning of this section I told you that there were two major theories that attempt to explain gravity, but we don't know which (if either) is really correct. Well, I want to briefly tell you about them to finish this module.

The first theory is called quantum gravity and it attempts to explain gravity at the smallest scale (called quantum mechanics). Remember the quantum mechanical model of the atom from module 3? Well, the quantum gravity theory attempts to explain the gravitational force as interactions of subatomic particles. Quantum theorists' postulate that a small force-carrying particle called a graviton is responsible for the force of gravity. Keep in mind that there is no direct observable evidence of a graviton at this point. But, since scientists have been able to gather experimental evidence that describes the other three fundamental forces in terms of quantum mechanics (the Standard Model of particle physics), it seems like a possible explanation.

The other theory was developed by Albert Einstein in 1916. Einstein proposed his General Theory of Relativity which attempts to explain a different way of looking at physics. The details are far, far beyond the scope of this course. But, one of the byproducts of Einstein's General Theory of Relativity was an original explanation of what causes the gravitational force.

Einstein's theory states that space is not always the way it appears to us. You know that the Earth is round even though it looks flat as you look out across a field to the horizon. In the same way, Einstein postulated that although it does not appear to change at all, space actually bends in the presence of an object with mass.

Look at Figure 7.36. This is an illustration of the orbit of Earth around the sun according to general relativity. The blue graph-paper like substance represents space. General relativity describes space like a geometric framework in which massive objects could alter or bend that geometry. And if that isn't hard enough to wrap your mind around, the theory also says matter that bends space also bends time! Notice in the figure how the massive sun distorts space enough to create a sort of well around it. A planet, such as Earth, will travel around the curve in space created by the mass of the sun.

FIGURE 7.36
Earth on a Curved Path Around Our Much Heavier Sun
The General Theory of Relativity states that mass bends space. Other masses passing through this space, must follow the curvature of the space in order to follow a straight line. So the path of the second object bends towards the larger mass.

So in the general theory of relativity, objects do not move towards each other because of a force of gravitational attraction, but because they are following the curve of space around an object. If Einstein is right, then, gravity is not really a force at all. It is, instead, a consequence of how mass bends space and time. Einstein developed some highly complex mathematical equations that have correctly calculated the movement of objects (such as Mercury). While these equations are far too complex to discuss, the basic premise is that mass of an object tells space how to curve and space tells a mass how to move.

Is Einstein right? Well we really aren't sure. The general theory of relativity has a lot of success in explaining things about space that could not be explained before. Most physicists admit that Einstein's explanation is better right now, since it at least has some direct evidence supporting it. In fact, there are some who postulate that *both* theories are true. At the same time, of course, it is possible that *neither* theory is true. After all, the history of science is filled with theories that seemed to have a lot of evidence supporting them but were later found to be wrong. Finish up by completing On Your Own problems 7.13–7.14.

ON YOUR OWN

7.13 Which universal force can repel as well as attract?

7.14 Which universal force acts to hold the nucleus together?

SUMMING UP

You experience forces everywhere in creation. Scientists are still discovering things about the interactions between matter. If this topic interests you, you will definitely want to take a physics course in high school because we have only scratched the surface of this fascinating topic. Perhaps you will help to bring the particle and general relativity theories of physics together!

ANSWERS TO THE "ON YOUR OWN" QUESTIONS

7.1 A force can cause an object at rest to move. A force can cause a moving object to accelerate by changing its speed or direction.

7.2 The net force is zero.

7.3 The four types of friction are: static friction, sliding (or kinetic) friction, rolling friction, and fluid friction. Static friction is the strongest, then sliding friction, then rolling friction and they all affect solids. Fluid friction affects objects in liquids or gases and in air it is called air resistance. All types of friction are forces that oppose motion.

7.4 Step 1   Write the list of knowns and the unknown.

$$t = 1.1 \text{ s}$$

$$a = 32 \text{ ft/s}^2$$

$$d = ? \text{ in ft}$$

Step 2   Write out the equation (use 7.1) and rearrange if necessary.

$$d = \tfrac{1}{2} \times a \times t^2$$

Steps 3 & 4   Write out the equation substituting the numbers from step 1 and solve.

$$d = 0.5 \times (32 \tfrac{ft}{s^2}) \times (1.1 \text{ s})^2 = 0.5 \times (32 \tfrac{ft}{s^2}) \times (1.1 \text{ s}) \times (1.1 \text{ s}) = 19.36 \text{ ft}$$

7.5 The cowboy will fall forward off the horse. While the horse is galloping, the cowboy and the horse have the same velocity. When the horse suddenly stops, the only force that can stop the cowboy is the friction between him and the saddle. If the horse stops quickly enough, friction will not have time to do this. As a result, the cowboy will continue to travel at the velocity he had, which is much faster than the horse's velocity once the horse has stopped. Thus, the cowboy falls forward, right over the horse.

7.6 Before the truck hits, the passengers in the car are traveling with the car at 30 mi/h. When the truck comes up from behind and hits the car, it will push the car forward, accelerating the car. Thus, the car will begin traveling faster than 30 mi/h. The passengers, however, are still traveling at 30 mi/h, so they will be flung backward in their seats until the backs of their seats apply enough force to accelerate them to the same velocity as the car.

7.7 The supplies should be dropped from point a. Remember the supplies have been traveling with the plane. Thus, they have the same velocity as the plane. When

MOD 7

they are dropped, they will still have that velocity, because no outside force (other than air resistance, which we will ignore) pushes against it. Since it takes time for the supplies to fall, if they were dropped at point b, they would pass by the hikers, being carried on by their initial velocity. If the supplies are dropped at point a, however, they will continue to approach the hikers as they fall. If the pilot times it right, the supplies will land on the X where the hikers are by the time they reach the ground.

7.8   Since the box is not being pushed, *the only force acting on it is friction.* Thus, the acceleration is due completely to friction. Since the box is moving, we also know this is the kinetic frictional force, which is what the problem is asking for. Now remember that the word acceleration does not mean speeding up. It means a change in velocity. If you reread the problem, you will see that the direction of the velocity is north, and the acceleration is south. Thus, the acceleration is opposite to the velocity, which means the box is slowing down. That should make sense, since friction opposes motion.

Step 1   List knowns and unknown and check units.

$$m = 15 \text{ kg}$$

$$a = 1.1 \text{ m/s}^2 \text{ south}$$

$$F_{kf} = ? \text{ in N}$$

Step 2   Write the equation (7.2) and rearrange so the unknown is on the left side of the equals sign, if needed. Remember friction is the only force acting on the box so $F = F_{kf}$.

$$F = F_{kf} = m \times a$$

Steps 3 & 4   Add knowns from step 1 to equation. Double check units and solve.

$$F_{kf} = (15 \text{ kg}) \times (1.1 \tfrac{\text{m}}{\text{s}^2}) = 16.5 \text{ N}$$

Now that you found the force of kinetic friction acting on the box, you need to determine the direction in which the force acts. The problem tells us that the box is moving north, so the direction of the force is south, since friction opposes motion. This should make sense, as the acceleration is south. Thus, the kinetic frictional force is 16.5 N south.

7.9   The goal is to keep the box moving at a constant velocity. What does that tell us about acceleration? When the velocity is *constant*, there is *no change*. This means that accelerations (which is the change in velocity) must be zero. Thus, the box must have *zero* acceleration. How much total net force leads to an acceleration of 0? Use equation 7.2 to find out.

Step 1 List knowns and unknown and check units.

$$m = 15 \text{ kg}$$

$$a = 0 \text{ m/s}^2 \text{ south}$$

$$F = ? \text{ in N}$$

Step 2 Write the equation (7.2).

$$F = m \times a$$

Steps 3 & 4 Add knowns from step 1 to equation. Double check units and solve.

$$F = (15 \text{ kg}) \times (0 \, \frac{m}{s^2}) = 0 \text{ N}$$

Remember that the net force is the sum of all the forces acting on the box. What are the forces acting on the box? Well a force must be applied to the box, so call that F_a, and the kinetic frictional force opposes the applied force. So the net force is equal to the applied force minus the frictional force.

Step 1 List knowns and unknown and check units.

$$F = 0 \text{ N}$$

$$F_a = ?$$

$$F_{kf} = 16.5 \text{ N south}$$

Step 2 Write the equation and rearrange for the unknown.

$$F = F_a - F_{kf} \quad \text{so} \quad F_a = F + F_{kf}$$

Steps 3 & 4 Add knowns from step 1 to equation. Double check units and solve.

$$F_a = 0 \text{ N} + 16.5 \text{ N} = 16.5 \text{ N}$$

In what direction will this applied force go? It must be in the same direction that the box is moving, which the previous problem said was north. Thus, a force of 16.5 N north must be applied. This will counteract friction, allowing the box to move at a constant velocity.

7.10 To get the block moving, the child must overcome static friction, which is resisting motion. Since static friction can resist with a force of 30 N west, the child must exert a force of slightly more than 30 N east.

7.11   We know that the racket exerted an action force on the ball because the ball's velocity changed. The ball had to slow down, stop, and then start moving in a new direction. This is a change in velocity, which means there was acceleration, which means there was a force. The equal and opposite reaction force demanded by Newton's third law was applied by the ball on the racket. We know that the ball exerted a force on the racket because the strings on the racket bowed.

7.12   If the ice skater throws the ball, he must exert an action force on it. Newton's third law states that the ball will apply an equal and opposite reaction force on the skater. Since there is no friction, that force will cause the skater to accelerate. Thus, the skater will begin to move in the opposite direction as compared to the ball. You do not normally get shoved backward when you throw a ball because the action force does not overcome the friction between you and the ground. Thus, the ball does exert a force on you, but you don't notice it because friction resists the force.

7.13   Electromagnetic force is the only force that can both attract and repel.

7.14   The strong nuclear force acts within the nucleus to hold it together.

STUDY GUIDE FOR MODULE 7

1. Match the following terms to their definitions.

    a. Force

    b. Friction

    c. Static friction

    d. Kinetic friction

    e. Free fall

    f. Inertia

    Friction that opposes motion once the
    motion has already started

    The motion of an object when it is falling
    solely under the influence of gravity

    A push or pull that acts on an object

    The tendency of an object to resist changes in
    its velocity

    Friction that opposes the initiation of motion

    A force that results when surfaces of objects
    rub against each other and opposes motion

2. What is the height of a building (in meters) if it takes a dropped rock 4.1 seconds
    to fall from its roof?

3. A hot-air balloonist drops a rock from his balloon. It takes 7 seconds for the rock
    to fall to the ground. What is the balloonist's altitude in feet?

4. State Newton's three laws of motion.

5. In space, there is almost no air, so there is virtually no friction. If an astronaut
    throws a ball in space with an initial velocity of 3.0 m/s to the west, what will the
    ball's velocity be in a year? Assume there are no nearby planets.

6. A boy is running north with a beanbag in his hands. He passes a tree and at the
    moment he is beside the tree, he drops the beanbag. Will the beanbag land next to
    the tree? If not, will it be north or south of the tree?

7. Suppose the situation in question 6 is now changed. The boy is running, but now
    his friend stands beside the tree with the beanbag. As the boy passes, he barely taps
    the beanbag, causing it to fall out of his friend's hands. Will the beanbag land next
    to the tree? If not, will it be north or south of the tree?

8. A busy shopper is driving down the road. Many boxes lie piled on the back seat of
    the car—evidence of shopping activity. Suddenly, the shopper must hit the brakes
    to avoid a collision. Will the boxes be slammed farther back into the back seat, or
    will they slam into the front seat where the driver can feel them? Explain.

9.   When roads get wet, they get slick. Obviously, then, the friction between a car's tires and the road decreases when the road is wet. Why?

10.   In order to slide a refrigerator across the floor, a man must exert an enormous amount of force. Once it is moving, however, the man need not exert nearly as much force to keep it moving. Why?

11.   A child is pushing her toy cross the room with a constant velocity to the east. If the static friction between this toy and the floor is 15 N, while the kinetic friction is 10 N, what force is the child exerting? How do you know?

12.   A father is trying to teach his child to ice skate. As the child stands still, the father pushes him forward with an acceleration of 2.0 m/s^2 north. If the child's mass is 20 kg, what is the force with which the father is pushing? (Since they are on ice, assume you can ignore friction.)

13.   The Mars Exploration Rover (MERA) landed Mars in 2004 to explore and take pictures and samples of the rocks and soil. If MERA has a mass of 185 kg and the acceleration due to gravity on Mars is 3.7 m/s^2, what is the weight of MERA on Earth and on Mars?

14.   In order to get a 15 kg object moving to the west, a force of just more than 25 N must be exerted. Once it is moving, however, a force of only 20 N accelerates the object at 0.1 m/s^2 to the west. What is the force that static friction can exert on the object? What is the force of kinetic friction?

15.   Static friction can exert a force of up to 700 N on a 500 kg box of bricks. The kinetic frictional force is only 220 N. How many newtons of force must a worker exert to get the box moving? What force must the worker exert to accelerate the box at 0.1 m/s^2 to the south?

16.   In order to shove a rock out of the way, a gardener gets it moving by exerting just slightly more than 100 N of force. To keep it moving at a constant velocity eastward, however, the gardener needs only to exert a 45 N force to the east. What are the static and kinetic frictional forces between the rock and the ground?

17.   Two men are trying to push a 710 kg rock. The first exerts a force of 156 N east and the second exerts a force of 220 N east. The rock accelerates at 0.20 m/s^2 to the east. What is the kinetic frictional force between the rock and the ground?

18.   A child pushes against a large doghouse, trying to move it. The doghouse remains stubbornly unmoved. What exerts the equal and opposite force which Newton's third law of motion says must happen in response to the child's push? What is that force exerted on?

19. A man leans up against a wall with a force of 20 N to the east. What is the force exerted by the wall on the man?

20. Name the four fundamental forces in creation. Which is the weakest of the fundamental forces? Which is the strongest?

---

[1] J.A. Garraty and P. Gray, eds, *The Columbia History of the World*. New York: Harper & Row, 1972, p. 709.

[2] Sir Isaac Newton, *Theological Manuscripts*, Ed. H. McLachlan. Liverpool: Liverpool University Press, 1950, p. 56.

[3] Newton, Isaac. "Letter from Sir Isaac Newton to Robert Hooke". *Historical Society of Pennsylvania* (https://digitallibrary.hsp.org/index.php/Detail/objects/9792). Retrieved 14 June 2019.

PHYSICS— ENERGY

In the last module you learned that forces cause motion. Well, all moving objects have energy. In module 2 you learned that, at the atomic level, everything is in motion. Atoms of solids have only a small amount of energy, so they simply vibrate back and forth around a fixed point. Atoms of liquids and gases have even more energy and so their atoms and molecules are able to move more. The amount of energy determines the amount of movement, which determines the phase of the substance. This type of kinetic energy is only one type of energy we will look at in this module. We'll also talk about how forces can do work on an object if part of the force is acting in the direction of motion. Finally, you'll learn about the relationship between energy, work, power, and machines.

Natural Notes

Without energy, nothing would ever happen. You are using energy right now to read these words. When you think of energy you may think of solar energy, wind energy, or even batteries. Scientists describe how and why things behave the way they do in terms of energy. You read about the force-carrying particles that hold atoms together in the last module—they are made of energy. Energy and matter are part of the created world.

FIGURE 8.1
Energy
Energy comes in many forms. How many do you see in this picture?

IN THIS MODULE YOU WILL READ ABOUT THE FOLLOWING MAIN IDEAS:

- Energy
- Energy, Work, and Power
- Work and Machines

ENERGY

What is energy? Unlike matter, energy isn't a physical thing that you can touch. However, energy can cause change—sometimes great change. In science, energy is defined as the ability to move or change matter in some way. Energy is more commonly defined as the ability to do work.

Energy—The ability to do work

We'll talk much more about work in the next section of this module, but in science, work is done any time an object is moved a distance by a force. When work is done on an object, energy is transferred. Thus, work and energy are closely related. In fact, both energy and work are measured in the same units. The SI unit for measuring energy is the joule (J), which is equal to a newton × meter (N·m). We'll see how in the next section.

Look at the woman in Figure 8.2. It requires energy for her to swing the racket and hit the tennis ball. Where did that energy come from? It came from the energy stored in the chemical bonds of the food she ate. That chemical energy was transferred to energy in her muscles, which allowed her to swing the racket. As she hits the ball, some of the energy she put into the swing transfers from the racket to the ball, which alters the direction and the speed at which the ball moves. That's the amazing thing about energy—it can be transferred from one thing to another.

FIGURE 8.2
Energy Changes Things
The ball changes direction when hit by the racket.

Types of Energy

The many forms of energy can be classified into two general types: kinetic energy and potential energy. You've already been introduced to kinetic energy in module 2 when we talked about the energy of motion of solids, liquids, and gases. Well, it turns out that any object in motion will have kinetic energy. Let's talk about kinetic energy first.

Kinetic Energy

When you throw a ball, like the pitcher in Figure 8.3, you give it speed as it leaves your hand. Because the ball is moving, it has kinetic energy. The kinetic energy (*KE*) of any

energy as he climbed the ladder to the diving board. As soon as he jumps, the diver's potential energy will be converted to kinetic energy as he falls.

An object's gravitational potential energy depends on the object's mass, its height above the Earth, and the acceleration due to gravity (9.8 m/s²). You can calculate an object's gravitational potential energy (PE) in joules by using Equation 8.2.

Equation 8.2

$$PE = m \times g \times h$$

In other words, the gravitational potential energy of an object is equal to its weight (mg) times its height. Now the height of an object is relative. What do I mean? Well the height of the apples in the tree would be measured from the ground (surface of the Earth). However if you are on the second story of a building and you pick up a book and carry it up to the third floor of the building, then the height you would measure to find the added potential energy is from the second floor to the third floor. So you will always measure height from a reference point, most often it will be the ground. Study the problems in Example 8.2 to see what I mean.

EXAMPLE 8.2

A. **Suppose the diver in Figure 8.6 is at the top of a 10.0 m high diving platform and has a mass of 80.0 kg. What is his potential energy relative to the ground?**

Step 1   Write the list of knowns and the unknown.

m = 80.0 kg

g = 9.8 m/s²

h = 10.0 m

PE = ? in J

Step 2   Write out the equation (use 8.2).

$$PE = m \times g \times h$$

Step 3   Write out the equation substituting the numbers from step 1.

$$PE = (80.0 \text{ kg})(9.8 \tfrac{\text{m}}{\text{s}^2})(10.0 \text{ m})$$

Step 4   Solve the problem.

$$PE = (80.0 \text{ kg})(9.8 \tfrac{\text{m}}{\text{s}^2})(10.0 \text{ m}) = 7{,}840 \tfrac{\text{kg·m·m}}{\text{s}^2} = 7{,}840 \text{ J}$$

Again notice the units. Just as with kinetic energy these units are equal to a N·m and a N·m is equal to a joule (J). So the **potential energy of the diver is 7,840 J.**

B.   After he dives, the diver climbs out of the pool and is standing on the ground. What is his potential energy relative to the ground now?

Since the diver is standing on the ground, his height above the ground would be zero. Therefore, **his gravitational potential energy relative to the ground would also be zero.**

Elastic Potential Energy

The potential energy of the strings of the harp in Figure 8.5 is called elastic potential energy. Any object that can be stretched or compressed has elastic potential energy. In case you're not entirely sure what elastic means—it refers to objects that spring back to their original shape after being stretched or compressed. Think about a rubber band. You can stretch out a rubber band but when you let it go, it springs back to its original size. When you stretched the rubber band you gave it potential energy. The farther an elastic object is stretched (or compressed), the greater its potential energy.

Look at the bow in Figure 8.7. The boy has pulled the string back stretching it. That gives it potential energy. Because the arrow is connected to the string, it also has potential energy. When the boy releases the bow string, it springs back to its original position. The potential energy of the arrow is converted to kinetic energy as it flies through the air.

You also add elastic potential energy to things such as springs when you compress them. Wind-up toys have a spring connected to the winder. As you turn the winder, the spring is compressed. Then when released, the spring returns to its original shape. As the spring unwinds, the potential energy is converted to kinetic energy and the toy moves.

Bouncing balls also have elastic potential energy (Figure 8.8). When you bounce a ball against the floor, the ball squishes a bit compressing the air inside. Then the compressed air forces the ball to spring back into shape after hitting the ground, thrusting the ball back up. So the elastic potential energy of the compressed ball (and air inside) is converted to the

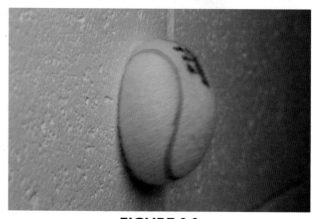

FIGURE 8.7
Elastic Potential Energy of Bow String
When the boy pulls the string and arrow back, he gives them potential energy.

FIGURE 8.8
Elastic Potential Energy of A Tennis Ball
The tennis ball (traveling at 28.95 m/s) collides with the wall and compresses.

kinetic energy of the ball as it bounces back into the air. Now review what you've learned by completing On Your Own problems 8.3–8.5. Then Conduct Experiment 8.1 to see elastic potential energy in action.

ON YOUR OWN

8.3   What factors determine the gravitational potential energy of an object?

8.4   What type of energy does a compressed pogo stick (Figure 8.9) have?

8.5   A 55.00 kg stunt man walks up the steps from the ground to the roof of a 72.8 m tall building. How much gravitation potential energy does he have at the top of the building?

FIGURE 8.9
Pogo Stick

EXPERIMENT 8.1
ENERGY OF A RUBBER BAND

PURPOSE:
To investigate the elastic potential energy and kinetic energy of a rubber band.

MATERIALS:
*   1—5 rubber bands (all must be the same thickness and length)
*   A metric ruler
*   Tape measure (one with metric units on it would be best)
*   Masking tape
*   Safety glasses or goggles

BACKGROUND:
It would be best to do this experiment outside or in a long hallway because the rubber band will fly some distance. Make sure to never point the rubber band at anyone! You may also want a helper to help you spot and mark where the rubber band lands as sometimes it will bounce a bit.

QUESTIONS:
What is the relationship between the potential energy of a stretched rubber band and its kinetic energy once the rubber band is released? In other words, how will the potential and kinetic energy of a stretched rubber band affect the distance it travels?

HYPOTHESIS:
Write what you predict will happen to the rubber band (how far will it travel when released) when it is stretched to different lengths.

PROCEDURE:

1. Locate a long straight area to conduct your experiment. A driveway or sidewalk on a nice day is perfect. If that is not an option, choose a room that has a long, unobstructed area for you to shoot the rubber band. Select a starting spot and mark it with a strip of masking tape.

2. With your feet behind the masking tape line, hook the rubber band over the front edge of the metric ruler and stretch it back to the 10 cm mark on the ruler. Keep the ruler level and let the rubber band go.

3. If you have a helper, have them place a masking tape mark where the rubber band lands and return the rubber band to you. If you don't have a helper, you will need to mark the landing place and retrieve the rubber band. (You may also use other rubber bands as long as they are the same thickness and length.)

4. Repeat steps 2—3 four more times for a total of 5 trials stretching the rubber band to 10 cm.

5. With the tape measure, measure the distance in centimeters from the starting line to the landing point for each of the 5 trials. Record these distances in your data table. Pick up the masking tape marks after recording the distance.

6. Repeat steps 2—5, but stretch the rubber band on the metric ruler to 15 cm.

7. Repeat steps 2—5, but stretch the rubber band on the metric ruler to 20 cm.

8. Repeat steps 2—5, but stretch the rubber band on the metric ruler to 25 cm.

9. Average your distances for each stretch length by adding the distances together and then dividing by 5. Record the average in your data table.

10. Make a graph of your results by putting the stretch length (in cm) on the x-axis and the average launch distance (in cm) on the y-axis. Plot your data points. What trend do you notice? Do your data points look like they form a straight line? If so draw a line of best fit. (There is more help for making your graph in the student notebook.)

CONCLUSION:

What do your results show? What trend did you see on your graph? What does this tell you about the relationship between potential energy and kinetic energy? Write a paragraph explaining what you found and make connections to what you learned in the text.

What happened in your experiment? You should have seen that the rubber band stretched to 25 cm traveled farther than it did at the other stretch lengths. When you stretched the rubber band you gave it elastic potential (stored) energy. When you released the rubber band, the potential energy was quickly converted to kinetic (motion) energy and the rubber band flew a distance. The more you stretched it, the more potential energy you gave the rubber band. The more potential energy you inputted, the more kinetic energy the rubber band had. Remember that kinetic energy and velocity squared are directly related. So, since the mass of the rubber band did not change, the greater kinetic energy meant greater velocity. And since velocity is equal to distance over time, the greater velocity meant greater distance traveled.

Why did I have you do 5 trials of each stretch length? Well, it was to reduce experimental error. What is experimental error? Every experiment has some errors in it. Hopefully, there aren't too many errors, and hopefully those few errors are small. However, sometimes the errors can be large. When you do experiments involving measuring, there is always some differences in exactly where to read the tape measure from one measurement to the next. And what if there was a slight bend in the tape measure? Error is introduced. Also, maybe the wind was blowing a bit harder during one of the trials. More error is introduced. Look back at your data. Do you notice how your measurements for the same stretch length varied? They varied because of experimental error. So doing multiple trials and averaging the measurements helps to reduce the effect of experimental error on your results.

Now what did the straight line (or almost straight line) of your graph mean? It means that there is a direct relationship between potential energy and kinetic energy. Think about it. The stretch length represents the potential energy you put into the rubber band. The launch distance represents the kinetic energy, because kinetic energy is directly related to speed which is directly related to distance. So the straight line shows us that the more potential energy an object has the more kinetic energy it will have once potential energy is converted to kinetic energy. Not only can energy be converted from potential to kinetic, but energy can also change from one form of energy to another.

Forms of Energy

You are using light energy to read this sentence. When you listen to music, you hear it because of sound energy. When you ride your bike, you use kinetic energy. When you pick up a book from the floor and place it on a shelf, you've given it potential energy. When a plant photosynthesizes, it takes energy from the sun and converts it to chemical energy (Figure 8.10). When you turn a light on in your house, you are using electric energy. As you can see, energy can take many forms.

FIGURE 8.10
The Sun's Energy
Plants convert the sun's energy into chemical energy.

Mechanical Energy

Together, the energy of the motion and position of everyday objects makes up what is called mechanical energy. Now you may think the term "mechanical" means that this is the energy associated with machines, but that is not the whole picture. Machines do have mechanical energy, but mechanical energy is not limited to machines. Mechanical energy is the sum of an object's potential energy and kinetic energy.

Think about what you did in Experiment 8.1. When you stretched the rubber band you gave it potential energy. But before you released it, the rubber band had no kinetic energy—it was all potential. Once released, the potential energy converted to kinetic energy. The sum of the potential and kinetic energy of the rubber band was mechanical energy. This energy could cause change. Imagine if you shot the rubber band at a paper cup sitting on a table. If you hit the cup, the mechanical energy of the rubber band could cause the cup to fall over. The same is true of a bouncing ball, a speeding car, a running child—they all have mechanical energy.

YOU DO SCIENCE

Ball Bounce

You'll want to do this activity outside or in a space with a high ceiling and hard floor. All you need is a basketball (a soccer ball will also work), a tennis ball, and a yard stick or tape measure. First drop the basketball from a height of 1 meter (~39 inches). Observe how high it bounces. Try to measure the height to which the basketball bounced and record. Now drop the tennis ball from a height of 1 meter. Again observe and record the height of the bounce. Now place the tennis ball on top of the basketball and drop both together from a height of 1 meter. How high did the balls bounce in each instance? How can you explain what happened in terms of mechanical energy–potential and kinetic energy?

The tennis ball had more mechanical energy when dropped with the basketball than it did when dropped by itself. Why do you think that is? Well, the tennis ball received some elastic potential energy from the basketball when they were dropped together. That extra elastic potential energy converted into more kinetic energy allowing the tennis ball to bounce higher than it did when dropped alone. It also was able to bounce higher than the basketball did when dropped alone because the tennis ball's mass is much smaller than the mass of the basketball. So that increased kinetic energy, but smaller mass, allowed the tennis ball to reach a greater speed and so a greater height than the basketball.

Thermal Energy

Remember from module 2 that everything is made up of atoms that are always in random motion. So everything has kinetic energy at the atomic or molecular level. The total kinetic energy of the moving atoms and molecules of an object make up its thermal energy. The more heat you add to an object, the more its particles move and the more kinetic energy (and so thermal energy) the object has. Likewise the more an object's atoms and particles move, the more kinetic energy (or thermal energy) it has and so the warmer it becomes. All matter has thermal

FIGURE 8.11
Thermal Energy
Molten metal can get so hot that it can emit visible light.

energy, even objects that feel cold (such as an ice cube). That's because the atoms and particles of all matter are in constant motion and have kinetic energy. Sometimes things become so hot some of the thermal energy converts to light energy (Figure 8.11).

Chemical Energy

Chemical energy is the energy stored in the chemical bonds of the molecules that make up a substance. Since this is stored energy it is actually potential energy, and you might hear it called chemical potential energy. For example, the source of energy for the fire in Figure 8.12 is the chemical energy stored in the wood. When the wood is burned, the chemical energy is released and some of it is converted to thermal energy so the boy can cook his hotdog.

FIGURE 8.12
Chemical and Thermal Energy
Chemical energy stored in the bonds of the wood molecules is converted to thermal energy to heat food when the wood is burned.

All chemical compounds store energy in their bonds. Fuels such as coal and gasoline have a large amount of chemical potential energy. When the gasoline in your car is burned in the car's engine, the energy stored in the chemical bonds of the gasoline is released and some of it is converted to mechanical energy which moves the car. Some of the released chemical energy is also converted to thermal energy which is why the car's engine gets hot.

Electrical Energy

If you use a hair dryer to dry your hair, or a toaster to toast your bread in the morning, you have used electricity or electrical energy. Electrical energy is the energy associated with moving charged particles. All appliances and the lights in your house use electrical energy to operate. The powerful bolts of lightning shown in Figure 8.13 are produced by electrical energy. The electrical potential energy in the clouds is converted to light energy (you see the bolt of lightning), sound energy (you hear the crack of thunder), and thermal energy as the lightning bolt strikes. In batteries, the chemical energy stored in the battery is converted to electrical energy to power your clock or flashlight. You will learn more about electric energy in a later module.

FIGURE 8.13
Electrical Energy
Lightning bolts transfer electric charge from the clouds to Earth.

Electromagnetic Energy

Electromagnetic energy is a form of energy that is reflected or emitted from objects and travels through space in the form of waves. This form of energy is also called radiant energy or light energy. The sun is the source (either directly or indirectly) of most of the Earth's energy supplies because it radiates electromagnetic energy through space in waves. These waves have some electrical properties and some magnetic properties.

What does it mean that electromagnetic energy can travel through empty space? It means that unlike the other forms of energy we've talked about, radiant energy does not need to touch other matter to transfer the energy. Examples of electromagnetic energy include radio waves, microwaves, infrared radiation, visible light, ultraviolet light, x-rays, and gamma radiation.

Light energy is the only form of energy that we can see directly (visible light). Light is made up of tiny photons which contain lots of energy. Light waves are always moving and so cannot be stored. Thus light energy is kinetic energy. But light energy can be converted into other forms of energy. That is exactly what plants do when they photosynthesize. They convert light energy into chemical energy in the bonds of glucose. You will learn more about light energy in a later module.

FIGURE 8.14
Electromagnetic Energy
The Andromeda galaxy contains billions of stars all giving off enormous amounts of electromagnetic energy.

Sound Energy

Sound energy is a form of mechanical energy and it is energy carried by sound waves. It is produced when an object (such as a cello string, Figure 8.15) vibrates. When the cello string vibrates, or moves back and forth, it pushes nearby air molecules together, creating a series of compressions which travel through the air as waves. You usually hear sound waves through the medium of air, but

FIGURE 8.15
Sound Energy
Sound energy travels in waves produced when an object vibrates.

ENERGY AND WORK

Remember energy is defined as the ability to do work. You may think it's work to read this textbook and answer the questions, but that is not the definition of work in science. In physics, *work is a transfer of energy.* You do work when you use a force to move something. The bigger the force, or the further you move an object, the more work you do.

> **Work**—The product of a force (applied in the direction of motion of an object) and the distance the object moves

To be clear, in science, work is only done when two conditions are met. First, an object must move. Second, a force must be acting on the object (either the whole force or part of the force) in the direction of motion. For example, the seagull in Figure 8.18 does work on the oyster when it lifts it up into the air. Work is done on the box in Figure 8.21 by the man as he lifts it. Once he lifts the box and is holding it, the man is no longer doing work on the box. That may seem surprising. He is still exerting an effort to hold the box, but because the box is not moving, the man is not working. Even if he walks down the hall holding the box, he does no more work on the box because the direction of motion is not in the same direction as the force applied. Now if he pushes the box along the floor, then he does work on the box because the force applied is in the same direction as the box is moving. *If a force does not act in the direction an object is moving, it does no work on the object.*

FIGURE 8.21
Work Is Done to the Box
The man does work on the box as he uses a force to lift it a distance. He is lifting it against gravity.

This is an important concept to keep in mind. Work depends on direction. Study Figure 8.22.

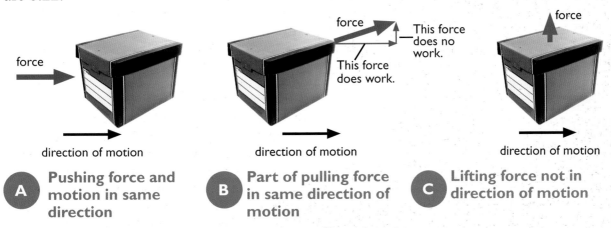

A Pushing force and motion in same direction

B Part of pulling force in same direction of motion

C Lifting force not in direction of motion

FIGURE 8.22
Work Depends on Direction
When force is applied in the direction of motion (A), the work done is maximized. Only the horizontal part of the pulling force in situation B does work to move the box to the right. Because the lifting force (C) is not in the direction the box moves, no work is done on the box.

Notice in situation B of Figure 8.22 that work can be done even if only a part of the force is acting in the direction of motion. It will be a smaller amount of work because the part of the force that is acting in the same direction as the box is moving is smaller than if you pushed the box (as in situation A). Since both the vertical part of the pulling force in B and all of the lifting force in C are not acting in the direction of motion, these forces do no work on the box.

In science, work can also be defined as the change in energy of an object. Let's look at another example of work being done to see what I mean. When the diver in Figure 8.6 climbed the ladder to the diving board, he did work. His muscles moved a force (his weight) up a certain distance (up to the top of the ladder). That is the definition of work. The diver gave himself potential energy. *Potential energy is energy with the potential to do work.* When the diver dives into the water, the energy changed from potential to kinetic energy. As the diver falls, gravity is now doing work on him since it is supplying the force (again his weight) and the direction of motion is down. Both the force of gravity and the direction of the diver's motion is down, so gravity does work on the diver as potential energy is changed to kinetic energy.

Calculating Work

We can calculate the amount of work (W) done by multiplying the force acting in the direction of motion by the distance that the object move. The equation is shown below.

Equation 8.3

$$W = F \times d$$

The units for work are the same as the units for energy. Notice that force units are newtons and distance units are meters. So work units are N·m which is equal to a joule. Study Example 8.3 to see how to calculate the work done on an object.

EXAMPLE 8.3

You lift a book from the floor to a bookshelf 1.5 meters above the ground. You exert a 19.6 N upward force in lifting the book. How much work did you do?

Step 1   Write the list of knowns and the unknown.

F = 19.6 N

d = 1.5 m

W = ? in J

Step 2   Write out the equation (use 8.3).

$W = F \times d$

Steps 3 & 4   Write out the equation substituting the numbers from step 1 and solve.

$W = (19.6 \text{ N})(1.5 \text{ m}) = 29.4 \text{ N·m} = \textbf{29.4 J}$

Power

Suppose you had to plow a large driveway after a snowstorm. Which of the ways shown in Figure 8.23 would you want to use to remove snow? Why? If you said "snow blower" so you could get the work done faster, then you have an idea of what power is. In science, power, like work, has a specific meaning.

> **Power**—The amount of work done each second

In other words, power is the rate of doing work. To do work at a faster rate requires more power. You can increase power in two ways. You can increase the amount of work done in a given time or decrease the time it takes to do a given amount of work.

If you've ever shoveled snow, then you know moving snow from one place to another requires work. The person with the snowblower, however, can do the same amount of work much faster. Since the man with the snowblower can do more work in less time than the man shoveling means the snowblower has more power.

Notice that the source of the power for the man shoveling is the man himself (his muscles and energy). The source of power for the snowblower is a gas-powered engine. The gas in the engine supplies the chemical potential energy which the engine converts to mechanical energy enabling work to be done. Machines that have engines are often rated by how much power they provide. Think about a snowplow. The powerful engine of the truck pushing the snowplow allows it to remove more snow faster than the snow blower with the much smaller engine.

FIGURE 8.23
Work and Power
The snow blower can remove more snow in less time than shoveling so it has more power.

Calculating Power

You can calculate power (P) simply by dividing the amount done by the time needed to do the work. This is shown in Equation 8.4.

Equation 8.4

$$P = \frac{W}{t}$$

The SI unit of power is the watt (W) which is equal to one joule per second (J/s) since work is measured in joules and time in seconds. The power unit was named after the Scottish scientist James Watt.

You are probably most familiar with the watt when referring to light bulbs. A 65 watt light bulb burns 65 joules of energy every second. Study Example 8.4 to see how to calculate power in an everyday situations. Then complete Experiment 8.2 and On Your Own questions 8.8–8.10 before going on.

EXAMPLE 8.4

A. **You lift a book from the floor to a bookshelf 1.8 m above the floor using a force of 16.5 N. You lift the book in 2.0 s. How much power (in watts) did you use?**

Step 1 Write the list of knowns and the unknown.

$F = 16.5$ N

$d = 1.8$ m

$t = 2.0$ s

$P = ?$ in W

Step 2 Write out the equation. Since we aren't given the value for work in the problem we will have to use both equation 8.3 and 8.4 to solve the problem.

$$P = \frac{W}{t} \quad \text{...and...} \quad W = F \times d \quad \text{...so...} \quad P = \frac{F \times d}{t}$$

Steps 3 & 4 Write out the equation substituting the numbers from step 1 and solve.

$$P = \frac{(16.5 \text{ N})(1.8 \text{ m})}{2.0 \text{ s}} = 14.85 \frac{\text{N·m}}{\text{s}} = 14.85 \frac{\text{J}}{\text{s}} = 14.85 \text{ W}$$

Notice how we can substitute the $F \times d$ for W in the power equation to solve for P. You will often see equation substitutions like this when you take a high school physics course. Also notice how the units worked out for this problem.

B. **A girl runs up a flight of stairs in 2.6 minutes. If the work she has done is equal to 320 J, how much power did she use to climb the stairs?**

Step 1 Write the list of knowns and the unknown. Check units and convert if needed.

$W = 320$ J

$t = 2.6$ min

$P = ?$ in W

Step 1B Notice that the time is given in minutes, but work is in joules which is equal to N·m and newtons are equal to kg·m/s², so we need to convert minutes to seconds.

$$\frac{2.6 \text{ min}}{1} \times \frac{60 \text{ s}}{1 \text{ min}} = 156 \text{ s}$$

Step 2 Write out the equation.

$$P = \frac{W}{t}$$

Steps 3 & 4 Write out the equation substituting the numbers from step 1 and solve.

$$P = \frac{320 \text{ J}}{156 \text{ s}} = 2.05 \, \frac{\text{J}}{\text{s}} = \textbf{2.05 W}$$

Your answer may have more decimal places than mine. I rounded to the hundredths position.

think about this

You may have heard of the horsepower unit for some machines, such as snowblowers and lawn mowers. Well, that unit was devised by the same scientist the SI power unit is named after. James Watt (1736–1819) was working on the design of the steam engine in the late 1700s to improve its efficiency. He needed a way to compare or explain the power of the steam engine to people. Since horses were the most commonly used source of power at that time (Figure 8.24), Watt compared the power of his engine to the power of a very strong horse so potential buyers (mostly farmers and miners) would see the benefit of the engine. So Watt set about determining how much work the typical draft horse could do by seeing how much weight (force) the horse could lift a distance of 1 foot in 1 minute. According to Watt's observations one typical horse could lift roughly 33,000 pounds a distance of 1 foot in 1 minute. He called this 1 horsepower (hp). He then showed his potential buyers that his steam engine could do 5 times (or sometimes more) work than a single draft horse. In other words, his one steam engine could do the work of 5 horses and so had a power rating of 5 hp. His comparison worked and Watt's steam engine soon became a very valuable tool of the Industrial Revolution. So when it came to naming the SI unit for power in 1960, it's easy to see why scientists decided to name the power unit the watt. Of course we still use the term horsepower today to describe the power of different machine engines, but in science 1 hp = 746 watts.

FIGURE 8.24
Horsepower
One horse can do about 746 J of work each second.
So three horses can do 2,238 J of work each second.
Although they can't keep that up indefinitely.

EXPERIMENT 8.2
HOW FAST CAN YOU DO WORK?

PURPOSE:
To explore the relationship between work, energy, and power using your own body.

MATERIALS:
- A 1 lb hand weight (You can also use a 16 ounce box of spaghetti or other 1 lb substance.)
- A piece of string 70 cm long
- Pencil or dowel rod
- Tape
- Tape measure or metric ruler
- Stopwatch
- Bathroom scale
- A clear stairway (You will be running up the steps so make sure the area is safe and you have proper shoes on.)
- A helper

BACKGROUND:
Any time you use a force in the direction of motion to move an object a distance you are doing work. In this investigation you will use your arms to supply the force to lift a 1 lb object. You will also use your legs to lift yourself (you are the object) up a flight of stairs. Since you will be doing your work against gravity lifting your body from the first floor to the second floor, we will only need the vertical height of the stairs, not the horizontal distance. We'll compare the power of your arms and legs.

QUESTIONS:
What is the relationship between work, energy, and power?

HYPOTHESIS:
Write what you predict will have more power, your arms or your legs.

PROCEDURE—PART A, ARMS:
1. Attach one end of the string to the 1 lb weight or box of spaghetti by tying the string around the center.
2. Tie the other end of the string around the pencil and secure with tape.
3. Measure the distance by measuring the string from the hanging weight to the pencil. You should have a distance of at least 50 cm. Record this measurement in your data table.
4. Record the mass in kilograms of your weight or box of spaghetti. (1lb = 16 oz = 0.45 kg)
5. With the stopwatch, have your helper time how quickly you can lift the 1 lb mass by rolling the string onto the pencil as you turn the pencil in your hands. Record the time in seconds.
6. Calculate the work and power (in watts and horsepower) that you produced as you lifted the 1 lb mass and record in the data table.

PROCEDURE—PART B, LEGS:

1. Using a bathroom scale, measure your weight. You will need to convert your weight in pounds to kilograms. (1 pound = 0.45 kg) Record your weight in kilograms.

2. Since we are going to determine the work and power required to lift your weight from the first floor to the second floor (red arrow on Figure 8.25), we are only concerned with the vertical height of the stairs, not the horizontal distance of the stairs. Remember that, although the force you will be applying is in the direction of the orange vector in Figure 8.25, the only part of the force that is used to lift you is the red arrow. The force represented by the yellow arrow does not help to lift you up the stairs. So to determine the vertical height of the stairs, measure the height of each step (blue arrows) and add them together. (You should find that each step is the same height, so once you measure one or two—

FIGURE 8.25

to be certain they are the same height—you can simply count the number of steps and multiply the number of steps by the height of one step to find the total vertical height.) Record the distance (total vertical height of the stairs) in your data table.

3. With the stopwatch, have your helper time how quickly you can get from the first floor to the second floor. Use common sense when running up the steps. Hold onto the railing and go up the steps quickly and safely. Record your time in the data table.

4. Calculate the work and power (in watts and horsepower) that you produced as you lifted your body up the stairs and record in the data table.

5. Clean up and put everything away.

CONCLUSIONS:

In a paragraph or two, answer the following questions and make connections to the text.

1. Which activity required the most work? Explain why using the terms force and distance.
2. Which activity produced the most power? Explain why.
3. If you wanted to produce more power in either part A or B, what could you do to maximize power?
4. If you went up the stairs twice as fast as you did, would you be doing more work? Why or why not?

ON YOUR OWN

8.8   What conditions are required for a force to do work on an object?

8.9   A book is sitting on a table. The table is exerting an upward force on the book to support it as it rests on the table. Does this force do work? Explain.

8.10   How much work (in joules) do you do when you use a 25 N force to lift a bag of potting soil from the floor to a shelf 1.5 m high? If you lift the bag in 2.0 s, how much power (in watts) do you generate?

WORK AND MACHINES

We've talked a little about machines, but I want to spend a bit of time discussing how machines and work are related. You see a machine is any device that makes work easier to do. That is because a machine either changes the size of a force, changes the direction of a force, or changes the distance over which the force is applied.

Imagine you are out with your mom running errands and one of the tires on your car goes flat. In order to change the tire, the car must be lifted off the ground. That would require much more force than you and your mom together could provide. That's why every car is equipped with a small but mighty little machine called a jack (Figure 8.26).

FIGURE 8.26
Machines Increase Force
The woman turns the crank a large distance to raise the car a small distance, but the force applied by the woman on the jack is much less than the force applied by the jack on the car.

When you use a jack you apply a rather small force to the jack handle by rotating the handle a fairly large distance (a full rotation). The jack magnifies this force applying it to the car. The much stronger force is used to lift the car, but only by a short distance. So the jack takes a small force exerted over a large distance and makes it a large force over a short distance. This is what allows you and your mom to lift a car when you normally would not be able to.

Some machines do the opposite of what the jack did. These machines decrease the applied force but increase the distance over which the force acts. Look at the rake in Figure 8.27, for example. The boy is applying a force to the handle end of the rake and moving it a short distance. But the other end of the rake moves a much greater distance, however it applies much less

FIGURE 8.27
Machines Decrease Force
The boy applies a force to the handle end of the rake, then moves it over a short distance. The other end of the rake moves a greater distance but with less force.

Well, think about a field hockey stick (Figure 8.31) which is a class 3 lever. The input force on the handle of the hockey stick is greater than the output force at the blade end of the stick. But the output distance of the stick is greater than the input distance. The benefit of the hockey stick is that the blade end travels farther and faster than the player's hands do. The hockey stick transfers this kinetic energy to the hockey ball. So the ball travels a greater distance at a faster speed than it would have if the player hit the ball with her hand or foot.

Efficiency

Remember when work is done energy is transferred. A machine increases the potential or kinetic energy of an object by doing work on it. You do work on the machine when you supply a force over a distance. The ramp in Example 8.5A, for example, increases the distance that the man must apply a force to lift the boxes, but it decreases the force he must apply. In this way he can "lift" heavier objects with the ramp than he could directly.

Because some of the work input to a machine (input force × input distance) is always used to overcome friction, the work output of a machine (output force × output distance) is always less that the work input. The percentage of work input that becomes work output is the efficiency of a machine. Would you ever expect a real machine to 100% efficient? No because friction exists. Because there is always some friction, all machines will have an efficiency less than 100%.

Efficiency is usually expressed as a percentage and can be found using Equation 8.7.

Equation 8.7

$$\text{Efficiency} = \frac{\text{Work output}}{\text{Work input}} \times 100\%$$

For example, if a machine has an efficiency of 80%, then you know that 80% of the work you put into the machine becomes work output. So if you put 10.0 J of work into a machine with an efficiency of 80%, then the work output would be 80% of 10.0 J, or 8.0 J.

Simple Machines

You have likely learned a little about simple machines in earlier science courses. We'll review a bit here so we can talk about their mechanical advantage—or how well they help us. There are six types of simple machines. Many mechanical devices are combinations of two or more of these machines. The six types of simple machines are the inclined plane, the wedge, the screw, the lever, the wheel and axle, and the pulley. Compound machines are machines made up of two or more simple machines that operate together.

Study Infographic 8.1 to see the types of simple machines and the general ideal mechanical advantage of each type. Notice that the input and output distances are determined differently for each machine. In this course you will not need to memorize how to find the input and output distances, except for the inclined plane. For other types of machines, the input and output distances will be given to you so you can determine the ideal mechanical advantage of machines using equation 8.6.

1 INCLINED PLANE

A simple machine consisting of a sloping surface that connects lower and higher elevations.

$$IMA = \frac{input\ distance}{output\ distance} \qquad IMA > 1$$

output distance

input distance

2 WEDGE

A simple machine that consists or two incline planes that work when they move.

$$IMA = \frac{length\ of\ wedge}{maximum\ thickness}$$

$$IMA > 1$$

input force

output force

3 PULLEY

A simple machine that consists of a rope and grooved wheel. The rope fits into the groove in the wheel, so pulling the rope turns the wheel.

MA is equal to the number of sections of rope (N) on the pulley system.

$$IMA = N$$

input

output

The wheel of the screwdriver is the handle. The axle is the shaft.

4 WHEEL AND AXLE

A simple machine that consists of 2 connected rings or cylinders, one inside the other. Both wheels turn in the same direction around a single point. The smaller, inner cylinder is called the axle while the bigger, outer ring is called the wheel.

$$IMA = \frac{diameter\ of\ input}{diameter\ of\ output}$$

If force is applied to the wheel, **MA > 1**
If force is applied to the axle, **MA < 1**

The wheel of the Ferris wheel is the ring where the seats are. The axle is the center where the spokes originate.

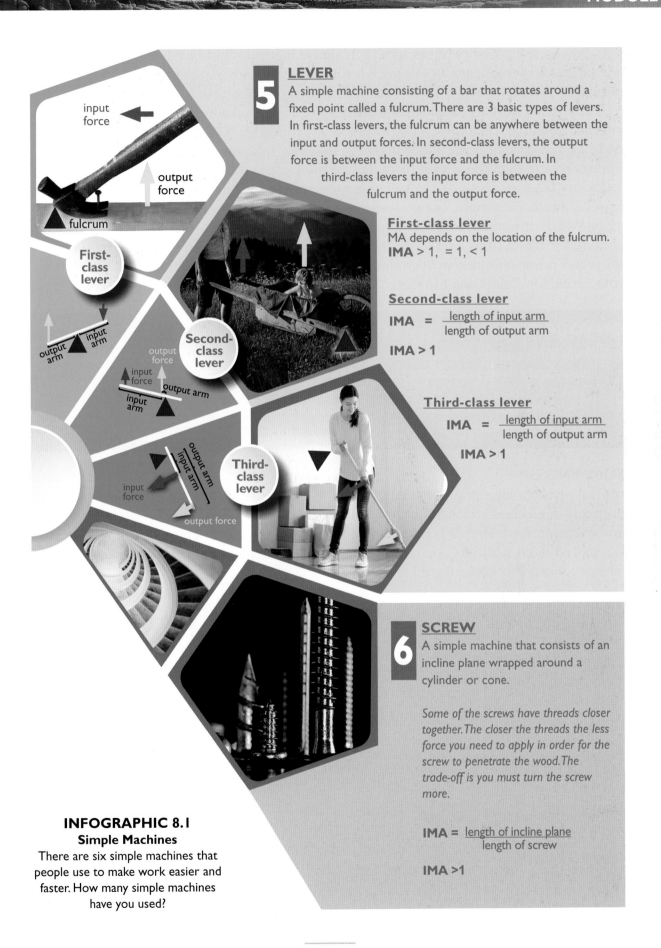

LEVER

5

A simple machine consisting of a bar that rotates around a fixed point called a fulcrum. There are 3 basic types of levers. In first-class levers, the fulcrum can be anywhere between the input and output forces. In second-class levers, the output force is between the input force and the fulcrum. In third-class levers the input force is between the fulcrum and the output force.

First-class lever
MA depends on the location of the fulcrum.
IMA > 1, = 1, < 1

Second-class lever

$$IMA = \frac{length\ of\ input\ arm}{length\ of\ output\ arm}$$

IMA > 1

Third-class lever

$$IMA = \frac{length\ of\ input\ arm}{length\ of\ output\ arm}$$

IMA > 1

input force

output force

fulcrum

First-class lever

output arm   input arm

Second-class lever

output force

input force

input arm

output arm

Third-class lever

output arm   input arm

input force

output force

MOD 8

SCREW

6

A simple machine that consists of an incline plane wrapped around a cylinder or cone.

Some of the screws have threads closer together. The closer the threads the less force you need to apply in order for the screw to penetrate the wood. The trade-off is you must turn the screw more.

$$IMA = \frac{length\ of\ incline\ plane}{length\ of\ screw}$$

IMA > 1

INFOGRAPHIC 8.1
Simple Machines
There are six simple machines that people use to make work easier and faster. How many simple machines have you used?

As you can see from Infographic 8.1, simple machines can have mechanical advantages less than, equal to, or greater than 1. A mechanical advantage greater than 1 means the machine increases the input force, so you do not have to exert as much effort to do the same work. A mechanical advantage equal to 1 means the machine does not increase the force you apply (input force) but it redirects it so that you can do the job easier or faster. A mechanical advantage of less than 1 means that although your input force is greater than the output force, the machine offers other desirable advantages such as greater reach or speed. We talked about the hockey stick as one example. The Ferris wheel is another example. The greater input force is applied to the axle of the Ferris wheel which then applies a lesser output force to turn the wheel (where the seats are). But, because the wheel turns over a greater distance, it turns faster than the axle. The speed of the wheel is one reason many people enjoy riding a Ferris wheel. Finish up this module by completing On Your Own problems 8.11–8.12.

ON YOUR OWN

8.11   Why is the actual mechanical advantage of a machine always less than its ideal mechanical advantage? And why can no machine be 100% efficient?

8.12   What is the ideal mechanical advantage of a ramp if its length is 4.0 m and its higher end is 0.5 m above its lower end?

SUMMING UP

You've learned a lot about energy, work, and machines. These are concepts that you probably don't think much about but come in contact with every day. Without energy, nothing happens. Energy is transferred or converted in many different ways and energy is required to do work. As you go about your daily activities, see if you can recognize the energy conversions occurring all around you.

ANSWERS TO THE "ON YOUR OWN" QUESTIONS

8.1 Kinetic energy is found by multiplying half of an object's mass by the square of its speed. Or $KE = \frac{1}{2} \times m \times v^2$

8.2 Step 1   Write the list of knowns and the unknown.

$m = 75$ kg

$v = 3.5$ m/s

$KE = ?$ in J

Step 2   Write out the equation (use 8.1).

$KE = \frac{1}{2} \times m \times v^2$

Steps 3 &5   Write out the equation substituting the numbers from step 1 and solve.

$KE = (0.5)(75 \text{ kg})(3.5 \frac{\text{m}}{\text{s}})^2 = (0.5)(75 \text{ kg})(3.5 \frac{\text{m}}{\text{s}})(3.5 \frac{\text{m}}{\text{s}}) = 459.375$ J

8.3 Gravitational potential energy is determined by the objects mass, acceleration due to gravity, and the height relative to a reference level (often the ground).

Or $PE = m \times g \times h$

8.4 Anything that is compressed or stretched has elastic potential energy.

8.5 Step 1   Write the list of knowns and the unknown.

$m = 55.0$ kg

$h = 72.8$ m

$g = 9.8$ m/s^2

$PE = ?$ in J

Step 2   Write out the equation (use 8.2).

$PE = m \times g \times h$

Step 3   Write out the equation substituting the numbers from step 1 and solve.

$PE = (55.0 \text{ kg})(9.8 \frac{\text{m}}{\text{s}^2})(72.8 \text{ m}) = 39{,}239.2 \frac{\text{kg}\cdot\text{m}\cdot\text{m}}{\text{s}^2} = 39{,}239.2$ J

8.6   a. thermal energy; b. chemical energy; c. electrical energy; d. mechanical energy; e. sound energy; f. electromagnetic energy (you could also have said light or radiant energy for f)

8.7   The law of conservation of energy states that when energy is transformed from one form to another, or transferred from one object to another, no energy is created or destroyed in the process.

8.8   Some of the force must act in the same direction as the object moves.

8.9   No work is done by the table because the object that the force acts on (the book) does not move. Remember in order for work to occur a force (acting in the direction of motion) must move an object a distance.

8.10   Step 1   Write the list of knowns and the unknown.

$F = 25$ N

$W = ?$ in J

$d = 1.5$ m

$P = ?$ in W

$t = 2.0$ s

Step 2   Write out the equation. This problem is asking for both work and power so you will need both Equations 8.3 and 8.4.

$P = \dfrac{W}{t}$ ...and... $W = F \times d$

Steps 3 & 4   Write out the equation substituting the numbers from step 1 and solve.

$W = (25$ N$)(1.5$ m$) = 37.5$ N·m $= 37.5$ J

$P = \dfrac{37.5 \text{ J}}{2.0 \text{ s}} = 18.75 \dfrac{\text{J}}{\text{s}} = 18.75$ W

8.11   The actual mechanical advantage of a machine is always less than its ideal mechanical advantage because of the presence of friction. The efficiency of a machine is always less than 100% because there is always some friction.

8.12   Step 1 Write the list of knowns and the unknown.

> *Input distance* = 4.0 m
>
> *Output distance* = 0.5 m
>
> *IMA* = ?

Step 2   Write out the equation. Since it problem asked for IMA we'll use Equation 8.6.

$$IMA = \frac{Input\ distance}{Output\ distance}$$

Steps 3 & 4   Write out the equation substituting the numbers from step 1 and solve.

$$IMA = \frac{4.0\ m}{0.5\ m} = 8$$

MOD 8

STUDY GUIDE FOR MODULE 8

1. Match the terms to their definitions.

   a. Energy   The force exerted by a machine

   b. Potential energy   The distance the output force is exerted
                                through, or how far the load moves

   c. Kinetic energy   The distance the input force is applied

   d. Input force   The ability to do work

   e. Output force   Energy that is stored as a result of position
                                or shape

   f. Input distance   The force a person exerts on a machine

   g. Output distance   The energy of an object due to its motion

2. If the speed of an object doubles, what happens to its kinetic energy?
   a. KE doubles   c. KE is halved
   b. KE stays the same   d. KE quadruples

3. Which of the following is an example of an object with elastic potential energy?
   a. a stretched spring   c. a moving arrow
   b. books on a shelf   d. a falling oyster

4. Which of the following is an example of electromagnetic energy?
   a. a speeding car   c. a falling stone
   b. sunlight   d. a stretched bowstring

5. Friction causes kinetic energy to be converted into what?
   a. potential energy   c. chemical energy
   b. mechanical energy   d. thermal energy

6. What is the energy stored in the bonds between atoms and molecules called?
   a. kinetic energy   c. chemical energy
   b. mechanical energy   d. thermal energy

7. Which of the following is an example of the conversion of gravitational potential energy to kinetic energy?
   a. striking a match
   b. kicking a soccer ball
   c. a falling raindrop
   d. a gasoline-powered engine

8. What does the law of conservation of energy state?

9. What is work?
   a. the product of speed and force
   b. the sum of power and force
   c. the product of force and distance
   d. the sum of motion and force

10. Which of the following is a unit of work?
    a. joule
    b. watt
    c. horsepower
    d. newton

11. Power is equal to work divided by which of the following variables?
    a. time
    b. force
    c. distance
    d. mechanical advantage

12. How is the work output of a machine related to its work input?
    a. work output is always less than work input
    b. work output is always greater than work input
    c. work output is about the same as work input
    d. work output is always zero

13. What can you say about the output force of a machine with a mechanical advantage much larger than 1?
    a. the output force is much less than its input force
    b. the output force is much larger than its input force
    c. the output force and input force are about the same
    d. the output force is in the same direction as its input force

14. What other type of simple machine can a screw be considered a type of?
    a. lever
    b. inclined plane
    c. pulley
    d. wedge

15. Does a weightlifter do work on the weight bar as he lifts it over his head? Is work done on the weight bar as he stands still holding the weights over his head for 5 seconds? Explain.

16.   A small meteoroid is approaching Earth. It has a mass of 120.0 kg and a speed of 20.0 km/s. How much kinetic energy does the meteoroid have? (Hint: 1 km = 1000 m)

17.   Suppose a 200.0 kg building supplies are lifted in the air to be placed onto a workstation. How much energy is needed to lift the supplies 3.00 meters into the air?

18.   A machine has an efficiency of 75%. What happens to 75% of the work put into the machine, and what happens to the other 25%?

19.   Say you are cracking nuts with a nutcracker.
   a. You apply an input force of 12.5 N to the nutcracker while the output force is 50.0 N. What is the actual mechanical advantage of the nutcracker?
   b. If the input distance of the nutcracker is 15.0 cm and the output distance is 3.0 cm. What is the ideal mechanical advantage of the nutcracker?

20.   You exert a force of 500.0 N to walk 4.0 m up a flight of stairs in 4.0 s. How much power do you use?

PHYSICS—WAVES AND SOUND

Have you ever seen the ocean? It's an amazing sight! Water stretches out as far as the eye can see, and waves crash against the shore on a regular basis. No doubt you have seen a water droplet or stone hit the water and send ripples out from the center. Look at the images in Figure 9.1. Both show waves. There is energy in those waves. It turns out that a great deal of the energy in creation is in the form of waves, and that's what we are going to learn about in this module.

FIGURE 9.1
Waves in Water
Energy from wind (left) and water drops (right)
travel in waves.

Natural Notes

Stop for just a minute and listen. What do you hear? Possibly there are birds singing, horns honking, siblings playing, or maybe nothing but your own breathing. In each instance you are experiencing sound energy. You learned in the last module that energy is everywhere and without it nothing would happen. That includes the sounds you hear. Sound energy is energy that moves in waves through matter from a vibrating object, whether you hear it or not. Every time you speak, the vibration of your vocal cords creates sound energy that moves through the air. All of creation began with the spoken word of God. And the Bible tells us that the words God speaks live forever.

For he spoke and it came to be; he commanded, and it stood firm.
Psalm 33:9

Heaven and earth will pass away, but my words will never pass away.
Luke 21:33

Although waves like those pictured in Figure 9.1 are the ones you are most familiar, the waves you see in water are just one type of waves that exist. You'll learn about the

most prevalent kind of waves in the next module when we discuss light. In this module you'll learn about mechanical waves—waves that include water waves and sound waves.

IN THIS MODULE YOU WILL READ ABOUT THE FOLLOWING MAIN IDEAS:

- Mechanical Waves
- Properties of Mechanical Waves
- Sound

MECHANICAL WAVES

The waves you see in Figure 9.1 are examples of mechanical waves.

Mechanical wave—A disturbance in matter that transfers energy through the matter

Mechanical waves start when a source of energy disturbs matter in some way and causes a vibration to travel through the matter. A vibration is a repeating back-and-forth (or up-and-down) motion.

Where does the energy come from in Figure 9.2? It comes from the person skipping the stone across the water. Basically the person gives the stone kinetic energy (there's more to it than that, such as spin, angle, etc., but without that energy there would be no skipping). Some of that energy is transferred to the water each time the stone hits the

water surface. When the stone pushes down on the surface of the water, the water surface pushes back up on the stone causing it to skip again. Each time some energy is transferred to the water, it causes a disturbance in the water and we see the ripples of energy. With each transfer of energy, the stone slows down. Eventually the stone falls through the surface of the water.

FIGURE 9.2
Energy in Waves
A skipping stone causes disturbances in the water sending ripples of vibration.

Mechanical waves need matter to travel through. We call the matter through which a wave travels the medium. A medium in which a wave travels can be solid, liquid, or gas. Water is the medium in Figures 9.1 and 9.2. When you hear thunder, air is the medium through which the mechanical wave travels. A solid door is the medium when someone knocks.

Types of Mechanical Waves

Scientists classify mechanical waves by the way they move through a medium. There are three main types of mechanical waves: transverse waves, longitudinal waves, and surface waves.

Transverse Waves
Look at Figure 9.3.

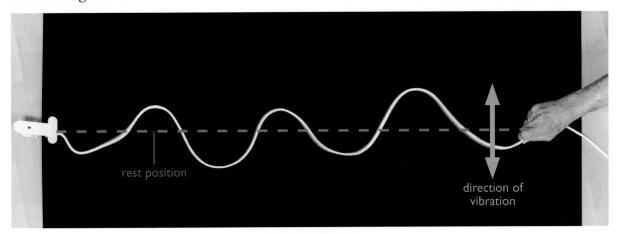

FIGURE 9.3
Transverse Wave
In transverse waves, the medium vibrates in a direction perpendicular to the direction in which the wave travels.

When you shake one end of a rope up and down, the vibration causes a wave to travel down the rope. But notice that the wave carries the energy from right to left in Figure 9.3. The direction the wave travels is perpendicular to the up-and-down motion of the vibration. This is a transverse wave.

Transverse wave—A wave in which the medium vibrates at right angles to the direction the wave travels

Now look at Figure 9.4. In a transverse wave, you have both **crests** which are the highest points on the wave and **troughs** (trawf') which are the lowest points on the wave. The distance between the crests (or the distance between the troughs) is called the wavelength (λ) of the wave. The height of the wave is called the **amplitude (A)**. We'll look at how these are related in the next section.

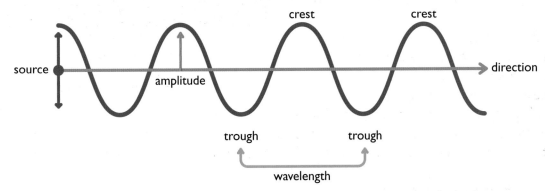

FIGURE 9.4
Parts of a Transverse Wave
The high points of a transverse wave are called the crests. The low points of the wave are called the troughs.

Longitudinal Waves

Have you ever played with a Slinky® toy? If you stretch it out on an uncarpeted floor and then add energy to the spring by pushing or pulling the end of the Slinky, you should see something similar to Figure 9.5.

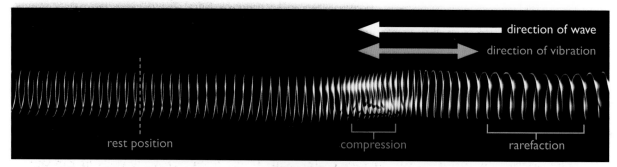

direction of wave

direction of vibration

rest position   compression   rarefaction

FIGURE 9.5
Longitudinal Wave
In longitudinal waves, the medium vibrates in a direction parallel to the direction in which the wave travels.

When you compress or stretch the end of the Slinky, you disturb the spring adding energy to it. In Figure 9.5, the wave carries the energy along the spring from right to left. The wave started on the right side and as it moves to the left, the coils bunch together as the energy of the wave passes through and then separate out farther apart. The vibration of the coils is in the same direction as the wave is traveling. This is a longitudinal (lawn juh too' duh nul) wave.

Longitudinal wave—A wave in which the vibration of the medium is parallel to the direction the wave travels

Notice (on Figures 9.5 and 9.6) the section where the coils are closest together. These compressed sections are called compressions, and they are similar to the crests of a transverse wave. Compressions are the places where particles of the medium (coils of the Slinky) crowd close together. The section to the right of the compression on Figure 9.5 and between the compressions in Figure 9.6 are where the coils are pulled further apart. These areas are called rarefactions (rayr' uh fak' shunz). Rarefactions are similar to troughs in transverse waves.

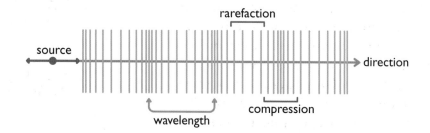

rarefaction

source   direction

compression

wavelength

FIGURE 9.6
Parts of a Longitudinal Wave
The compressed sections of a longitudinal wave are called compressions.
The spaced areas of the wave are called rarefactions.

$$v = (331.5 + (0.6 \cdot 20)) = (331.5 + 12) = 343.5 \frac{m}{s}$$

Notice that I did not put the units for T into the equation. I am supposed to do that with most equations. With this equation, however, it is *set up* assuming that the temperature will be in Celsius. As a result, there is no need to include the unit in the equation, because the units have been worked out already. This is one of the *few* equations in which you need not carry the units through. You must remember, however, that the equation *requires* the temperature to be in Celsius. So the answer is **343.5 m/s**.

In your experiment, you probably got an answer between 290 and 400 m/s. The experiment you performed was not all that accurate, however, so do not be concerned about the actual answer you got. One of the more important things to draw from the experiment is the experience of seeing the cause of a sound before hearing the *sound itself*.

The technique you used in Experiment 9.2 can also be used when watching a thunderstorm. If you've ever watched lightning before, you probably have experienced seeing a flash of lightning (Figure 9.16) and then hearing the thunderclap a few moments later. Thunder and lightning are actually formed at the same time. Since we're studying sound in this module, let's talk about the sound of thunder you hear. As the electrical charge of the lightning heats the air around the storm cloud very quickly, the added thermal energy causes the air to quickly expand. This causes a wave which, when it hits your ear, gets translated into the "boom" of thunder.

FIGURE 9.16
Frequency
We see lightning before we hear thunder unless the lightning strike is less than 1/5th of a mile away.

If lightning and thunder are created at the same time, the delay you experience between seeing a lightning flash and hearing the thunder is due to the time it takes sound to travel to your ears. Remember, light travels very quickly. The speed of light is so great that the time it takes for light to travel even several miles is simply too small for you to measure. Thus, as far as you are concerned, you see a lightning bolt essentially the same instant it is formed. Sound travels much more slowly, however. As a result, you often do not hear the thunder until much later. Study the following example to see what I mean.

EXAMPLE 9.3

A physicist is watching a thunderstorm. She sees a flash of lightning and then hears a thunderclap 2.0 seconds later. If the air temperature is a cool 15 °C, how far away from the physicist was the lightning forming?

Because light travels so quickly, we can assume that the lightning was formed at the instant in which the physicist sees it. The time delay that the physicist observes, then, is simply the time it took for the sound to travel from the point at which the lightning was created to the physicist. First, we need to know the speed of sound which can be determined using equation 9.2. Once you know the speed, you can use equation 6.1 to find the distance traveled. So, this will be a two-part problem.

Step 1 Write the list of knowns and the unknown. Remember the temperature must be in Celsius.

$$T = 15\,°C$$

$$t = 2.0\,s$$

$$v = ?\ \text{in m/s}$$

Step 2 Write out the equation to find the speed (use 9.2).

$$v = (331.5 + 0.6 \cdot T)\,\frac{m}{s}$$

Steps 3 & 4 Write out the equation substituting the numbers from step 1 and solve.

$$v = (331.5 + (0.6 \cdot 15)) = (331.5 + 9) = 340.5\,\frac{m}{s}$$

Step 5 Write out the equation for speed (use 6.1) and rearrange it to solve for distance.

$$v = \frac{d}{t}\ \dots \text{multiply time to both sides} \dots\ d = v \times t$$

Steps 6 & 7 Write out the equation substituting the numbers from steps 1 and 4 and solve.

$$d = (340.5\,\frac{m}{s}) \times (2\,s) = 681\,m$$

The lightning, therefore, was formed **681 m** from the position of the physicist.

Although the way I solved the example is the most accurate way to determine how far away a lightning strike is, there is an easy method that gives relatively good results as well. It turns out that thunderstorms usually result when cold air (called a cold front) moves in under warm air (warm front). Thunderstorms, therefore, usually result in cooler temperatures. A "good guess" for the temperature in a thunderstorm is about 16 °C. At that temperature, sound travels at about 341 m/s. Well, 341 meters is about 1/5 of a mile. In other words, during a thunderstorm, you can estimate the speed of sound to be 1/5 of a mile per second. As a result, for every second of delay between the lightning strike and the thunder, the lightning strike was about 1/5 of a mile away. If you count 2 seconds between a lightning flash and the resulting thunder, then, the lightning struck about 2/5 of a mile away. Although you will not be able to use this simple estimation to answer problems, you can use it when you are watching lightning strikes! Practice what you've learned so far by completing On Your Own problems 9.6–9.7.

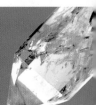

ON YOUR OWN

9.6   What is the speed of sound in air when the temperature is 28 °C?

9.7   During a thunderstorm, the temperature is 18 °C. If you see a lightning flash and hear the thunder 1.5 seconds later, how far away did the lightning actually strike?

The Speed of Sound in Other Substances

When we hear a sound, it is usually the result of waves traveling through the air. That's not always the case, however. Although we usually think of sound traveling through air, it is important to realize that sound can travel through any substance in which it can oscillate in order to make waves. Look through Table 9.1 which lists a few substances and the approximate speed of sound in each.

Do you notice a trend in the data? Air is a gas, while alcohol and water are liquids. The rest of the substances in the table are solids. Notice that the speed of sound in the liquids is about three times the speed of sound in air. In addition, the speed of sound in the solids is somewhere between two and five times higher than the speed of sound in the liquids. Thus, sound travels faster in liquids than it does in gases, and it travels faster in solids than it does in liquids.

Also notice how sound travels faster when temperatures are warmer. Why do you think we see these trends? Remember that the kinetic theory of matter states that all substances have atoms that are in motion. When temperatures are warmer, the added thermal energy causes atoms to vibrate faster. This means sound waves can travel faster too because the molecules bump into each other more easily to transfer energy. Also remember that atoms in a solid are closer together than atoms in a liquid or gas, so the sound wave can travel through solids more quickly.

TABLE 9.1 The Speed of Sound in Certain Mediums	
Medium	Speed (m/s)
Dry air, 0 °C	331
Dry air, 25 °C	346
Alcohol, 25 °C	1143
Fresh water, 0 °C	1401
Saltwater, 0 °C	1449
Fresh water, 30 °C	1509
Saltwater, 30 °C	1546
Wood (oak)	3848
Steel	5029
Aluminum	5093
Iron	5128
Glass	5503

MOD 9

Traveling Faster than the Speed of Sound

If an object (such as a jet airplane) travels in a medium (such as air) faster than the speed of sound in that medium, we say that the object is traveling at supersonic speeds.

Supersonic speed—Any speed that is faster than the speed of sound in the medium of interest

Some jets routinely travel through the air faster than sound. In aviation, the speed of these jets is often measured in terms of the speed of sound. This speed unit is known as the Mach (mahk) number. When a jet travels at the speed of sound in air, it is said to be traveling at Mach 1. If a jet is traveling at twice the speed of sound, it is said to be traveling at Mach 2. The F-18 Super Hornet jet (Figure 9.17), for example, is flown by the U.S. Navy's

Blue Angels and has a maximum speed of Mach 1.8 (1,190 mi/h). This means it can travel 1.8 times faster than the speed of sound. The NASA space shuttle exceeded Mach 10 after dropping out of orbit and coming in for a landing!

An interesting phenomenon is shown in Figure 9.17. It is known as a sonic boom and is generated when an object travels through air faster than the speed of sound in air.

Sonic boom—The thunder-like sound produced as a result of an object traveling at or above Mach 1

As a jet travels, it produces pressure waves that travel, at the speed of sound, away from the plane in all directions—similar to how a boat creates a wake in the water. As long as the jet travels slower than the pressure waves it produces (in other words, less than Mach 1), the waves travel in all direction, including ahead of the jet. Because of the jet's motion, though, the wave compressions in front of the jet are closer together than the wave compressions behind the jet. When the jet reaches Mach 1, however, it moves right along with the pressure waves it produces. This causes the compressions of waves to "pile up," making a huge cone-shaped wave called a shock wave that moves outward and rearward from the jet all the way to the ground. You can see the shock waves of the T-38C jet in Figure 9.18. Like a thunderclap, the shock wave of air creates a very loud boom—a sonic boom. When the jet exceeds Mach 1, it actually outruns the sound waves it produces. This causes the waves to pile up at the edge of a cone. When that cone reaches your ears, you hear the sonic boom.

Sonic booms can be destructive to human ears, and they can also be destructive to buildings, etc. Because sound travels through air, when the huge wave associated with a sonic boom hits a building, it can shake the building rather dramatically and may cause damage. As a result, jets try to travel at or above Mach 1 only in areas of little or no populations.

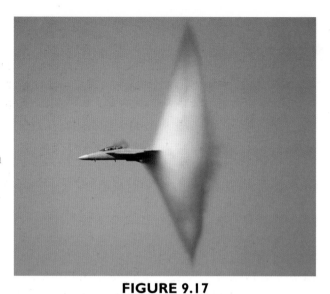

FIGURE 9.17
Breaking Sound
An F-18 Super Hornet creating a sonic boom. The cloud forms as water in the air condenses in the low-pressure area behind the jet.

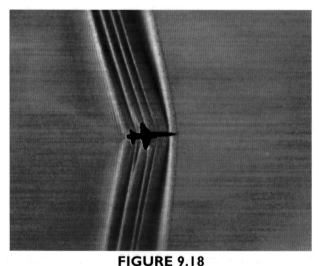

FIGURE 9.18
Shock Waves
A T-38C aircraft in supersonic flight. The shock waves are made visible by a new photographic technique and a computer using special mathematical equations.

Intensity and Loudness

A sonic boom is loud because when the sound waves produced by a supersonic jet begin to bunch up, their amplitudes add together. As a result, the amplitude of the sound wave that comes from a supersonic jet is huge. The same can be said for a thunderclap. The reason a thunderclap is so loud stems from the fact that the heat produced in a lightning strike is so large that it bunches up a lot of air in the compressions (crests) of the sound wave.

TABLE 9.2 Sound Intensity Level	
Sound	**Intensity (dB)**
Threshold of hearing	0
Whisper	15–20
Normal Conversation	40–50
Busy traffic	60–70
Heavy machinery	80–120
Typical rock concert	115
Threshold of pain	120
Jet plane (take-off)	120–160
Possible damage to ears	130

Remember that the amplitude of a wave tells us how much energy the wave carries. Waves with very large amplitudes (like thunder) carry a lot of sound energy. The rate at which a wave's energy flows through a given area is called intensity. Sound intensity depends on the wave's amplitude, so really, intensity is another way of expressing wave amplitude. Intensity also depends on how far away you are from the sound source. Thunder sounds louder (which means it has a higher intensity) the closer you are to the lightning strike.

Sound intensity is measured in units called decibels (dB). The decibel is 1/10th of the unit bel (remember, the prefix *deci-* means 1/10th) The bel scale of intensity measurement was named for Alexander Graham Bell, the inventor of the telephone. In the bel scale, an increase in one bel corresponds to a 10-fold increase in sound wave intensity. The threshold of human hearing is defined as 0 decibels, meaning the sound can just barely be heard. A 20 dB sound has 100 times (10 ×10) more energy per second than a 0 dB sound. A 30 dB sound has 1,000 times (10 × 10 × 10) more energy than a 0 db sound. Table 9.2 shows the intensity levels of some common sounds.

Intensity measures the energy or amplitude of sound waves. Loudness, however, is the physical response to the intensity. It's how each person perceives the sound intensity. Of course, the loudness you hear depends on the sound intensity. In other words as amplitude increases intensity increases, and loudness increases as well. Explore the effects of amplitude on loudness by conducting Experiment 9.3.

EXPERIMENT 9.3
AMPLITUDE AND LOUDNESS

PURPOSE:

To investigate the relationship between a sound wave's amplitude and its intensity.

MATERIALS:

- Eye protection such as goggles or safety glasses
- If you have access to a stringed instrument such as a violin, guitar, cello, or banjo, use it for this experiment. If you do not have access to such an instrument, you will need:

- Rubber band
- Plastic tub (like the kind whipped cream comes in)

QUESTION:
How does changing the amplitude of a sound wave affect the sound produced?

HYPOTHESIS:
Write your prediction of what will happen as you increase the amplitude of a sound wave.

PROCEDURE:
1. If you do not have a stringed instrument, make a simple one by stretching the rubber band all the way around the plastic tub. Do this so that the rubber band stretches tightly across the open end of the tub as well as across the bottom of the tub.
2. Hold the instrument so that you can watch a string (or the rubber band) when you pluck it.
3. Pluck a string only slightly. Watch how the string vibrates and listen to the sound it produces. Record your observations (draw a picture of the string vibration).
4. Using the same string each time, pluck the string harder and harder. Do not pluck the string so hard that it will break, however. Each time you pluck harder, listen to how the sound changes, and observe how the string vibrates. Record your observations drawing pictures of the vibrating string.
5. Put everything away.

CONCLUSIONS:
Explain what you saw and heard in terms of amplitude, intensity, and loudness. Make connections to the text.

What did you see and hear in the experiment? When you plucked the string only slightly, you only added a small amount of energy. So, the string vibrated only slightly, and the sound produced was not very loud. As you plucked the string harder, however, you added more energy and the string vibrated a lot more. In addition, the sound was louder. The more energy you add, the greater the change in volume. What does this mean? When the string vibrates more vigorously, it pushes more air than when it vibrates only slightly. Thus, the sound waves produced by a vigorously vibrating string have more energy and a larger amplitude than the sound waves produced by a string that vibrates only slightly.

Large-amplitude sound waves have greater intensity and are loud; small-amplitude sound waves have less intensity and are relatively quiet. Remember, though, that intensity (and so loudness) also depends on how far you are from the source of a sound. If you are farther away from a sound source, the sound is not as loud as if you are close. Why? Because as a sound wave travels through air, its amplitude decreases. In an open space, then, the volume you hear can be reduced by simply moving away from the source of the sound. In closed spaces like auditoriums, however, moving further from the source will reduce the direct volume of the sound, but sometimes reflections off walls or in corners can actually increase the volume.

Loudness also depends on the health of your ears and how your brain interprets the signals sent from your cochlea. When you turn the volume up on your television, radio, or electronic devise, you are simply causing the device to produce sound waves of larger and larger amplitude. The larger the amplitude of the sound waves, the louder the sound is. Extremely loud sounds can damage your hearing because of the amplitude of the waves. Remember, your ear detects sound waves with the tympanic membrane. The larger the amplitude of the wave, the more violently the tympanic membrane vibrates. Extremely loud sounds such as explosions can cause the membrane to tear painfully due to the sudden increase in the violence of its vibrations. Worse, however, the constant onslaught of loud sounds such as power tools and loud stereo systems (Figure 9.19) can destroy the delicate cells in the cochlea (see Figure 9.15) that are responsible for turning those vibrations into signals the brain can understand. If those cells die, they can never be replaced, and that will result in severe hearing loss and continual ringing in your ears. Ringing in your ears, then, is a sign that you have been exposed to sounds loud enough to damage your hearing.

FIGURE 9.19
Loudness
Loud music that reaches intensities of greater than 120 dB can damage your hearing.

Now although it is possible to harm or destroy your hearing, your ears have a remarkable range when it comes to the loudness they can withstand. They have a remarkable range because the cells in the cochlea do not respond linearly with increasing sound intensity. In other words, when the amplitude of a sound wave doubles, the response of the cells does not double. They are designed to reduce the sensitivity of their response as the amplitude of the sound waves that hit the ear increase. As a result, a sound wave with ten times more amplitude does not sound ten times louder.

think about this

You just learned that an increase of 10 decibels results in a sound wave intensity increase of a factor of 10. So if the sound waves that come from a soft whisper has an intensity of 20 dB, it has 10 × 10 or 100 times the intensity of the sound waves at the threshold of human hearing (0 dB). If you think about that for a moment, you should get a really good appreciation for how well our ears are designed! Since the threshold of human hearing is 0 dB, and since physical damage can occur at 130 dB, that tells us the human ear has a range of 130 db. In other words, the human ear can detect sound waves as much as 10 × 10 × 10 × 10 × 10 × 10 × 10 × 10 × 10 × 10 × 10 × 10 × 10 = 10,000,000,000,000 times its threshold before it might be damaged! That is an incredible range.

Make sure you understand how intensity is measured by studying Example 9.4 and then complete On Your Own problems 9.8–9.9.

EXAMPLE 9.4

The sound from a typical vacuum cleaner is about 60 decibels, while the sound of a rifle firing is about 140 decibels. How many times larger is the intensity of the waves coming from the rifle as compared to those coming from the vacuum cleaner?

Remember that in the bel scale, every increase of 10 dB is the same as a tenfold increase in the intensity of the sound wave. So you need to find the difference in intensity first, and then find the tenfold increase.

Step 1   Write the list of knowns and the unknown.

intensity of vacuum cleaner = 60 dB

intensity of rifle firing = 140 dB

How many times larger = ?

Step 2   We don't have any equation other than subtraction.

intensity of rifle firing − *intensity of vacuum cleaner*

Steps 3 & 4   Substituting the numbers from step 1 and solve.

140 dB − 60 dB = 80 dB

Step 5   The rifle then, is 80 dB louder than the vacuum cleaner. Since each 10 dB represents a 10 fold increase in sound wave intensity, we need to determine how many factors of 10 we need by dividing 80 by 10 to get 8. So, the total increase is calculated by taking 10 and multiplying it by itself 8 times.

10 × 10 × 10 × 10 × 10 × 10 × 10 × 10 = 100,000,000

This means the intensity of the rifle's sound wave is **100,000,000 times larger** than the intensity of the vacuum cleaner's sound wave.

ON YOUR OWN

9.8   A jet is traveling at Mach 1.8 when the temperature of the surrounding air is 0 °C. What is its speed in m/s?

9.9   The sound from a typical power saw has a loudness of 110 dB. How many times larger is the intensity of the sound waves from a power saw as compared to those of normal conversation (40 dB)?

Wavelength, Frequency, and Pitch

How do wavelength and frequency of a sound wave affect what we hear? You already learned that wavelength and frequency are inversely proportional to each other. When wavelength is large, frequency is small, and vice-versa. Thus, we often think of wavelength and frequency together. Perform Experiment 9.4 to see how the wavelength of a sound wave affect how you hear the sound.

EXPERIMENT 9.4
WAVELENGTH AND SOUND

PURPOSE:
To explore how changing wavelength (and thus frequency) affects sound.

MATERIALS:
- Water
- Glass or plastic bottle (A glass bottle is best, and 2 liter is the ideal size. It must have a narrow neck. A jar will not work well.)
- Eye protection such as goggles or safety glasses

QUESTION:
What happens to the sound we hear when the wavelength of a sound wave changes?

HYPOTHESIS:
Write your prediction of how the sound you hear will change when you increase the wavelength (decrease the frequency) of the wave.

PROCEDURE:
1. Empty the bottle and rinse it out with water.
2. Hold the bottle up to your mouth so that the top edge of the bottle opening just touches your bottom lip.
3. Pursing your lips, blow across the top of the bottle. It may take some practice, but you will eventually produce a sound that sounds like it is coming from a horn. Blow a few times to get an idea of what that sound sounds like.
4. Fill the bottle ¾ full of water and repeat steps 2 and 3. Blow a few times to get a good idea of what the sound sounds like.
5. Write in your data table how this sound differed from the first one.
6. Empty some of the water out of the bottle so that the bottle is now only half full. Repeat steps 2 and 3 again.
7. Write in your data table how this sound differed from the previous one you made.
8. Empty some of the water out of the bottle so that the bottle is now only ¼ full. Repeat steps 2 and 3 again.
9. Write in your data table how this sound differed from the previous one you made.
10. Empty the rest of the water out and repeat steps 2 and 3 one more time. The sound you get now should be essentially the same as what you started with. Record any observations.
11. Clean up and put everything away in its proper place.

CONCLUSIONS:

Write a paragraph explaining what differences in sound you encountered. Make references to what you learn in the text.

What was the difference in the sounds you produced with the bottle? The sound should have had essentially the same volume in each case. The difference should have been in the pitch of the sound you heard.

Pitch—An indication of how high or low a sound is, which is primarily determined by the frequency of the sound wave

The terms "high" and "low" in this definition do not refer to volume. Instead, they refer to a musical scale. When the bottle was empty, the sound produced should have been deep and low, much like the low notes a singer would sing. When the bottle was nearly full, the sound produced should have been higher and more shrill, like the high notes a singer would sing. The less water the bottle had in it, the lower the sound should have become.

Why was there a difference in pitch? Well, when you blew across the top of the bottle, you moved air around inside the bottle. The air began traveling up and down in the bottle in response to how you were blowing. Since you blew at a reasonably constant rate, air began traveling up and down in the bottle forming a wave. The wavelength of the wave produced was determined by how far the air could travel up and down the bottle. When the bottle was empty, air could travel all the way to the bottom of the bottle. Thus, you produced sound waves with a long wavelength. When the bottle had a lot of water in it, there wasn't much distance over which air could travel. As a result, the waves produced had a *short* wavelength.

The experiment, then, demonstrates that sound waves with a long wavelength have a low pitch, while sounds with a short wavelength have a high pitch. Remember, wavelength and frequency are inversely proportional to one another. This means that sound waves with long wavelengths have low frequencies and low pitch. Sound waves with short wavelengths have high frequencies and high pitch. This is something you need to remember.

Sound waves with low pitch have low frequency.

Sound waves with high pitch have high frequency.

We usually think of pitch in terms of frequency, however, since it is the frequency of the waves that your ear detects.

Pitch and Music

Look at the tubular bells in Figure 9.20. Also known as chimes, tubular bells are a percussion instrument made of pipes. Each pipe is a different length. When struck with a mallet, the pipe oscillates, and the vibrations travel through the air and hit your ear. The length of the pipe determines the frequency of the sound wave. The shorter the pipe, the shorter the

FIGURE 9.20
Musical Chimes
The longer pipes create sound with longer wavelengths, lower frequencies, and lower pitch. The shorter pipes create waves with shorter wavelengths, higher frequencies, and higher pitch.

FIGURE 9.21
Flute Keys
By pressing the different keys, the flutist changes the frequency and so the pitch of the wave.

FIGURE 9.22
Guitar Strings
By shortening the guitar string, the guitarist changes the frequency and so the pitch of the wave.

wavelength, the higher the frequency, and the higher the pitch. The longer pipes have longer wavelengths, lower frequencies, and so lower pitch.

Nearly all instruments utilize some method to change the wavelength of sound waves in order to change the pitch of the sounds being generated. Woodwind instruments, such as the flute shown in Figure 9.21, are those that you blow into in order to create the sound. By pressing different keys, the flutist changes the distance over which the air travels in the instrument. This changes the wavelength of the sound, which changes the frequency and, therefore, the pitch. Even stringed instruments do this, just in a slightly different way.

A stringed instrument (like a guitar shown in Figure 9.22) has a series of strings. When the string is plucked, it begins to vibrate. This causes the string to push air back and forth, making a sound wave. If you watch a guitar player, he or she will change the length of the string that is plucked by holding the string down at different positions along the neck of the guitar. Since the length of the string that vibrates changes, the wavelength of the sound wave produced changes. This changes the pitch of the sound.

Now it is important to realize that what scientists call "sound" is not necessarily what people think of when they hear the word "sound." Most people think of sound as what people hear. Scientists, however, think of sound simply as waves in the air. As a result, there are plenty of "sounds" we do not hear. Remember, what we hear as sound is actually a result of the signals sent from the cochlea to the brain. We do not hear the waves themselves. The signals made by the cochlea transmit the frequency of the wave to the brain, and the brain interprets this as pitch.

The human ear, though elegantly designed, cannot detect all frequencies of waves in the air. In general, human ears are sensitive to waves with frequencies between 20 Hz and

20,000 Hz. Longitudinal waves with these frequencies are called sonic waves. The musical notes with which we are most familiar have frequencies in the range of several hundred Hz. Middle C, for example, has a frequency of 264 Hz. Waves with frequencies higher than 20,000 Hz are called ultrasonic waves, and waves with frequencies below 20 Hz are called infrasonic waves. The only difference between these waves is their frequencies. Nevertheless, only sonic waves produce what most people call sound. Some animals, however, can hear waves that are not sonic. Bats, for example, can hear sounds with frequencies up to 100,000 Hz, while cats can hear sounds with frequencies up to 40,000 Hz. Whales and elephants, on the other hand, can hear infrasonic waves. Check your understanding by completing On Your Own problems 9.10–9.11.

ON YOUR OWN

9.10 Many flautists (a person who plays a flute) also play the piccolo, an instrument that looks like a very small, short flute. Which instrument (the flute or the piccolo) can produce notes with the highest pitch? Why?

9.11 Are the wavelengths of ultrasonic waves shorter or longer than the wavelengths of sonic waves?

The Doppler Effect

The fact that the pitch of the sound you hear is related to the frequency of the sound wave leads to an interesting effect known as the Doppler effect.

> **Doppler effect**—A change in sound frequency caused by the motion of the sound source, motion of the listener, or both

Perhaps you have heard the pitch of an ambulance siren change as it passed you. That is the Doppler effect. It was named after Austrian physicist Christian Doppler who discovered it. Figure 9.23 show what happens in the Doppler effect.

The ambulance in Figure 9.23 is emitting a constant frequency sound wave from the siren. As the ambulance moves, the siren emits those waves as the ambulance travels. Thus, after it has emitted one wave, it moves forward to emit the next. This causes the compressions and rarefactions of the sound waves to be bunched up in front of the ambulance and stretched out behind it.

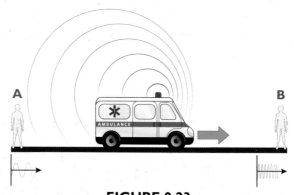

FIGURE 9.23
The Doppler Effect
As the ambulance approaches, observer B hears a higher pitch because the sound waves bunch together (have a higher frequency). When the ambulance passes, observer A hears a lower pitch because the sound waves stretch out having a lower frequency.

Since the sound waves get bunched up in front of the ambulance, the wavelength is shorter, so the frequency is higher. You can see the shorter wavelength, higher frequency waves under observer B. As the ambulance approaches observer B in Figure 9.23, the observer will hear the siren at a pitch that is higher than the pitch the siren actually produces and that the ambulance driver hears.

When the ambulance passes, the sound waves that reach the ear of observer A are the ones traveling behind the ambulance. They are stretched out, which gives them a larger wavelength and thus a lower frequency. This results in a pitch that is suddenly lower than the pitch the siren produces. So as you stand still while an ambulance with its siren on passes by, you will hear the pitch change from high to low. Test your understanding by trying the You Do Science activity and completing On Your Own question 9.12.

YOU DO SCIENCE
THE DOPPLER EFFECT

You can try this yourself if your parent is willing to drive the car while honking the horn past you. You'll need to find a street or parking lot where the horn noise will not bother anyone. Once you find a street or parking lot, stand to one side and have your parent drive to one end of the street. Be careful—do not get too close to the street. Have your parent drive down the street toward you with a speed of at least 20 mi/h. A few seconds before the car reaches you, have your parent blow the horn in a single blast until he has completely passed you. Note how the horn sounds before the car passes you and after the car passes you. If you can, have your parent drive the car past you in the opposite direction, blowing the horn as before. Then have your parent stop the car by you and blow the horn. Note the pitch and compare it to what you heard when the car was moving.

ON YOUR OWN

9.12 Suppose an ambulance with its siren blaring is sitting still. You are running as fast as you can toward the ambulance. Would the horn sound like it had a higher pitch, lower pitch, or the same pitch as it had when both you and the car are standing still?

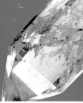

Uses of Sound Waves

Sound waves are useful to us in ways other than hearing. Remember, we can't hear ultrasonic or infrasonic sound waves, but they are sound waves nevertheless. Because of the way sound waves travel, we can use them to "see" things we otherwise could not see. We can use sound waves to understand what the inside of the Earth looks like, even though we have never seen it. Typically, the sound waves used for this purpose are infrasonic, so they have frequencies lower than 20 Hz.

When sound waves encounter an obstacle, a portion of the wave travels through the obstacle, but another portion is reflected backward (see Figure 9.24). The fraction of the wave reflected depends on the type of obstacle encountered. The device shown in Figure 9.24 is an ultrasonic ruler. The circuitry in the device measures the temperature of the air and determines the speed of sound

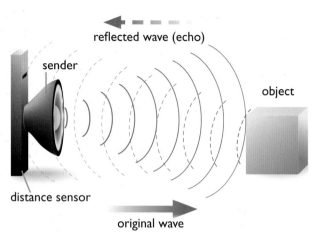

FIGURE 9.24
Ultrasonic Ruler
The ultrasonic transmitter emits a short burst of sound. The waves bounce off an object and return to the receiver which calculates the distance.

for that temperature. When the wave hits a wall or other obstruction, part of the wave is transmitted through the obstruction, and part of the wave is reflected back. That part that is reflected back is detected by the ultrasonic ruler, and the time it took to travel to the obstruction and back is measured by the circuitry. The ultrasonic ruler then uses the speed of sound and the time it measured to calculate the distance from the device to the obstruction. Thus, a person simply holds the device and points it to a wall, and the device determines the distance to that wall with a precision better than 0.5 cm.

think about this

One way you can experience the phenomenon of reflected waves is to stand at the edge of a canyon and yell. You will hear an echo that results from the sound waves you produced reflecting off the canyon walls and coming back to your ears again. It turns out that when you talk in your house, a portion of the sound waves you form is reflected off the walls and back into your ears. You do not hear an echo, however. Why? Well, the walls in your home are simply too close. Since sound travels relatively quickly, it hits the walls and bounces back to your ears so fast that your brain cannot tell the sound wave leaving your mouth from the one reflected off the walls. If you go to a canyon, however, the sound waves bounce back to your ears from a much greater distance. As a result, your brain can distinguish between the original wave and the reflected one.

In general, a sonic wave must take about 0.1 seconds to reflect off an obstacle and travel back to your ears for your brain to perceive it as an echo. Based on the average speed of sound in air, then, you need to be about 34 meters away from an obstacle in order for you to hear an echo as a result of sound waves bouncing off the obstacle. That's why you only hear echoes in settings like canyons or long, empty hallways.

Medical Ultrasound

Ultrasonic waves can also be used as a medical imaging tool. When a sound wave hits an obstruction, part of the wave is reflected, and part is transmitted. If the obstruction is stationary, the reflected and transmitted waves are the same frequency, but they each have lower amplitudes than the original wave. If ultrasonic waves are directed at a person, a portion of the waves gets transmitted into the person's body. As those waves travel through the body, they will continue to travel until they hit another obstruction. At that point, a portion of the waves will be reflected, and a portion will be transmitted. If wave sensors are tuned to detect that portion of the waves that were transmitted through the body but reflected back by an obstruction encountered in the body, the detectors can use the same principles the ultrasonic ruler uses to determine the distance to the obstruction within the body.

If several such waves are directed across a large area in the human body, this procedure can determine the general shape of the obstruction within the body. The most popular application of this is used for pregnant mothers. Using this technique, an ultrasonic imager can produce the general shape of a fetus in the mother's body. Figure 9.25 shows you 3D ultrasonic images of a preborn baby.

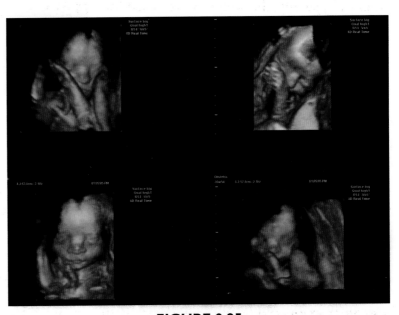

FIGURE 9.25
Sonogram of a Human Fetus
Ultrasound waves map a 3D image of a baby inside its mother's body.

Sonar

Another application that uses reflected sound waves (similar to the ultrasonic ruler shown in Figure 9.24) is sonar. In sonar, ultrasonic waves are emitted, and sensors detect the reflected portions of those waves. The sensors end up creating an image of any obstruction in their path. Figure 9.26 is a map of the ocean floor created by sonar imaging. Scientists are able to identify volcanoes on the ocean floor. The volcano circled in the image is the West Mata volcano, the deepest erupting volcano known to date. It was discovered

FIGURE 9.26
Sonar Map
Knowing the speed of sound in saltwater, scientists use sonar to map the ocean floor.

in 2009 by sonar and is nearly 4000 feet below the surface of the Pacific Ocean. The Tonga Trench in the upper right side of the map is nearly seven miles deep.

Sonar is used in other ways too. Professional fishing ships use sonar to detect schools of fish. And although sonar is best known as the way a submarine tracks ships and other submarines, the most efficient sonar known to humankind exists in bats.

Since bats tend to feed at night, they need to be able to "see" things in the dark (Figure 9.27). The way they do it is through a sonar system that produces images like that of the sonar in a submarine. The differences between a submarine's sonar and a bat's sonar, however, are substantial. For example, the bat's sonar provides significantly more information than a submarine's sonar and is significantly more efficient. First of all,

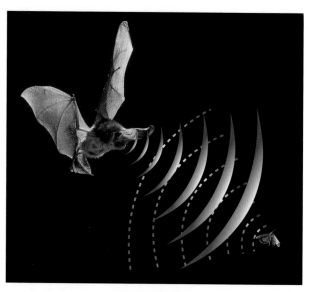

FIGURE 9.27
Bat Sonar
A bat emits a series of high-pitched sounds (solid semi-circles) which are reflected off of nearby insects (dashed semi-circles). Well-developed sensory organs in the bat's inner ears allow the bat to locate the insect and distinguish it from other objects.

rather than just emitting one or a few frequencies of ultrasonic waves, bat sonar produces a wide range of ultrasonic frequencies. Because materials react differently to different frequencies of sound waves, this allows the bat to use the amplitude of the reflected waves to determine the nature of the obstacle from which the ultrasonic waves are reflected. A bat's sonar is so precise in this regard that it can distinguish an insect from a stick or leaf by simply analyzing the amplitudes of the reflected sound waves for each frequency!

In addition, the bat can process the information given by its sonar system much more quickly than the fastest computer man can create. This allows it to identify obstacles and insects so quickly that it can fly around without running into anything and still detect, target, and eat up to five insects each second! All this is done in a sonar system that has a mass of less than 1 gram! This makes the bat's sonar system significantly more efficient than the best sonar human science can produce, and at the same time, it gives the bat a *lot* of information.

SUMMING UP

You should now have a better appreciation for how sound energy travels and all that we can do with sound—even sound we can't hear. Although the bat's sonar system is the most efficient known to humankind, it is not the only natural sonar system. Porpoises use sonar to navigate as well, because their eyesight is limited underwater. I hope that when you think about how these technological marvels are sprinkled throughout nature, you consider how elegantly designed they are and how great is their designer.

ANSWERS TO THE "ON YOUR OWN" QUESTIONS

9.1   Mechanical waves are formed when a source of energy causes a vibration to travel through a medium.

9.2   In transverse waves, the medium vibrates perpendicular to the direction that the wave travels. Shaking the end of a rope up and down is an example of a transverse wave. In longitudinal waves, the medium vibrates parallel to the direction the wave travels. An example would be the compressions and rarefactions of a Slinky spring. In surface waves, the medium vibrates both perpendicular and parallel to the wave direction, so it has circular motion. Deep water waves in an ocean are examples of surface waves.

9.3   The more energy a wave has, the greater its amplitude.

9.4   Wavelength and frequency are inversely proportional to one another. Thus, if wavelength increased, frequency is decreased.

9.5   Step 1   Write the list of knowns and the unknown.

λ = 0.25 m

f = ? in waves per second

v = 0.5 m/s

Step 2   Write out the equation (use 9.1). You will need to rearrange it to solve for f.

$v = \lambda \times f$ ... dividing both sides by λ gives us ... $f = \dfrac{v}{\lambda}$

Steps 3 & 4   Write out the equation substituting the numbers from step 1 and solve.

$$f = \frac{0.5\ \frac{m}{s}}{0.25\ m} = 2.0\ \frac{1}{s}$$

This tells us that 2 waves will hit you every second.

9.6   Step 1   Write the list of knowns and the unknown. Remember the temperature must be in Celsius.

T = 28 °C

v = ? in m/s

Step 2   Write out the equation (use 9.2).

$$v = (331.5 + 0.6 \cdot T) \frac{m}{s}$$

Steps 3 & 4   Write out the equation substituting the numbers from step 1 and solve.

$$v = (331.5 + (0.6 \cdot 28)) = (331.5 + 16.8) = 348.3 \frac{m}{s}$$

9.7   To determine how far away the lightning struck, we will assume that the light from the lightning bolt reaches the physicist's eyes pretty much instantaneously. Thus, the time delay between seeing the lightning and hearing the thunder tells us the distance. First, however, we need to determine how quickly the sound travels. Then, once we know the speed, we can determine the distance the sound traveled.

Step 1   Write the list of knowns and the unknown. Remember the temperature must be in Celsius.

$T = 18\,°C$

$v = ?$ in m/s

$t = 1.5$ s

$d = ?$ in m

Step 2   Write out the equation (use 9.2).

$$v = (331.5 + 0.6 \cdot T) \frac{m}{s}$$

Steps 3 & 4   Write out the equation substituting the numbers from step 1 and solve.

$$v = (331.5 + (0.6 \cdot 18)) = (331.5 + 10.8) = 342.3 \frac{m}{s}$$

Step 5   Write out the equation for speed (use 6.1) and rearrange it to solve for distance.

$$v = \frac{d}{t} \text{ ... multiply time to both sides } ...d = v \times t$$

Steps 6 & 7   Write out the equation substituting the numbers from steps 1 and 4 and solve.

$$d = (342.3 \frac{m}{s}) \times (1.5 \text{ s}) = 513.45 \text{ m}$$

The lightning, therefore, was formed **513.45 m** from the position of the physicist.

9.8   To determine the speed of the jet, we first must determine the speed of sound. After all, Mach 1.8 means 1.8 times the speed of sound. Thus we need to find the speed of sound and multiply it by 1.8.

Step 1   Write the list of knowns and the unknown. Remember the temperature must be in Celsius.

$T = 0 \, °C$

$v = ?$ in m/s

Step 2   Write out the equation (use 9.2).

$v = (331.5 + 0.6 \cdot T) \dfrac{m}{s}$

Steps 3 & 4   Write out the equation substituting the numbers from step 1 and solve.

$v = (331.5 + (0.6 \cdot 0)) = (331.5 + 0) = 331.5 \dfrac{m}{s}$

Step 5   Multiply the speed of sound by 1.8.

$v = (331.5 \dfrac{m}{s})(1.8) = 596.7 \dfrac{m}{s}$

9.9   The bel scale states that every 10 decibels correspond to a 10 times increase in the intensity of the sound wave. So first find the difference in intensity and then determine the 10-fold increase.

Step 1   Write the list of knowns and the unknown.

intensity of power saw = 110 dB

intensity of conversation = 40 dB

How many times larger = ?

Step 2   We don't have any equation other than subtraction.

intensity of power saw – intensity of conversation

Steps 3 & 4   Substituting the numbers from step 1 and solve.

110 dB – 40 dB = 70 dB

Step 5   The power saw then, is 70 dB louder than normal conversation. Since each 10 dB represents a 10-fold increase in sound wave intensity, we need to determine how many factors of 10 we need by dividing 70 by 10 to get 7. So, the total increase is calculated by taking 10 and multiplying it by itself 7 times.

10 × 10 × 10 × 10 × 10 × 10 × 10 = 10,000,000

This means the intensity of the power saw's sound wave is 10,000,000 times larger than the intensity of normal conversation.

9.10   A high pitch means a high frequency. Waves with high frequency have short wavelengths. In general, then, the shorter the wind instrument, the higher the pitch. Therefore, the piccolo produces the notes with the highest pitches.

9.11   Ultrasonic waves have *higher (larger) frequencies* than sonic waves. This means they have shorter (smaller) wavelengths.

9.12   As you run towards the ambulance, you will encounter the crests of the waves faster than if you were standing still. This means that the waves will seem to have a higher frequency when you run toward the ambulance. Thus the siren's pitch will sound higher than the pitch it actually produces. There is another way to think about this question. Remember from module 6 that velocity is relative. Whether you approach the ambulance or the ambulance approaches you, you are both approaching each other. Thus, the physics is similar either way.

STUDY GUIDE FOR MODULE 9

1. Match the following terms to their definition.

    a. Mechanical wave

    A wave in which the medium vibrates at right angles to the direction the wave travels

    b. Transverse wave

    A change in sound frequency caused by the motion of the sound source, motion of the listener, or both

    c. Longitudinal wave

    An indication of how high or low a sound is, which is primarily determined by the frequency of the sound wave

    d. Surface wave

    A disturbance in matter that transfers energy through the matter

    e. Supersonic speed

    A wave in which the vibration of the medium is parallel to the direction the wave travels

    f. Pitch

    A wave that travels along the surface of a medium

    g. Doppler effect

    Any speed that is faster than the speed of sound in the medium of interest

2. In designing a car's horn, the engineers test the sound of the horn and decide that its pitch is too low. To adjust the horn, should the engineers change the electronics so as to produce sound waves with longer or shorter wavelengths?

3. A sound wave is traveling through air with a temperature of 30 °C. What is the speed of the sound wave?

4. If the sound wave in problem 3 has a wavelength of 0.5 meters, what is its frequency?

5. A sound wave has a speed of 345 m/s and a wavelength of 500 meters. Is this wave infrasonic, sonic, or ultrasonic?

6. A physicist takes an alarm clock and puts it in an airtight chamber. When the chamber is sealed but still full of air, the physicist is able to hear the alarm despite the fact that he is outside of the chamber. If the physicist then uses a vacuum pump to evacuate essentially all the air out of the chamber, will the physicist still be able to hear the alarm? Why or why not?

7. What type of wave are sound waves?

8.   You are watching the lightning from a thunderstorm. You suddenly see a flash of lightning, and 2.3 seconds later, you hear the thunder. How far away from you did the lightning strike? (The temperature at the time is 13 °C.)

9.   Sound waves are traveling through the air and suddenly run into a wall. As the sound waves travel through the wall, do they travel faster, slower, or at the same speed as when they were traveling in the air?

10.   In the situation described above, what happens to the amplitude of the wave? Is the amplitude of the wave smaller, larger, or the same as the amplitude before the wave hit the wall?

11.   A jet aircraft is traveling at Mach 2.5 through air at 1 °C. What is the jet's speed in m/s?

12.   A jet travels through air at 464.1 m/s. If the air has a temperature of 0 °C, at what Mach number is the jet flying?

13.   Why do jets travel at speeds of Mach 1 or higher only in sparsely populated regions?

14.   A guitar player is plucking on a string. If he takes his finger and pinches the string to the neck of the guitar so as to shorten the length of the string, will the pitch of the sound emitted increase, decrease, or stay the same?

15.   You hear two musical notes. They both have the same pitch, but the first is louder than the second. If you compare the sound waves of each sound, what aspect(s) of the wave (wavelength, frequency, speed, and amplitude) would be the same? What aspect(s) would be different?

16.   The horn on your neighbor's car is stuck, so it is constantly blaring. You watch your neighbor get into the car and drive away from you, heading toward the nearest place for automobile service. Compare the pitch of the horn before he starts to drive away to the pitch you hear as he is driving away from you.

17.   You are riding your bicycle toward a stationary police car with a siren that is blaring away. Will the pitch of the siren sound lower, higher, or the same as it will sound when you actually stop your bicycle? (Assume the actual pitch of the siren stays constant.)

18.   You are standing near an interstate highway trying to talk on your cell phone. You have raised your voice because of the noise, so the loudness of your voice is about 80 decibels. The sound of the traffic on the highway is about 100 decibels. How many times larger is the intensity of the traffic's sound waves as compared to those of your voice?

19.   An amplifier can magnify the intensity of sound waves by a factor of 1,000. If a 30 dB sound is fed into the amplifier, how many decibels will come out?

think about this

Do you remember Einstein's Theory of Special Relativity from module 8 ($E = mc^2$)? One of the fundamental assumptions of this theory is that the speed of light in a vacuum represents the *maximum speed* that can *ever* be attained by any object that has mass. Thus, the Theory of Special Relativity states that nothing with mass can travel faster than 3.00×10^8 m/s. In essence, then, this theory says that the speed of light is the ultimate speed limit because no object with mass can travel faster than light.

The details of this incredible theory are beyond the scope of this course, but it is important to realize that its fundamental assumption does, indeed, seem to be true. Many experiments confirm the predictions of special relativity, and no data contradicting the theory can be found (to date). Therefore, most scientists consider it to be a valid scientific theory. As a result, the general view of science is that no matter how much energy you expend, you can never travel faster than the speed that light travels in a vacuum.

Wavelength and Frequency

All electromagnetic waves traveling in a vacuum travel at the same speed—the speed of light. But this doesn't mean that all electromagnetic waves are the same. The wavelength and frequency of different electromagnetic waves vary even though their speed is the same.

Just like with sound waves, the speed of electromagnetic waves is the wavelength times the frequency (Equation 9.1). Remember that frequency and wavelength are inversely proportional. Also remember that the speed of electromagnetic waves is constant (3.00×10^8 m/s) and that we represent the speed of light (or any electromagnetic wave) with the symbol c. So, if you know the wavelength of an electromagnetic wave, you can calculate its frequency using Equation 9.1 and $v = c = 3.00 \times 10^8$ m/s.

The Dual Nature of Light

Scientists know that electromagnetic radiation (such as light) travels as a wave. But they also have evidence that electromagnetic radiation behaves like a stream of particles. So, which is it? Well, let's look at what scientists have discovered about how electromagnetic radiation behaves.

The first serious scientific investigations of light were done by none other than Sir Isaac Newton. In 1704, Newton published a book called *Optiks* in which he reported the conclusions of his research on light. In this book, Newton concluded that a beam of light behaved the same as a stream of particles that all moved in the same direction. This came to be known as the particle theory of light. According to this theory, light comes in little packets. We cannot see the individual packets of light, because they are simply too small to distinguish. Thus, just like a stream of water is really composed of individual water molecules, a beam of light is really composed of individual light particles.

The Dutch mathematician and physicist Christian Huygens, who lived at the same time as Newton, disagreed with Newton's conclusions. He considered light to be a wave. He published his own work in which he could explain all of Newton's experiments assuming that light was a wave and not a particle. This was called the wave theory of light, and it was largely ignored at the time. In a few years, however, scientists began to do experiments that indicated light does, indeed, behave as a wave. As a result, by the early 1800s, most scientists believed in the wave theory of light.

Evidence for the Wave Model

In 1801, the English physicist Thomas Young showed in an experiment that light behaved like a wave. To understand how he did that, first look at the vibrations in the water created by raindrops in Figure 10.5. Notice what happens when vibrations from one drop run into vibrations from another drop. When these waves meet each other, they interact. The interaction of waves with other waves is called wave interference.

When two waves traveling in opposite directions meet, they pass through each other, which affects their amplitude. How the amplitude is affected depends on the type of interference. There are two types of wave interference: constructive interference and destructive interference. Study Figure 10.6 to see the difference.

FIGURE 10.5
Wave Interference
When vibrations meet, they interfere with each other.

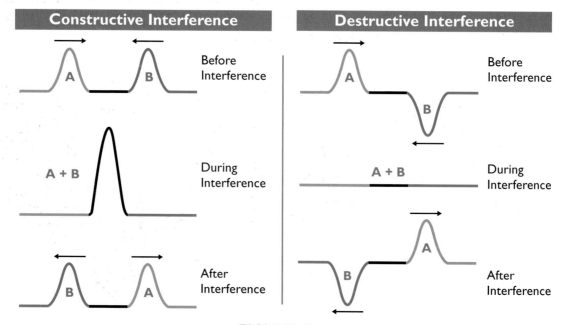

FIGURE 10.6
Constructive and Destructive Wave Interference
When the crests of one wave meets the crest of another wave traveling in the opposite direction constructive interference occurs. If a crest of one wave meets a trough on another wave, destructive interference occurs.

When the crest of one wave overlaps the crest of another wave, constructive interference occurs. Notice that the waves combine as they pass through each other and the amplitude of the combined waves is greater than the individual wave's amplitudes. When the crest of one wave overlaps the trough of another wave, destructive interference occurs. What happens to the combined wave then? The amplitudes cancel each other out and the resulting wave has an amplitude of zero.

So how does this help us understand how Young determined that light was a wave? Well, where waves interfere, they create interference patterns. Remember where crests meet crests, there will be larger amplitudes and where crests meet troughs there will be no amplitudes. This creates a pattern. You can see this happen in oceans (Figure 10.7) where the interference of waves coming from opposite directions causes a phenomenon known as square waves or a cross sea. Just so you know, square waves are rather rare. However, if you should see this while at the ocean, get out of the water as soon as possible because this phenomenon causes dangerous swimming and boating conditions.

FIGURE 10.7
A Cross Sea
Square waves result from the interference of waves coming from different directions.

Now let's talk about Young's experiment. If light behaves as a wave, Young expected to see an interference pattern as the waves overlapped. If light did not behave as a wave, then he would expect to see the light travel in a straight path (see Figure 10.8A and B).

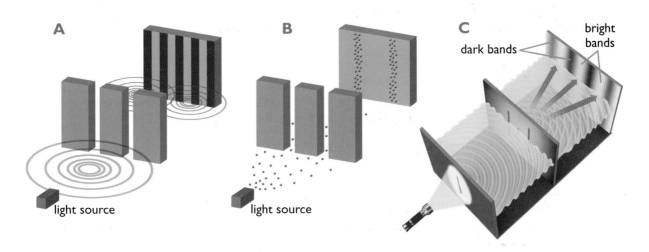

FIGURE 10.8
Wave or Not?
A. If light behaves as a wave, Young expected to see an interference pattern as shown in A.
B. If light does not behave as a wave, Young expected to see a pattern similar to B.
C. When Young performed the experiment, he observed that when light is passed through slits, it produces an interference pattern, confirming that light behaves like a wave.

So, Young set up three boards (see Figure 10.8C), one with a single slit in it, one with a double slit in it, and a solid one to be a screen. He then passed a light beam through the slits to see what would show up on the screen. Figure 10.8C shows Young's results. He observed alternating bands of light and dark. In other words, Young observed an interference pattern. The bright bands on the screen show constructive interference and the dark bands show destructive interference. Therefore, Young's experiment showed that light behaves like a wave.

Evidence for Wave-Particle Duality

By the mid-1880s most scientists were convinced of the fact that light is a wave. However, in 1887 Heinrich Hertz (the same scientist that the frequency unit is named after) discovered something puzzling. Hertz discovered that when blue light hit the surface of a metal, electrons were emitted. The brighter the blue light that hit the surface of the metal, the more electrons were emitted as shown in Figure 10.9. The interesting part was that if bright red light hit the surface of the metal, no electrons were emitted. This is called the photoelectric effect.

FIGURE 10.9
The Photoelectric Effect
Electrons are emitted from metal when blue light hits it but not when red light hits the metal.

Scientists could not understand how blue light could cause this but red light could not if light behaves like a wave.

Then, in 1905, Albert Einstein proposed a new theory often called the wave-particle theory. The wave-particle theory explains that electromagnetic radiation, including light, could behave as both a wave and a particle. How can that be? Well, remember the quantum mechanical model of the atom from module 3? That model explains that when electrons return to a lower energy level, they release energy. Einstein argued that the energy released from the electron returning to a lower energy level was given off in "packets" of energy. We now call such packets of energy photons (foh' tawnz).

Photons do not represent a fixed amount of energy. Rather each photon's energy depends on the frequency of the electromagnetic wave. The greater the frequency of an electromagnetic wave, the more energy each of its photons has. As it turns out, blue light has a higher frequency than red light. This means that photons of blue light have more energy than photons of red light. Blue light photons have enough energy to cause electrons to be emitted from the surface of a metal. Red light photons, on the other hand, do not have enough energy to cause electrons to be emitted from metal surfaces. This is because the frequency of red light is low.

According to Einstein then, a photon is a packet of energy released when an electron returns to a lower energy level. After released, the photon travels outwards as a wave (Figure 10.10). Then as waves of photons travel through space or matter, they make up electromagnetic radiation.

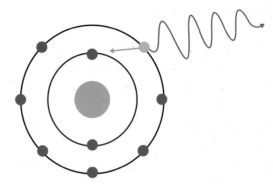

Since Einstein proposed this theory, there has been quite a bit of evidence gathered to support it. For example, using modern technology, scientists performed something similar to Young's experiment. They used a very sensitive camera to take photos of laser light passing through two slits. The photos showed tiny pinpoints of light passed through the slits, seeming to indicate that light consists of particles. However, if they left the camera lens open for a long time, the pinpoints of light formed bands just like interfering waves (Figure 10.11).

FIGURE 10.10
Wave-Particle Duality
When an electron returns to a lower energy level, a photon (particle) is released and travels like a wave.

It shouldn't surprise you that this is called the quantum-mechanical theory of light and it is the currently accepted theory on the nature of light. Since this can seem quite confusing, let's sum it up. Light is composed of little packets of waves. Each individual packet can be thought of as a particle, called a photon. At the same time, however, since each packet is composed of electromagnetic waves, light can also be thought of as a wave. Thus, light will sometimes behave as a particle, and at other times it will behave as if it is a wave. Since waves within a photon are electromagnetic, there is no need for atoms or

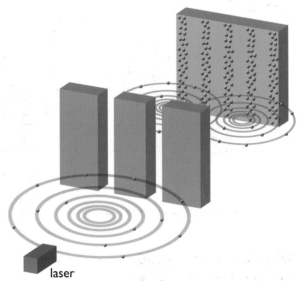

laser

FIGURE 10.11
Quantum-Mechanical Theory of Light
Light sometimes behaves as a particle and sometimes as a wave.

molecules in order for light to travel. As a result, light can travel through any region of space, regardless of what occupies that portion of space. Review what you've learned by answering On Your Own questions 10.1–10.3.

ON YOUR OWN

10.1 What produces an electromagnetic wave? What do all electromagnetic waves have in common and what makes electromagnetic waves differ from one another?

10.2 Suppose a photon is traveling through air. If the particle suddenly hits a lake, what will happen to its speed?

10.3 How does photon energy relate to frequency? What experiment first showed this?

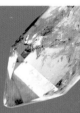

THE ELECTROMAGNETIC SPECTRUM

You now know that electromagnetic waves are waves that carry packets of energy through matter or space as vibrating electric and magnetic fields. But did you know that electromagnetic waves have a wide range of wavelengths and frequencies? The complete range of wavelengths of electromagnetic waves is called the electromagnetic spectrum. Sunlight contains the complete electromagnetic spectrum, though we can see only a small portion of those wavelengths. Figure 10.12 shows the electromagnetic spectrum and we will discuss the varying wavelengths and frequencies of this spectrum in this section.

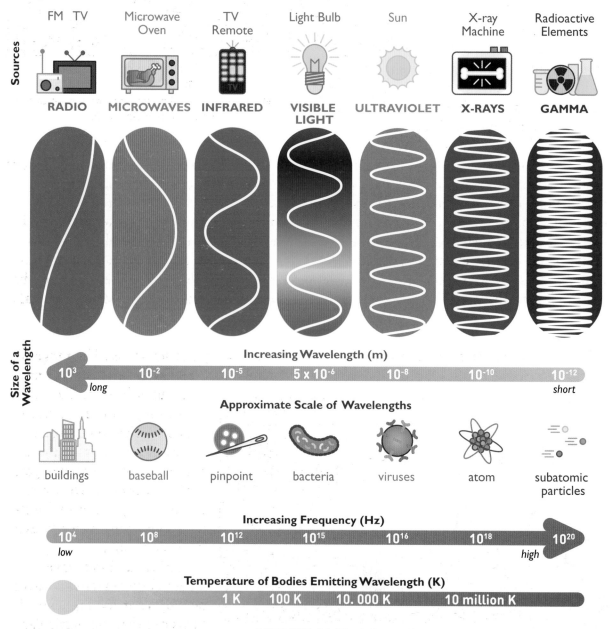

FIGURE 10.12
The Electromagnetic Spectrum
The electromagnetic spectrum consists of radio waves, microwaves, infrared waves, visible light, ultraviolet waves, X-rays, and gamma rays.

Radio Waves

RADIO

The electromagnetic waves with the longest wavelengths are radio waves. The range of radio wave wavelengths can go from longer than a football field to as short as a football. These long wavelength, low frequency waves are used to transmit radio and television signals as well as allow you to talk on your cell phone. It might surprise you that the radio and television signals that are captured with an antenna, a digital satellite dish, a digital cable box, or even

FIGURE 10.13
Radio Waves
When you talk on a cell phone, your phone sends out and receives radio waves.

your smart phone are just electromagnetic waves. You can't see these waves, of course, but without them, you would never hear a radio or watch a television program. When you tune a radio or change the channel on a television, you are telling the electronics in the device to look for a particular frequency (thus, a particular wavelength). Electromagnetic waves of that frequency that strike the antenna are then picked up by the electronic circuitry in the device. The information in that signal is decoded, and the result is the radio or TV program you wanted to hear or watch. Television signals have shorter wavelengths than radio signals, and FM radio signals have shorter wavelengths than AM radio signals.

Microwaves

Microwaves are sometimes considered the shortest-wavelength radio waves. The range of microwave wavelengths goes from about 1 meter to about 1 millimeter. Microwaves have

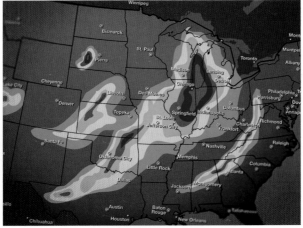

MICROWAVES

FIGURE 10.14
Microwaves
The Doppler-radar image seen on TV weather news uses microwaves to gather and send data.

many uses. The weather radar image on your evening news is one application of microwaves. The GPS system your parents might use to navigate in the car uses microwaves. But probably the most familiar application of microwaves is to cook food.

How do long-wavelength electromagnetic waves heat up your food quickly? It turns out that the particular wavelengths used in microwave ovens are absorbed by water molecules in food.

MOD 10

When the waves are absorbed, the water molecules spin due to the energy absorbed with the waves. When they start spinning, there is a lot of friction between them and the other molecules in the food, and that generates heat. That heat cooks your food. A microwave oven heats food quickly compared to a conventional oven because, in a conventional oven, the heat must travel into the food being cooked. As a result, the food must get hot on the outside before it can get hot on the inside. In a microwave oven, the microwaves are causing the water molecules *throughout* the food to spin. Thus, the food is exposed to heat all over right away. That makes the food cook a *lot* more quickly.

Infrared Light

Electromagnetic waves with wavelengths just shorter than microwaves are called infrared (in' fruh red) light. The term *infrared* means "below red" because infrared light waves have lower frequencies (and longer wavelengths) than red light in the visible range of light waves. Infrared rays have higher frequencies than microwaves and their wavelengths vary from about 1 millimeter to about 750 nanometers. (Remember that a nanometer is one millionth or 10^{-9} meters.)

INFRARED

When a hot object gives off heat, most of the energy is in the form of infrared light. A space heater, for example, gives off a lot of heat. You can see the wires of the space heater glow red, but that is only a small portion of the energy it is emitting. Much

FIGURE 10.15
Thermogram
A thermogram can be used to diagnose heat loss in homes.

of the energy the space heater emits is in the form of infrared radiation, which you cannot see, but you can sense its warmth on your skin. Restaurants use infrared lamps to keep food warm. Zoos use infrared lamps to keep reptiles and other cold-blooded animals warm.

A device called a thermograph uses infrared sensors to create a type of infrared map called a thermogram. In Figure 10.15, a thermograph uses infrared radiation to determine if a house is losing too much thermal energy. The yellow and red colors show that heat is being lost to the outside. The human body is usually warmer than the surrounding area, so thermographs can be used to help search-and-rescue teams to locate victims missing after a natural disaster such as an earthquake or tsunami.

Visible Light

Visible light is the part of the electromagnetic spectrum that the human eye can see. Conduct Experiment 10.1 to investigate visible light.

EXPERIMENT 10.1
VISIBLE LIGHT

PURPOSE:
To explore and observe the wavelengths of visible light. Note: this experiment is difficult to perform near noon.

MATERIALS:
- A flat pan, like the kind you use to bake a cake
- A medium-sized mirror (4 inches by 6 inches is a good size)
- A sunny window (A flashlight will work, but it will not be as dramatic.)
- A plain white sheet of paper
- Water
- Eye protection such as goggles or safety glasses

QUESTION:
What will the wavelength of light waves determine about the property of visible light?

PROCEDURE:
1. Fill the pan with water. The water level should be high enough so that a significant portion of the mirror can be submerged.
2. Place the pan of water in direct sunlight from the window.
3. Immerse at least a portion of the mirror in the water and tilt it so that it reflects the light from under the water up and back toward the window.
4. Use one hand to hold the plain white paper above the pan of water, between the pan and the window. Use the other hand to hold the mirror in the water so that it stays tilted.
5. Play with the tilt of the mirror and the position of the white sheet, trying to reflect sunlight with the mirror and land it on the white sheet of paper as shown in Figure 10.16.

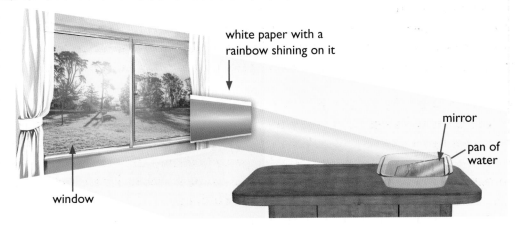

white paper with a rainbow shining on it

mirror

pan of water

window

FIGURE 10.16

6. If you play with the position of the paper and the tilt of the mirror enough, you should eventually see a rainbow, as shown in the figure above. This may take a little work.

7. If you can have a parent or sibling take a photo of the rainbow on your white sheet that you can attach to your data table. If you can't take a picture, then draw what you saw in your data table.
8. Clean up and put everything away.

CONCLUSION:

In a paragraph, describe what you were able to capture on the white sheet. Read the paragraphs below and then make connections to the text as to what happened.

What did you see in the experiment? If everything went well, you should have seen a rainbow, which is actually the result of separating light according to its wavelengths. What made the rainbow you saw in the experiment? When light travels through different substances, it tends to bend. I will discuss this in much greater detail later on in this module. The amount that the light bends depends, in part, on the wavelength of the light. Thus, when the sunlight hit the water, it bent. Certain wavelengths bent farther than others. The mirror then reflected the light and it traveled back out of the water. When that happened, the light bent again. Once again, the amount the light bent depended on the wavelength. That was enough to partially separate one wavelength of light from another. As a result, the reflected light was split into different wavelengths. When it shined on the paper, then, it appeared to you as a rainbow.

What we see as white light, then, is really light that is made up of many colors. If we separate the wavelengths, we get different colors. The longest wavelengths of light we see are made up of various shades of red, while the shortest wavelengths of light we see are made up of various shades of violet. The other colors (orange, yellow, green, blue, and indigo) have wavelengths in between (see Figure 10.17).

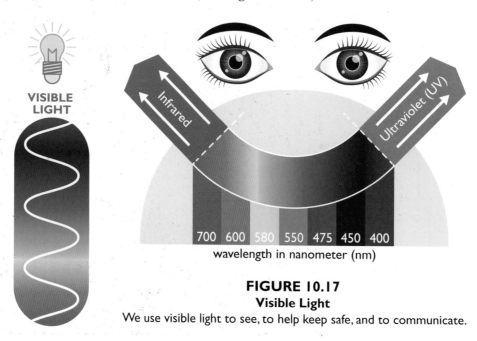

FIGURE 10.17
Visible Light
We use visible light to see, to help keep safe, and to communicate.

Although you needn't memorize the wavelength of each color, you *do* need to memorize the *relative* size of the wavelengths in question. In other words, you need to know that red light has the longest wavelength, orange light has shorter wavelength, and so on. This is easy to do if you think about the colors as a single name. If you start with the color that corresponds to the longest wavelength (red) and you put the first letter of each color together, you come up with a man's name: ROY G. BIV. So, if you think of ROY G. BIV every time you think of the colors of visible light, you will always know that red light has the longest wavelength, violet the shortest, and you will also know the order of all colors in between.

The wavelengths of visible light are quite small. They range in size from about one hundredth the thickness of a human hair to the length of a bacterium. Each wavelength of visible light corresponds to a specific frequency and a specific color. Obviously, we use visible light to see. Plants use different frequencies of visible light to photosynthesize. We use lights to read by at night and to keep from stumbling when its dark. Red traffic lights tell us when to stop and green traffic lights tell us when to go.

think about this

Did you know that the different colors of the rainbow have different temperatures? It shouldn't surprise you since each color corresponds to a different frequency of energy. In fact, in 1800 the German-born English astronomer, William Herschel, discovered infrared radiation because he was curious about the temperatures of different wavelengths of light. Herschel is depicted in Figure 10.18 placing a thermometer on the colors of visible light he separated using a prism. He observed that the temperature was lower at the blue end and higher toward the red end. He then wondered if the temperature would be even higher if he placed the thermometer beyond the red end of the spectrum. He found that the temperature was indeed higher. This led Herschel to conclude that there must be invisible radiation beyond the red end of the visible spectrum. If you look back at Figure 10.12, you can see the thermometer at the bottom indicating the temperature (in Kelvin units) of the various wavelengths of electromagnetic radiation. You can try Herschel's experiment too! Just complete the You Do Science activity.

FIGURE 10.18
Herschel's Infrared Experiment

363

YOU DO SCIENCE

THE TEMPERATURE OF THE RAINBOW

All you need to try Herschel's experiment for yourself is a prism, a thermometer (if you have 2 or 3 that is even better), a plain white piece of paper, and the sun. If you don't have access to a prism (glass prisms work the best), then a CD cut in half will work too. If you have some black paint, put a light coating of black paint on the bulb of the thermometer. You can use black magic marker, but paint works better. This will help the thermometer to absorb heat energy better. If you don't have the paint or marker, you will still see a temperature change, just not as quickly. You need to do this on a sunny day (few clouds) and close to noon. Go outside and set the paper on the ground. With your thermometer, take an initial temperature reading in the shade and record in your data table. Hold the prism or CD, angling it, until you can get a nice band of rainbow colors on the white paper. You will need to hold it there for a while, so if you can set it (or lean it) on a book or something that would be best. Place the thermometer in a band of the purple-blue area and wait about 3–5 minutes. Record the temperature. Repeat with the thermometer in the yellow-orange band of light. Then repeat with the thermometer just beyond the red band of light. Record your temperatures. If you have 2 or 3 thermometers, you can set all three of them up at the same time. Compare your temperature readings to the wavelengths and frequencies of the light waves.

Ultraviolet Light

Ultraviolet radiation has wavelengths shorter than those of visible light. The term *ultraviolet* means "above violet" because the frequencies of ultraviolet light are higher than the frequency of violet light. Ultraviolet wavelengths range from about 400 nanometers to about 4 nanometers, the size of some viruses. Because of the higher frequencies, ultraviolet light has more energy than visible

ULTRAVIOLET

FIGURE 10.19
UV Protection
When in the sun for a long time, protect your eyes with sunglasses and your skin with sunscreen.

light. It turns out that the higher the frequency (shorter the wavelength) the more energy a wave has.

Ultraviolet (UV) light has enough energy to kill living tissue. Medical professionals often use ultraviolet lamps to sterilize things. If you put something under an UV lamp, the ultraviolet light will kill most of the germs (bacteria, viruses, etc.) that live on it. Your skin makes vitamin D when it is exposed to the ultraviolet light from the sun. Our bodies use vitamin D to help us absorb calcium from foods to produce strong bones and teeth. However, too much exposure to the sun's ultraviolet rays can cause sunburn, wrinkles, and eventually skin cancer. Excessive UV exposure can also damage your eyes. So, enjoy your time in the sun, but remember that moderation is the key, along with wearing sunglasses and the proper use of sunscreen.

think about this

All living things need the light energy from the sun to survive. But you just read that too much ultraviolet radiation is harmful, potentially even deadly, to living cells. How is it that living things can overcome this problem? Well, the Earth was designed with a type of filter layer surrounding it called the ozone layer.

Ozone, a molecule composed of three oxygen atoms, makes up this amazing filter. It turns out that ozone is a molecule that breaks down in the presence of the ultraviolet light most damaging to living tissue. This ultraviolet light has just enough energy to break apart one of the bonds that holds the oxygen atoms together. The bond, in order to break, must absorb the ultraviolet light. In other words, when ultraviolet light encounters an ozone molecule, it uses its energy to destroy the ozone molecule instead of harming living tissue. One truly incredible thing about this wonderful filter is that ozone cannot be broken down by visible or infrared light because their waves do not carry as much energy. As a result, they pass right by ozone without interacting

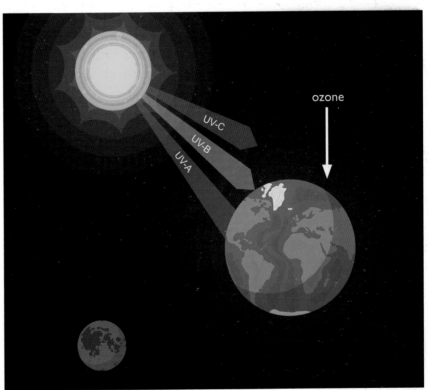

FIGURE 10.20
Earth's Ozone Layer
UV-C waves, the most damaging of the ultraviolet waves, are blocked from Earth's surface by the ozone layer.

with it. So, the most damaging ultraviolet light is stopped by ozone, but the kind of light Earth needs (visible and infrared) is allowed to hit the surface of the Earth where its energy is used by plants and animals. Notice in Figure 10.20 that not all of the UV light from the sun is stopped by this filter. Some does end up getting through, even on cloudy days. This is why you must protect your skin from sunburn.

X-Rays

X-rays have very short wavelengths and high frequencies. X-rays, used in medicine so that doctors can see your bones (and other internal structures) without actually opening up your body, have wavelengths even shorter than ultraviolet light. Because they are high frequency waves, X-rays have even more energy than do ultraviolet rays. So, while ultraviolet light will affect your skin, X-rays have enough energy to pass through your skin and other soft tissues, but not enough energy to pass through dense structures such as bones or teeth.

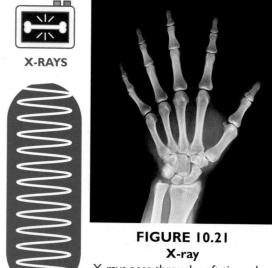

X-RAYS

FIGURE 10.21
X-ray
X-rays pass through soft tissue but are stopped by bone and teeth.

Because X-rays have so much energy, and can penetrate human cells, too much X-ray exposure can be dangerous. Have you had a dental X-ray taken? If you have then you may remember that a heavy apron was placed over your body to protect you from stray X-rays while the X-ray of your mouth was taken. The heavy apron contains lead, which X-rays cannot penetrate, and so protects your body. This is also why X-ray technicians who perform X-rays all day long, stand behind a lead shield to avoid exposure to the X-rays.

Gamma Rays

Gamma rays have the shortest wavelengths (shorter than the diameter of the nucleus of an atom) and highest frequencies in the electromagnetic spectrum. This makes them the most energetic electromagnetic wave. With that much energy, gamma rays can penetrate just about anything. This makes gamma rays very dangerous.

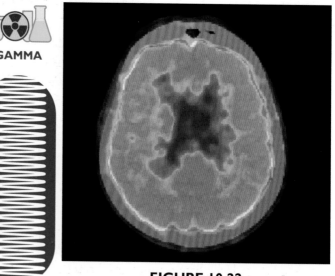

GAMMA

FIGURE 10.22
Brain Scan
Gamma rays emitted by radioactive tracers in the brain are used to produce color-coded images.

Believe it or not, it is because gamma rays can be deadly that medical science uses them to kill cancer cells. The goal of radiation therapy is to use gamma rays to target and kill cancer cells without harming nearby healthy tissue. Gamma rays are also used to make color-coded pictures of the brain to aid in diagnosing disease. The different colors indicate different levels of brain activity. Review what you've learned in this section by completing On Your Own problems 10.4–10.5.

ON YOUR OWN

10.4 Without looking at Figure 10.17, order the following colors in terms of *increasing frequency:* yellow, indigo, red, green.

10.5 If radio signals are really made up of electromagnetic waves, why doesn't a radio station's antenna glow when it transmits it signals?

THE BEHAVIOR OF LIGHT

Without light, nothing is visible. When you look at something, what you are really seeing is light. When light passes through an object (such as a window) you can see through that object. But if light does not pass through an object, you cannot see through it. The way light behaves when it strikes an object depends, in part, on the type of material the object is made up of. There are three types of materials when talking about how light strikes them. Materials can be transparent, translucent, or opaque.

Transparent materials are those that you can clearly see through because these materials allow most of the light that strikes it to pass through. The fishbowl and the water in Figure 10.23 are both transparent materials because you can clearly see the objects inside.

FIGURE 10.23
Transparent
Light waves pass through transparent materials.

A translucent material allows light waves to pass through, but it scatters the light waves as they pass. The glass in Figure 10.24 is an example. You can see through the glass but the objects you see are not clear or distinct. Notice how you can tell that someone is sitting on a chair at a table with an umbrella, but the images are fuzzy and lack detail. The glass window is translucent.

Most materials are opaque, meaning they absorb or reflect all of the light that strikes it. The chair you're sitting on, this book, and the floor beneath your feet are all examples of opaque materials. An opaque object does not allow any light to be transmitted through it. Therefore, you cannot see through opaque objects.

Interactions of Light

Let's look a little more closely at the way light interacts with objects. Remember, light waves are photons of energy. So, when light hits a material, some or all of the energy in the light can be transferred to the material. What happens to the light? When light hits an object, depending on whether the object is transparent, translucent or opaque, the light will either be transmitted (pass through), reflected (bounce back), or be absorbed (enter the medium but not exit). When light is transmitted, it can be refracted, polarized, or scattered.

FIGURE 10.24
Translucent
Light waves pass through but scatter, so objects are out of focus.

MOD 10

Reflection

When you were studying sound waves in the previous module, I told you that when sound waves encounter an obstacle, a portion of the sound waves bounces off the obstacle and starts traveling in another direction. That's how we hear echoes. Another portion of the sound waves begins traveling through the obstacle. Well, under the right conditions, the same thing happens to light waves. When light (or sound) waves bounce off an obstacle, we call it reflection. Conduct Experiment 10.2 to learn more about reflection.

EXPERIMENT 10.2
THE LAW OF REFLECTION

PURPOSE:
To investigate and observe where reflected waves will go.

MATERIALS:
- Eye protection such a goggles or safety glasses
- A flat mirror. The mirror can be very small, but it needs to be flat. You can always tell if a mirror is flat by looking at your reflection in it. If the image you see in the mirror is neither magnified nor reduced, the mirror is flat.
- A white sheet of paper
- A pen
- A protractor
- A ruler
- A flashlight
- Black construction paper or thin cardboard
- Scissors
- Tape
- A dark room

QUESTION:
When light waves reflect off of an obstacle, how do the reflected waves travel?

HYPOTHESIS:
Predict where the reflected light wave will go when a flashlight is shown on a mirror by drawing its path.

PROCEDURE:
1. Cut the construction paper into a circle that fits the face of the flashlight. Make it that when the circle is taped to the face of the flashlight, little or no light will be able to escape.
2. At the edge of the circle, cut a small, thin slot. The circle of paper should look something like the one shown in Figure 10.25A.
3. Now tape the circle to the face of the flashlight, so that light escapes only through the slot.

FIGURE 10.25A

4. Lay the white piece of paper on a rectangular table or desktop so that its edge is even with the straight edge of the table.

5. Tape the paper down so that it does not move from this position. NOTE: Check with your parents before doing this. Tape can harm some tabletops.

6. Use the protractor to make a line that is perpendicular to the edge of the table and centered on the paper. In the end, your setup should look like Figure 10.25B.

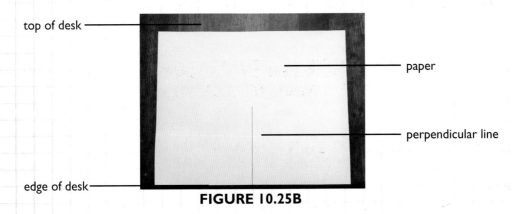

top of desk

paper

perpendicular line

edge of desk

FIGURE 10.25B

7. Push the mirror up against the edge of the table so that the line you just drew is centered on the mirror and perpendicular to it. Tape the mirror to the edge of the table so it stays there.

8. Turn on the flashlight and turn out the lights.

9. Hold your flashlight so that the slot is on the bottom of the face, touching the paper. Play with the tilt of the flashlight until the light coming from the slot causes a beam on the paper that hits the mirror at the same point where the line touches the mirror. You should then see the beam reflect off the mirror back onto the paper, as shown in Figure 10.25C.

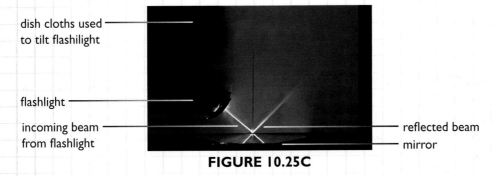

dish cloths used to tilt flashilight

flashlight

incoming beam from flashlight

reflected beam

mirror

FIGURE 10.25C

10. Use your pen to carefully trace the path of the beam as it travels from the flashlight and reflects off the mirror.

11. Turn on the lights.

12. Use your protractor to measure the angle of the line representing the part of the incoming beam relative to the perpendicular line you originally drew. Record the angle in your data table.

13. Use your protractor to measure the angle of the line representing the reflected beam relative to the same perpendicular line. Record the angle in your data table.

14. Do the experiment twice more, changing the position of the flashlight so that the angle that the incoming beam makes with the perpendicular line is different each time. In each case, record and compare the angle made by the incoming beam to that of the reflected beam.

15. Clean up and put everything away. Save the black cover you made for the flashlight in steps 1 and 2 as you will use it again in Experiment 10.3.

CONCLUSION:

In a paragraph, explain how the refracted beam and the incoming beam are related. Make connections to the text after reading the paragraphs that follow.

Within experimental error, the angles you measured in each trial of the experiment should have equaled each other. Scientists call the angle the light ray from the flashlight made with the perpendicular line the **angle of incidence**. The angle the reflected ray made with the perpendicular line is called the angle of reflection. With that terminology, I can say your experiment should have indicated that the angle of reflection equals the angle of incidence. That is the **law of reflection**.

Law of reflection—The angle of reflection equals the angle of incidence

Believe it or not, this simple law is responsible for how mirrors work.

To understand why the law of reflection works, you first need to understand how we see things in the first place. As you look at the words on this page, light reflects off the page and up toward your eye. The pattern of reflected light is read by your eye and is converted to electrical impulses sent to your brain. I will discuss this process a bit more in a later section of this module. Your brain then converts these electrical impulses into an image. That's how you see. That's also why you cannot see things without the aid of light. Your eyes cannot send any signals to your brain unless light reflects off the thing you are observing and enters your eyes. Only then can a message be sent to your brain so that it can form an image.

With this in mind, consider a woman looking at herself in a mirror (Figure 10.26). Why does she see her foot, for example? Well, light reflects off of her foot, hits the mirror, reflects off of the mirror, and enters her eyes. The thing to realize here is that the woman's brain will think that the light travels in a straight line.

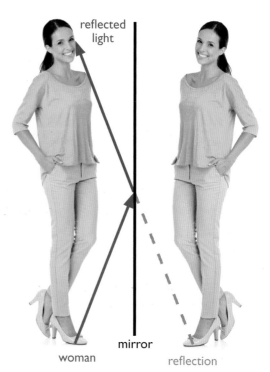

FIGURE 10.26
Reflection in a Mirror
Light waves travel from her shoe, reflect off of the mirror, and travel to the woman's eyes.

370

As a result, her brain extends the light backward, as illustrated by the dashed line in the figure. This makes the woman's brain think that the image of her foot is actually behind the mirror because it thinks that the light hitting her eyes is coming from the start of the dotted line. Review what you've learned by completing On Your Own problems 10.6–10.7.

Refraction

As I mentioned before, when light or sound waves encounter an obstacle, reflection is not the only thing that can happen. In addition to bouncing off an obstacle, light and sound waves can be transmitted through an obstacle, provided certain conditions are met. When a wave enters an obstacle, it usually bends in response to its changes in speed. Perform Experiment 10.3 to understand the process of refraction.

ON YOUR OWN

10.6 Explain the following.

   a. Explain the difference between opaque, transparent, and translucent materials. Give an example of each type.

   b. Explain what three things can happen to a light wave when it enters a new medium.

10.7 Draw the path of the light ray in the diagram below to show where the light eventually hits the screen.

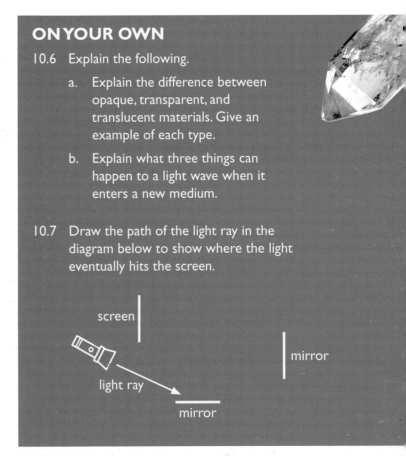

EXPERIMENT 10.3
REFRACTION OF LIGHT

PURPOSE:
To explore what happens when light encounters a transparent obstacle.

MATERIALS:
- A square or rectangular glass or clear plastic pan (If you have a flat bottle, it will work as well. It just needs to be something with clear, flat sides that can hold water.)
- Water
- Milk
- Spoon
- Flashlight with the same cover you used in Experiment 10.2
- A sheet of plain white paper
- Pen
- Protractor
- Ruler
- Eye protection such as goggles or safety glasses

QUESTION:
What happens to light when it is transmitted through transparent objects?

MOD 10

HYPOTHESIS:
Draw what you predict the path of the light beam will be when light is transmitted through a glass pan and water.

PROCEDURE:
1. Draw a line lengthwise down the middle of the plain white sheet of paper.
2. Use your protractor to draw another line perpendicular to the line you just drew. This line should be about 3 inches from one of the edges of the paper, and it should span the entire width of the paper.
3. Use your protractor and ruler to draw a third line that starts at the edge of the paper nearest the line you just drew and travels through the intersection of the lines you drew in steps 1 and 2. This new line should make a 45 degree angle with each of the other lines. In the end, your paper should look something like what is shown in Figure 10.27.
4. Fill the pan half full of water and add ½ teaspoon of milk. Stir it so the water is a little cloudy. This will allow you to see the beam of light as it travels through the water.
5. Set the pan on the paper so one of its flat edges is sitting right on the line you drew in step 2.
6. Fix up your flashlight again so that it is just like what you used in Experiment 10.2.

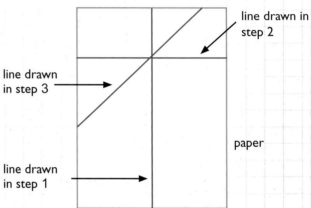

FIGURE 10.27

7. Lay the flashlight on the table with its slot down and then turn off the lights.
8. Position the flashlight so that the light beam shines on the paper and follows the line you drew in step 3 from where it leaves the flashlight until it hits the pan.
9. Look down into the water from directly above the pan. You should see that when the beam hits the pan, two things happen. First, part of the beam is reflected off the pan. The other part of the beam is refracted into the water.
10. Look at the refracted beam relative to the line you drew in step 3. Does the light beam follow that line? Draw what you see in your data table.
11. Follow the light beam until it hits another one of the pan's sides. What happens there? Draw what you see and record your observations.
12. Clean up and put everything away.

CONCLUSION:
In a paragraph, describe the path that the refracted line took. Read the following paragraphs and make connections to what you learn in the text.

What did you see in this experiment? First, you should have seen that when the light beam hit the pan, part of it was reflected and part was refracted. This is what hap-

side. This will only happen when the sun shines on the water droplets from behind you. And the sun also needs to be at a certain angle. This is why you do not see a rainbow after every rain shower. It depends on how high the sun is in the sky and where that position is relative to your position.

You should also realize that you do not see all the colors of the rainbow from one water droplet. Of all the rays drawn on the left-hand side of the Figure 10.32, only one reaches your eyes. There are, however, many water droplets in the air. Thus, you see the different colors from different water droplets. Look at Figure 10.32 again. Which light is bent the lowest when it leaves the water droplet? The red light is bent the lowest. What water droplets will you see the red light from, then? If the red light is bent low, then in order for it to reach your eyes, the red light will have to come from the *highest* water droplets in the sky. Since the violet light is bent the least, you will see that light coming from the *lowest* water droplets in the sky. Now look at Figure 10.33. A rainbow will always appear with the red light on the top and the violet light on the bottom, because you will see the red light coming from the highest water droplets and the violet light coming from the lowest water droplets.

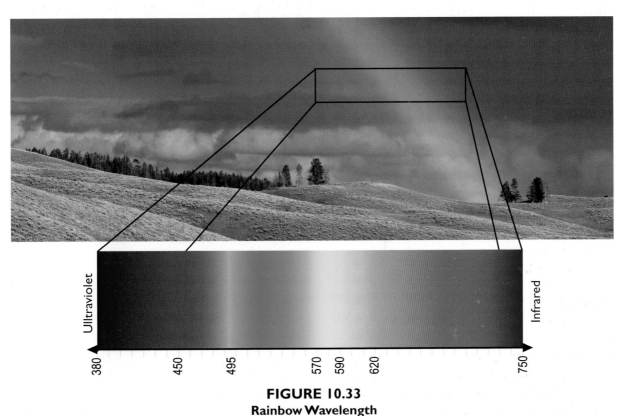

FIGURE 10.33
Rainbow Wavelength
Rainbows always appear with red light on the top and violet light on the bottom.

Polarization

Have you ever been "blinded" by the sun reflecting off of snow or water? That's because light waves from the sun vibrate in all directions. This is called unpolarized light. Remember light waves are electromagnetic waves with electric fields vibrating in one direction and magnetic fields vibrating at right angles. When light hits the snow or water (a horizontal surface) it reflects horizontal light waves more strongly than the rest of the sunlight. Because these reflected light waves vibrate mainly in the horizontal plane, they are said to be polarized. In other words, polarized light is light waves that vibrate in only one plane.

See what I mean by looking at the simplified representation in Figure 10.34. You can see two polarizing filters. The vertical polarizing filter allows only vertically vibrating waves (vertically polarized light) to pass through. It blocks the waves vibrating horizontally. The horizontal polarizing filter, on the other hand, allows only horizontally vibrating waves (horizontally polarized light) to pass through, blocking the vertically vibrating waves. So, after the unpolarized light passes through the vertical polarizing filter it is now considered polarized light.

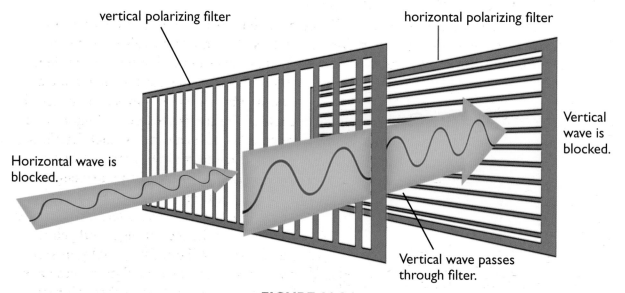

vertical polarizing filter

horizontal polarizing filter

Horizontal wave is blocked.

Vertical wave is blocked.

Vertical wave passes through filter.

FIGURE 10.34
Polarizing Filters
A polarizing filter blocks light waves that are not vibrating in the same direction.

What do you do to reduce the glare of the sun off of snow? You wear sunglasses. It turns out that polarizing sunglasses use polarizing filters that block waves with electric fields vibrating in the horizontal plane. So, since the glare from the snow is actually light waves reflected horizontally, polarizing sunglasses use vertically polarized filters which block the horizontally polarized glare. What do you think will happen if you look at light through a horizontally polarizing filter and a vertically polarizing filter at the same time?

You can try this if you have two pairs of polarizing sunglasses available. If not look at Figure 10.35. Notice how you can see the diagonal lines through the lens on the top left and bottom. They are filtering light reflecting off of the lined surface, but you can still see through them because some of the polarized light reaches your

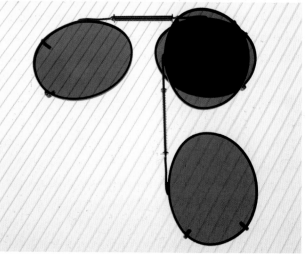

FIGURE 10.35
Polarizing Sunglasses
When you turn two polarizing filters perpendicular to each other, no light passes.

eyes. But look at what happens when two lenses are placed at right angles to each other. No light passes through so you can't see anything! Since both the horizontal and vertical light waves are blocked, no reflected light reaches your eyes.

Scattering

Earth's atmosphere contains many tiny particles and molecules such as dust and water. When light rays from the sun pass through these molecules or particles, the particles can redirect the light waves. This is called scattering.

Look at the sunset in Figure 10.36. Remember that visible light is made up of different wavelengths that correspond to different colors. As sunlight travels to Earth, it encounters many tiny particles that scatter the shorter-wavelength blue light more than larger particles that scatter longer-wavelength light waves. At sunrise or sunset, the angle of the sun is greater, and light must travel a longer distance to reach Earth. So, by the time the sunlight reaches your eyes, most of the blue and green wavelengths have been scattered out and away from your line of sight. What is left for your eyes to detect are the red, orange, and yellow wavelengths of light. That is why, at sunrise and sunset when the light waves have farther to travel and move through more particles, you see such beautiful red, pink, and orange skies.

FIGURE 10.36
The Colors of Sunset
You see the colors of visible light that have not been scattered by tiny particles as the waves travel through the atmosphere.

Scattering of light also explains why the sky looks blue. We know that the air around us is colorless, but the sky on a sunny day looks quite blue. When the sun is high in the sky, the light waves travel more directly and so have a shorter distance to get to Earth. The tiny particles in Earth's atmosphere scatter light of blue wavelengths in all directions more than other colors of light and so we see a blue sky. Review by completing On Your Own questions 10.8–10.10.

ON YOUR OWN

10.8 The following is a diagram of how a light ray travels from substance **A** through substance **B**:

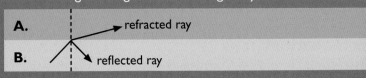

Does light travel more quickly in substance **A** or **B**?

10.9 A man is spear fishing. He looks into the water and sees a fish in front of him. When he aims his spear, should he aim it at the fish, in front of the fish, or behind the fish?

10.10 What happens to light that passes through a horizontal polarizing filter?

YOUR EYES AND COLOR

There are many, many marvelous facets of the eye, but we will concentrate on one: the way it focuses light. Remember, the reason we see things is that light reflects off them and enters our eyes. Our eyes then detect the light and send signals to the brain, which forms an image in our mind. We will study how the eye handles light. But before we do that, we should discuss how lenses work because our eyes have a truly amazing lens.

Lenses

The fact that light rays tend to bend when they travel through transparent objects can be quite useful. For example, consider a light ray traveling through the object in Figure 10.37, which is made of glass. When the ray strikes the transparent object, it will be refracted. This means the light will bend toward a line perpendicular to the surface at the point of contact.

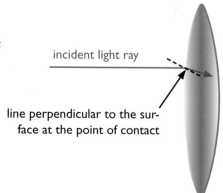

FIGURE 10.37
Light Hitting Glass

Now, the light ray will travel through the glass along the path indicated in Figure 10.37. At some point, however, the light ray will reach the edge of the glass object and exit. At that point the substance through which the light is traveling will change. Thus, the light will be refracted again. Since light travels faster in air than it does in glass, the refracted light ray is bent away from the perpendicular. The result is pictured in Figure 10.38A.

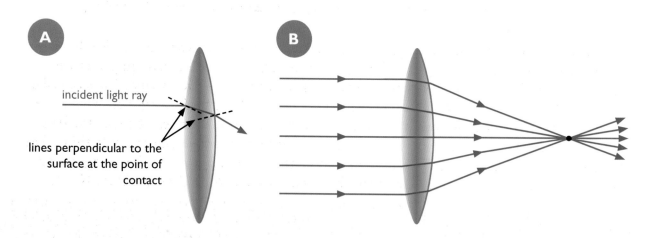

FIGURE 10.38
Light Refracting Through A Converging Lens
When light rays refract through a converging lens, they are focused to one spot.

If you were do this for several light rays traveling horizontally toward the object, you would have what is shown in Figure 10.38B. It turns out that a transparent object shaped like the ones in Figures 10.37 and 10.38 will always focus horizontally traveling light rays through a single point, called the focal point. We call such an object a converging lens, because it makes all horizontal light rays converge to a single point. You should know that the converging lens drawn in the figures above are drawn very wide to easily illustrate how the light ray refracts twice as it travels through the lens. Generally, converging lenses are much thinner than what is shown here.

If I change the situation a little bit, I get a completely different result. Suppose I have a glass object shaped like that in Figure 10.39. When light rays hit this object, refraction causes a completely different situation from what I got with the converging lens. This kind of lens, called a diverging lens, bends light rays outward, causing them to diverge away from one another. Once again, please realize that most diverging lenses are much thinner than what I have pictured here.

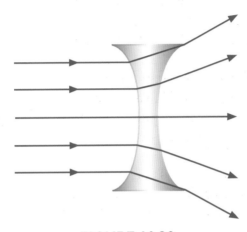

FIGURE 10.39
Light Refracting Through a Diverging Lens
When light rays refract through a diverging lens, they are spread away from each other or diverge.

Converging lenses and diverging lenses each have their applications. Notice the difference between converging and diverging lenses. The sides of a converging lens are curved outward. As a result, we say converging lenses have a convex shape. The sides of a diverging lens are curved inward. We call this a concave shape. This should tell you something. Lenses work because of their curvature. If the curvature changes, the way the lens works changes. In fact, the *type* of curvature (concave or convex) is not the only thing that affects the way a lens works. The *amount* of curvature also plays a role. Try to figure out how the amount of curvature plays a role by answering On Your Own problem 10.11.

ON YOUR OWN

10.11 Consider the two lenses pictured below. Which one focuses light rays closest to the lens?

a.   b.

The Human Eye

The most elegant application of a converging lens in all of God's creation can be seen in the eye. Examine Figure 10.40. In simple terms, the eye contains several different optical elements that all work together to produce vision. The eye is covered by a thin, transparent substance called the cornea. It protects the eye from abrasions and the like. It also participates in the focusing of light by refracting light that enters the eye. The iris is a cover that can open up wide or close down to just a small hole. This regulates how much light gets into the eye. The opening left by the iris is called the pupil. When you are in the presence of bright light, the iris closes down to allow only a small amount of light into the eye. This makes your pupil small. When there is little light, the iris opens wide, allowing a larger percentage of the light in. This makes your pupil look large. Once light enters the pupil, it is focused by

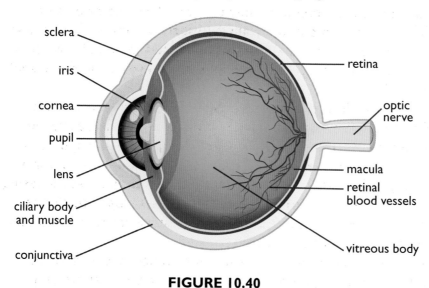

FIGURE 10.40
A Human Eye
Light is refracted through the converging lens and focuses the image on the retina.

a converging lens. The light is focused on the retina, which is made up of light-sensitive cells called rods and cones. When these cells sense light hitting them, they send electrical messages down the optic nerve to the brain, which decodes the messages and forms them into images.

Now here's the really neat thing about the way the eye handles light. Have you ever watched a photographer focus their camera? The focus works by moving a converging lens back and forth inside a tube. As the converging lens moves, the point at which the light rays converge moves. A photographer moves the lens of their camera back and forth until the light rays converge so as to put the image right on the film of the camera. That results in a sharp, in-focus image on the film. If the object moves in relation to the lens, the image will form someplace else. As a result, the lens must be moved again, in order to get the light rays to converge at the right place.

Just as a camera must focus images on its film in order to take a picture, your eye must focus images on its retina in order for you to see the image clearly. The retina has light-sensitive cells that receive light and send signals to the brain based on the nature of that light. This allows your brain to form the image you see. If you are to see an image clearly, then, it must be focused on your eye's retina. How does your eye focus the light to your retina?

Believe it or not, the eye *can actually change the shape of the lens* in order to keep the image in the same place, regardless of where the object is! This is accomplished with the ciliary (sil' ee air ee) muscle. It squeezes or expands the lens, which changes the lens' focal point. When the lens is squeezed down so that it is small and fat, the focal point is close to the lens.

Thus, when an object moves in relation to the eye, the ciliary muscle changes the shape of the lens, which in turn changes the focal point of the lens to compensate. This keep the image focused on the retina! This is an amazing feat of physics. To give you some idea of just how amazing this is, think about modern-day cameras. Technology has given us very sophisticated cameras. In fact, it is common now for even the cameras on smart-phones to have autofocus. The camera can automatically adjust the position of the lens so that the image stays in focus on the film. Even the most sophisticated camera, however, is still significantly slower in its autofocus capability as compared to the eye, and the image's focus is significantly less resolved.

Part of the reason for this is the difference between the way a camera focuses and the way your eye focuses. Remember, a camera focuses by moving the lens. The eye, on the other hand, changes the very shape of the lens in order to change how the light rays focus. Moving a lens in order to change where the light converges is not nearly as fast or as accurate as changing the shape of the lens. Unfortunately, cameras cannot use the faster, more accurate technique because *human science cannot make a lens as sophisticated as that which you find in the eye!* Thus, even the best that today's science has to offer cannot come close to mimicking the marvelous design of the eye.

Even the best of designs, however, can have problems. Sometimes, due to flaws in genetics or due to overuse under the wrong types of circumstances, an eye can develop myopia (nearsightedness) or hyperopia (farsightedness). These conditions develop when the eye's lens cannot be adjusted enough to make sure the image stays focused on the retina (Figure 10.41). For example, if you are nearsighted, your eye can use it ciliary muscle to change the lens enough to keep the image of objects close to you focused on the retina. However, as the object moves farther and farther away, the lens's focal point cannot be changed enough to keep the image there. As a result, the image gets blurry because the light is focused *in front of* the retina, *not on* the retina.

To compensate for this, corrective lenses are put

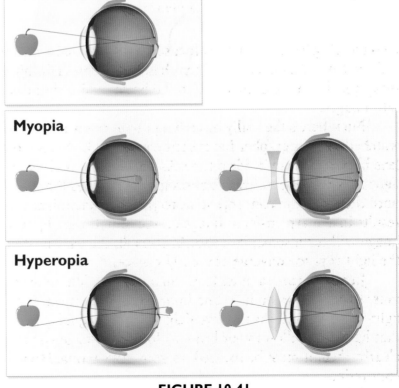

FIGURE 10.41
Myopia and Hyperopia
Lenses can correct nearsightedness and farsightedness.

in front of the eye. Because light is being refracted too strongly and thus focuses in front of the retina, diverging lenses are used. A diverging lens, such as the one shown in Figure 10.39, refracts light rays so that they diverge from on another. This compensates for the fact that the eye refracts light too strongly, and the result is an image that can be focused on the retina.

A similar situation happens when a person is farsighted. In this case, the eye's lens can adjust to objects far away, but it cannot focus on objects that are close. As a result, corrective lenses are used. As you might imagine, since nearsightedness is caused by the eye refracting light too strongly, farsightedness is caused by the eye refracting light too weakly. As a result, a converging lens must be used to correct farsightedness, as it helps refract the light in the right direction before the light hits the eye. This makes up for the fact that the eye cannot refract light strongly enough on its own.

How We Perceive Color

Another remarkable aspect of the eye is how it perceives color. To get an idea of how this marvelous process works, perform the following experiment.

EXPERIMENT 10.4
HOW THE EYE DETECTS COLOR

PURPOSE:
To explore an optical illusion to see how the eye perceives color.

MATERIALS:
- Two plain white sheets of paper (there shouldn't be any lines on them)
- A bright red marker (A crayon will also work, but a marker is better.)
- Timer or stopwatch

PROCEDURE:
1. Use the marker to draw a thick cross on one of the plain sheets of paper. The cross should be about 6 inches long, and the two legs that make it up should be about ¾ of an inch thick. Color the entire cross so that you have a large, solid bright red cross in the middle of a white sheet of paper.
2. Put the clean sheet of white paper underneath the sheet with the cross on it. Make sure the cross faces you so that you can see it.
3. Stare at the cross for a full 60 seconds.
4. After a full 60 seconds of staring at the cross, quickly pull the top sheet of paper out of the way so that you can only see the clean sheet of paper on the bottom.
5. Note what happened in your data table. There is a chance that you will see nothing. Most people, however, will see something rather dramatic.
6. Put everything away.

CONCLUSIONS:
In a paragraph, describe what you saw. After reading the following paragraphs, explain why you saw what you saw, making connections to the text.

ANSWERS TO THE "ON YOUR OWN" QUESTIONS

10.1   The vibration of an electric charge (like an electron) produces electromagnetic waves (EM). All EM waves have the same speed, but they differ in frequency and wavelength.

10.2   According to Table 10.1, light has a speed of 220,000,000 m/s in fresh water. Thus, when the photon hits the lake, it must slow down.

10.3   The greater the frequency of an EM wave, the more energy each of its photons has. This is shown in the photoelectric effect when unlike blue light, the frequency of red light is low, so the photons do not have enough energy to cause a metal to emit electrons.

10.4   You can remember the relative wavelengths of light with the acronym ROY G. BIV. Red has the longest wavelength, and violet has the shortest. With that knowledge then, we can say that for the colors given, red has the longest wavelength, yellow is next, followed by green. Indigo has the shortest wavelength. However, the question asked about frequency. The longer the wavelength, the lower the frequency. Thus, in terms of *increasing frequency* it is, red, yellow, green, indigo.

10.5   A radio station's antenna does not glow because the light it emits is not visible. Radio waves have wavelengths longer than visible light.

10.6   a.   Transparent materials (glass window, fishbowl, water) transmit light (allow light to pass through). Translucent materials (frosted glass) scatter light that passes through. Opaque materials (wood table, chair, desk, book, etc.) absorb or reflect all light. Note: the student could use other examples.

   b.   Light can be reflected (bounce off), it can be absorbed (enter but not exit), or it can be transmitted (pass through).

10.7   Each time the light is reflected, the angle it makes with the perpendicular must be the same before and after reflection. The drawing should look like:

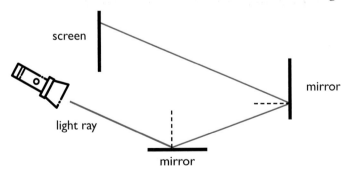

10.8   The refracted light ray bends away from the perpendicular when traveling from substance A to substance B. When light travels into a substance in which it moves more slowly, the light bends toward the perpendicular. When light travels into a substance in which it moves more quickly, the light bends away from the perpendicular. Thus, light travels more quickly in substance B than in substance A.

10.9　Because the light rays will be refracted away from the perpendicular when they leave the water, the light will bend. However, the man's brain will interpret the light as if it has been traveling straight (remember the reflection discussion). Thus, his eye will extend the light backwards, making the fish appear farther back (and shallower) than the fish truly is. This is what happened in the magic quarter activity. When you added water to the bowl, the quarter appeared. It looked like it was farther away from you than it was in reality. Thus, the man must aim in front of the fish he sees.

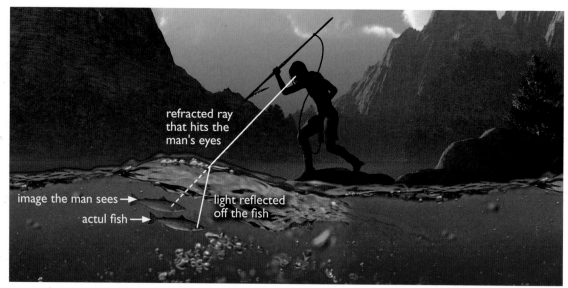

10.10　When unpolarized light passes through a horizontally polarizing filter, only horizontally polarized light (light waves vibrating in the horizontal plane) comes out the other side of the filter. All other light is blocked by the filter.

10.11　Lenses work because of their curvature. The more curvature they have, the more they will do their job. Thus, lens (b) will focus the light rays closest.

10.12　The mirror reflects all wavelengths that hit it. When the green hits it, it will reflect green. When the red hits it, it will reflect red. When both hit it, it will reflect both. When your eyes see both colors, your brain will add them to make yellow.

10.13　The red shirt is red because when light strike it, it absorbs all wavelengths except red. It does this by mixing yellow and magenta. The yellow absorbs all wavelengths except red and green, and the magenta absorbs all wavelengths except red and blue. Thus, red is the only wavelength reflected from the shirt. When the green light shines on it, the green light will be absorbed by the magenta. Nothing will be reflected back. Thus, the shirt will look black. In fact, it won't even look like a shirt. Without any light reflecting back from it, you will not even see the shirt!

STUDY GUIDE FOR MODULE 10

1.   Define the following terms.

    a. Electromagnetic wave

    b. Law of reflection

2.   Explain the wave theory of light, the particle theory of light, and the quantum-mechanical theory of light.

3.   Sound waves cause air to oscillate. What do light waves oscillate?

4.   What does Einstein's Theory of Special Relativity say about the speed of light?

5.   Light is traveling through water and suddenly breaks the surface and travels through air. Did light's speed increase, decrease, or stay the same once it left the water?

6.   Order the following colors in terms of increasing wavelength: orange, violet, yellow, green. In other words, list the color corresponding to the smallest wavelength first, and end with the color that corresponds to the longest wavelength.

7.   Order the colors in problem 6 in terms of increasing frequency. Once again, start with the lowest frequency and end with the highest frequency.

8.   Do radio waves have higher or lower frequencies than visible light? What about X-rays?

9.   Infrared light is given off by any object that is losing heat. The human body is almost always losing heat to the environment. Why, then, don't human bodies glow at night, since they are emitting light?

10. Light hits a mirror, making an angle of 15 degrees relative to a line drawn perpendicular to the mirror's surface. What angle does the reflected light make with the same line?

11. In the following diagram, will the man see his foot, despite the fact that the mirror does not reach the ground?

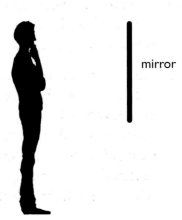

mirror

12.   When light travels from one substance to another, what two things can happen to the direction of the light ray's travel?

13.   In a physics experiment, a light ray is examined as it travels from air into glass. If the angle that the light ray makes with a line perpendicular to the glass surface is measured, will the refracted ray bend toward or away from that line?

14.   When you look at objects underwater from above the water, they appear to be at a different position. Why?

15.   A mountain climber finds that her sunglasses are not blocking glare from a vertical rock wall. What can you hypothesize about the polarizing filters in her sunglasses?

16.   Why does the sky look blue on sunny days?

17.   In order for you to see a rainbow, what three conditions must be met?

18.   What is the difference between a converging lens and a diverging lens?

19.   Which of the following lenses is a converging lens? Which is a diverging lens?

a.    b.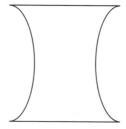

20.   What is special about the way the eye focuses light as compared to the way a camera focuses light?

21.   Suppose the cone cells on your retina that sense red light no longer work. If you look at a white piece of paper, what color would it appear to be? If you look at a red piece of paper, what color would it appear to be?

22.   A shirt is dyed so that it looks violet. What colors of light does the dye absorb?

23.   A cyan dye is made of a mixture of substances that absorb all light colors except blue and green. If you took a cyan piece of paper and placed it in a dark room and shined red light on it, what would you see? What would you see if you shined green light on it?

PHYSICS— ELECTRICITY AND MAGNETISM

Y ou've already learned a bit about the electro-magnetic force—one of the four fundamental forces. I'm sure you are at least somewhat familiar with this force. It is the force that makes electricity flow in an electrical circuit, holds electrons in an atom, and makes lightning. It is also the force that attracts the north pole of a magnet to the south pole of a magnet. This causes the compass needle to point north, refrigerator magnets to stick to the refrigerator, and electrical motors to turn. But did you know that at one time, physicists thought the force that governs electricity was completely different from the force that governs magnetism? After all, electricity and magnetism seem so different; how could they both be governed by the same force? We'll take a more in depth look at the electromagnetic force and how electricity and magnetism work.

Natural Notes

You probably don't think about electricity or magnetism much, but you use them every day. Electric and magnetic fields are everywhere. You already learned that each generates the other in electromagnetic waves. And together they make up the electromagnetic force, one of the four fundamental forces in creation. Now we'll look more closely at how electric fields can produce heat, light, chemical changes, and are even part of your body. Earth has a magnetic field that migrating birds, fish, bees, and some butterflies can sense. And beautiful auroras (northern lights) are produced, in part, because of electrical charges and magnetic fields.

MOD 11

FIGURE 11.1
Auroras
Energetic electrically charged electrons accelerate along magnetic field lines into the upper atmosphere, where they collide with gas atoms, causing the atoms to give off light.

IN THIS MODULE YOU WILL READ ABOUT THE FOLLOWING MAIN IDEAS:

- A Detailed Look at the Electromagnetic Force
- Electric Charge
- Electric Circuits
- Magnetism

A DETAILED LOOK AT THE ELECTROMAGNETIC FORCE

It took the genius of a Scottish physicist named James Clerk Maxwell to demonstrate that both electricity and magnetism are, in fact, different facets of the same force. When Maxwell demonstrated this fact, enormous advances were made in the study of electrical and magnetic phenomena in physics. As a result, many people refer to Maxwell as the founder of modern physics. He is often ranked with Albert Einstein and Sir Isaac Newton as one of the three most important figures in the history of science. Because of his importance, let's look at a brief biography.

James Clerk Maxwell

Born in a remote region of Scotland in 1831, Maxwell was home-educated until being accepted to Edinburgh University at the age of 16. The university offered him admission when a group of scientists there read a paper he had written about geometric curves when he was 14 years old. They were so impressed with it that they immediately accepted him as a student. When he came to the university, all the professors were amazed at his ability to design experiments that explained whatever interested him. He quickly outgrew the experimental facilities at Edinburgh University and transferred to Cambridge University in England to continue his studies.

FIGURE 11.2
James Clerk Maxwell
Scottish physicist best known for his formulation of the electromagnetism.

After graduating from Cambridge, he took a teaching post at King's College and met Michael Faraday, the inventor of the electrical generator and the electrical transformer. Although great with experiments, Faraday lacked the mathematical insight of Maxwell. Together, they made a great team. Maxwell put Faraday's theories on a firm mathematical foundation, and as a result, real advances were made in the study of electricity and magnetism.

When he was 42, he published a book titled *Treatise on Electricity and Magnetism.* In it, he used forty mathematical equations to show that electricity and magnetism were, indeed, governed by exactly the same force. As with most revolutionary works, it was not accepted right away. The later experiments of Heinrich Rudolph Hertz lent so much weight to Maxwell's work, however, that it eventually became the guiding force of electromagnetic study. With time, Maxwell's forty equations were reduced to only four, but they still bear the name "Maxwell's Equations." With two to four years of post-calculus mathematics, you can *begin* to understand Maxwell's Equations.

James Clerk Maxwell was also known for many other things. He provided the mathematical foundation for the kinetic theory of gases, which allows chemists and physicists to explain the behavior of a gas under almost any set of conditions. That theory was later expanded to apply to all matter. It is now called the "kinetic theory of matter," and you learned a bit about it in module 2. In addition, Maxwell was the first to explain how we see in color, which led him to be able to make the first color photograph in 1861. Maxwell also developed several advances in the field of thermodynamics (thur' moh dye nam' iks), which you will learn about in chemistry.

salt and light

Clearly, Maxwell is a genius of the caliber of Newton. Like Newton, he was also a devoted Christian. As was the case with Newton, Maxwell studied science as a means of serving Christ. Indeed, when Maxwell founded the Cavendish Laboratory at Cambridge University, he wanted to remind all scientists who entered that they should perform their duties with reverence to the Lord. As a result, Maxwell insisted that the Scripture verse, "Great are the works of the Lord; they are pondered by all who delight in them" (Psalm 111:2) be carved in Latin on the great door that leads into the laboratory. Science always needs people like James Clerk Maxwell!

The Electromagnetic Force

As I said before, everyone has some experience with the electromagnetic force. But in order to delve a little deeper, let's go over the basics. The best way to start is by having you perform an experiment.

EXPERIMENT 11.1
ELECTRICAL ATTRACTION AND REPULSION

PURPOSE:
To observe the electromagnetic force. Specifically to observe when electrically charged objects attract one another and when they repel one another.

MATERIALS:
- Two balloons (Round balloons work best, but any kind will do.)
- Thread
- Cellophane tape
- Eye protection such as goggles or safety glasses

QUESTION:
What happens when objects with like charges come near each other? What happens when objects with unlike charges come near each other?

HYPOTHESIS:
Write your predictions of what will happen when objects with like charges are brought together and when objects with unlike charges are brought close together.

PROCEDURE:

1. Blow up the balloons and tie them off so they each stay inflated.
2. Tie some thread to one of the balloons and attach the other end of the thread to the ceiling or the center of a door frame with some tape so that the balloon hangs from the thread. Make the length of the thread so that balloon one hangs at about the same height as your chest.
3. Take the balloon that is hanging by the thread and rub it in your hair a little. This will cause the balloon to pick up some electrical charge. Now back away from the balloon and allow it to hang there.
4. Take the other balloon and rub it in your hair just a little.
5. Hold this second balloon in both your hands and slowly bring it close to the balloon that is hanging from the thread. What happens?
6. Play with the situation a bit, trying to see what kind of motion you can induce in the hanging balloon. Record your observations in the data table.
7. Vigorously rub the balloon that is in your hands in your hair. Spend significantly more time doing it this time as compared to what you did in step 4.
8. Once again, bring the balloon in your hands close to the balloon that is hanging on the thread. Note what happens and note how the motion of the hanging balloon compares to its motion in steps 5 and 6.
9. Put away the balloon that is in your hands.
10. Take a piece of tape that is at least 15 cm long and tape it to the top of a table. Leave a little part of it unfastened, so that you can remove it in a moment. Be sure to ask your parents which table you should use for this, as what you will do in the next step can damage the finish on some tables.
11. Quickly rip the tape off the table and grasp it at both ends. Hold the tape near the hanging balloon, with the sticky side facing the balloon. What happens this time?
12. Once again, play with the situation a bit to see what kind of motion you can induce in the hanging balloon. Record your observations.
13. Clean up and put everything away.

CONCLUSIONS:

Write a paragraph explaining your observations. Read the paragraphs below and then tie your observations into what you learned in the text.

Why did the hanging balloon behave the way it did in the experiment? Well, when you rub a balloon in your hair, it picks up some stray electrons in your hair. This causes the balloon to pick up an overall negative charge. Since you rubbed both the hanging balloon and the balloon in your hand in your hair, both of them developed a negative charge. When you brought one close to the other, they began to repel each other, because charges that have the same sign repel each other. The closer the balloons got together, the greater the repulsion. Also, when you rubbed the balloon in your hand more vigorously in your hair, it picked up more negative charge, which also increased the repulsion. This brings me to the first rule of electrical charge:

Charging by Friction

When you rubbed the balloon in your hair in Experiment 11.1, you charged the balloon by friction. The electrons in your hair were transferred to the balloon as you rubbed it against your hair, because atoms in the latex rubber have a greater attraction for electrons than atoms in hair. Thus, the balloon picks up a negative charge and your hair becomes positively charged. This type of charging by friction can happen just by walking across a carpet in your socks on a dry day. If you've ever been shocked by touching a door handle after walking across the carpet, then you've been charged by friction. Jumping on a trampoline in your socks on a dry day can make your hair stand on end because of frictional charging (Figure 11.8).

FIGURE 11.8
Charge by Friction
Jumping on a trampoline on a dry day can cause your hair to lose electrons and become positively charged!

Charging by friction—Charging an object by rubbing two items together where one transfers electrons to the other

Charging by Conduction

When you charge something by touching it to an electrically charged object and allowing the charge to flow between them, physicists say that you are charging by conduction. This is also known as charging by contact.

Charging by conduction—Charging an object by allowing it to come into contact with an object that already has an electrical charge

FIGURE 11.9
Charge by Conduction
By touching the Van de Graaff generator, charge is transferred from the sphere to the girl. Her hairs repel each other because like charges repel.

In other words, by allowing electrons to be conducted between the object you are charging and the object that already has a charge, you are charging by conduction.

The Van de Graaff generator pictured in Figure 11.9 uses a moving belt to remove electrons and accumulate a positive charge on the metal sphere. When the girl touches the sphere, she acquires a positive charge large enough to make her hairs repel each other. The sphere is still charged, but because some of the charge has transferred to the girl, the net charge on the sphere is reduced while the net charge on the girl is increased by the same amount.

Charging by Induction

Think about a time that you were shocked when you touched a metal doorknob. First, you picked up extra electrons by friction when your feet moved over the carpet and so your hand became negatively charged. When your hand comes near (but does not yet touch) the doorknob, the net negative charge of your hand repels the electrons in the doorknob. Look at Figure 11.10. Notice that the electrons in the doorknob move to the base of the door-knob, leaving a net positive charge on the part of the doorknob closest to your hand. Count the charges on the doorknob. It is still neutral, but the charge has rearranged within it. If you were able to separate the base of the doorknob from the handle at this point, the handle would have a positive charge. This is charging by induction.

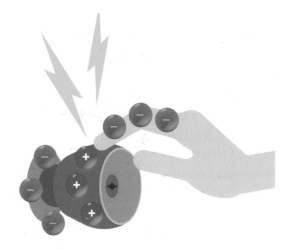

FIGURE 11.10
Charge by Induction
Induction occurs when the charges within a neutral object rearrange themselves as a charged object is brought near but not touching.

Charging by induction—Charging an object without direct contact between the object and a charge

think about this

Why do you get a shock from the doorknob? Well, when the gap between your negatively charged hand and the doorknob is small, the air between them suddenly becomes charged. This charged air, then, provides a path for the electrons on your hand to flow to the doorknob. This is called a **static discharge.** A static discharge can appear as if it jumps from your hand to the doorknob. In fact, if the room is dark, sometimes you can even see the spark.

To better understand charging objects, complete Experiment 11.2.

EXPERIMENT 11.2
MAKING AND USING AN ELECTROSCOPE

PURPOSE:
To gain practice in building a device that detects the presence of electrical charge and to observe the basic methods used to charge an object.

MATERIALS:
- Tape
- A clear glass
- A plastic lid that fits over the glass. This lid can be larger than the mouth of the glass, but it cannot be smaller. The top of a margarine tub or something similar works quite well.
- A paperclip

- Two 5 cm × 1.5 cm strips of aluminum foil (the thinner the better—do not fold the foil, rather cut it to this size)
- A balloon
- A pair of pliers
- Eye protection such as goggles or safety glasses

PROCEDURE:

1. Using your hands and the pliers, straighten out and then bend the paper clip so that it ends up looking something like what is shown in Figure 11.11A.
2. Cut a thin slot in the plastic lid. Slide the loop of the twisted paper clip into the slot, then twist it 90 degrees so that the slot holds the loop in place. The loop should stand perpendicular to the lid. You may need to use some tape to hold it in this position (see Figure 11.11B).
3. Poke a hole near one end of each strip of foil and hang the foil strips on the tiny hooks that are at the bottom of the twisted paper clip.
4. Place the lid on top of the glass, so that the foil strips hang on the inside of the glass. You have just made an electroscope (ih lek' truh skohp). It should look something like what you see in Figure 11.11B.

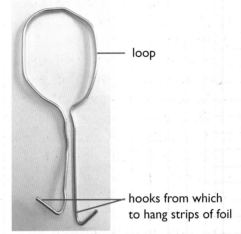

loop

hooks from which to hang strips of foil

FIGURE 11.11A

plastic lid

loop on the twisted paper clip

glass

foil strips

FIGURE 11.11B

5. What does an electroscope do? An electroscope detects the presence of electrical charge. To see this, inflate the balloon and tie it off so that it stays inflated.
6. Rub the balloon in your hair to charge it.
7. Slowly bring the balloon close to the loop of the twisted paper clip without actually touching it. The foil strips should start to move. If they do not, your balloon is probably not charged well. Rub it more vigorously in your hair or rub it in someone else's hair.
8. Note how the foil strips move as you bring the balloon closer to the loop. Don't actually touch the loop with the balloon! Record your observations.
9. Pull the balloon away from the loop and note how the foil strips move. Do steps 8 and 9 a couple of times so that you can describe the motion of the foil strips well. Record your observations.

10. Bring the balloon near the loop one more time. This time, however, allow the balloon to touch the paper clip. Record what happens to the foil strips.

11. Pull the balloon away. This time, the behavior of the foil strips should be noticeably different from what it was in step 9. Record the difference.

12. I want you to do one more thing. These next few steps might be a little tricky. Touch the loop with your finger. You should notice that the foil strips respond to your touch. Record what they do.

13. Take your finger away from the loop.

14. Bring the balloon close to the loop, but do not touch it with the balloon. When you see the foil strips move significantly, hold the balloon where it is and touch the paper clip with a finger from your other hand. As soon as your finger touches the paper clip, the foil strips should move again. Keep your finger resting on the paper clip for a moment.

15. Pull your finger away so that it is no longer touching the paper clip.

16. Now pull the balloon away. The foil strips should move yet again and behave similarly to what you saw in step 11. This doesn't always work the first time, so try it a few times until it eventually works. Record your observations.

17. Clean up and put everything away in its proper place.

CONCLUSION:

Write a paragraph describing what you observed and explaining what happened in terms of how the charges were transferred. Make connections to the text.

What happened in the experiment? The foil and the paper clip, like all forms of matter, have both positive and negative charges in them. We know that the number of positive charges and negative charges are equal, so the foil and paper clip have no overall charge. However the balloon picked up some electrons by friction when you rubbed it in your hair, so the balloon had more negative charges than positive ones, giving it an overall negative charge. When you brought it in close proximity to the paper clip, the balloon induced the electrons in the paper clip to move. The negative charge of the balloon repelled the negatively charged electrons in the paper clip and the foil. Since they were repelled, they traveled away from the balloon, which caused the ends of the foil to be rich with electrons. At the same time, since electrons moved away from the atoms in the paper clip, those atoms lost electrons and therefore became temporarily positively charged. In the end, then, the foil strips developed a temporary overall negative charge, and the paper clip developed a temporary overall positive charge, as shown in Figure 11.12.

FIGURE 11.12
First Part of Experiment 11.2
When the negatively charged balloon was brought near the paper clip, a temporary negative charge was induced when electrons in the paper clip were repelled and traveled away from the clip to the foil. The excess negative charges in the foil made the strips repel each other.

If you did not touch the balloon to the paper clip, as soon as you pulled the balloon away, the foil strips should have relaxed back to their normal position. That's because once the negatively charged balloon moved away, the electrons that were crammed together in the foil were no longer repelled by anything. The paper clip had an overall positive charge, however, and this positive charge attracted electrons back to the paper clip. This made everything neutral again. When that happened, the foil strips hung down normally again.

What happened in the next part of the experiment? When you touched the balloon to the paper clip, the foil strips moved apart again and, after you removed the balloon, they stayed apart. This is because when you actually touched the balloon to the paper clip, some of the balloon's extra electrons were able to flow into the paper clip and into the foil strips by *conduction*. This gave the paper clip and foil strips a bunch of extra electrons. When you pulled the balloon away, those extra electrons stayed. This caused a permanent negative charge to develop on the foil strips. Since the foil strips stayed negatively charged, they still repelled each other. Thus, they stayed away from each other. You ended up getting rid of the charge by touching the paper clip with your finger. When you did that, the extra electrons flowed into your body. This got rid of the negative charge on the foil strips, and the strips relaxed.

FIGURE 11.13
Charging by Induction
A temporary charge is induced when the negatively charged balloon is brought near but not touching the paper clip. When you touch the paper clip, electrons travel through your hand leaving the foil and paper clip. The foil and paper clip now have a positive charge caused by induction.

In the last part of the experiment (illustrated in Figure 11.13), you also ended up charging the foil strips. In that case, when the balloon was moved near the paper clip, the electrons in the paper clip and foil moved away from the balloon, concentrating negative charge in the foil strips, causing the strips to repel each other. When you touched your finger to the paper clip, however, the electrons could travel farther away from the balloon by traveling through your finger and into your body. Thus, you actually removed some of the electrons from the foil and paper clip. When you moved your finger and then the balloon away, the paper clip and foil were left with fewer electrons than they should have had, because some of those electrons stayed in your hand. This gave the foil strips and the paper clip an overall positive charge. Since the strips were both positively charged, they repelled each other, and they moved away from each other again.

When you performed the experiment in this way, you induced the negative charges to leave the foil by giving them an escape route: your hand. This caused the foil strips to become positively charged when you took your hand and the balloon away. Thus, you caused the foil to have a positive charge by *induction*. Answer On Your Own problem 11.4.

ON YOUR OWN

11.4   If you want to give an object a positive charge, but the only source of charge you have is negative, would you charge the object by conduction or induction?

ELECTRICAL CIRCUITS

One of the most useful aspects of the force that exists between charged particles is that you can use it to make electrical circuits. In an electrical circuit, charges flow through a wire. The energy those charges have can be used by electrical devices, and the result is something useful. For example, when a light bulb is hooked up to an electrical circuit, the bulb glows. In order to understand how this works, you need to understand two things: how the charges begin moving in the first place, and how the energy of the moving charges is used by the light bulb. We'll start with the former concept and end with the latter.

FIGURE 11.14
Batteries
Batteries contain chemicals on the positive side that will lose electrons and chemicals on the negative side that gain electrons.

In order to get electrical charges moving, you need something that uses the electromagnetic force. One device that does this is a battery. A battery stores electrical charge. The description of how a battery does this is a bit too difficult to explain here, but you will learn about it in chemistry. For right now, just realize that one side of the battery contains chemicals that want to lose electrons, while the other side contains chemicals that want to gain electrons. As a result, one side of the battery is a source of electrons, so it is considered negative. The other is the place where the electrons want to go, so it is considered positive. When the two sides of a battery are hooked together with a metal, electrons will flow through the metal from the negative side of the battery to the positive side. So a battery is a device that converts chemical energy to electrical energy.

Voltage

As you no doubt already know, a battery is rated by its voltage. Most cylindrical batteries are rated at 1.5 volts, while the small, rectangular batteries with electrical posts at the top are typically 9 volts. But what does voltage mean? It tells you how hard the battery "pushes" electrons through an electrical circuit. The higher the voltage, the harder the battery "pushes" electrons through the metal.

Now remember why we want the electrons to travel from one end of the battery to the other. We want to use their energy to do work. Thus, the more voltage the battery has, the more energy the electrons have, and the more we can do with them. If you think about it, however, the voltage of a battery is not the only factor that determines how much gets done in an electrical circuit. Not only does the energy of each electron influence what gets done, but so does the *number* of electrons that travel through the circuit. After all, when ten electrons travel through an electrical circuit, ten times more work will get done than when only one electron travels through the circuit. Thus, not only the voltage of the battery, but also the number of charged particles flowing through the circuit will determine what the circuit can do.

Electric Current

The number of electrons that flow through a circuit in a given amount of time can be determined by examining the electrical current in a circuit.

> **Electrical current**—The amount of charge that travels past a fixed point in an electric circuit each second

Electrical current is usually measured in Amperes, which are abbreviated as "amps" or "A." When you look at an electrical circuit, then, you need to know both the current (amps) and the voltage (volts) of the circuit. They each work together to tell you how much an electrical circuit can do.

For example, if you are playing with an electrical toy that works on a 9 volt battery (Figure 11.15) and accidentally touch a bare wire while the toy is running, you might get shocked, but you won't be seriously hurt. That's because both the voltage and the current running through the toy's electrical circuit is low. On the other hand, if you were unfortunate enough to touch the bare wire of a fan that is plugged into a wall socket and running, you would almost certainly be seriously hurt, because the voltage and current running through that circuit are quite high.

It is important to realize that *only one* of these two quantities needs to be large for an electrical circuit to pack a good punch. The voltage in your car's battery is probably 12 volts. That's not much more than the 9 volt battery that runs an electrical toy. There are several hundred amps of current that flow through the ignition circuit when the car is being started, however. That's about a million times more current than what's flowing through the circuit of an electrical toy! Thus, even though the voltage of a car's electrical circuit is low, the current is high, and the circuit can therefore provide a lot of energy. As a result, touching an exposed battery cable in a car that is being started can be

FIGURE 11.15
9 volt Battery
You won't get seriously hurt if you touch both sides of a 9 volt battery.

very dangerous! This should make perfect sense. After all, the voltage simply tells you the energy of the electrons in the circuit. Thus, if the energy per electron is really large, just a few electrons can pack a lot of energy. As a result, a circuit with low current but high voltage can be harmful. In the same way, if the voltage is low, the circuit could still have a lot of energy just by having an enormous number of electrons flowing through it. In that case, voltage would be low, but current would be high. Such a combination is still harmful.

Now that you know about voltage and current, it is time to learn about electrical circuits. Suppose I take two metal wires and connect one side each side to a battery and the other side of each wire to a small light bulb. The result might look something like Figure 11.16.

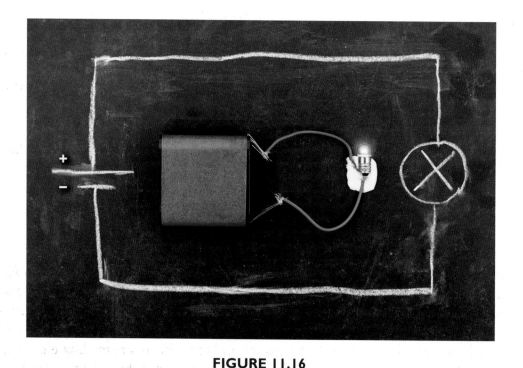

FIGURE 11.16
A Simple Circuit
One wire connects the negative side of a battery to a lamp. The other wire connects the positive side of a battery to a lamp to make a simple circuit.

This is a very basic electrical circuit. Electrons will flow through the wire from the negative side of the battery through the lamp to the positive side. The electrons flowing through the lamp cause it to light up. Notice the chalk drawing around the circuit. This is how physicists draw circuits. They have developed symbols to represent the major components of an electrical circuit. A battery is symbolized with two parallel lines, one longer than the other. The positive side of the battery is usually represented by the longer line. The lamp is symbolized by the circle with an X in it. Figure 11.17 shows you the electronic circuit symbols. You will not need to know all of these, but I thought you might like to see them. You will become more familiar with many of them when you take physics in high school.

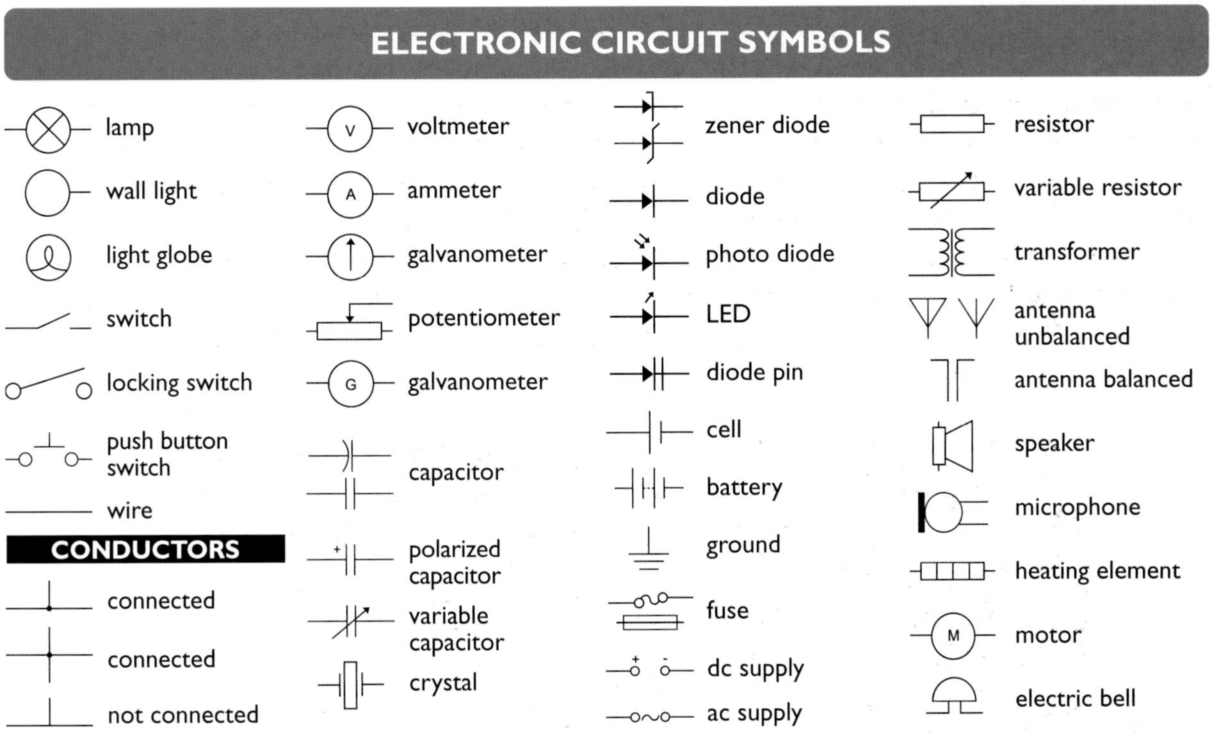

ELECTRONIC CIRCUIT SYMBOLS

lamp	voltmeter	zener diode	resistor
wall light	ammeter	diode	variable resistor
light globe	galvanometer	photo diode	transformer
switch	potentiometer	LED	antenna unbalanced
locking switch	galvanometer	diode pin	antenna balanced
push button switch	capacitor	cell	speaker
wire		battery	microphone
CONDUCTORS	polarized capacitor	ground	heating element
connected	variable capacitor	fuse	motor
connected	crystal	dc supply	electric bell
not connected		ac supply	

FIGURE 11.17
Circuit Symbols
Physicists have developed symbols for circuit components.

How Current Flows

The first thing you need to be able to do when you look at a circuit like the one in Figure 11.16 is determine how the current flows. Unfortunately, Benjamin Franklin caused a great deal of confusion over this very point. Although he is best remembered for his political endeavors as one of the United States' Founding Fathers, Franklin was actually one of the most respected scientists in his time. His theories and experiments regarding electricity were known and admired the world over. Many of his ideas laid the groundwork for our modern theories of electricity.

You see, batteries were invented long before anyone really understood electricity. As a result, scientists attempted to learn about electricity by studying batteries and the electricity they produced. In Franklin's studies, he theorized that batteries had a positive and a negative side, and that electricity was composed of particles that flowed from one side of a battery to the other. These ideas were readily accepted and highly regarded by scientists around the world.

Now, although Franklin's concept of positive and negative sides of a battery helped revolutionize the way scientists studied electricity, it also caused a bit of confusion. You see, Franklin thought that the positive side of a battery had too many of these mysterious particles and the negative side had too few. Thus, he said that electricity must flow through a circuit from the positive side of the battery to the negative side. Since his ideas were highly regarded, this idea was accepted the world over. Scientists everywhere began drawing electrical circuits assuming that the electricity flowed from the positive side of the battery, through the circuit, and back to the negative side.

As is usually the case with technology, people began finding uses for electricity long before science had figured out electricity. Thus, engineers began designing electrical circuits, and they, too, drew the circuits assuming that electricity flowed from the positive side of the battery to the negative side. As time went on, however, science slowly showed the error of this assumption. The electron was discovered, and it was determined that electricity is actually the flow of electrons. Thus, in reality, electricity flows from the negative side of the battery (the source of electrons) to the positive side of the battery (where the electrons go).

This conclusion, however, contradicted thousands of circuit drawings that had been made over the years. Engineers had always drawn current as flowing from the positive side of the battery to the negative side. They didn't want to stop doing it just because science had shown that the reverse was true. As a result, people just kept on drawing electrical current as starting from the positive side of the battery and flowing to the negative side, even though they knew it was wrong.

Illustrating the current as flowing from positive to negative came to be known as conventional current, and it is still the way circuits are drawn today.

> **Conventional current**—Current that flows from the positive side of the battery to the negative side; this is the way current is drawn in circuit diagrams, even though it is wrong

The point to this long, drawn-out discussion is that Benjamin Franklin's inaccurate assumption regarding how current flows forces us to draw current in an electric circuit as flowing from the positive side of the battery to the negative side. Even though we know this is not what happens physically, we do it so as not to break with tradition. Thus, in our original circuit diagram, the current can be pictured as shown in Figure 11.18. In this diagram, the red line shows the path of the current in the wire. Of course, even though the red line is not drawn right on top of the lines representing the wire, it is still understood that the current is actually flowing in the wire, not where the red line is drawn. Review what you've learned by completing On Your Own problem 11.5.

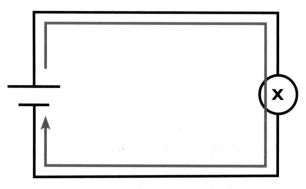

FIGURE 11.18
Conventional Current
Even though current flows from the negative side of a battery to the positive side, conventional current is shown flowing from positive to negative.

ON YOUR OWN

11.5 For the following circuit diagram, draw the current flow with a dashed line. Then draw the actual flow of electrons with a solid line.

Conductors and Insulators

Have you wondered why metal wire is usually coated with plastic or rubber? You already learned that metals are good conductors of electricity. Remember that metals make positive ions easily by giving up electrons. It turns out that metal ions form a type of lattice structure where their loosely bound valence electrons can easily move back and forth (Figure 11.19). This is why electrical conductors are materials through which electrons can easily flow. The plastic or rubber coating are electrical insulators. Electrical insulators are materials in which electrons *cannot* easily flow. The coating around the wire helps to keep the metal's valence electrons where they need to be. The coating also protects you from getting a shock when working with a circuit.

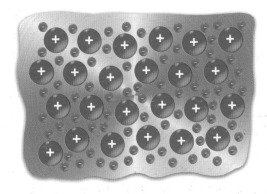

FIGURE 11.19
Metal Lattice
In a metal, cations (red) are surrounded by loosely bound shared valence electrons (blue). This makes them good conductors.

Resistance

Now that you know how to get electrons moving (by using an energy source such as a battery) and that metal wires are good conductors of moving electrons; you might be wondering what actually happens to those electrons as they move through the wire? And how can we use the energy in the electrons to do work (something useful)?

Well, once you get electrons moving using an energy source, the electrons move through the conducting wire (Figure 11.20). As they move they collide into other electrons and the ions in the wire. Remember that energy of movement is kinetic energy, so the moving electrons have kinetic energy. As they collide, some of the kinetic energy is converted into thermal energy (which can be used to do work, such as cooking). However, now that some of the kinetic energy has been converted, there is less energy available to move electrons through the wire which means the current will be reduced. This is called resistance.

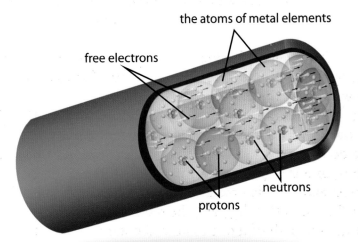

FIGURE 11.20
Current and Resistance
Electric current is the flow of electrons. In electric circuits this charge is carried by moving electrons in a wire. Collisions with other electrons and ions reduce kinetic energy and cause resistance.

Resistance—A material's ability to impede the flow of charge

MOD 11

Try this simple experiment to see what I mean.

EXPERIMENT 11.3
CURRENT AND RESISTANCE

PURPOSE:
To investigate properties of current and resistance.

MATERIALS:
- A 1.5 volt battery (Any AA-, C-, or D-cell battery will work. Do not use any battery other than one of those, though, because a higher voltage can make the experiment dangerous.)
- Aluminum foil
- Scissors
- Eye protection such as goggles or safety glasses
- Gloves (optional)

QUESTION:
What will you feel when aluminum foil connects both ends of a battery?

HYPOTHESIS:
Write your prediction of what you will feel when you touch aluminum foil connecting the positive and negative ends of a battery.

PROCEDURE:
1. Cut a small strip of aluminum foil about 1.3 times the length of the battery and only about 1 cm wide.
2. Lay the foil across the battery and, using your thumb and forefinger, pinch the foil so that it contacts both ends of the battery, as shown in Figure 11.21.
3. Hold the foil there for a few moments. Note what you feel. **Do not hold the foil for too long, as it can get painful!** Record your observations.
4. Clean up and put all of your materials safely away.

FIGURE 11.21

CONCLUSION
Was your prediction correct? In a paragraph, describe what you felt and then explain why, making connections to the text.

NOTE OF CAUTION

Before you go on, I want to caution you. You could touch the aluminum foil only because both the voltage *and* the current would be too low to cause you serious harm. Do not do this in any other situation! Since you still have a lot to learn about electricity, you will not know what is safe and what is not. Playing with electricity is dangerous. Don't do *anything* else with electricity; please keep safe by only letting professionals and experts work with electricity.

The heat you felt in the experiment comes from the electrons moving in the foil. As soon as you touched the aluminum foil to both ends of the battery, electrons flowed through the aluminum from the negative side of the battery to the positive side. The electrons accelerated under the electromagnetic force of the battery and, as a result, started moving quickly. Now, as electrons flowed through the aluminum, they began colliding with the electrons in some of the aluminum atoms. They also collided with impurities in the metal. These collisions produced heat, and you felt that heat in your fingers. So the heat you felt in the experiment was a result of the aluminum *resisting* the flow of electrons. Each metal resists electron flow differently, therefore each metal has its own resistance.

It turns out that the type of metal is not the only thing that determines resistance. The resistance of a wide piece of metal, for example, is lower than the resistance of a narrow piece made out of the same metal. Think about it this way, which straw would be easier to drink a milkshake through, a thin straw or a thick, wide straw? It is easier to drink a milkshake through a wide straw. In the same way, a thick wire allows the electrons that move through the metal to "spread out" as they move through, reducing congestion and thus the number of collisions.

Two other things, besides thickness, affect resistance. As you might expect, the longer the metal wire, the larger the resistance. After all, the longer the metal, the more chance the electrons have to collide with things in the metal. Finally temperature will affect resistance. As the temperature of the wire increases, more electrons can collide more often. Because electron collisions increase, resistance increases too.

With the knowledge of current, electrical circuits, and resistance that you now have, let's look at how the simplest electrical devices work. For example, consider an electrical heater. This could be a space heater used to warm up a room, a coil on an electric stove, or even the wires on the inside of a toaster. When such a device is turned on, the heater begins to glow, emitting a large amount of heat. This works because the material used to make the heater has a certain amount of electrical resistance. Since there is resistance, there is heat and often light. The light causes the heater to glow, and the heat energy warms the room, cooks the food, or browns the bread.

FIGURE 11.22
A Stovetop Burner
As electrons flow through the coil on this burner, the resistance of the metal produces heat and light.

One way we get electrons to do something useful in an electrical circuit, then, is to use a metal's resistance to convert the kinetic energy of the electrons speeding through the circuit into thermal (heat) and light energy. The type of metal used to do this will influence the effect you get. For example, most metals will resist the flow of electrons in such a way as to produce mostly heat and only a small amount of light. Those metals are used in heaters, stoves, and toasters. Other metals tend to produce more light than heat. Those metals are typically used in the filaments of light bulbs.

It is important that you really see what's going on in an electrical circuit. Most people think that electrical devices "use up" electrons. Thus, you plug your appliance in, and it "eats up" the electricity it pulls from the electrical socket. That's not what happens. The same number of electrons flow out of a toaster as the number that flowed into it. What the toaster does use up, however, is energy. As electrons flow through a circuit, the collisions they experience convert the energy produced by the electromagnetic force into heat. Answer On Your Own question 11.6.

ON YOUR OWN

11.6 When we work with most circuits, we assume that the resistance of the wire in the circuit is zero. Thus, the only resistance we consider is that of the device (or devices) in the circuit. Suppose a wire was made of aluminum. Would it have zero resistance? How do you know? Hint: Think about Experiment 11.3.

Switches and Circuits

With the tools you have learned so far, you can look at a simple circuit and determine in which direction the current flows. So let me ask you a question: In what direction does the current flow in the circuit in Figure 11.23? You should realize that I just asked you a trick question. No current flows in the circuit in Figure 11.23. Why? Remember, in order to have electricity, electrons must travel from one place to another. In the circuits we have discussed so far, they flow from one end of the battery to the other. The reason they do this is because there is metal linking the two sides of the battery.

In the circuit drawn in Figure 11.23, the metal does not link the two sides of the battery, because there is a break in the wire. Thus, electrons cannot flow from one side of the battery to the other, because they cannot jump over the "gap" in the wire. As a result, there is no current in the circuit. Physicists call circuits such as the one drawn on the right open circuits. An open circuit is shown in Figure 11.24 using a switch.

FIGURE 11.23

Open circuit—A circuit that does not have a complete connection between the two sides of the power source; as a result, current does not flow

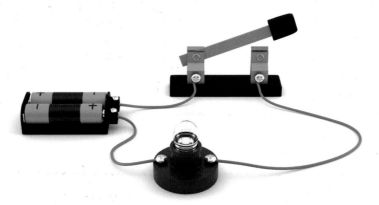

FIGURE 11.24
An Open Circuit
Electrons are unable to flow through the circuit when there is a break in the circuit, as with a switch.

could be produced is through resistance. Thus, the aluminum foil had resistance. in fact, *all wires (under normal conditions) have resistance*. Nevertheless, we typically ignore the resistance of a wire in an electric circuit, because compared to the devices in the circuit, the resistance of the wire is very small.

11.7   Since modern Christmas tree lights can continue to work even after a few bulbs are burnt out, modern Christmas tree lights are wired in parallel. Since the old ones would cease to work when one burnt out, old Christmas tree lights were wired in series. This was a real problem, because if one light bulb burnt out, you would have to go through the string and replace each bulb one at a time to figure out which one didn't work.

11.8   You could not make a magnet that way. The one wire will certainly cause a magnetic field, as will the other. However, since the currents are opposite of each other, the magnetic forces generated will be opposite as well. Thus, they will cancel each other out, resulting in no net magnetic force.

11.9   The difference is the number of atoms or domains aligned in each magnet. Remember, the larger the number of aligned domains, the stronger the magnet. Since the magnets are identical in size, shape, mass, and composition, magnet 2 must have more domains aligned than magnet 1.

11.10   Remember, the electrical and magnetic forces are really different aspects of the same force. Thus, their properties are the same. Notice that the only real difference between this picture and Figure 11.34 is that we have a positive and negative charge instead of a north and south pole. Since magnetic and electric forces are really the same, however, the resulting field lines should be essentially the same.

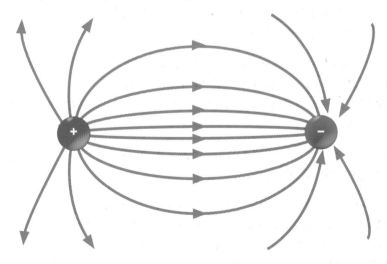

MOD 11

STUDY GUIDE FOR MODULE 11

1. Define the following terms.

    a. Photon

    b. Charging by conduction

    c. Charging by induction

    d. Electrical current

    e. Conventional current

    f. Resistance

    g. Open circuit

2. For the following situations, use a solid arrow to draw the force exerted by the circle with the solid line. Use a dashed arrow to draw the force exerted by the circle with a dashed line.

    a.   b.

3. The force between the south pole of a magnet and the north pole of another magnet is measured. If the distance between the poles is increased by a factor of 3, how does the new force compare to the old one? Is the force attractive or repulsive?

4. Two charged particles are placed 10 centimeters from each other and the resulting force is measured. The charge on object 1 is then doubled and the charge on object 2 is left the same. Also, the distance between the objects is reduced to 5 centimeters. How does the new force compare to the old force?

5. What causes the electromagnetic force?

6. Given your answer to question 5, why don't charged particles glow?

7. If you were to use a positively charged rod to charge an object by induction, what charge will the object have?

8. If you were to use a positively charged rod to charge an object by conduction, what charge will the object have?

9.   An electrical circuit uses a large voltage but a small current. Is the energy of each electron high or low? Are there many electrons flowing through the circuit, or are there few? Is the circuit dangerous?

10.   Under what conditions is an electrical circuit reasonably safe?

11.   Draw the conventional current flow in the following circuit:

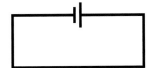

12.   What is wrong with conventional current?

13.   You have two wires. One is long and the other is short. Other than that, they are identical. Which has more resistance?

14.   You have two wires. One is thin, and the other is very thick. When the same current is run through each wire, which will get hotter?

15.   In which circuit will the light bulb glow?

a.

b.

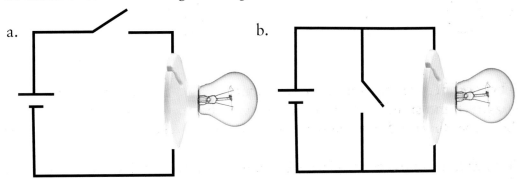

16.   Three lights are in a circuit. When one burns out, they all go out. When the burnt-out one is replaced with a good light, the other two lights work again. Are the lights wired in a parallel circuit or a series circuit?

17.   If it takes a flow of charged particles to make a magnet, where is the charged particle flow in a permanent magnet?

18.   Is it possible to have a permanent magnet with only a north pole?

19.   Is it possible to make a magnet from something that is not a magnet?

20.   If a material does not respond to a magnet, what can you conclude about the atoms in that material?

EARTH SCIENCE— OUR EARTH

You have probably learned a bit about Earth in previous science courses. That's good, because we're going to pay particular attention to how chemistry and physics help geologists (scientists who study planet Earth) understand our planet. Geology is the study of planet Earth, including its physical structure, its composition, its history, and the processes that act on it. Geochemists study the composition, structure, processes, and other physical aspects of the Earth. Geophysicists study the Earth using gravity, magnetic, electrical, and sound methods. In this chapter we will review Earth's structure and composition. We will also look a little more closely at the chemical and physical processes that go on. We'll look at the surface of Earth and consider how matter, such as rocks and water, moves through cycles. And we'll learn about how forces can change Earth's surface. The goal is to gain a better understanding of how our beautiful planet works.

Natural Notes

The study of Earth science involves multiple branches of science. Earth science combines geology, chemistry, physics, and biology. From its core to its atmosphere, Earth is a complex system of interconnected processes that involve the exchange of matter and energy between layers. We've spent the last 11 modules learning the basics of chemistry and physics. In the next two modules, we'll look at some of the chemical and physical processes that occur on our home, the Earth. It's important to understand how these processes work so that we can be responsible stewards of the majestic world God created.

How great are your works, Lord, how profound your thoughts!
Psalm 92:5 (NIV)

FIGURE 12.1
Earth
Many chemical and physical processes occur on our planet every second!

IN THIS MODULE YOU WILL READ ABOUT THE FOLLOWING MAIN IDEAS:

- Earth's Structure
- Rocks and Minerals
- Processes of the Lithosphere

EARTH'S STRUCTURE

You might find it interesting to know that scientists understand more about microscopic cells and the composition of distant stars than they do about the structure of the Earth beneath them. Think about that. We have instruments, such as microscopes and telescopes, that allow us to see things we cannot normally see. But we do not yet have an instrument that allows us to see into the layers of the Earth. Why? Remember from module 10 that we see through things when light is transmitted through them. Well, light does not travel through rocks (at least not most of them).

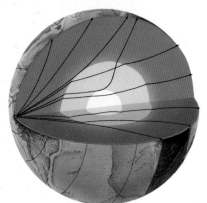

FIGURE 12.2
Seismic Waves
Artwork showing the movement of seismic waves through the Earth.

However, remember from module 9 that scientists have been able to use sound waves to "see" deep into the Earth. Seismic (size' mik) waves from earthquakes vibrate through the Earth in a similar way that longitudinal sound waves travel. These seismic waves travel through the Earth and reach the surface where vibration detectors, called seismographs (size' muh grafs), can be used to analyze the vibrations. By analyzing the vibrations at different points on Earth's surface, scientists can determine the speed at which the seismic waves traveled, how much energy they lost as they traveled, and how their courses changed in different parts of the Earth. You might also remember that sound travels faster through solids than liquids, so scientists can use this information to determine what type of material the wave passed through. In this way, scientists are able to "map" the interior and learn about the composition of the Earth (Figure 12.2).

Scientists have also been able to drill into the Earth to about 13 km (8 mi) using large drilling machines. They then lower instruments deep into the Earth to take readings and learn about its structure and make-up that way. Now keep in mind that the center of the Earth is about 6,400 km (4,000 mi) deep, so we really are not able to gather data based on direct observation much below the surface. Nevertheless, scientists have collected enough data based on indirect observation that they have divided Earth up into three compositional layers or five mechanical layers (Figure 12.3). The compositional layers are determined by the chemical make-up of components of each layer. These layers are called the crust, mantle, and core. The mechanical layers are determined by each layer's physical properties. This is because the physical conditions in Earth's interior vary from layer to layer. As you go deeper and deeper into the Earth, temperature and pressure increase. Because of this increase in temperature and pressure, the properties of the materials in each layer change. The mechanical layers include the lithosphere (lith' us sfeer), asthenosphere (as then' us sfeer), mesosphere, outer core, and inner core.

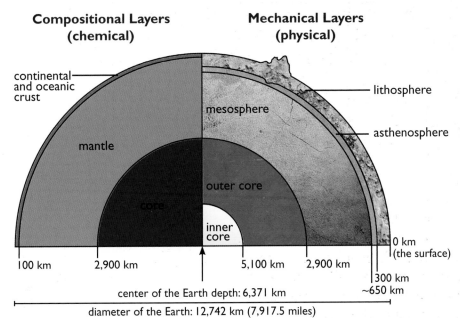

Compositional Layers (chemical)

continental and oceanic crust

mantle

core

Mechanical Layers (physical)

lithosphere

mesosphere

asthenosphere

outer core

inner core

100 km 2,900 km 5,100 km 2,900 km

0 km (the surface)

300 km
~650 km

center of the Earth depth: 6,371 km

diameter of the Earth: 12,742 km (7,917.5 miles)

FIGURE 12.3
The Structure of the Earth
A cross section of the Earth showing two different views. On top the Earth is divided into it compositional layers. The bottom shows Earth divided into mechanical layers.

The Crust

The crust is the only section of the Earth that we really know well because it is the only section of the Earth we can actually observe directly. The crust is composed of Earth's outermost layer of rock. Most of the rocks that make up the crust are composed of silicates—chemical compounds containing silicon and oxygen. Silicon dioxide is known as silica and it is very prevalent in the crust. Silica is the principal component of sand and glass. Often silicates will also contain metals such as iron, calcium, or aluminum.

The thickness of the crust varies depending on where you are. The majority of it ranges in thickness from about 90 km (55 mi) to about 20 km (12 mi), although it can be a bit thicker (under mountain chains) or as thin as 5 km (under the deepest parts of the ocean). There are two different types of crust: continental crust and oceanic crust. Continental crust, as you can guess from the name, makes up the continents. It is composed mainly of less-dense silicate rocks such as granite (Figure 12.4). Oceanic crust is much thinner than continental crust. It is composed mostly of dense silicate rocks like basalt.

FIGURE 12.4
Granite and Basalt
Granite (left) and basalt (right) rocks make up different parts of Earth's crust.

The Mantle

Directly beneath the Earth's crust is the mantle. Remember, scientists have never directly studied the mantle. But just like other things we cannot see, like atoms and distant galaxies, scientists make indirect observations and design theories to explain them. Then they devise experiments to predict the results based on the theories. If the results of the experiments agree with the theory's predictions, the theory is considered to be a good one. If not, the theory is refined or discarded for a new one that can explain the experimental results.

So, as far as what we know about the mantle, the first scientist to really make use of the information gathered by seismographs was a Croatian scientist named Andrija Mohorovicic (moh' huh roh' vuh chich). He carefully studied the seismographic recordings of

MOD 12

435

seismic waves from several different locations. Based on his study, he concluded that the Earth's interior was not the same throughout. He postulated that many miles beneath the surface, there was a border beyond which the composition of the Earth was much different from that of the Earth's crust. That border became known as the Mohorovicic discontinuity, or Moho (moh' ho) for short. (In geology, the term discontinuity indicates a surface where seismic waves change velocity.) We now know that Moho marks the boundary between the Earth's crust and the beginning of the Earth's mantle. See Figure 12.5.

As time went on and the study of seismic waves became more detailed, scientists began proposing models of the Earth's mantle. Eventually, the calculations based on the models were in excellent agreement with the data. Thus, even though we have never directly seen the mantle, we think we know its composition and its general properties simply because we have analyzed how certain waves travel through it.

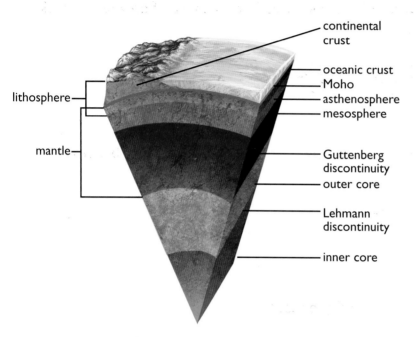

FIGURE 12.5
The Layers of Earth's Interior
The Earth's mantle is divided into three layers. The lithosphere (which also includes the crust), the asthenosphere, and the mesosphere.

Like the crust, the rock of the mantle is composed mostly of silicates, however these rocks are rich in iron and magnesium. Therefore, these rocks are much denser than those of the crust. This makes sense because the deeper we go into the Earth the more tightly packed matter becomes. At the same time, the temperature of the rock in the mantle increases the deeper you go. At the Moho, the temperature is about 500 °C (1,000 °F), while the lower portion of the mantle gets as hot as 4,000 °C (7,000 °F). That makes for some very hot rocks! The pressure (force applied per unit area) that the rocks of the mantle are under increases with depth as well. After all, the more rock that's above, the more weight that's pressing down on it. By the time you reach the bottom of the mantle, the pressure is about 1.4 *million* times that of pressure at the Earth's surface!

The fact that pressure and temperature increase as you travel deeper into the mantle leads to some very interesting effects on the physical properties of the rock. Therefore, geologists divide the mantle up into three layers (Figures 12.3 and 12.5). The lithosphere includes the uppermost part of the mantle as well as Earth's crust. The lithosphere is composed of relatively cool, solid, rigid rock. Below the lithosphere, there is a small portion of the mantle called the asthenosphere. At the pressure and temperature found in the asthenosphere, the rock there is softer, weaker, and not completely solid. It behaves more like warm taffy candy, flowing around in the mantle. It's important to note that these rocks in the mantle are not liquid, just as taffy is not liquid. When subjected to an abrupt force, the flowing rocks can harden into a firm solid. After the force passes, the rock returns to its flowing state. Scientists call this *soft* plastic rock.

Plastic rock—Rock that behaves like something between a liquid and a solid

Most theories that describe Earth's mantle have this plastic rock moving about in huge currents in the asthenosphere.

Below the asthenosphere is the mesosphere. The rocks of the mesosphere are stiffer than those of the asthenosphere. Despite being stiffer, these rocks can still flow only much more slowly. Scientists call these rocks *stiff* plastic rock. To get an idea of how plastic rock behaves, perform the following experiment.

EXPERIMENT 12.1
A SIMULATION OF PLASTIC ROCK

PURPOSE:
To explore the properties of plastic rock by producing a mixture that simulate such behavior.

MATERIALS:
- A shallow pan (a pie pan, for example)
- Cornstarch
- Measuring cups
- Water
- Spoon for stirring
- Eye protection such as goggles or safety glasses

PROCEDURE:
1. Put one cup of cornstarch into the pan.
2. Add 2/3 cup of water.
3. Stir the water and cornstarch together. You should find it very hard to stir at first, but as you continue to stir, you should get to the point where you have an evenly mixed, white liquid in the pan.
4. Add an additional ½ cup of cornstarch to the mixture.
5. Stir the newly added cornstarch into the mixture. Now you should start seeing an interesting behavior. As you stir, the mixture should solidify, making it hard to stir. However, when you stop stirring and let the mixture sit, it should liquefy again. If you don't see that behavior, your mixture is not correct. If the mixture stays liquid, you have too much water. To fix this, add cornstarch a little at a time until you get the desired behavior. If the mixture never turns to liquid, you have too much cornstarch. Add water a little at a time until you get the desired behavior.
6. Explore this interesting behavior for a while. Describe your observations in the data table.
7. Pick up some of the mixture with your hand. As you pick it up, it should become solid.
8. Squeeze the solid into a ball, then relax your hand and watch what happens to the ball.
9. Repeat this a few times. Describe your observations in the data table.
10. To clean up everything, you will need to use hot water from the tap. As you add hot water to the pan, the mixture will become a liquid. Continue to add water until it is very fluid and you can

safely pour it down the drain. Make sure to leave the hot water running for several minutes after the mixture has been cleaned up, as you need to flush it down the drain. Failure to do so could clog your drain.

CONCLUSIONS:

Did this experiment help you understand the properties of plastic rock? Explain your observations and make connections to the text.

The Core

In 1914, a German geologist, Beno Gutenberg (goo' ten burg), analyzed seismic waves and concluded that there is another drastic change in the makeup of the Earth significantly below the Moho. The boundary marking that change is now known as the Gutenberg discontinuity (see Figure 12.6) and signals the beginning of the Earth's core. The core is remarkably different from the mantle. First, scientists think it is composed mostly of iron, not silicates, with lesser amounts of nickel and some lighter elements. Second, below the Gutenberg discontinuity, the core is actually *liquid*, not solid. It is a liquid because, at the depth of the Gutenberg discontinuity, the temperature is hot enough to melt iron and the other components of the outer core.

In 1936, Danish scientist Inge Lehmann's (lay' mahn) work with seismic waves led her to the realization that the core actually has a *solid* inner region beneath the liquid outer region. So, scientists now separate the core into the inner core and the outer core. Not surprisingly, the boundary between these two layers is called the Lehmann discontinuity. The outer core lies just below the Gutenberg discontinuity and is mostly molten iron. The inner core lies below the Lehmann discontinuity and is mostly solid iron.

How is that possible? The temperature of the outer core is hot enough for iron to melt, which is why it is liquid. And while the inner core is actually hotter than the outer core, it is the incredibly great pressure of the inner core that explains the solid nature of the iron there. Remember from module 2 that in almost all substances (except water), the molecules and atoms are close together when the substance is a solid, and they are farther apart when it is a liquid. Also remember that the reason substances melt is that you increase the kinetic energy of their molecules or atoms when you heat them which allows the atoms to move farther apart and liquefy. This is what happens in the outer core. But, when you add a lot of pressure (as exists in the inner core), the atoms or molecules will actually be forced back closer together and so become solid again. This is known as pressure freezing. So, because of the extremely high pressure in the inner core of the Earth (estimated to be 3.6 *million* times the pressure at Earth's surface), the iron rock stays solid, despite its extremely high temperature (estimated to be 5,500 °C).

FIGURE 12.6
Earth's Core
Earth's inner core is believed to be a solid ball of metal (mostly iron and nickel). The outer core is mostly molten (liquid) metal (iron and nickel).

Earth's Core and Magnetic Field

Probably the most interesting fact about the Earth's core is that most scientists agree that a large amount of electrical current flowing in the core generates Earth's magnetic field. Because we only have indirect data to help us understand where this electrical current in the core comes from, it is still one of science's great mysteries. There are two main theories that try to explain the data. If you are interested in reading about these theories, you can find a discussion on this information on the course website mentioned in the front of the text.

FIGURE 12.7
Earth's Magnetic Field
Earth's magnetic field (blue bands) deflects charged particles, called cosmic rays (yellow particles), that would destroy Earth if they reached the surface.

The area of Earth's atmosphere that is influenced by Earth's magnetic field is called the magnetosphere. It is important to know that life on Earth would not be possible without Earth's magnetic field. You see, along with ultraviolet rays, there are certain high-energy electrically charged particles, called cosmic rays. Some of the particles are emitted from the sun, but most come from sources outside the solar system. These cosmic rays travel toward our planet and arrive at the top of Earth's atmosphere. If they were allowed to strike the Earth, they would kill all life on the planet. Fortunately for us, however, the Earth's magnetic field deflects the vast majority of these particles, keeping them from hitting Earth. As a result, life can flourish. If the Earth's magnetic field were too small, it would not deflect enough of these cosmic rays. If it were too strong, it would deflect the cosmic rays, but it would cause deadly magnetic storms that would make life impossible! Thus, Earth has a magnetic field at *just the right strength to support life*. Review what you've read by completing On Your Own problems 12.1–12.2.

ON YOUR OWN

12.1   Would water be subject to pressure freezing? Why or why not?

12.2   Describe the three main layers of Earth.

ROCKS AND MINERALS

Along with studying the interior of the Earth, geochemists and geophysicists also study the Earth's lithosphere. Remember, the lithosphere includes the brittle upper portion of the mantle and the crust. The lithosphere is composed mainly of rocks and minerals. Rocks, like those pictured in Figure 12.8 may seem permanent, but they're not. Over time a rock will change from one type into another. But before we learn how that happens, we first need to look at rocks and minerals in a little more detail.

FIGURE 12.8
Rocky Mountains
Mount Robson is the highest point of the Canadian Rockies.

MOD 12

Rocks

Rocks are all around us. You can see them jutting out of the tops of hills and mountains, and they lie beneath the dirt you walk on and the mud beneath the ocean. The crust of the Earth often contains soil and sediment as well as rock. If soil is present, it is the top layer, and underneath that, there is often a layer of sediment.

Sediment—Small, solid fragments of rock-like gravel, sand, silt, mud, or clay

Rocks are made up of one or more of the following: different minerals (we'll talk about these next), broken pieces of crystals or other rocks, shells of once-living animals, or compressed pieces of plants. Rocks are classified into 3 major groups based on how they form. Study Infographic 12.1 to learn about **sedimentary** (sed uh men' tuh ree) rock, **igneous** (ig' nee us) **rock,** and metamorphic (met uh mor' fik) rock.

THE 3 MAJOR TYPES OF ROCKS

SEDIMENTARY ROCK

Sandstone (pictured above) is a type of sedimentary rock. Sedimentary rocks form when pressure (force) and chemical reactions cement sediments together. When layers of sand and mud (sediments) accumulate, the weight of the sediment presses down, compacting the layers underneath. Chemical reactions occur in the water in the spaces between the grains of sediment. Minerals (such as calcium carbonate, $CaCO_3$) precipitate and harden, binding the grains of sediment together. You can usually see the layers of compacted and cemented sediment in the sedimentary rock.

IGNEOUS ROCK

Igneous rock, such as granite (shown above), forms from molten (liquid) rock called magma. Magma forms deep underground where the temperature is hot enough and conditions are just right for solid rocks to melt. Because the liquid rock is less dense, the magma rises through cracks in the overlying rocks pressing down from above. As magma rises towards the surface, it cools and hardens. Magma that hardens underground usually cools slowly and large crystals can form. Magma that reaches Earth's surface is called lava. Lava cools very quickly as it comes in contact with oceans or air and so forms small crystals or glass.

METAMORPHIC ROCK

Metamorphic rock, such as the schist rock shown above, forms when existing sedimentary or igneous rocks are changed as a result of great pressure and temperature. These changes occur to the rock without the rock melting. This can happen because naturally occurring chemical substances in the rocks (called minerals) each have a specific range of temperature and pressure in which they are stable. So when minerals in sedimentary or igneous rock are heated or compressed beyond their range of stability, the minerals break down and form other minerals. This changes the sedimentary or igneous rock into a new, or transformed, metamorphic rock.

INFOGRAPHIC 12.1

Imagine a newly formed igneous rock like the large granite rock shown in Figure 12.10. In one pathway of the rock cycle, the granite rock is worn down by weathering and erosion into sand. Perhaps rain and wind carry the sand to a river which transports the sand to the ocean and deposits it as sediment. Eventually layers of sediment are deposited on top of each other and they become compacted, cementing together to become part of the sedimentary rock sandstone. If the sandstone is pushed deep underground, the heat and pressure can cause it to undergo metamorphism and form the metamorphic rock quartzite. Even this doesn't necessarily end the rock cycle. The quartzite could be pushed to the surface and be exposed to weathering and erosion, which again causes the rock to form sediment. Or the metamorphic rock quartzite could be heated past its melting point becoming magma, which upon cooling as it rises to the surface of the Earth, forms another igneous rock. You can get a visual representation of the rock cycle just described by looking at Figure 12.12.

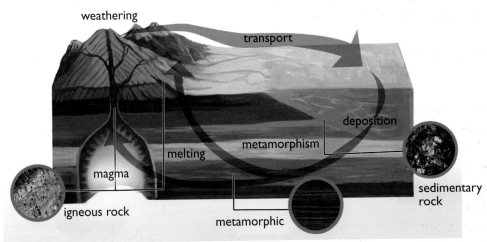

FIGURE 12.12
The Rock Cycle
The rock cycle describes the dynamic (always changing) transitions among the three main rock types: sedimentary, metamorphic, and igneous.

Water

You have already learned a good deal about water in module 4, but a discussion of the Earth's surface wouldn't be complete without talking about water. Look at Figure 12.13 and think about what an astronaut sees when they look back at the Earth's surface. How would you describe it? It's clear that there are mountains on the land in North and South America shown on the globe, but what do you see more of? Water! In fact, about 71 percent of the Earth's surface is covered with water. This is why Earth is sometimes referred to as the "water planet" or the "blue planet."

FIGURE 12.13
The Water Planet

As you already know, water occurs in three main states on Earth—liquid, solid, and gas—depending on the temperature. Most of Earth's water is the saltwater found in the oceans. Only about 3% of the water on Earth is fresh water in the form of lakes, ponds, rivers, creeks, and streams. But that's not all of Earth's fresh water! Some of the water on our planet isn't visible from above because it is underground. Clouds in our atmosphere are mostly made up of water. Finally, Earth has many icebergs and glaciers, which are made up of water in its solid phase. In short, our planet is "overflowing" with water. Collectively, all of these water sources are called the hydrosphere (hi' droh sfear), and they are essential for life's existence.

Hydrosphere—The sum of all water on a planet

The Hydrosphere and the Hydrologic (Water) Cycle

Since the hydrosphere is actually the sum total of all water (gas, liquid, and solid) that exists on the planet, it is important to take a look at all the sources of water on the Earth. Table 12.1 shows the breakdown of Earth's water supply.

TABLE 12.1		
Water Source	**Type of Water**	**Percent of Hydrosphere**
oceans	saltwater	97.250%
glaciers and icebergs	freshwater	2.050%
groundwater	freshwater	0.685%
surface water (not oceans)	mostly freshwater	0.009%
soil moisture	freshwater	0.005%
atmospheric moisture	freshwater	0.001%

Notice how the vast majority of Earth's water supply is contained in the oceans as saltwater so it isn't even drinkable! Only 2.75% of Earth's water supply is freshwater and therefore at least potentially drinkable. You may be surprised to see that almost ¾ of Earth's supply of freshwater is contained in glaciers and icebergs. A large fraction of the remaining freshwater is underground. Scientists call this groundwater. In the end, surface freshwater (what we typically think of when we think of Earth's freshwater supply—lakes, ponds, rivers, streams, and creeks) makes up less than 0.01% of the Earth's freshwater supply. While you don't need to memorize Table 12.1, you should remember the following key facts.

1. Most of Earth's water supply is contained in the oceans as saltwater.

2. Most of Earth's *freshwater* supply is stored in icebergs and glaciers.

3. The largest source of *liquid freshwater* is groundwater.

You may be wondering how these different sources of water interact with each other. Hopefully you are beginning to realize that everything on Earth is connected in different ways and these sources of water are not isolated from each other. Even though they are listed as different water sources in Table 12.1, they do interact with one another, which makes for some very interesting science. Scientists call the interaction between these sources of water the hydrologic (hi droh loj' ik) cycle.

Hydrologic cycle—The process by which water is continuously exchanged between Earth's various water sources

The best way to understand the hydrologic cycle is to study the illustration in Figure 12.14.

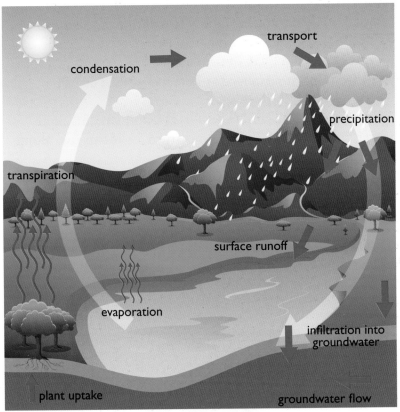

FIGURE 12.14
The Hydrologic Cycle
The hydrologic cycle is more commonly called the water cycle. It shows how the different sources of water interact with each other through various processes on Earth.

Just like with the rock cycle, there are several processes involved in changing water from one type to another. These processes include evaporation, transpiration, condensation, precipitation, and the eventual return of flowing water to the ocean. And just as forces and energy are responsible for the changes in the rock cycle, energy from the sun and the force of gravity power the water cycle. Refer to Figure 12.14 often as you read the following paragraphs as it shows the major processes of the hydrologic cycle.

Water gets into the atmosphere predominantly by evaporation. You learned about evaporation in module 2. It is solar energy that causes water on Earth's surface to heat up and change into water vapor in the air.

As the sun continues to warm the moist air, it expands and rises, carrying the water vapor higher into the atmosphere. Most evaporation occurs over the ocean and large lakes, but smaller amounts of water evaporate from ponds, rivers, and streams.

It is also important to note that water vapor enters the atmosphere when it evaporates from the leaves of trees and other plants in a process called transpiration.

Transpiration—Evaporation of water from plants

If you think about it, evaporation takes water out of the oceans, lakes, rivers, and streams, while transpiration takes water from the soil. After all, plants absorb water from the soil, so any water they emit must have originally come from there. Thus, transpiration depletes soil moisture. Soil moisture can also be depleted when it infiltrates (soaks down) into the groundwater sources and feeds into lakes, rivers, and streams by the process of groundwater flow.

MOD 12

When evaporation and transpiration take place, water vapor goes into the atmosphere. It then forms clouds by a process called condensation which you learned about in module 2. We'll discuss cloud formation in more detail in the next module, but for now, just realize it occurs when gaseous water (water vapor) cools and turns into a liquid that stays suspended in the air. Eventually, the oceans, lakes, rivers, streams, and soil moisture all get replenished when gravity causes the water in the clouds to fall out of the atmosphere as precipitation.

Precipitation—Water falling from the atmosphere as rain, snow, sleet, or hail

Some of the precipitation falls directly into the oceans, lakes, rivers, and streams, and some of it falls onto land. That water can replenish the soil moisture, or it can run along the surface of the land into a body of water as **surface runoff**.

think about this

Let's step back and look at the "big picture" of the hydrologic cycle one more time. Picture a drop of water in the ocean. That water drop that started in the ocean can evaporate and become part of a cloud. When the cloud finally precipitates, that water drop might very well fall into a lake, river, or stream. It also might become surface runoff or groundwater which eventually feeds a river, lake, or stream. As a result, a water drop that starts out in the ocean can very easily be transferred to one of the freshwater sources in the

hydrosphere. In the same way, a freshwater river might dump into the ocean, allowing freshwater to be transferred to the ocean via river flow. Alternatively, a water drop that evaporated from a freshwater source might eventually precipitate in an ocean, once again transferring water from a freshwater source to the salty ocean. The point is that the hydrologic cycle constantly exchanges water between all the sources in the hydrosphere. Think about that. Because of the hydrologic cycle, the next drink you take might contain water that was once in the ocean!

If you think it odd that water can be transferred from the ocean to a freshwater source, perform the following experiment. Then answer On Your Own problems 12.5–12.8.

EXPERIMENT 12.2
EVAPORATION, CONDENSATION, AND PRECIPITATION

PURPOSE:
To investigate how water can be transferred from a saltwater source (the ocean) to a freshwater source in the hydrologic cycle.

MATERIALS:
*   Water

- Salt
- Ice
- Tablespoon
- Small saucepan
- Saucepan lid or frying pan lid larger than the saucepan used
- Large bowl (It should not be plastic and heat safe, as it will get hot.)
- Potholders
- Zippered plastic sandwich bag
- Stove
- Eye protection such as goggles or safety glasses

PROCEDURE:

1. Fill the saucepan ¾ full of water.
2. Add three tablespoons of salt to the water and stir to make as much salt dissolve as possible. Do not be concerned if you can't get it all to dissolve.
3. Taste a tiny bit of the saltwater you have made. Please note that you should NEVER TASTE THINGS IN AN EXPERIMENT UNLESS A PERSON OF AUTHORITY TELLS YOU THAT IT IS SAFE TO DO SO! Tastes bad, doesn't it? Record your observations.
4. Now set the pan of saltwater on the stove and start heating it up. Your goal is to have vigorously boiling water, so turn up the heat!
5. While you are waiting for the saltwater to boil, take the zippered sandwich bag and fill it full of ice. Zipper it shut so that no water from the ice can leak out.
6. Once the saltwater has started boiling vigorously, place the bowl next to the saucepan. The bowl should not be on a hot burner. You do not want to heat the bowl. You just want it close to the boiling water.
7. Now use the potholder to hold the saucepan lid and put the zippered sandwich bag full of ice on top of the lid. You may have to use a finger or two from the hand holding the lid to make sure that the bag of ice stays on top of the saucepan lid.
8. Hold the lid so that one end (the one with the most ice on it) is over the saucepan and the other end is over the bowl. Tilt the lid so that it tilts toward the bowl. In the end, your setup should look something like this:

9. Hold the lid there for a little while and watch what happens on the underside of the lid. **BE CAREFUL! EVERYTHING IS HOT!** Notice that water droplets are forming on the underside of the lid over the saucepan, and they slowly drip down the lid towards the bowl.

10. If your arm gets tired, you can set the lid down so that part of it rests on the saucepan and the rest sits on the bowl. Make sure that the bowl is lower than the saucepan so that the lid still tilts towards the bowl.

11. Eventually, you will see water dripping off the pan lid and into the bowl. Wait until there is enough water in the bowl to be able to take a sip. Once that happens, turn off the burner and wait a moment.

12. Using potholders, take the lid away and put it in the sink. Pour the half-melted ice out of the bag and throw the bag away (or recycle it). Still using potholders, take the bowl away from the stove and set it on the counter. Empty the saucepan and put it in the sink as well.

13. Allow the bowl to cool down completely, and then taste the water in the bowl. **Once again, you can only do this because I am telling you to!**

14. What does the water taste like? Record your observations.

15. Clean up and put everything away.

CONCLUSIONS:

Write a paragraph describing what you did and explaining your observations. Make connections to the text.

What happened in the experiment? Well, the water in the saucepan was supposed to represent ocean water. When you tasted it, did it taste salty? If you allowed the pan of salt-water to sit out long enough, eventually the water would all evaporate away. It would take a while for that to happen, however, so in the experiment, we accelerated things by heating the pan until the water started boiling. Thus, boiling the saltwater was just a way to speed up the rate at which the water would evaporate from the pan. When the steam (water vapor) hit the pan lid, the coolness of the ice caused the water to turn from vapor back into liquid. This process is condensation, and it is basically the same thing that happens to form a cloud. Thus, the cool pan lid was supposed to represent the clouds formed when ocean water evaporates into the atmosphere. Eventually, so many drops of water formed that they trickled down the pan lid into the bowl. This, of course, represents precipitation. In the end, when you tasted the water in the bowl, there was no salt taste at all. The bowl, therefore, represents a freshwater source.

The point of the experiment was to show you that even though water might start out as part of a saltwater source, through the process of evaporation, condensation, and precipitation, it can very easily be transferred to a freshwater source. How can this happen? Water evaporates but salt does not. So in a mixture of saltwater, when the water evaporates, the salt stays behind. This keeps the salt in the ocean but allows the water from the ocean to be exchanged with the many other water sources in the hydrosphere.
The experiment you performed is actually a very standard technique in chemistry. It is called distillation (dis tuh lay' shun).

Distillation—Evaporation and condensation of a mixture to separate out the mixture's individual components

When chemists do distillations, they typically have a mixture of two or more substances that need to be separated. When the mixture is boiled, the substances tend to evaporate one at a time, allowing the chemist to separate them. In the distillation you performed, you could have allowed all the water to boil away and condense into the bowl. In the end, you would have had freshwater in the bowl and nothing but salt in the saucepan; thus, the saltwater mixture would have been separated into its components: salt and water.

ON YOUR OWN

12.5 Describe a path through the rock cycle that begins with magma and ends with a sedimentary rock.

12.6 Suppose you are given a sample of water taken from somewhere in Earth's hydrosphere.

a. Would it most likely be saltwater or freshwater?

b. If it is freshwater, where did it most likely come from?

c. If the person who collected the sample tells you it is freshwater that originally came from a liquid source, where did it most likely come from?

12.7 Water that was originally in a plant ends up in a cloud. What two processes of the hydrologic cycle caused it to be transferred that way?

12.8 Rain that hits the land can travel as a liquid into a lake, river, stream, or ocean in two different ways. What are they?

Weathering

We've talked a bit about weathering and erosion already, but since these are major processes in how rocks are transformed, they warrant a little more discussion. I waited until after you learned about the hydrologic cycle, because that comes into play as well.

Have you ever seen curious rock structures like the ones in Bryce Canyon in Utah (shown in Figure 12.15)? Have you wondered how that could happen? Well, it starts with weathering.

FIGURE 12.15
Bryce Canyon Rocks
Unique rock formations called *hoodoos* result from weathering and erosion.

Weathering—Any process that breaks down rocks and creates sediment

Weathering helps shape the Earth's surface. While weathering is responsible for breaking down rocks where they are located, it does not move rock pieces from one place to another. There are two forms of weathering: mechanical weathering and chemical weathering.

Mechanical Weathering

Mechanical weathering is the physical process of breaking rock into smaller fragments. With mechanical weathering, the composition of the rocks does not change. This should make sense if you think back to the types of changes in matter you learned about in module 2.

Weathering refers to physical changes that occur in rocks. Physical changes do not alter the composition of the rock, just its size, shape, etc. Chemical changes, on the other hand, will alter the composition of the rock.

Mechanical weathering can occur in several ways. The main agents of mechanical weathering are water, ice, and wind. The most common form of mechanical weathering is called ice wedging or frost wedging. This happens when water makes its way into pours or cracks in the rock. The liquid water freezes into solid ice when temperatures drop below freezing. Remember as water freezes it expands, so the ice begins wedging the rock crack farther apart until it could crack completely in half (Figure 12.16). This type of weathering is most common in mountain areas where water often freezes at night and then the ice thaws during the day. If you live where winters are cold, you may notice potholes on your roads. Potholes form in part due to ice wedging.

FIGURE 12.16
Ice Wedging
Ice wedging causes rocks to crack and potholes to form.

Another type of mechanical weathering is called abrasion. Abrasion occurs when one rock bumps, grinds, or scrapes against another. Gravity causing rocks to tumble down hills will cause rocks to bump into each other. Strong winds can blast sand and small rocks against larger, stationary rocks causing abrasion. It may surprise you that the movement of glaciers can cause abrasion when the small rocks embedded in the ice scrape against the rock below. Have you ever noticed very smooth stones or smooth pieces of glass (like those shown in Figure 12.17) while walking at the beach? If you have, then you've seen evidence of abrasion as the ocean waves grind the rocks or glass over the sandy bottom.

Mechanical weathering can occur in other ways too. Plants and animals can play a part in weathering. This is often called biomechanical weathering. Plant roots can grow into cracks in rocks and exert such a powerful force that rocks are slowly

FIGURE 12.17
Abrasion
Smooth stones and beach glass are formed by abrasion.

slopes than lower elevations. As streams flow toward the sea, the slopes over which they travel become smaller, so the water moves slower and more sediment settles to the stream bottom. As a stream reaches flatter, more gently sloping areas, a flood plain can form. A flood plain is the flat area around a stream that is only entirely covered by water during floods. Often this occurs when there are periods of heavy rains.

Sometimes mechanical weathering of the rocks and soil on one side of a river causes a bend or curve to form. Where a river curves (Figure 12.24), the water on the outside of the curve moves faster than the water on the inside. And as you already know, fast moving water causes more erosion. So, the faster moving water picks up more sediment and carries it downstream where it is deposited on the slower-moving water side of the river (the inside curve). The deposited sediment on

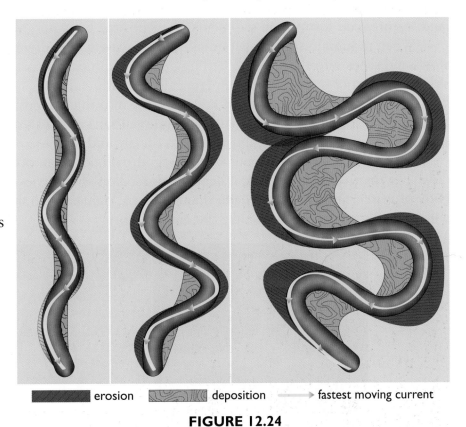

erosion · · · · deposition ——→ fastest moving current

FIGURE 12.24
Meanders Change the Path of a River over Time
Meanders form when faster waters erode the stream bank causing curves to form. Slower waters deposit sediments on the inside of curves.

the slow side starts to build up causing the water to move even faster on the fast side. Downstream, the fast water slams into the far side of the river with enough speed to begin to carve out another curve. These curves are called meanders. The faster the water flows the greater the curve can get. Sometimes (often during floods) the river erodes through a narrow neck of land at the base of a meander, forming a new path. As sediments build up along the new channel, the old meander is cut off from the river and a curved lake is formed. These types of lakes, pictured in Figure 12.25, are called oxbow lakes.

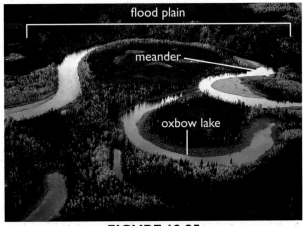

FIGURE 12.25
Rivers Change the Land
Rivers often form winding meanders across their flood plain. During floods, rivers may cut new channels, leaving oxbow lakes to form from old meanders.

Features Formed by Sediment Deposition

We've already talked a bit about how slower water deposits sediment, but did you know even that can change the land? As streams flow down from mountains to flatter areas, they carry a lot of sediment. Larger particles of sediment are deposited first, but as the river or stream slows even further, smaller particles of sediment can be deposited. Two different land features can form when sediments are deposited by water: alluvial fans and deltas.

When mountain snows melt quickly, flood waters flow downhill to a plain where it slows and seeps into the ground, settling out the sediments it carries. What results is a fan-shaped deposit of sediment on the plain called an alluvial fan (Figure 12.26, left). If this happens often enough, the alluvial fan can grow into thick deposits of sediment. Sometimes smaller mountain streams will form alluvial fans as they reach a plain where the stream ends and the water is absorbed into the ground.

When a stream or river ends by flowing into a lake or an ocean, the water slows down. As the river water slows, it deposits the sediment it carries just before entering the body of water. This is called a delta (Figure 12.26, right). Often, but not always, the delta will form in a triangular shape like the one shown.

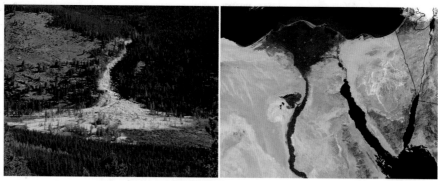

FIGURE 12.26
Alluvial Fans and Deltas
When moving water deposits sediment, alluvial fans (left) or deltas (right) can form. The left image shows an alluvial fan caused by flooding (Rocky Mountain National Park). The right image shows the delta formed by the Nile River as it enters the Mediterranean Sea.

Features Formed by Groundwater Erosion

As water soaks into the ground or flows underground, chemical weathering can cause groundwater erosion. Remember as carbon dioxide in the air reacts with water it forms carbonic acid. As the acidic rainwater moves down through the ground, it reacts with different rocks and may become even more acidic. If this acidic water comes in contact with soft rocks such as limestone, the acid water can easily erode away much of the rock. When the groundwater level drops, it carries the sediment away and a cavern or cave is formed.

In many caves you can see spectacular mineral structures. Sometimes water drips into the cavern from the rock layers above, carrying dissolved minerals such as calcium carbonate. As the mineral laden water drips from the ceiling, an icicle-like formation called a stalactite (stuh lak' tyt) grows. If the water drips all the way down to the floor, a pillar of minerals called a stalagmite (stuh lag' myt) grows. (You can remember the difference between these two formations if you recall that stalactite has a "c" for ceiling, and stalagmite has a "g" for ground.) If a stalactite and a stalagmite join together, they form a column like the one shown in Figure 12.27. If you have a chance to visit a cave, you should just to witness the strangely captivating beauty of these amazing formations.

Another way you may have witnessed groundwater erosion is if you have ever seen a sinkhole. If erosion weakens a layer of limestone under the surface, entire portions of the ground can suddenly collapse swallowing cars or even buildings. Some areas of the United States have many sinkholes.

FIGURE 12.27
Groundwater Erosion
Left: The large column in this cave in Virginia is formed when stalactites and stalagmites meet. Right: A sinkhole formed on Highway 101 in Harbor, Oregon.

Features Formed by Glaciers

Glaciers form when more snow falls on a region over a period of time than melts. The weight of each additional layer of snow causes the bottom layers to turn to glacial ice. Although glaciers may look like they are stationary, they actually are constantly moving. And while they move much more slowly than rivers, they are quite effective at weathering, eroding, and depositing sediment. In fact, you can tell where a glacier has been by the landscape features it leaves behind. This is because a glacier can carry and dump an enormous amount of rocks and sediment.

As a glacier flows, mechanical weathering loosens rocks on the ground beneath it or on the valley walls surrounding it. Mechanical weathering occurs through abrasion or as the glacial ice widens cracks in the bedrock beneath the glacier in a process called plucking. Loosened rock become frozen to the bottom of the glacier and then carried away. Sometimes even very large boulders can be weathered off the sides of a valley by abrasion and fall onto the glacier. The glacier may then carry these rocks, as well as rocks and sediments frozen to the bottom, for many kilometers over many years. When the glacier melts, it deposits its load of sediment and rocks, creating a variety of landforms. Look at Figure 12.28 on the next page to see some of the landforms mentioned in the next paragraphs.

MOD 12

FIGURE 12.28
Glacial Formations
Top Left: The Matterhorn in Switzerland. Top Right: An erratic from
California's Lassen Volcanic National Park. Bottom: View from Mount
Temple in Banff National Park, Alberta, Canada

Unlike rivers and streams that erode the surface by cutting V-shaped valleys, glaciers carve U-shaped valleys as they move through mountainous areas. The glacier can actually carve the stone into a rather smooth bowl-shaped surface called a cirque. Ridges form between cirques that are sculpted close together. Sometimes several ridges will connect to form a pyramid shape called a horn. The Matterhorn in the Swiss Alps is a famous horn chiseled by glaciers. Often water will collect in the large depressions left by glaciers. When that happens glacial lakes will form. You will find glacial lakes in the mountains (called cirque lakes), but any land over which a glacier has moved can have a lake. The Great Lakes and the Finger Lakes in New York are called kettle lakes which were formed by chunks of glacier ice left behind in depressions as a glacier came and retreated.

Again like rivers, glaciers can form different features by depositing rocks and sediment. Large boulders called glacial erratics are eventually dropped by moving or melting glaciers. Erratics are noticeable for two reasons. They are often huge and because they are often carried for quite a distance, they are usually composed of a different type of rock from the surrounding bedrock. Besides the large boulders, the unsorted mixture of sediment, sand, gravel, and rocks deposited by melting glaciers is called **till.** Till deposits can leave several different formations in the landscape depending on where and how they are deposited. If you are interested in learning more about these landforms, check out the Book Extras website mentioned in the student notes.

Features Formed by Wind

Just like water, wind can carry sediment. Also like rivers, the speed of the wind determines the size of the material it carries. You've probably seen dust floating in the air on relatively calm days and larger pieces of debris being whisked about by stronger winds. Have you ever been on a sandy beach on a very windy day? If so, then you have felt the blast of the sand as it whipped against your skin. Mechanical weathering by abrasion is one of the ways wind can change landscape features.

Wind erosion occurs more often in dry areas where water and plants are not as able to bind the soil. It should be obvious that smaller particles, such as sand, will be more easily picked up higher and moved further by the wind than larger pebbles or rocks. So that means as the wind erodes away the smaller sediment, what is left is a hard surface of larger, gravel-sized rocks that are not easily moved by wind. This process is called **deflation.**

When you think of wind erosion and deposition, you should picture **sand dunes** like those shown in Figure 12.29. Over time dunes can move great distances and take many different shapes as the wind picks up sand from the back of the dune and blows it to the front. In non-sandy dry areas, dust can be blown about and form deposits called **loess** (les'). A dust storm like the one in Figure 12.29 can transport tons of dust over long distances. In fact, dust from the Sahara Desert in Africa regularly blows across the Atlantic Ocean and can be seen on satellite photos.

FIGURE 12.29
Wind Erosion
Top: Pink sand dunes in the desert in Utah. Middle: Dust storm in Texas in June 2009. Bottom: Dust plume off the Sahara Desert over the northeast Atlantic Ocean as seen from space.

MOD 12

SUMMING UP

We have only touched the surface of what happens on Earth's lithosphere. There is so much more for you to learn as you continue your study of science. Hopefully you now have a better understanding of the structure of Earth and how ever changing its landscape is. Knowing more about our dynamic planet can help us care for this remarkable creation. Finish this module by completing the On Your Own problems and then the Study Guide.

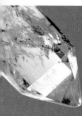

ON YOUR OWN

12.10 Suppose a stream erodes the land. What features are likely to form in steep mountainous areas? What features may form in more level areas?

12.11 List three features caused by glaciers.

12.12 How does deflation affect the land surface in dry regions?

ANSWERS TO THE "ON YOUR OWN" QUESTIONS

12.1 No, it would not. Water is one of the few substances in creation that has its molecules closer when it is a liquid compared to when it is a solid. Thus, if I press water molecules closer together they become more liquid. In fact, if you exert pressure on ice it will melt, because you are pushing the molecules closer together, like they are in liquid water. Please note that at *extreme* pressures, water can become a solid, but that solid is not what you and I would call ice.

12.2 The three main layers of Earth are the crust, the mantle, and the core. The crust is thin and composed of rocks and soil. The mantle is a thick layer of hot, solid rock. The core is a large sphere of metal with a liquid outer core and a solid inner core.

12.3 A mineral is a naturally occurring, inorganic solid with a regular crystal structure and a definite chemical composition. Rocks are classified as igneous, sedimentary, and metamorphic rocks.

12.4 A variety of tests are available—the student need only list two of the following. A streak test could be done using a streak plate. The density of each sample could be calculated by measuring the mass and volume. A Scratch test to determine the hardness of each sample could be done. You could also break each sample apart to see how they fracture.

12.5 Answers may vary but should be similar to the following. The magma cools to form igneous rock. The igneous rock is weathered to form sediment. The sediment is deposited and compacted to form sedimentary rock.

12.6 a. It would most likely be saltwater. After all, more than 97% of the Earth's water is ocean water, so the most likely source for water is the ocean.

b. If it is freshwater, it most likely came from an iceberg or glacier, since that's the largest source of freshwater on the planet.

c. If the person tells you it is from a liquid source, it is most likely groundwater, because groundwater is the largest source of *liquid* freshwater.

12.7 Transpiration and condensation put the water into the cloud. Since it was in a plant, the only way to get it into the atmosphere is by transpiration. At that point, however, it is water vapor, not in a cloud. To be in a cloud, the water vapor must condense.

12.8 Rain on the land can get into another water source via surface runoff or groundwater flow. If the rain never really gets absorbed by the soil, it becomes surface runoff. If it gets absorbed by the soil and enters into the groundwater, it will get to another water source by groundwater flow.

12.9   Both mechanical and chemical weathering break rocks down. Mechanical weathering breaks rocks into smaller pieces through physical processes like ice wedging and abrasion. Chemical weathering occurs when chemical reactions dissolve rocks or convert minerals in rocks into different minerals.

12.10   In steep areas, V-shaped valleys and waterfalls can form. In more level areas flood plains, oxbow lakes, and meanders can form.

12.11   Any three of the following would be correct: cirques, horns, U-shaped valleys, ridges, glacial lakes, kettle lakes.

12.12   Deflation is a process of wind erosion where wind removes sand and dust from the ground and leaves a hard surface of larger rocks behind.

Now, not all the atmosphere's weight is pressing down on any one thing. After all, the weight of the atmosphere is distributed across the entire planet. Nevertheless, if you were to weigh a column of air with an area of 1 inch by 1inch from sea level to the top of Earth's atmosphere, you would find that it weighs 14.7 pounds. What does that mean? It means that at sea level, the atmosphere exerts an average of 14.7 pounds of weight on every square inch it touches.

think about this

Think about that for a moment. At sea level, every square inch of the Earth is being pressed down with an average weight of 14.7 pounds. What does that mean? Well, suppose you were standing at sea level. Depending on your build, each of your shoulders is about 3 inches wide by 4 inches long. This gives each shoulder an area (length times width) of 12 square inches. This means that on each of your shoulders, the atmosphere is pressing down with a weight of 12 × 14.7, or about *176 pounds!* This is atmospheric pressure. Now please note that the weights I am talking about here are averages. Depending on weather conditions, the atmospheric pressure can be higher or lower than 14.7 pounds per square inch. However, at sea level, that is the *average* amount of atmospheric pressure.

What do you think causes air pressure? Since we know air is composed of gases, you should guess that it has something to do with them. Remember the Kinetic Theory of Matter from module 2? Well, gas particles have a lot of energy and so are constantly moving, bumping into things. In other words they exert pressure. So why don't you *feel* the gases applying pressure on you? If you think about it, you should realize that you don't *feel* any weight pushing on you—especially not 176 pounds. It doesn't *feel* that way because there is equal pressure pushing on you from all sides, including from within! How does that help? Well, think back to what you learned about forces in module 7 (see Figure 7.4). When two equal forces are pushing on each other from opposite directions, they cancel each other out and there is no net force. In the same way, the pressure pushing on you in one direction is canceled by pressure pushing on you in the opposite direction. The net effect is that you do not *feel* any pressure. Nevertheless, the pressure is there. To see what I mean, perform Experiment 13.2.

EXPERIMENT 13.2
ATMOSPHERIC PRESSURE

PURPOSE:
To observe that the atmosphere actually does exert pressure on everything it touches.

MATERIALS:
- Stove
- Frying pan
- 2 empty, 12 ounce aluminum cans (like soft drink cans)
- 2 bowls
- Tablespoon
- Water
- Ice cubes

- Tongs
- Eye protection such as goggles or safety glasses

HYPOTHESIS:

Predict what will happen if air pressure on the inside of a mostly empty can is less than the atmospheric pressure on the outside of the empty can.

PROCEDURE:

1. Put 1 tablespoon of water in each aluminum can.
2. Place the two aluminum cans in the frying pan so that they stand up.
3. Put the frying pan on the stove and turn the heat up to high. This will heat up the water in the cans.
4. While you are waiting for the water in the cans to heat up, fill each bowl half full of water.
5. Place a few ice cubes in each bowl so that the water becomes ice cold.
6. Wait for steam to start rising out the opening of each can. That will tell you the water inside is boiling vigorously. Allow the water to boil for about 30 seconds.

7. After 30 seconds, turn off the heat. Use the tongs to grab one can and place it upright in one of the bowls of water.
8. Record what happens.
9. Use the tongs to grab the other can and place it upside down in the bowl of water.
10. Record what happens.
11. Clean up and put everything away.

CONCLUSIONS:

In a complete paragraph, discuss your results and explain what happened in terms of pressure. Make connections to the text.

What happened in your experiment? Well, when you put the first can in the water upright, nothing exciting happened. The can obviously cooled off, and the water in the bowl got warmer, but there should have been no noticeable change. However, when you put the second can in the water upside down, the can should have crumpled noticeably. Depending on how much water you put in the can, how long you let it boil, and how cold the water in the bowl was, it might have crumpled only a little, or it might have really been crushed.

What explains the results of the experiment? Well, remember that the air around you is exerting pressure on everything it touches, including the cans. The cans do not crumple from this pressure, however, because there is air *inside* the cans as well. The air outside each can pushes in on the can, and the air inside the can pushes *out* on the can. The pressure from the air outside is counteracted by the pressure from the air inside. As a result, the can does not crumple. This is, in fact, why you don't feel air pressure pushing in on you. The air inside your body is pushing out on you, and the air outside your body is pushing in on you. Thus, the air pressure inside your body counteracts the air pressure outside your body.

In the experiment, we changed this situation a bit. The results, however, depended on *how* we changed the situation. You see, as the water boiled, the steam rising from the boiling water pushed the gas molecules in the air out of each can. Thus, once a steady stream of steam came billowing out of the cans, each can was mostly full of steam (water vapor) and had only a little air inside. The steam exerted pressure, however, so the cans did not crumple, because the pressure of the steam pushing out on the cans still counteracted the atmospheric pressure pushing in on the cans.

When you placed the first can upright in the water, the steam rapidly condensed and turned back into liquid, but as it did so, air was able to rush into the can through the opening in the top. Thus, steam was replaced by air, which means that the pressure being exerted in the can by the steam was replaced with pressure being exerted by the air that came inside the can. As a result, the pressure pushing out from the inside of the can did not change much. This meant that the air pressure pushing in on the can from the outside was still counteracted by pressure pushing out from the inside of the can, so the can did not crumple (Figure 13.4 top).

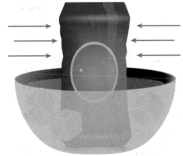

When you placed the second can upside down into the second bowl, the steam once again rapidly condensed into liquid. Unlike what happened with the first can, however, air could not rush in to replace the steam, because the opening of the can was under water. As a result, there was little air pressure inside the can. This meant that there wasn't much pressure inside counteracting the pressure being exerted on the can by the air outside. Since there was nothing to push against the air pressing in on the can, the pressure exerted by the air outside the can crushed it (Figure 13.4 bottom).

FIGURE 13.4
Cans in Experiment 13.2
When air could rush into the can, it did not crush because the pressures inside and out were equal. (top). When air was prevented from entering the can, the pressure inside was less than the atmospheric pressure outside and the can collapsed (bottom).

Scientists measure air pressure (atmospheric pressure) with an instrument called a barometer. Meteorologists use changes in air pressure (sometimes called barometric pressure because it is measured by barometers) to help predict changing weather. You may have seen a barometer, like the one shown in Figure 13.5, that shows what the weather may be like based on the pressure reading. Notice how low pressure signifies rainy weather and high pressure denotes sunny weather. Notice also the units on the barometer in Figure 13.5. It turns out that there are many, many units that can be used to measure atmospheric pressure.

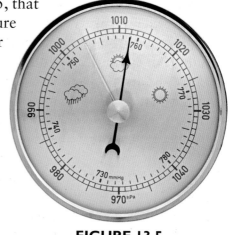

FIGURE 13.5
A Barometer
Barometers measure atmospheric pressure.

Units of Pressure

When I originally mentioned atmospheric pressure, I gave its average value at sea level as 14.7 pounds per square inch (psi). Since pressure is force per unit of area (P = F/A), many applications give the measurement of atmospheric pressure based on how much weight it exerts over a certain area. For example, some barometers (including the original barometer invented in 1643 by the Italian scientist Evangelista Torricelli) measure how much a column of mercury (Hg) rises or falls inside a tube (measured in millimeters) depending on the change in atmospheric pressure. As air pressure increases, the column of mercury in the barometer rises. As air pressure decreases, the column of mercury falls (see Figure 13.6).

A barometer that uses mercury is much easier to work with than one that uses water because mercury is a much denser liquid. That means a barometer made of mercury will be much shorter than one made of water. So, since this method of reporting atmospheric pressure simply involves measuring the height of mercury in a tube, the units are most often reported as millimeters of mercury, abbreviated mmHg. In those units, average atmospheric pressure at sea level is 760 mmHg. This same height measured in inches is 29.9, which you will sometimes hear reported by weathermen. Thus, 14.7 psi = 760 mmHg = 29.9 inches of Hg. You can see the barometer in Figure 13.5 uses mmHg units on the inner circle.

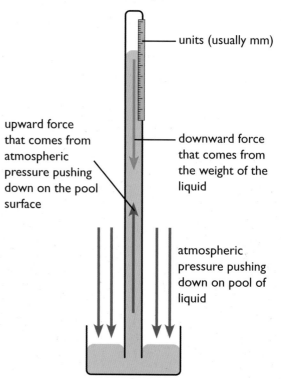

units (usually mm)

upward force that comes from atmospheric pressure pushing down on the pool surface

downward force that comes from the weight of the liquid

atmospheric pressure pushing down on pool of liquid

FIGURE 13.6
A Simple Barometer
As the atmosphere pushes down on the mercury in the pool, it pushes the mercury in the tube upwards against the weight of the liquid (downward).

That's not the end of it, however! Since we often worry about the atmospheric pressure only in terms of whether it is above or below the average sea-level atmospheric pressure, there is another unit we can use. This unit, called the atmosphere (abbreviated atm), is very easy to compare to the average sea-level atmospheric pressure. You see we call the atmospheric pressure at sea level 1.0 atm. So, 1 atm = 14.7 psi = 760 mmHg = 29.9 in. If the atmospheric pressure is less than 1.0 atm, you know it is less than its average sea-level value. For example, an atmospheric pressure of 0.9 atm indicates that the atmospheric pressure is only 90% of its average sea-level value. In the same way, a value of 1.1 atm indicates that atmospheric pressure is 110% of the average sea-level value.

Finally, if you noticed the units on the bottom circle of Figure 13.5 are hPa and wondered what they stand for—they are hectopascals. The pascal is a unit of pressure named after the French physicist, Blaise Pascal who validated Torricelli's work with air pressure. The pascal (Pa) unit is the SI unit of pressure. Another unit was also named after Torricelli and is called the torr. For this course, you will not need to know any of the pressure units except atmosphere and pounds per square inch, but when you take chemistry and physics, you will see all of the ones mentioned here and even more.

Altitude and Air Pressure

I mentioned that air pressure changes with the weather, but atmospheric pressure also changes with altitude. The gas molecules that make up our atmosphere are densest near Earth's surface and become less dense as altitude increases. In other words, at greater altitudes, the same volume of air contains fewer molecules of the gases that make up the atmosphere. Examine Figure 13.7.

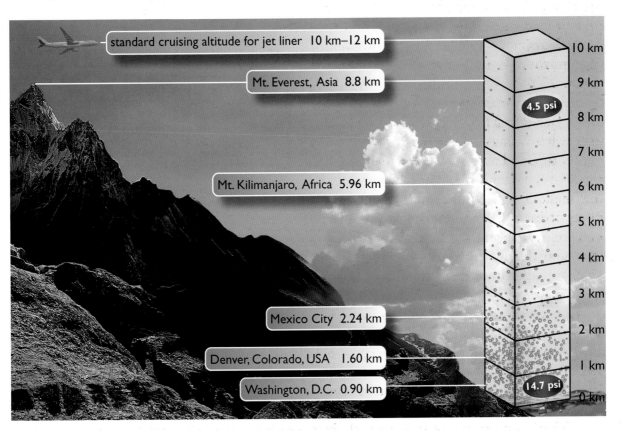

FIGURE 13.7
Air Pressure Decreases with Altitude
Atmospheric pressure is greatest at Earth's surface. As altitude increases, air pressure decreases.

MOD 13

Why do you think this is the case? Well, because air is made of gases, it can be compressed or squished together. This is because the atoms and molecules in gases are much more spread out than in solids or liquids (review the Kinetic Theory of Matter section in module 2 if you need to). Near Earth's surface, the column of air includes the entire depth of the atmosphere, so the weight of all the air above it increases the density of gas and so the pressure is higher. As altitude increases, the depth of the air above it decreases, so the density and pressure decrease as well. The higher you go, the less air there is in the column of atmosphere above you, so the lower the air pressure.

To see what happens to a sealed bottle as it descends a mountain, look at the plastic water bottle in Figure 13.8. The image on the left shows the empty bottle sealed at an elevation of 4,267 m (14,000 ft). The bottle (filled with air) was then carried down the mountain to an elevation of 2,743 m (9,000 ft) shown in the center image. Notice how the increased atmospheric pressure on the outside of the bottle begins to collapse it. Finally, in the image on the right, you see what happened to the bottle when it was brought down to 305 m (1,000 ft). The increased atmospheric pressure caused the bottle to be crushed because the atmospheric pressure (outside the bottle) was greater at the lower altitude than it was when the bottle was sealed at the higher altitude (where the pressure inside the bottle was lower).

FIGURE 13.8
Bottle Crushes as Altitude Decreases
Plastic bottle sealed at 4,265 m (left) on Mauna Kea in Hawaii.
Taken down to 2,743 m (center) and then 305 m (right),
where the change in air pressure crushed it.

Now notice Mount Everest in Figure 13.7. It has an altitude of 8.9 kilometers above sea level. At that altitude, the atmospheric pressure is only 4.5 psi, about a third of what exists at sea level. Look at the density of the air molecules at that altitude. Because of this fact, mountain climbers who climb Mount Everest (and other mountains) must bring their own oxygen supply. Even at more common altitudes, you can notice that the amount of air decreases with increasing altitude. For example, athletes who are used to playing their sport at low altitudes find it much more difficult to play the same sport in cities like Denver, Colorado, where the elevation is approximately 1610 meters (1 mile) above sea level. This is because the density (amount of air per unit volume) at that altitude is 90% of the amount at sea level, so the athletes must breathe harder to get the amount of oxygen to which they are accustomed. Keep in mind though, that the composition of air in Denver is still the same as at sea level, but the total amount of air is less, which means there are fewer oxygen molecules in the same volume of air available to breathe.

Check your understanding by trying the You Do Science activity and completing On Your Own problems 13.2–13.4.

YOU DO SCIENCE
AIR PRESSURE

Demonstrate the effect of air pressure and impress your friends at the same time by trying this activity. You'll need a plastic cup, index card, water, and a sink. Over the sink, completely fill the plastic cup with water. (It needs to be overflowing for this to work.) Then place the index card on top of the cup. Make sure that no air is trapped between the water and the card. What do you think will happen when you turn the cup upside down? Ask your friends or family what they think. Write down everyone's predictions. Now, holding the cup over the sink, place the palm of one hand on the card. Then use your other hand to turn the cup upside down so that the cup rests on the card in your hand. Holding the bottom of the cup and card over the sink (now on the top because the cup is inverted), slowly remove your hand from the card. Observe what happens. Explain what happened in terms of air pressure.

ON YOUR OWN

13.2   How does the atmosphere protect life on Earth?

13.3   In general, how does air pressure change with altitude?

13.4   The atmospheric pressure is 1.1 atm. Which of the following values for atmospheric pressure would you see in the weather report: 29.9 in, 32.9 in, or 28.1 in?

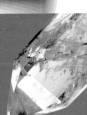

ENERGY AND THE ATMOSPHERE

Just as you may not have noticed that air has pressure and is pushing on you all the time, you also may not think of the air around you as having energy, but it does. It's hard to see energy moving, but energy is the reason that the air moves. The wind and weather result from changes in the energy in the atmosphere. Remember, all molecules, including the invisible gas molecules making up our atmosphere have energy—and that energy is always changing. Temperature differences in the atmosphere occur because solar energy is absorbed as it moves through the atmosphere. The transfer of heat energy within the atmosphere, hydrosphere, and the Earth's surface (and interior) occurs due to radiation, conduction, and convection (Figure 13.9).

Radiation—The transfer of energy by waves through air or empty space

MOD 13

Conduction—The transfer of heat energy from molecule to molecule by contact

Convection—The transfer of heat energy, through a liquid or gas, by currents

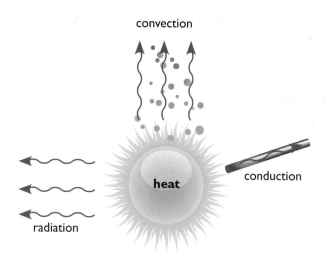

FIGURE 13.9
Methods of Heat Transfer
Heat energy can be transferred by radiation, conduction, or convection.

You read about light energy traveling in electromagnetic waves in module 10 and how this is a form of solar radiation. Heat energy can be transferred by waves through air or space as well. In fact after the sunlight heats Earth's surface, some heat energy radiates back into the atmosphere.

In conduction, heat energy moves from one molecule to another as they are touching. Warmer molecules vibrate faster than cooler ones. As the warmer molecules bump into the cooler ones, they transfer some of their energy. Think about how hot the metal handle of a pot gets when you're heating soup on the stove. The heat energy was transferred from one molecule to the next until the handle became hot too.

Convection is the transfer of heat energy by currents. This type of energy transfer is only possible with liquids and gases as they have more freedom of movement. When the air near Earth's surface is warmed by heat radiating from the ground, the warmer air is less dense so it rises. As it rises, it cools. The cool air is denser, so it sinks back down to the surface. This creates a convection current. Convection is the most important way heat travels in the atmosphere and is responsible for many weather conditions. Look at Figure 13.10. Cold, dense air (blue arrows) sinks downwards to be warmed by radiation from the warm ground or sun. The warm, less dense air (red arrows) rises and carries moisture upwards. As the warm, moist air rises, it

FIGURE 13.10
Convection Cloud Formation
Convection currents contribute to the formation of clouds.

cools. The water vapor in the cooling air condenses to form clouds and the cooler, denser air falls to the ground to be warmed again.

Now you know a bit about how energy moves in the atmosphere. In this course, we'll look at how temperature and pressure changes in the different layers of the atmo-

The Temperature Gradient in the Atmosphere

Now that you have a good understanding of what temperature is and you've reviewed the layers of the atmosphere, you can better understand why there is a temperature gradient in the atmosphere. What do I mean by temperature gradient? The term gradient refers to a gradual change, so a temperature gradient refers to a gradual change in temperature. Look at the red line in Infographic 13.1. That red line indicates the average temperature as the altitude increases in the atmosphere.

Remember, the amount of air in the atmosphere decreases with increasing altitude. The troposphere is the shortest layer of the atmosphere, rising only about 12 km. Even so, it contains 75% of all the gas molecules in the atmosphere, making it the densest layer. While the troposphere is characterized by a drop in atmospheric pressure as altitude increases, there is also a steady drop in temperature as altitude increases. In general, for every kilometer you increase in altitude, the temperature decreases by about 6.5 °C. The temperature gradient of the troposphere is responsible for snow existing on the upper parts of a mountain even in the summertime (Figure 13.12). By the time you reach altitudes of about 5 kilometers, the temperature is easily 30 °C lower than the temperature at sea level. Since summer temperatures are usually in the range of 25–30 °C, and since water freezes at 0 °C, you can see that even on a summer day, the temperature at altitudes of 5 km stays well below the freezing point of water. By the time you reach the tropopause, the air is so thin and cold that an unprotected person would quickly lose consciousness and die.

FIGURE 13.12
Mountains in Summer
Despite the fact that this photograph was taken in the summer (note the green grass in the foreground), the mountains in the background are still covered with snow and ice because of the altitude.

Now one reason the atmosphere is warm is the greenhouse effect, as discussed in the beginning of this module. As you increase altitude, the amount of greenhouse gases decreases, so there are fewer molecules absorbing energy. As a result, the energy content of the troposphere decreases with increasing altitude. Since the energy content of the troposphere decreases with increasing altitude, and since temperature is really a measure of the energy in the molecules of a substance, the temperature decreases with increasing altitude.

Notice what happens, though, when you reach the stratosphere—the temperature gradient reverses. Instead of decreasing with increasing altitude as it does in the troposphere, the temperature begins *increasing* with increasing altitude in the stratosphere. Why is that? Does the amount of air increase in the stratosphere? No. The amount of air in the stratosphere still decreases with increasing altitude. Something else is responsible for the change in the temperature gradient. You can see in Infographic 13.1, that the temperature gradient reverses when the ozone layer is reached. Even though the *total* amount of air

MOD 13

decreases with increasing altitude, the ozone layer introduces an increase in the amount of one particular gas: ozone.

Remember, ozone protects us from the ultraviolet rays of the sun by absorbing them before they reach the planet's surface. When ozone absorbs ultraviolet rays, it absorbs the ultraviolet rays' energy as well. Thus, even though the total amount of air decreases with increasing altitude, the amount of the greenhouse gas, ozone, increases in the stratosphere. As a result, the energy of the gases in the ozone layer and upper stratosphere is higher than the energy of the gases below the ozone layer (and top of the troposphere), because the ozone is absorbing more energy from the sun. This increased energy causes the temperature to increase with increasing altitude in the stratosphere. Once you reach the stratopause, however, the amount of ozone falls away again, and the temperature begins to decrease with increasing altitude in the mesosphere, as it does in the troposphere.

What happens in the thermosphere? An interesting effect occurs in the thermosphere. The number of molecules in the air is so small there that a thermometer would read incredibly low temperatures, because there would be very few collisions between the thermometer and the molecules in the thermosphere. In fact, the density of the molecules in the thermosphere is so low that it's been estimated one gas molecule can travel about 1 km before it collides with another molecule. Nevertheless, the average energy of the few molecules in the thermosphere is very high because they absorb huge amounts of high energy solar radiation (X-ray and UV radiation). This radiation is converted into heat energy and temperatures can reach higher that 1,000 °C. But, if you were to space walk in the thermosphere, you would be very cold because there are aren't enough gas molecules to collide with you and transfer the heat to you. So, if you define temperature as the average energy of each molecule in the thermosphere, the temperature of the thermosphere is very high. If, on the other hand, you define temperature as what a thermometer measures, the thermosphere has a very low temperature. This interesting effect is the source of the name: thermosphere.

Infographic 13.1 doesn't include a temperature gradient for the exosphere because the temperatures there vary greatly by day and night. The air in the exosphere is extremely thin and composed mainly of helium, and hydrogen. The temperature in the exosphere varies greatly and can range from −157 °C at night to over 1,700 °C during the day when the sun radiates its energy. Again, the energy of the individual molecules is very high (so they are moving very quickly), but there are so few molecules (even fewer than in the thermosphere) that a thermometer would not collide with enough to show an increase in temperature and a space walker would feel cold. Spacesuits, like the one shown in Figure 13.13, protect astronauts from those extreme temperatures. In fact, people live for quite a while in the International Space Station and other space stations that orbit in the thermosphere or lower exosphere.

FIGURE 13.13
Astronaut in Space
Astronaut Bruce McCandless II, participating in a historic untethered spacewalk in 1984.

think about this

Not all scientists agree that the exosphere is really a part of Earth's atmosphere. Some scientists consider the thermosphere to be the uppermost layer of our atmosphere, and that the exosphere is part of space. Yet, other scientists do consider the exosphere part of Earth's atmosphere. You see, the atoms and molecules in the exosphere actually orbit around the planet. Sometimes, the atoms and molecules escape their orbits and go into interplanetary space. This tends to blur the distinction between the exosphere and interplanetary space. As a result, it is really hard to say where the exosphere ends and interplanetary space begins.

The Ionosphere

Before we end this section on the energy of the atmosphere, we need to discuss the ionosphere. Within the upper portions of the mesosphere, the thermosphere, and the lower portions of the exosphere is a region called the ionosphere. Notice that this name has the word ion in it. Recall from module 4 that when an atom becomes electrically charged, it becomes an ion. When an atom turns into an ion, we say that it has been ionized. So, the ionosphere is a very active region of the atmosphere where solar radiation ionizes gases. The ionosphere can grow or shrink depending on the energy it absorbs from the Sun and ranges roughly from 60 km to 1,000 km above Earth's surface.

The ionosphere is actually a very useful portion of Earth's atmosphere, because radio transmitters can use it to increase their range. Radio signals (part of the electromagnetic spectrum, module 10) travel in straight lines. Thus, most radio signals (AM and FM radio, for example) can only be received by radios that are relatively close (within a few hundred miles) of the transmitter. Certain radio signals (such as strong AM signals, especially at night), however, can actually bounce off the ionosphere. As a result, these radio signals can be transmitted a great distance. Shortwave radios emit signals with the ideal properties for bouncing off of the ionosphere, so shortwave radios can really broadcast around the world.

We've already discussed the auroras a bit before in previous modules, but this phenomena occurs in part due to the ionosphere. You see, parts of the ionosphere overlap with Earth's magnetic field at the north and south poles. The northern lights, called the aurora borealis (baw ree al' is), is in the Northern Hemisphere, and the southern lights, called the aurora australis (aw stray' lis), appear in the Southern Hemisphere (Figure 13.14).

FIGURE 13.14
Auroras
Spectacular light displays are visible as the aurora borealis in the Northern Hemisphere (left). The aurora australis encircles Antarctica as seen from space (right).

MOD 13

If you have never seen them, they appear in the night sky as glowing regions of brilliant colors that tend to move over the sky in interesting ways. The auroras are the result of high-energy collisions between ionized particles in the ionosphere that are affected by the magnetic fields of both Earth and the sun. The collisions involve a lot of energy, and some of that energy is converted to light, which makes up the auroras. Because these collisions occur in the ionosphere above the north and south poles, they are usually visible in places far to the north (such as Canada and Alaska) or to the south (such as Australia and New Zealand). However, depending on the energy involved, they can sometimes be visible in regions farther away from the poles.

Before continuing, complete On Your Own problems 13.7–13.9.

ON YOUR OWN

13.7 List the major layers of the Earth's atmosphere in order, beginning with the layer closest to Earth's surface.

13.8 Compare (generally) the way temperature changes with altitude in the troposphere and in the stratosphere.

13.9 Sometimes, disturbances in the sun's magnetic field can cause disturbances in the ionosphere. Suppose you were listening to an FM radio at the time of such a disturbance. Would you notice? What if you were listening to a shortwave radio transmission from another continent?

BEYOND OUR ATMOSPHERE

You now have an overview of Earth and its atmosphere. But what about beyond our planet's atmosphere? There is a whole branch of science devoted to exploring our solar system (Figure 13.15). So just how do scientists discover things in space? What do they look for?

FIGURE 13.15
Our Solar System
The planets of our solar system. From left to right: the sun, Mercury, Venus, Earth, Mars, Jupiter, Saturn, Uranus, Neptune.

Planetary science is the study of planets and their systems, including moons, rings, gas clouds, and so on. Modern technology, including complex telescopes, along with piloted spacecrafts and unpiloted space probes, have allowed scientists to explore beyond our planet. Although humans have not yet traveled across our solar system, scientists have gathered a lot of information about different planets and moons. The National Aeronautics and Space Administration (NASA) has been exploring space since 1958. Other countries and groups of countries also have space exploration agencies. Since NASA's first Apollo missions took people to the moon, all of the planets and nearly all of the moons of our solar system have been photographed by space probes. A space probe is an unpiloted spacecraft that carries scientific instruments and computers into space and transmits information back to scientists on Earth. Space probes are generally less expensive to send to space than piloted space vehicles.

For example, look at the image of Jupiter in Figure 13.16, captured by NASA's Juno space probe on September 11, 2019. Notice the swirling clouds and other details. We live

in an amazing time that allows us to see distant planets in such detail! The Juno is a solar powered spacecraft, launched on August 5, 2011 that reached Jupiter in July 2016. Since then it has been orbiting Jupiter and has been transmitting images and other scientific data about Jupiter's magnetic field and atmosphere. Scientists rely on space probes like Juno and telescopes to gather new information about the solar system.

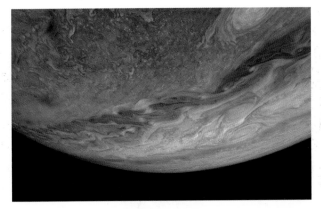

FIGURE 13.16
Jupiter
An image of Jupiter captured by the Juno spacecraft in 2019.

One of the many things scientists in this field look for when exploring another planet is whether it has signs of life. What do they look for? Scientists study the atmospheres of the planets to determine if conditions are adequate to support life, even tiny microbes. Because Earth is the only planet with life, and oxygen is a necessary gas, one of the atmospheric gases they look for is oxygen. They also look for water, specifically liquid water. The Juno space probe is equipped with instruments that are taking measurements

FIGURE 13.17
Opportunity Rover
An artist's rendering of the Mars Exploration Rover (MER) taking photographs and gathering data on Martian soil (left). An actual photograph of Opportunity's track on the surface of Mars (right).

deep into Jupiter's Great Red Spot to see if there is any evidence of even water vapor. In 2004, NASA successfully landed two space probes, robotic rovers named Spirit and Opportunity, on Mars (Figure 13.17). They were each to have a 90-day mission of geological

MOD 13

and atmospheric exploration. But Spirit worked until 2010 and Opportunity stopped transmitting in June 2018. What did they find? They found evidence that Mars was wetter long ago and that conditions on Mars may have been able to sustain microbial life (although no evidence of life was found). NASA has since sent two other probes to Mars, the Insight Lander and the Curiosity Rover. The Mars 2020 Rover is scheduled to launch in July 2020.

So far we've talked about unpiloted space probes and the information they transmit to Earth. But scientists still travel into space, although they now conduct near-Earth space missions. Also, rather than different countries all having their own space programs, a time of cooperation exists in the exploration of space. Astronauts from various countries are currently living and conducting scientific experiments aboard the International Space Station (ISS), shown in Figure 13.18, as it orbits Earth in the thermosphere.

FIGURE 13.18
Alluvial Fans and Deltas
The International Space Station (left) in orbit over the Earth. Astronauts Christina Koch and Andrew Morgan stow biological research samples into a science freezer located inside the U.S. Destiny laboratory module of the ISS.

Future space missions include testing microgravity conditions and how it affects 3D printing, the effects of microgravity on key organ tissues (colon, heart, lung, liver, kidney), and testing a new vest that could protect astronauts' vital organs from deep-space radiation. These vests may have applications for X-ray technicians and those patients undergoing radiation therapy. There are many other experiments taking place on the ISS. If you are interested in learning more about what happens on the ISS or our current explorations of space, visit the Book Extras website for links.

Finish up this module by completing On Your Own problem 13.10.

ON YOUR OWN

13.10 What are some ways that scientists are currently learning more about the solar system?

SUMMING UP

The Earth and its atmosphere are fascinating places. Earth is the only known planet that supports life and that is because of God's marvelous design. There is so much more for you to investigate, weather, climate, astronomy, and so on. We've only covered the basics, but I hope you have found that Earth is a very special place to call our home.

ANSWERS TO THE "ON YOUR OWN" QUESTIONS

13.1 Plants may grow better when their caretakers talk to them because when someone talks to a plant, he exhales some carbon dioxide on it. This increases the concentration of carbon dioxide in the plant's vicinity, which might make some plants grow better.

13.2 The atmosphere protects life on Earth from bombardment by meteors and high-energy radiation from space. It also filters out much of the harmful ultraviolet radiation before it can reach Earth's surface.

13.3 In general, atmospheric pressure decreases as altitude increases. Think of atmospheric pressure as the weight of air pressing down on what it touches. As you increase altitude, there is less air above you. As a result, there is less weight pressing down on you.

13.4 The atmospheric pressure will be reported as 32.9 inches. Remember, an atmospheric pressure of 1.0 atm means that atmospheric pressure is at its average sea level value, which is the same as 29.9 inches of Hg. Since the atmospheric pressure is 1.1 atm, we know that it must be higher than its average sea level value. The only number given that is greater than 29.9 inches of Hg is 32.9 inches of Hg.

13.5 There will be heat in this system, because energy will be transferred from the warmer brick to the colder brick. Since they are touching the heat energy will be transferred by conduction. Despite the fact that both bricks are cold, one is warmer than the other. Thus, energy will flow from the warmer brick to the colder brick. Since heat is energy that is being transferred, heat is present.

13.6 The observer is correct. When the thermometer was put into the substance, some energy got transferred from the substance to the thermometer. That's what caused the liquid in the thermometer to rise. Since energy went into the thermometer's liquid, it left the substance. This resulted in some small amount of cooling. In other words, since the thermometer took a little energy from the substance, it cooled the substance slightly. Thus, the substance was slightly warmer the instant the thermometer was placed in it, and then it cooled as a result of transferring energy to the thermometer.

13.7 The major layers from Earth's surface outward are: troposphere, stratosphere, mesosphere, thermosphere, and exosphere. The ionosphere is not a layer, but a region that overlaps several layers.

13.8 In the troposphere, the temperature decreases as the altitude increases. In the stratosphere (once you reach the ozone layer), the temperature increases rapidly as the altitude increases.

13.9   You will not really notice the disturbance while listening to the FM radio, but you will notice it while listening to the shortwave radio. Remember, short-wave radios bounce their signals off the ionosphere. A disturbance in the ionosphere will affect the shortwave radio's signal.

13.10   Piloted spacecraft, unpiloted space probes, and telescopes are used to gather new information on the solar system.

FORMS OF CARBON

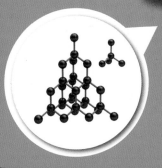

DIAMOND

Diamond is a form of carbon in which each carbon atom is covalently bonded to four other carbon atoms. This three-dimensional form is strong, compact, and rigid. Remember, diamond has a hardness of 10 because no other natural substance is harder than diamond. This hardness comes from the fact that cutting a diamond requires breaking many covalent bonds. For this reason many cutting, grinding, and drilling tools are coated with diamond. And, of course, diamonds are used in jewelry.

GRAPHITE

Graphite has very different properties than diamond. In graphite, the carbon atoms are arranged in widely spaced layers. The covalent bonds between carbons within each layer are strong. However, each of the layers is only weakly bonded to the other layers. The weak bonds between layers allow them to easily slide over each other. This gives graphite soft, slippery properties that make it a good lubricant for moving metal parts in machinery. You should recognize it as being used in pencil "lead" where the stacked structure of graphite allows you to easily make and erase marks on paper.

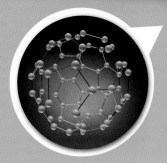

FULLERENES

Fullerenes were discovered in 1985 in the soot produced when some carbon compounds burn. In this form of carbon, the carbon atoms are arranged in pentagon and hexagon patterns that form hollow spheres. These carbon spheres resemble soccer balls and have been found in meteorites. The one pictured here contains 60 carbon atoms (20 hexagons and 12 pentagons) and is called buckminsterfullerene after Buckminster Fuller, an American architect who designed similarly shaped domes.

INFOGRAPHIC 14.1
Forms of Carbon

Hydrocarbons

You learned a bit about hydrocarbons in module 5. Remember, hydrocarbons are compounds that contain only carbon and hydrogen. They are the simplest type of organic compounds, yet they can greatly vary in size. Methane (CH_4), for example, is a hydrocarbon with only one carbon and is produced by microorganisms in the stomachs of cows. Grass contains a compound called cellulose which grazing cows (Figure 14.3) are not able to digest. However,

FIGURE 14.3
Cows and Methane
Microorganisms in the stomachs of a cow produce up to 0.23 kilograms (0.5 pounds) of methane per day.

microorganisms in the cow's stomachs break down cellulose into smaller molecules that the cow can digest, but they produce methane as a byproduct. You may recall that methane is a greenhouse gas and once in our atmosphere tends to absorb the infrared light the Earth radiates.

Saturated Hydrocarbons

Methane is considered a saturated hydrocarbon because all of the bonds in the compound are single bonds. Notice in Figure 14.4, methane has only one carbon atom, ethane has two carbon atoms, propane has three carbon atoms, and butane has four carbon atoms—each single bonded and having the maximum number of hydrogen atoms possible for each carbon atom. In other words, they are saturated with hydrogen atoms. Look at each of the names of the hydrocarbons in Figure 14.4. What do you notice about them? They each end in –*ane*. Another name for a saturated hydrocarbon is an alkane. The names of alkanes end in –*ane*.

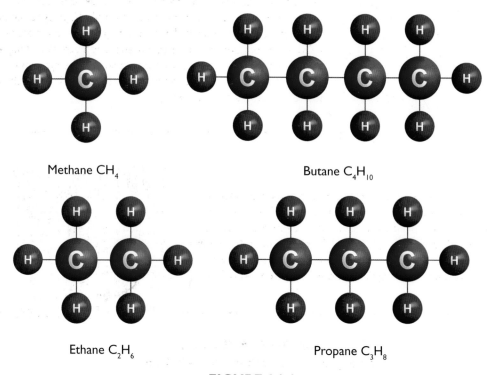

Methane CH_4

Butane C_4H_{10}

Ethane C_2H_6

Propane C_3H_8

FIGURE 14.4
Some Straight-Chain Alkanes
Molecules of methane, ethane, propane, and butane.

Different hydrocarbons have different properties, such as the boiling and melting points. The properties of hydrocarbons depend on two things: the number of carbon atoms and how those atoms are arranged. The carbon atoms can be arranged in a straight chain, a branched chain, or a ring. Study Infographic 14.2 to learn more about the arrangement of carbon atoms in alkanes.

ARRANGEMENT OF CARBON ATOMS IN ALKANES

In **straight-chain molecules**, all the carbon atoms are lined up in a row and form the backbone of the molecule. The number of carbon atoms in a straight-chain alkane affects its state at room temperature. The alkanes shown in Figure 14.4 are all gases at room temperature, while pentane (C_5H_{12}) and octane (C_8H_{18}) are liquids at room temperature. The more carbon atoms, the higher the boiling point.

STRAIGHT CHAINS
Butane C_4H_{10}

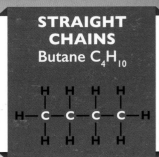

BRANCHED CHAINS
Isobutane C_4H_{10}

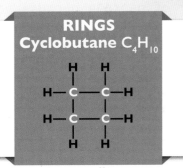

Branched-chain molecules have at least one of the carbon atoms off to the side from the backbone. Look at isobutane. Notice that it has the same molecular formula (C_4H_{10}) as butane, but its structural formula is different. One of the carbon atoms in isobutane is bonded to the three other carbon atoms making a branch. (Recall that a molecular formula shows the type and number of atoms in a molecule and the structural formula show how those atoms are arranged.)

In **ring molecules** such as cyclobutane the chain of carbon atoms is joined at the two ends to form a ring. Because each carbon atom forms bonds with two other carbon atoms, it can only bond with two hydrogen atoms. So cyclobutane (C_4H_8) has two fewer hydrogen atoms than butane or isobutane. Most ring alkanes (also called cyclic hydrocarbons) have rings with five or six carbons.

RINGS
Cyclobutane C_4H_{10}

INFOGRAPHIC 14.2
Arrangement of Carbon Atoms in Alkanes

Look again at butane and isobutane in Infographic 14.2. Both molecules have four carbon atoms and ten hydrogen atoms, but the atoms are arranged differently. Compounds with the same molecular formula but different structural formulas are called isomers. Butane and isobutane are isomers. As you might expect, the difference in the structure of these molecules can affect their properties. For example, the boiling point of butane is –0.5 °C, but the boiling point of isobutane is –11.7 °C. With butane there is only one possible isomer, but the number of possible isomers increases rapidly with each additional carbon atom added to the chain. For example, octane (C_8H_{18}) has 18 isomers, while decane ($C_{10}H_{22}$) has 75! Try the You Do Science activity to model the isomers of hexane (C_6H_{14}).

YOU DO SCIENCE
MODELING ISOMERS

In this activity, you will build models to describe the isomers of hexane (C_6H_{14}). You will need 30 marshmallows, 70 raisins (or dried cranberries), and 50 toothpicks. Break the toothpicks in half. Each ½ toothpick represents a single bond. Use marshmallows to represent carbon atoms, and raisins to represent hydrogen atoms. Using your supplies, build five different isomers of hexane. Each model should have 6 carbon atoms and 14 hydrogen atoms. For each model attach all six carbon atoms to each other first. Then attach hydrogen atoms until each carbon atom has four bonds. Keep in mind that you only build a new isomer if it is structurally different than the others. Look at Figure 14.5. All of the structures shown are the same isomer of pentane because you can create each one simply by rotating or flipping the first one. So make sure you have five different isomers. Draw the structural formula for each isomer in your notebook. (You can find the correct structural formulas after the answers to the On Your Own problems at the end of this module.)

FIGURE 14.5
The Same Pentane Isomer

Unsaturated Hydrocarbons

Knowing that saturated hydrocarbons are those that have only single bonds between carbon atoms (and so have the maximum number of hydrogen atoms for each carbon atom), can you guess what an unsaturated hydrocarbon is? Unsaturated hydrocarbons have at least one double or triple bond between carbon atoms, so the carbon atoms are not bonded to the maximum number of hydrogen atoms. These type of hydrocarbons are classified by the type of bond (double or triple) and the arrangement of their carbon atoms. There are three types of unsaturated hydrocarbons: alkenes, aromatic hydrocarbons, and alkynes.

Study Infographic 14.3 to learn more about these types of unsaturated hydrocarbons and then complete On Your Own problems 14.1–14.4.

TYPES OF UNSATURATED HYDROCARBONS

ALKENES
Ethene C_2H_4

Alkenes are unsaturated hydrocarbons that contain one or more double bonds. The name of any alkene always ends in –ene. Most fruit and vegetable-bearing plants produce ethene. Ethene (also called ethylene) speeds up ripening. You can see evidence of ethene production (brown spots) on the bananas.

AROMATIC HYDROCARBONS
Benzene C_6H_6

Aromatic hydrocarbons are also called cyclic hydrocarbons and they contain at least one double bond so their names also end in -ene. Although the formula for these compounds show six carbon atoms in a ring with alternating single and double bonds, the six bonds in the ring are the same. That is because the six valence electrons are shared by all six carbon atoms. Benzene is the smallest aromatic hydrocarbon with just one ring. Larger aromatic hydrocarbons consist of two or more rings. Their name, aromatic hydrocarbons, comes from the fact that many of them have strong odors.

ALKYNES
Ethyne C_2H_2

Alkynes are unsaturated hydrocarbons that contain one or more triple bond. The name of specific alkynes ends in –yne. Ethyne is the smallest alkyne. It is burned in acetylene torches that are used by welders. Alkynes are the most reactive hydrocarbon compounds and are relatively rare in nature. The ethyne in the acetylene torch produces a flame so hot that most metals can be melted and welded together.

INFOGRAPHIC 14.3
Types of Unsaturated Hydrocarbons

ON YOUR OWN

14.1   Name three forms of carbon.

14.2   What are three ways that that carbon atoms can be arranged in a hydrocarbon molecule?

14.3   Explain what an isomer is.

14.4   A scientist discovered a new unsaturated hydrocarbon? She determined that there were two triple bonds between carbon atoms in the molecule. What type of unsaturated hydrocarbon did she discover?

MOD 14

Fossil Fuels

Where do hydrocarbons come from? The main source of hydrocarbons is fossil fuels. Fossil fuels are mixtures of hydrocarbons that formed from the remains of plants or animals. When plants die, they generally decay or are eaten by other organisms. But when floods or volcanic eruptions bury large masses of plants and animals, and this organic material is crushed so that most of the hydrogen and oxygen atoms are pressed out, carbon in the form of fossil fuel is left. Three types of fossil fuels exist. They are coal, natural gas, and petroleum. The type of fossil fuel depends on the organic material and how it decayed.

Coal is a solid fossil fuel like that shown in Figure 14.6. You can see the fossil of the fern in the large chunk of coal. Giant tree ferns and other plants that were buried after catastrophic events and then subjected to great amounts of pressure, produced the coal we're using today. Most of the hydrocarbons in coal are larger aromatic hydrocarbons with a high ratio of carbon to hydrogen atoms. So when burning coal, more soot is produced than when burning other fossil fuels. The majority of electric power in the United States is generated by burning coal in power plants.

FIGURE 14.6
Coal from Plants
Ferns, like the ones shown, have left fossilized imprints on coal formations as they were compressed under layers of rock.

Natural gas, the second main fossil fuel, is formed from the remains of marine organisms. Natural gas is mostly methane—the same compound produced in cow's stomachs as they digest grass. Natural gas also contains ethane, propane, and isomers of butane. It is often found along with coal or oil in underground deposits but it can form at higher temperatures. Natural gas burns with a blue flame as shown on the gas range in Figure 14.7. Many homes also have gas furnaces, fireplaces, and water heaters. Natural gas is distributed to homes through underground pipes. Like coal,

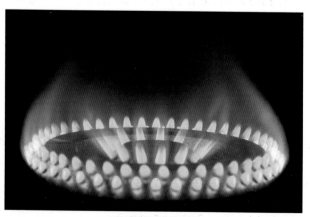

FIGURE 14.7
Natural Gas Flames
Natural gas burns cleaner, less soot, than coal—making it a desirable fuel.

natural gas is also used in power plants to produce electricity. However, natural gas burns cleaner than coal does, with much less soot.

Petroleum, also known as crude oil, is a liquid fossil fuel. Like natural gas, petroleum is formed from the remains of marine animals such as plankton and algae. Petroleum is pumped by oil rigs from deep below Earth's surface, both on land and offshore. Petroleum is a mixture of mainly long, branched alkane and alkene hydrocarbons. Once pumped out of the ground, petroleum is processed and separated into simpler mixtures, such as gasoline, kerosene, and heating oil.

FIGURE 14.8
Gasoline from Petroleum
Gasoline is made from crude oil. It is one of the most readily seen fossil fuels.

Combustion of Fossil Fuels

We burn fossil fuels to release energy used to power cars, cook food, and heat buildings. You learned about combustion reactions in module 5. Energy from the combustion of the hydrocarbon propane is used to heat the air in a hot air balloon.

$$C_3H_8 + 5O_2 \longrightarrow 3CO_2 + 4H_2O$$

When hydrocarbons of fossil fuels are burned in the presence of adequate oxygen, the primary products are carbon dioxide and water. This is called complete combustion.

Sometimes, however, in stoves and furnaces that are not cleaned or properly ventilated, there may not be enough oxygen available for complete combustion of all the fuel. When that happens, a deadly gas, carbon monoxide, is produced. This is called incomplete combustion.

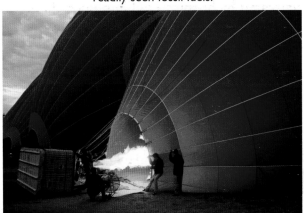

FIGURE 14.9
Hot Air Balloons
Energy from propane combustion heats the air, which causes hot air balloons to rise by convection.

$$2C_3H_8 + 7O_2 \longrightarrow 6CO + 8H_2O \text{ (incomplete combustion)}$$

Carbon monoxide (CO) is a colorless, odorless gas that can be inhaled and absorbed by blood. If carbon monoxide is absorbed by blood, it prevents the blood cell from carrying oxygen throughout the body. People whose homes are heated by natural gas or heating oil should have carbon monoxide detectors to alert them to the production of carbon monoxide. In addition to the production of carbon monoxide, incomplete combustion of fossil fuels also produces tiny particles of carbon called soot. Review this section by completing On Your Own problem 14.5.

ON YOUR OWN

14.5   What are the three main fossil fuels? What phase state are each type in?

MOD 14

BIOCHEMISTRY

Biochemistry is the chemistry of life. *Bio–* means life, so biochemistry deals with the chemistry of living things. You've already learned about molecules and compounds. Well, living organisms have specific molecules and compounds that are necessary to carry on life functions. In this section you will learn about some of the most important compounds and processes that go on inside living organisms like you.

Biochemical Compounds

You will learn about these compounds in great detail when you take biology. But for this course, you should know that all biochemical compounds contain carbon, hydrogen, and oxygen. Some biochemical molecules may also contain nitrogen, phosphorus, or sulfur. The molecule in Figure 14.10 is one of the most important biomolecules, glucose ($C_6H_{12}O_6$). Without glucose, living things would not have the energy they need to survive. In the model in Figure 14.10, red balls represent carbon atoms, green balls represent oxygen atoms, and blue balls represent hydrogen atoms.

Almost all biochemical compounds are polymers. Polymers are large molecules composed of repeating smaller molecules called monomers. The prefix *mono–* means one, and the prefix *poly–* means many.

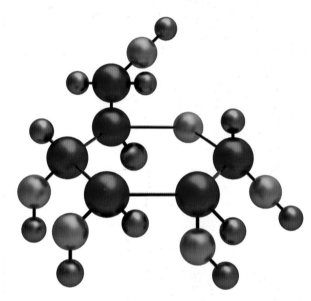

FIGURE 14.10
A Glucose Model
Glucose is the energy molecule of the cell. It is composed of carbon (red), oxygen (green), and hydrogen (blue) atoms.

Monomer—A single molecule that can react with other molecules to form a large molecule

Polymer—A large molecule that is made out of many smaller molecules joined together by covalent bonds

Glucose is a monomer. When many glucose molecules bond together, they form the polymer starch that is found in plants like potatoes, corn, and rice. Glucose monomers also form the polymer cellulose found in the cell walls of plants. The same cellulose that microorganisms break down in the stomachs of grass eating cows.

Although there are millions of biochemical compounds, all of them can be grouped into four main classes: carbohydrates, proteins, lipids, and nucleic acids. These molecules make up the cells and tissues of living things. They are also involved in all life process, such as making and breaking down food for energy. Study Table 14.1 to learn more about the four classes of biochemical compounds.

TABLE 14.1
Classes of Biochemical Compounds

Class	Elements	Examples and Functions
CARBOHYDRATES	carbon oxygen hydrogen	sugars—provide energy to cells starches—store energy in plants cellulose—makes up cell walls of plants
PROTEINS	carbon oxygen hydrogen nitrogen sulfur	tissues—main component of muscle enzymes—speed up biochemical reactions hormones—regulate life processes antibodies—defend against infections
LIPIDS	carbon oxygen hydrogen phosphorus (some)	fats—store energy in animals and a main part of cell membranes oils—store energy in plants
NUCLEIC ACIDS	carbon oxygen hydrogen nitrogen phosphorus	DNA—stores genetic information in cells RNA—helps cells make proteins

Chemical Reactions in Cells

Besides fossil fuels, people in the past have burned animal fats (called tallow) to make candles or as fuel for their lamps. This is a combustion reaction in which the fat combines with oxygen and produces carbon dioxide, water, and energy in the form of heat and light. Our bodies also release energy from fat in controlled chemical reactions within our cells. Some of the energy released helps maintain your internal body temperature to around 37 °C (98.6 °F). Chemical reactions that take place in the cells of organisms follow the same rules as reactions that you learned about in module 5. Energy may be required or produced in these reactions, or it may be transferred or converted from one form to another. All living things need energy and they get this energy through chemical reactions.

Chemical reactions that take place in living things are called biochemical reactions. Living organisms depend on chemical reactions for more than just energy, though. Every function and structure of living creatures depends on thousands of biochemical reactions that occur in each cell. Some of the most important biochemical reactions are the reactions involved in making food, photosynthesis, and releasing energy from food, cellular respiration.

Photosynthesis and Cellular Respiration

Most of the energy used by living organisms comes, either directly or indirectly, from the light energy provided by the sun. During photosynthesis, plants use the energy from sunlight to chemically combine carbon dioxide and water to produce carbohydrates, specifically glucose. A green pigment in plant leaves called chlorophyll is required for photosynthesis to occur. The equation below summarizes the complex series of chemical reactions for photosynthesis.

$$6CO_2 + 6H_2O + \text{energy (light)} \longrightarrow C_6H_{12}O_6 + 6O_2$$

Notice what happens during photosynthesis. Energy from sunlight is converted into the chemical energy stored in the covalent bonds of the glucose molecule.

Plants are able to make glucose, their own energy storing compound, but how do plants and animals release the energy stored in those bonds? Plants and animals break bonds in glucose and release the stored energy in the process of cellular respiration. Like photosynthesis, cellular respiration is a complex series of reactions. The following equation is a summary of the overall process.

$$C_6H_{12}O_6 + 6O_2 \longrightarrow 6CO_2 + 6H_2O + \text{energy (heat)}$$

Notice how the reactants of cellular respiration are the products of photosynthesis, and the products of cellular respiration are the reactants of photosynthesis. Figure 14.11 summarizes the relationship between photosynthesis and cellular respiration. Each process produces the reactants for the other process.

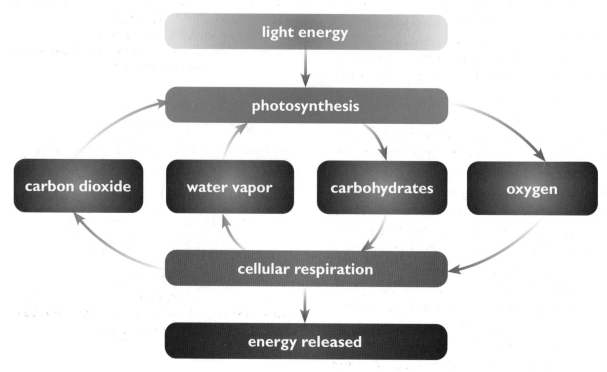

FIGURE 14.11
Related Processes
Photosynthesis and cellular respiration are related. The products of one are the reactants of the other.

think about this

What does your body need energy for? If you answered everything, you're right! It takes energy to keep your body temperature steady. It takes energy to smile, laugh, or cry. Every time you have a cut, it takes energy for your body to heal the skin. It takes energy to ride your bike, climb the stairs, eat your lunch, or even to breathe and sleep. So, from the second you started life as a single cell, the reactions of cellular respiration have been going on inside your cells, nonstop. The energy your body needs to thrive you get from glucose and oxygen; the products of photosynthesis. As your cells convert the chemical energy in glucose to the usable energy for life functions, they release carbon dioxide and water—exactly what plants need to produce glucose and oxygen. What a remarkable design!

Reaction Helpers

Many of the reactions that take place in your cells would not happen fast enough to keep your cells alive if they didn't have help. You worked with a reaction helper in Experiment 5.2 when you added yeast to a decomposition reaction. I told you that the yeast was a catalyst, which is a substance that speeds up reactions without being used up. Our bodies use protein catalysts called enzymes.

Without enzymes, our bodies could not break down or digest food. Enzymes are also used in cellular respiration. Enzymes allow reactions inside cells to take place faster and at much lower temperatures than they normally would. Thousands of enzymes help reactions take place in your cells. When you eat a sandwich, an enzyme in your saliva (amylase) aids in the breakdown of the bread and lettuce. Digestion continues in your stomach where another enzyme (pepsin) catalyzes the breakdown of proteins.

Our bodies need vitamins in order to produce certain enzymes. Vitamins are organic compounds that organisms need in small amounts, but they cannot produce themselves. We must get vitamins from the foods we eat. For example, vitamin B (found in eggs, dairy, and meat) helps in forming the enzymes needed for cellular respiration. Vitamin C (found in citrus foods) is needed by the enzyme that makes a protein in your skin. Vitamin C is also necessary for the growth, development, and repair of all body tissues.

To get an idea of how much vitamin C there is in different fruit juices, conduct Experiment 14.1. Then review what you've learned by completing On Your Own problems 14.6–14.8.

FIGURE 14.12
Digestion Enzymes
Enzymes aid in the breakdown of food to release energy stored in the bonds.

FIGURE 14.13
Vitamin C
Vitamin C, found in citrus fruits, is needed by your body for health and growth.

EXPERIMENT 14.1
COMPARING VITAMIN C IN FRUIT JUICES

PURPOSE:
To use an indicator to determine the relative amount of vitamin C in fruit juices.

MATERIALS:
- Tincture of iodine—1 ounce bottle (You can find this at any drug store.)
- Lemon juice
- Apple juice
- Orange juice
- Grapefruit juice or pineapple juice (or another juice of your choosing)
- 100 mg vitamin C pill
- Medicine dropper
- A 1 quart jar
- Measuring cup with milliliter markings
- Water
- Six 8 ounce clear plastic cups

BACKGROUND:
Different fruits or fruit juices all contain vitamin C, but which is the best source? Vitamin C is an organic acid called ascorbic acid. Like other acids, vitamin C reacts with indicators to produce a color change. Tincture of iodine is a brownish-red colored indicator. When vitamin C is added, it becomes colorless. This reaction can be used to test for the presence of vitamin C and to give some idea of the amount that can be found in the fruit or fruit juices.

Note: Do not consume any of the fruit or fruit juices during this experiment. Tincture of iodine can stain and *should NOT be ingested*, so you may want to place plastic under your lab area.

HYPOTHESIS:
Predict which fruit juice contains the most vitamin C. Record your prediction.

PROCEDURE:
1. Prepare an iodine solution by mixing a bottle of tincture of iodine with 500 mL of water in the quart jar.
2. Pour 50 mL of the iodine solution into each of 5 clear plastic cups. Line them up on your work area.
3. Using a spoon, crush a vitamin C tablet and then dissolve it in 100 mL of water in the other clear plastic cup. This will be your control.
4. Using the medicine dropper add one drop of the vitamin C control solution to a cup of iodine. Swirl the cup and note the color change. If the iodine solution did not become clear, continue adding drops of the vitamin C solution one at a time (and swirling after each drop) until the iodine solution turns clear or almost clear. Make sure to count the drops and then record the total number of drops required to turn the iodine solution clear.

5. Rinse out the medicine dropper thoroughly so that your results will not be contaminated. If you have more than one medicine dropper, use a different one for the next juice while the first one dries.
6. Repeat steps 4 and 5 for each of the juices.
7. Clean up and put everything away.

CONCLUSIONS:

Make a bar graph of your results. Which fruit juice had the most vitamin C? Write a paragraph explaining how your results showed the juices with the most vitamin C. Make connections to the text.

What did you find in your experiment? The control should have required the fewest number of drops to make the iodine solution turn from reddish-brown to clear. That is because the vitamin C pill is 100% vitamin C. So when testing the juices, you should expect that it will require more drops of the juice to turn the iodine solution clear than it did of the control. But the juice(s) that turn the iodine solution clear in the fewest number of drops will contain the most vitamin C. The juice(s) that require the most drops to turn the iodine solution clear will have the least amount of vitamin C.

ON YOUR OWN

14.6 What happens to sunlight during photosynthesis?

14.7 Describe the relationship between photosynthesis and cellular respiration.

14.8 Amino acids are the monomers of proteins (proteins are polymers). What would happen to the reactions in a person's body if they did not have enough of the essential amino acids?

PHYSICS AND LIFE

Biological physics, or biophysics, is becoming one of the leading sciences of the 21st century. Biophysics combines the study of physics and biology to examine systems (such as cells, organisms, ecosystems) of living things. You've already read a bit about how physics and biology are interrelated. For example, you learned that bats use sound waves to locate insects to eat. Understanding sound waves also helps doctors know how the ear works and how to help those with hearing loss. Optical lenses help correct vision problems. Even in your everyday actions of walking, driving, or using a cell phone, physics is at work. Let's take a look at how physics interacts with your everyday life.

Physics at the Park

You can see examples of simple machines at any neighborhood park. The seesaw in Figure 14.14 is an example of a simple lever. Swings are examples of pendulums.

FIGURE 14.14
Seesaws and Swings
Examples of physics in the park.

To swing, you use a force, whether your feet or someone pushing you, to overcome friction and to get you started. Swings work by converting potential energy into kinetic energy, then kinetic energy into potential energy over and over again. Remember all the way back to Experiment 1.2? You found that mass did not affect the pendulum's swing. That means no matter how big or small your friend is, they will swing at the same time as you do as long as you start your swing from the same height. Try it next time you're at a swing set—physics in action!

While we're talking about parks, an amusement park is a great place to see physics happening. You can see all three of Newton's laws occurring when you ride bumper cars. Spinning rides are thrilling because of a center-seeking force called centripetal force. The ride shown in the top right of Figure 14.15 plasters the rider against the back wall as it spins at high speeds. Look back at your results from Experiment 7.2. The inertia of the marble caused it to fly off of the pie pan when there was no wall to keep it moving in a circle. When you are on a spinning ride, your inertia wants to send you flying off, but the walls of the ride keep you whirling. You will learn a lot more about this force when you take a physics course.

FIGURE 14.15
Amusement Park Physics
You can experience a lot of what you study in physics when you visit amusement parks.

Roller coasters are the perfect place to see Newton's laws, the force of gravity, and mechanical energy at work. Many roller coasters only use engines to tug you to the top of the first hill—the highest point of the ride. After that gravity and the laws of physics take over. You'll feel heavier as you are pulled up to the top and then experience a feeling of weightlessness as you plummet down the track. If the roller coaster has loops and twists in it, the track provides the centripetal force that keeps you going around the bends. Because of your inertia, you will feel the car jerk and pull as you are pressed into the seat through the turns. It really is the result of the laws of physics that makes these rides so exhilarating.

Transportation and Physics

From tires to jet engines, people have used physics to imagine better, faster ways to travel. You've already learned how Newton's third law explains how rockets can take off. But physics can also explain how airplanes fly. Examine Figure 14.16. Notice the shape of the bird's wing and airplane wing (red cross sections). The shape of an airplane's wing is called an airfoil. This curved shape causes fluids, such as the gases in air (blue lines), to move faster over the tops of wings. The fast-moving air causes the air pressure above the wings to decrease. The slower-moving air below the wings causes air pressure to be greater below than above the wings. Now, the pressure exerted downwards on the wing by the air above it (red arrow) is less than the pressure exerted upwards from below it (green arrow). This difference creates an upward force called lift that pushes the wing upwards. It was a Swiss mathematician named Daniel Bernoulli who discovered that *the pressure of a moving fluid decreases if the fluid moves faster.* This is called Bernoulli's principle. So, the faster an airplane moves, the more lift there is. When the force of lift is greater than the force of gravity, the airplane is able to fly. Keep in mind that this is a simplified explanation and there is more to it, including Newton's laws. You will learn more about speed and pressure and how they are related when you take physics. But, if you ever ride in an airplane, you will know that the laws of physics can explain how the airplane flies.

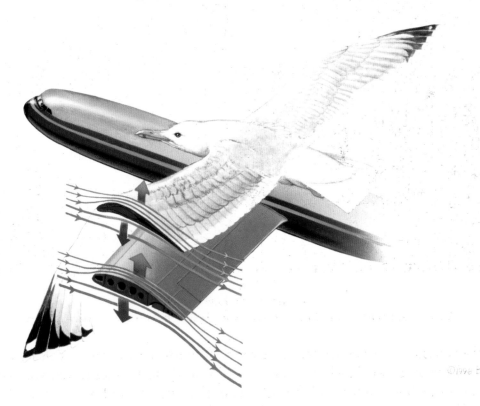

FIGURE 14.16
Wing Aerodynamics
Faster moving air creates a pressure difference that causes lift.

YOU DO SCIENCE
BERNOULLI's PRINCIPLE

You can see Bernoulli's principle in action if you have a funnel (or an empty 2 liter soda bottle) and a ping-pong ball. If you don't have a funnel, cut the top of the 2 liter soda bottle (about 6 inches from the neck of the bottle) to make a funnel. Place the ping-pong ball in the funnel. With your head tilted back, and the wider end of the funnel pointed upwards, blow air forcefully through the narrow end of the funnel to try to lift the ball out. Observe what happens and record your observations. Now, place the ball in the funnel as before, but this time hold the funnel by the narrow neck in front of you. Place your lips on the rim of the wider end of the funnel and blow forcefully across the top of the wider end. What happens? Record your observations. You should have noticed that when blowing from underneath the ball, the ball stayed at the bottom of the funnel. This was because the faster moving air caused a decrease in pressure under the ball so the higher pressure above the ball pushed it down into the funnel. When you blew across the wider top of the funnel, the faster moving air caused a decrease in pressure above the ball. The greater pressure below the ball, then lifts it up to the top of the funnel.

think about this

While we're talking about traveling, did you know that Einstein's theories of relativity are crucially important to your GPS (Global Positioning System)? The Global Positioning System is a network of about 30 satellites that orbit Earth above the exosphere at about 20,000 km. Wherever you are on the planet, at least four GPS satellites are able to "see" you at any time. Your GPS device takes radio signals (that travel at the speed of light) from at least three of these satellites and calculates your location depending on how long it took for the signals to reach it. Because the speed and height of the satellites can vary slightly, the GPS device uses equations from Einstein's theories to adjust the location results. Because of Einstein, your GPS is accurate to within several centimeters!

FIGURE 14.17
GPS Device
Smartphones are now equipped with GPS devices that can accurately direct you to any location using satellites.

Physics and Forensics

Crime scene investigators often use chemistry and physics as they examine crimes or accidents. Car accident reconstruction is an example where investigators analyze skid marks made as cars screech to a stop. A forensic accident reconstruction engineer starts by collecting data on the car's tires, the road surface, and the lengths of the skid marks. From this information, the forensics engineer can determine the coefficient of friction and then the frictional force applied to the car to stop it. Knowing the work done by friction to stop the car, they can then make a good estimate of the car's speed before the driver hit the brakes.

FIGURE 14.18
Skid Marks
Police can use the length of skid marks to determine the speed of a car using physics equations.

Forensic scientists also use physics for other things besides accident reconstruction. They use physics principles when they study ballistics, for example. Ballistics is the examination of evidence related to firearms at a crime scene. A ballistics expert will use Newton's laws (among other physics concepts) to determine the trajectory of a bullet or explosive devices. Much of what you study in a physics course can be applied to forensic science.

Physics and Health

We've already discussed a bit about how physics helps scientists and doctors know about human health. Biophysics has been essential to the development of many diagnostic techniques. We've already looked at how MRIs (Magnetic Resonance Imaging) use strong magnetic fields and radio frequencies to produce 3-D images of tissues.

CT (Computed Tomography) scans are another technology using physics. CT machines shoot narrow beams of X-rays into a patient as it rotates around the person's

body. Signals produced as the X-rays pass through the body are sent to a computer. The computer generates a cross-sectional image (or slice) of the area being X-rayed, and then stacks the slices together to create a 3-D image of the patient. This allows doctors to identify normal areas and locate any abnormalities. Biophysicists continue to work to make medical imaging safer, faster, and more precise so that we can learn more about how the body works.

In addition to creating tools to aid in imaging and diagnosing problems, physics has been instrumental in developing life-saving treatments and devices. Radiation

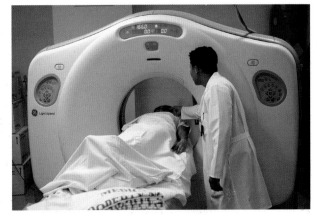

FIGURE 14.19
CT Scanner
Computed Topography scans help diagnose diseases and evaluate injuries.

therapy helps treat many types of cancer. Biophysicists developed kidney dialysis machines to help patients with kidney disease. Cardiac defibrillators, pacemakers, and artificial heart valves have been designed to help patients with electrical problems or issues with fluid (blood) flow in the heart. Computer models called neural networks help biophysicists model how the brain and nervous system work. In this way we can better understand how information is processed both with our eyes and our ears. Understanding how our bodies move has helped biophysicists design better prosthetic limbs and develop better ways to deliver drugs to the areas of the body that need it.

Biophysics also plays a part in understanding the environment. Scientists who work in environmental biophysics research and collect data on all aspects of our planet, from the microscopic organisms that live in deep ocean vents to pollutants in the stratosphere. They are even trying to find ways to convert algae into a renewable fuel source called bio-fuel. These are not the only areas that biophysicists are working in, but I hope you have a better picture of how interrelated the different branches of science really are. Finish up this chapter by completing On Your Own problem 14.9.

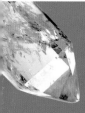

ON YOUR OWN

14.9 Two ping-pong balls are suspended from strings so they hang at the same height with a small space between them. When a hair dryer is used to blow air between the two balls, the balls come together and touch. Explain why this happens.

SUMMING UP

There are so many fascinating careers in the fields of biochemistry and biophysics. I hope you found this module interesting and inspiring. We only covered a few of the many possibilities. Nutritionists and dietitians use chemistry in their field of helping people with digestion problems to eat better. Optometrists use the physics of optics to determine which lenses will correct vision problems. Audiologists use the physics of sound to determine if hearing aids can help a person hear better. Physical therapists need to understand the physics of movement in order to help people regain their range of motion after an injury. If any of the science in this module is inspiring to you, consider exploring all the career opportunities that your study of physical science opens up!

ANSWERS TO THE "ON YOUR OWN" QUESTIONS

14.1 Carbon can exist as diamond, graphite, and fullerenes.

14.2 In hydrocarbon molecules, carbon atoms can be arranged in straight chains, branched chains, or in ring shapes.

14.3 An isomer is any molecules with the same molecular formula but different structural formulas. Isomers have the same type and number of atoms, but they differ in how they are arranged.

14.4 The three types of unsaturated hydrocarbons are alkenes (one or more double bond), alkynes (one or more triple bond), and aromatic hydrocarbons (ring structures of alternating double and single bonds). Since the hydrocarbon had a triple bond, the scientist must have discovered an alkyne.

14.5 The three types of fossil fuels are coal (a solid), natural gas (a gas), and petroleum (a liquid).

14.6 The energy of sunlight is converted into chemical energy that is stored in the bonds of glucose.

14.7 The products of photosynthesis are the reactants of cellular respiration and the reactants of photosynthesis are the products of cellular respiration.

14.8 The question told you that proteins are made from amino acids. You also know that enzymes are proteins. So, if there were not enough essential amino acids, the body would not be able to produce enzymes needed for cellular reactions.

14.9 Bernoulli's principle states that as the speed of a fluid increases, the pressure of the fluid decreases. According to Bernoulli's principle, the moving air between the balls has a lower pressure than the surrounding, nonmoving air. The greater pressure on the outside of the balls pushes them together.

You Do Science: Modeling Isomers

The five structural formulas for the isomers of hexane are shown below (without attached hydrogen atoms). The chemical name of each isomer is given beside the structural formula.

C – C – C – C – C – C n-hexane

C – C – C – C 2,3-dimethylbutane
      | |
      C C

C – C – C – C – C 2-methylpentane
    |
    C

C – C – C – C 2,2-dimethylbutane
        |
        C

C – C – C – C – C 3-methylpentane
        |
        C

STUDY GUIDE FOR MODULE 14

1.   Define the following terms:

   a. Monomer

   b. Polymer

2.   What is organic chemistry?

3.   Why is diamond extremely hard but graphite is extremely soft?

4.   What is a saturated hydrocarbon? What name is given to them?

5.   Describe the shapes that saturated hydrocarbons can take?

6.   What are isomers?

7.   Describe the types of unsaturated hydrocarbons.

8.   What are the three types of fossil fuels?

9.   Why is it important to make sure that there is plenty of air around a gas burner such as the one shown in the figure?

10.   What are the four classes of biochemical compounds?

11.   What are the products of photosynthesis? What are the products of cellular respiration?

12.   What role do enzymes play in cells?

13.   What are vitamins?

14.   What does Bernoulli's principle state?

15.   Hurricanes and tornadoes have very high-speed winds. Some people believe that these high-speed winds can cause houses to explode outward. Explain why they might think that can happen.

PHYSICAL SCIENCE RESEARCH

Why are we ending our physical science course with research? Well, in the last module you were introduced to some of the many career possibilities that a study of physical science can open up. Remember, science is a way of understanding the world, and that involves research! All scientists spend some time researching things they don't know, so they can formulate good questions. And writing, as you probably already know, is a very important part of any subject. In science, writing about their research and experiments is the main way scientists share what they have learned, both successes and failures. They write journal articles and conference presentations, so that any other scientist who is also researching the same topic can learn from them.

Natural Notes

You're about to start the final module in your physical science journey. You should feel a real sense of accomplishment—you've learned a lot of science! Believe it or not, there is still a lot of science you have yet to learn. I hope you've been inspired to keep on learning because this module is all about researching a physical science topic that interests you. We started our study of physical science by reviewing the basics. We'll end our journey by walking through how to do scientific research and write a paper on it. Researching is a great way to learn new things about our physical world and about the God who created it. Writing about your research is one important way to share what you've learned with others.

FIGURE 15.1
The Bible
Always remember, the greatest research you can do is in God's word.

Most often scientific research involves designing experiments to answer questions that you formulate during background study. You've done quite a few experiments in this course and have written lab reports for them. You will have more opportunities to design experiments and write formal lab write-ups in future science courses, so in this module we're focusing on conducting and presenting background research. Keep in mind that this is not the only way to conduct research, and other courses may give you slightly different information, but this will give you an overview to help you research a physical science topic of your choice. There will be no Study Guide questions or test for this module. Your final project for physical science will be sharing the research you do on a physical science topic that you find intriguing!

IN THIS MODULE YOU WILL READ ABOUT THE FOLLOWING MAIN IDEAS:

- Conducting Research
- Sharing Your Research
- Your Turn to Research

CONDUCTING RESEARCH

When you think of conducting research, you might picture the endless stacks of books in a library such as those shown in Figure 15.2. Where do you even start? For this project, you'll start with what you've already learned in physical science. You will use the information you've studied in this course as a springboard to investigate something you don't yet know.

It is important to understand that research is actually a process rather than something that just happens. You first need to form one or more questions. Then decide on resources and gather information from those resources. Next you need to

FIGURE 15.2
Research Library
Research can seem overwhelming if you start by walking through a library and hoping some topic jumps out at you.

sort the information you find and decide what is important—what information will answer your questions. Once you've collected the data, you need to think about it and start to organize it into a form that you can share. And then you write your research paper, create a project, or present your information in a way that others can see what you've learned. Of course this process can be adjusted as needed, but I will give you a little more detail on the steps before you start researching yourself.

Getting Started

Hopefully you found you were curious about more than a few things you learned about as you worked through this text. Take a moment and skim through your student notebook. Did you write any comments? Does anything you see spark some questions like, *I wonder if that can really happen or I wonder if the same thing would happen if...* These types of questions are the seeds that good research ideas can blossom from.

So the first thing you need to do is to find what you are interested in studying more about. Choose a topic that fascinates you. This probably seems obvious but choosing something you want to learn more about will make the research process far more fun and engaging! Once you have a general topic, keep asking yourself questions. Let your natural curiosity lead you to research ideas. Keep in mind that you don't want your topic to be too broad because you will likely find so much information that it will be difficult to focus your paper. You also don't want your topic to be too narrow as it may be hard to find any information at all.

Brainstorming and Narrowing

Once you think of a broad topic that interests you, try to brainstorm things that might be related to that topic. Write your ideas down. For example, if your topic is northern lights you might write down things like: *when do the lights appear, how do they move around, what colors can appear, where's the best places to see them?* Keep asking questions until you come up with some interesting research questions that you want to know the answers to.

Next write down what you already know about your topic. Your textbook will help you with this. You can even use the Book Extras website as a resource for information too. Then start your actual research.

Finding Credible Sources

The library is always a good place to begin research. The librarian can help you find good books on the topic you choose. Textbooks are also a good source for finding answers to questions. And of course, interviewing an expert on your topic is always fun—if you happen to know one. Today, however, most students can easily find answers to questions on the internet. Before we talk about finding good sources on the internet, you should check with your parents about any rules they may have for conducting internet searches.

FIGURE 15.3
Questions
Good research starts with questions you want to find the answers to.

FIGURE 15.4
More Questions
Ask many questions about your topic until you find some you want to research.

FIGURE 15.5
Internet Research
Make sure to find reliable sources on the internet for your research.

Not all internet sources are equal. What does that mean? Well, with the internet you can find a lot of information, but not all of it is accurate. Sometimes you will find something that looks like a good source, but it is really someone's opinion with no scientific evidence to back it up. Or you may find actual misconceptions presented as fact. You can't believe everything you read on the internet! So how do you find reliable sources? There are several things to look for when checking the credibility of a website.

- Author—Who wrote the web page? Does the author have credentials that they share on the webpage? Are they an authority on the topic? Does the information come from a school, business, or company site?

- Purpose—Why did the author publish the website? Is it to share information (data and results) or to give their opinion?

- Dates—When was the site published or updated? Sometimes websites are not updated in so long that their information is no longer valid. Look for current websites.

Search the web carefully. The most reliable sites belong to the government (.gov), universities (.edu), and well-known organizations (.org).

think about this

A note about Wikipedia. Wikipedia is a great resource for getting an overview of a topic. However, it is not considered a reliable source because Wikipedia allows anyone to create pages and these pages can be edited by anyone (even anonymously) at any time. And, while Wikipedia webpages may be accurate (and often are), there is really no way to know for sure. In fact, Wikipedia itself claims that it should not be considered a reliable source. So, for that reason Wikipedia is not permitted as one of the three sources needed for this project. However, sources sited on a Wikipedia webpage may indeed be a credible source, so use Wikipedia wisely.

Research

Once you've found three credible sources, begin to research. Read your sources and take notes. Use the note-taking skills you've been honing during your study of physical science. Make graphic organizers to help you remember important points you want to make in your paper. Use outlines as a way of making sure you are not missing anything significant.

Remember to write things in your own words. Do not copy word-for-word what you find in your sources as that is plagiarism. If you do want to use someone else's words in your paper, you must use quotations and let the reader know who's words they are. A good way to help you avoid copy and pasting words from sources is to try writing the points you want to

FIGURE 15.6
Notetaking
Take notes in your own words as you research the answers to your questions.

include "in a nutshell." Think about what you're reading and then figure out what the main point is and rewrite that in your own words, "in a nutshell." Research until you find the answers to all of the questions you had brainstormed. And make sure to cite all of your references. You will find pages in your student notebook to help you with this part of the process.

SHARING YOUR RESEARCH

There are many ways to share your research. Most scientists write journal articles or present posters to share their research. We're going to talk about writing a 1 to 2-page research paper. However, if you are already writing a research paper in another course, you can choose from the list below on how to present your research. Check with your parent, or if you're taking this class with a co-op, ask your teacher which option they would like you to do.

Using your graphic organizers and outlines, write out your topic sentence or thesis statement. The thesis statement explains what your paper is about and what problem or question your paper will answer. This should be the last sentence of your introductory paragraph. Don't write the introductory paragraph yet—you should always start with your thesis statement. You want your thesis statement to be the "hook" that makes your audience want to read the rest of your paper. Or, your thesis should be a statement telling the reader what the points they will learn by reading your paper.

Next you'll write your introductory paragraph, placing your thesis statement at the end of it. Introductory paragraphs give background information and can explain a bit about why you chose the topic. All the sentences in your introductory paragraph should lead up to your thesis statement.

Now use your thesis statement to help you determine three main points that you want to cover. Take your graphic organizers and outline and turn them into paragraphs that support your thesis statement. Choose one main point per paragraph.

Write a concluding paragraph. This paragraph should summarize the points you made in the previous paragraphs. Do not introduce any new information in your conclusion. You can, however, include how learning about your topic has impacted you. You can find an example paper in the student notebook.

While you're writing your paper, don't forget to use complete sentences with proper grammar. You will also want to use transition sentences (ones that start with words such as however, also, furthermore, in conclusion) between paragraphs. Once you have your first draft written, proofread your paper. Now is the time to check for spelling and grammar errors. When you've proofread and made any changes, make a final copy of your research paper. Now it's time to share what you've learned with others!

Alternate Research Presentations

If you've already written one (or several) research papers this year, you may want to choose an alternate way of sharing your research. Below is a list of ideas for you to choose. But, check with your parent before making a switch.

- PowerPoint presentation on the computer

- Poster

- Speech

- Brochure or informational pamphlet

- Children's storybook or flip-up book

- Videotaped presentation

- Play or skit

- Songs or Poems

The possibilities for presentations are limited only by your imagination. The goal is to learn something new in the physical sciences and share that information with others. Oh, and to have fun!

YOUR TURN TO RESEARCH
Now it's your turn.

- Look through your student notebook and textbook to find topics that you'd like to learn more about.

- Begin asking questions you want to know the answers to.

- Start some preliminary research. Don't be afraid to alter your questions once you start learning more about your topic.

- Once you have a better idea of what you plan to write about, develop a topic sentence or hook to get your reader interested in what you plan to share.

- Then complete in-depth research. Use 3 credible sources. As you research, write notes that you can use to write your research paper. Use some of the note-taking skills you developed during this course, such as graphic organizers or outlines. Don't forget to write the citations for the sources you choose.

- Start writing. Write a 1 to 2-page research paper that presents the information you learned through your research. Or, choose one of the other ways of sharing your research and go for it!

- Present your research to parents, friends, or co-op.

- Celebrate your accomplishment of successfully completing your physical science course!

There are pages in your student notebook (and a sample research paper) to help you with what we've talked about in this module. There is also a rubric for grading this paper in the *Solutions and Tests Manual*. So, get started on your own scientific research and enjoy the process!

SUMMING UP

Research is a very important part of the learning process, as well as being useful in real-life later on. You may have written research papers before. But hopefully this module has helped you to see how sharing what you've learned with others is an enjoyable and valuable way to really understand a topic. I also hope that you were able to see the bigger picture of how what you learn in science can uncover the fingerprints of God throughout all of creation.

DEAR PHYSICAL SCIENCE STUDENT,

Congratulations! You've accomplished a whole year of increasing your understanding of our physical world. You should be very proud of yourself—I know I am proud of you.

I hope you have enjoyed your science journey this year. More importantly, I hope that as you worked through this course you've been inspired to keep learning. I also hope that you have come to a deeper appreciation for the ingenuity and creative genius of God. Over and over again in this course, you learned about processes in creation that are simply too complex and too well designed to have occurred by chance. I hope that seeing some of these systems has filled you with awe and a deep respect for God's handiwork.

> The heavens declare the glory of God; the skies proclaim the work of his hands.
> —Psalm 19:1 (NIV)

But know this, as wonderful as the heavens and Earth are, you, dear student, are God's most precious creation!

> When I consider your heavens, the work of your fingers, the moon and the stars, which you have set in place, what is mankind that you are mindful of them, human beings that you care for them? You have made them a little lower than the angels and crowned them with glory and honor.
> —Psalm 8:3–5 (NIV)

God loves you and wants to have a relationship with you! And His word tells us that nothing can separate us from His love.

> No power in the sky above or in the earth below—indeed, nothing in all of creation will ever be able to separate us from the love of God that is revealed in Christ Jesus our Lord.
> —Romans 8:39 (NLT)

It has been a blessing and a joy to share this year with you. I hope you will always look for God's signature throughout all creation. And you will join me, and all of Apologia, to proclaim:

> Lord, our Lord, how magnificent is your name throughout the earth!
> You have covered the heavens with your majesty.
> —Psalm 8:1 (CSB)

Warmly,

Vicki Dincher

Matter – Anything that has mass and takes up space (has volume) (p. 41)

Mechanical wave – A disturbance in matter that transfers energy through the matter (p. 312)

Minerals – Solid, naturally-occurring, inorganic substances that have a definite chemical composition and a crystalline structure (p. 441)

Mixture – Two or more substances mixed together but not chemically bonded (p. 45)

Mole – An amount of a substance that contains approximately 6.02×1023 particles (known as Avogadro's number) of the substance (p. 172)

Molecule – The smallest unit of a chemical compound, composed of two or more atoms bonded together (p. 45)

Monomer – A single molecule that can react with other molecules to form a large molecule (p. 504)

Newton's first law – An object in motion (or at rest) will stay in motion (or at rest) until it is acted upon by an outside force (p. 240)

Newton's second law – When an object is acted on by one or more unbalanced forces, the net force is equal to the mass of the object times the resulting acceleration (p. 245)

Newton's third law – For every action, there is an equal and opposite reaction (p. 252)

Observation – Gathering information using senses or with the aid of instruments (p. 5)

Open circuit – A circuit that does not have a complete connection between the two sides of the power source; as a result, current does not flow (p. 416)

Orbitals – A region of space around the nucleus where electrons are most likely to be found (p. 97)

Output distance – The distance the output force is exerted through, or how far the load moves (p. 298)

Output force – The force exerted by a machine (p. 297)

Photon – A small "package" of light energy that acts like a particle (p. 400)

Pitch – An indication of how high or low a sound is, which is primarily determined by the frequency of the sound wave (p. 336)

Plastic rock – Rock that behaves like something between a liquid and a solid (p. 437)

Polar molecule – A molecule that has slight positive and negative charges due to an imbalance in the way electrons are shared (p. 131)

Polyatomic ions – A covalently bonded group of atoms that has a positive or negative charge and acts as a unit (p. 154)

Polymer – A large molecule that is made out of many smaller molecules joined together by covalent bonds (p. 504)

Potential energy – Energy that is stored as a result of position or shape (p. 276)

Power – The amount of work done each second (p. 291)

Precipitation – Water falling from the atmosphere as rain, snow, sleet, or hail (p. 448)

Pressure – The force (weight) applied over a unit of area (p. 472)

Products – New substances formed as a result of a chemical change (p. 117)

Qualitative observation – Observations made using one of the five senses: sight, smell, touch, taste, or hearing (p. 5)

Quantitative observations – Observations made with instruments such as rulers, balances, graduated cylinders, beakers, thermometers, etc. (p. 5)

Radiation – The transfer of energy by waves through air or empty space (p. 479)

Reactants – Substances that undergo a chemical change (p. 117)

Reference point – A point against which direction is measured (p. 189)

Resistance – A material's ability to impede the flow of charge (p. 413)

Rock cycle – A series of processes in which forces within Earth and at the surface cause rocks to continuously change from one type to another (p. 444)

Scalar quantity – A physical measurement that contains only magnitude (number) and does not contain directional information (p. 191)

Scientific law – A description of a natural phenomenon or relationship that is supported by a significant amount of evidence and often include mathematical terms (p. 14)

Scientific model – Useful simplification used to make it easier to understand things that might be too difficult to directly observe (p. 16)

LAB SUPPLY LIST

MODULE 1

Experiment 1.1
Alka Seltzer tablet
A small solid object (such as a pebble or eraser)
Magnifying glass
Centimeter ruler
Kitchen balance
Beaker of water
Stirring rod or spoon to stir

Experiment 1.2
String
Masking tape
Stopwatch or other 30 second timer
Pencil
Paper clip
5 Washers
Half a piece of cardstock paper (cut paper in
    half lengthwise) or cardboard 8.5" x 5.5"
Protractor
Metric ruler

MODULE 2

Experiment 2.1
4 beakers (250 mL) or clear glass cups (The
    beakers or cups must be the same size.)
Hot and cold water
Ice
Red, blue, green, and yellow food coloring
Measuring cup
Stopwatch (optional)
A helper

Experiment 2.2
Paper towels
4 beakers (250 mL size) or pint sized, large
    mouth glass jars
1 large quart jar
4 spoons
Measuring cup
Water
Vegetable oil
Corn syrup
Rubbing alcohol (isopropyl alcohol)
Red and blue food coloring
4 Small cork pieces
4 Pennies
4 Grapes (or raisins)
4 Small paper clips
4 Marbles
4 Washers
4 Ice cubes

You Do Science
A balloon
Water

Experiment 2.3
A beaker or a small, clear glass (like a juice glass)
Baking soda
Tap water
A 9 volt battery (the kind that goes in a radio,
    smoke detector, or toy. DO NOT use an
    electrical outlet, as that would be quite
    dangerous! A 1.5 volt flashlight battery will
    not work.)
Two 9 inch pieces of insulated wire. The wire
    itself must be copper.
Scissors
Some tape (preferably electrical tape, but
    cellophane or masking tape will work.)
A spoon for stirring
Eye protection such as goggles or safety glasses

MODULE 3

Experiment 3.1
2 small Styrofoam balls (Balls should be about 2 inches in diameter. Styrofoam balls from craft stores work well.)
Pipe cleaners (white or gray)
Plastic pony beads (These can be found at craft stores.)
2 bamboo skewers
Fishing line
2 wire hangers
Red and blue pushpins

Experiment 3.2
Color cards found in the student notebook
Scissors
Glue or tape

You Do Science
Table salt (sodium chloride)
Distilled water
A clean, clear glass container (a beaker or jam jar)
String
Wooden spoon

MODULE 4

Experiment 4.1
A Styrofoam or paper cup
Glass of water
Vegetable oil
Balloon
Pen
Eye protection such as goggles or safety glasses

Experiment 4.2
Stick of butter or margarine (It must be fresh from the refrigerator so that it is solid.)
2 beakers or microwave-safe glass bowls
Water
Ice cube
Microwave (A saucepan and stove can be substituted for the microwave.)
Knife (A serrated one works best. You will use it to cut the butter.)
Spoon
Eye protection such as goggles or safety glasses

Experiment 4.3
Water
Bowl
4 beakers or clear glasses
Paper towels
Wax paper
Pipette or eyedropper
Straw
2 microscope slides
Metal paper clip (Use a standard-sized paper clip. A big one will probably not work.)
Toilet paper
Dish soap
Vegetable oil
Toothpicks
Scissors
Blue and red food coloring
Spoon
Eye protection such as goggles or safety glasses

MODULE 5

Experiment 5.1
Water
9 volt battery (A new one works best.)
2 test tubes (You can purchase these at a hobby store. If you cannot get them, use the tubes that florists put on the stems of cut flowers.)
Beaker or glass (It must be deep enough so that when it is nearly full of water, the battery can stand vertically in the glass and still be fully submerged in the water.)
Epsom salts (You can get these at any drugstore or large supermarket.)
Tablespoon
Eye protection such as goggles or safety glasses

Experiment 5.2
Beaker or a clear glass
Water
White vinegar
Baking soda (A fresh box will work best.)
Salt substitute (Morton Salt Substitute, Nu-Salt, or NoSalt are brands you can find at your grocery store.)
Epsom salts
Hydrogen peroxide
Steel wool
Quick rising dry yeast (A new packet—check the expiration date—that has been kept refrigerated will work best.)

Thermometer
Tablespoon
Timer
Eye protection such as goggles or safety glasses
Optional—Acetone (Some fingernail polish removers contain acetone. You may be able to find it at a drug or grocery store, read the labels for ingredients.)
Optional—Styrofoam packing peanut

You Do Science
1 or 2 liter soda bottle
½ cup hydrogen peroxide
¼ cup dishwashing soap
Food coloring
Measuring cup
A packet of active yeast
Warm water

MODULE 6

You Do Science
A helper
A yard stick, meter stick, or tape measure
Masking tape
A stopwatch

Experiment 6.1
At least 4 eggs
2 pieces of reasonably strong cardboard (like the cardboard found on the back of writing tablets)
Several books
A pair of scissors
Ruler
A large tray or cookie sheet
Paper towels
Kitchen table
Eye protection such as goggles or safety glasses

Experiment 6.2
A large glass jar with a lid
Some dirt of outside (Dig straight down into the ground to get dirt from many depths.)
Some sand
Some gravel composed of various sizes of rocks
Water

MODULE 7

Experiment 7.1
A large heavy book (at least 21 cm by 27 cm)
A small piece of paper (about 3 cm by 3 cm)
Eye protection such as goggles or safety glasses

You Do Science
A stopwatch that reads hundredths of a second (many smartphones have this feature)
A chair or stepladder
A rock or other heavy object to reduce air resistance (make sure your choice will not damage your floor)
A tape measure

Experiment 7.2
A coin (nickels work well)
A 3 inch by 5 inch index card (note the units listed)
A small beaker or glass (like a juice glass)
A raw egg
A hard-boiled egg
An aluminum pie pan
A pair of scissors
A marble or other small ball
Eye protection such as goggles or safety glasses

Experiment 7.3
A plastic, 2 liter bottle
A stopper that fits the bottle (It could be rubber or cork, but you cannot use the screw-on cap. It has to be something that plugs up the opening of the bottle but can be pushed out by a pressure buildup inside the bottle. Modeling clay can work as well. You could also try a large wad of gum, as long as the gum has dried out and has the texture of firm rubber.)
A cup of vinegar
2 teaspoons of baking soda
Aluminum foil
Four pencils
Eye protection such as goggles or safety glasses

You Do Science
A balloon
some string or fishing line
A plastic drinking straw
Some scotch tape

MODULE 8

Experiment 8.1
1–5 rubber bands (all must be the same thickness and length)
A metric ruler
Tape measure (one with metric units on it would be best)
Masking tape
Safety glasses or goggles

You Do Science
A basketball (a soccer ball will also work)
A tennis ball
A yard stick or tape measure

Experiment 8.2
A 1 lb hand weight (You can also use a 16 ounce box of spaghetti or other 1 lb substance.)
A piece of string 70 cm long
Pencil or dowel rod
Tape
Tape measure or metric ruler
Stopwatch
Bathroom scale
A clear stairway (You will be running up the steps so make sure the area is safe and you have proper shoes on.)
A helper

MODULE 9

Experiment 9.1
Plastic wrap
Scissors
Tape
Match
Plastic 1 liter or 2 liter bottle (the kind soda pop comes in)
Candle
Large pot
Wooden spoon
Large bowl
Rice
Eye protection such as goggles or safety glasses

You Do Science
A balloon

Experiment 9.2
Two medium-sized rocks
A person to help you
A stopwatch
A 250 meter stretch of sidewalk, pavement, gravel road, or lawn that is relatively straight
A tape measure, meterstick, or yardstick

Experiment 9.3
Eye protection such as goggles or safety glasses
If you have access to a stringed instrument such as a violin, guitar, cello, or banjo, use it for this experiment. If you do not have access to such an instrument, you will need:
Rubber band
Plastic tub (like the kind whipped cream comes in)

You Do Science
A licensed driver
A vacant street or parking lot

Experiment 9.4
Water
Glass or plastic bottle (A glass bottle is best, and 2 liter is the ideal size. It must have a narrow neck. A jar will not work well.)
Eye protection such as goggles or safety glasses

MODULE 10

Experiment 10.1
A flat pan, like the kind you use to bake a cake
A medium-sized mirror (4 inches by 6 inches is a good size)
A sunny window (A flashlight will work, but it will not be as dramatic.)
A plain white sheet of paper
Water
Eye protection such as goggles or safety glasses

You Do Science
A prism (or a CD cut in half)
A thermometer (if you have 2 or 3 that is even better)
A plain white piece of paper
Black paint, or a black magic marker

Experiment 10.2
Eye protection such a goggles or safety glasses
A flat mirror. The mirror can be very small, but it needs to be flat. You can always tell if a

mirror is flat by looking at your reflection in it. If the image you see in the mirror is neither magnified nor reduced, the mirror is flat.
A white sheet of paper
A pen
A protractor
A ruler
A flashlight
Black construction paper or thin cardboard
Scissors
Tape
A dark room

Experiment 10.3
A square or rectangular glass or clear plastic pan (If you have a flat bottle, it will work as well. It just needs to be something with clear, flat sides that can hold water.)
Water
Milk
Spoon
Flashlight with the same cover you used in Experiment 10.2
A sheet of plain white paper
Pen
Protractor
Ruler
Eye protection such as goggles or safety glasses

You Do Science
A quarter
An opaque bowl
Some water in a pitcher or very large glass

Experiment 10.4
2 plain white sheets of paper (there shouldn't be any lines on them)
A bright red marker (A crayon will also work, but a marker is better.)
Timer or stopwatch

MODULE 11

Experiment 11.1
2 balloons (Round balloons work best, but any kind will do.)
Thread
Cellophane tape
Eye protection such as goggles or safety glasses

Experiment 11.2
Tape
A clear glass
A plastic lid that fits over the glass. This lid can be larger than the mouth of the glass, but it cannot be smaller. The top of a margarine tub or something similar works quite well.
A paperclip
Two 5 cm x 1.5 cm strips of aluminum foil (the thinner the better)
A balloon
A pair of pliers
Eye protection such as goggles or safety glasses

Experiment 11.3
A 1.5 volt battery (Any AA-, C-, or D-cell battery will work. Do not use any battery other than one of those, though, because a higher voltage can make the experiment dangerous.)
Aluminum foil
Scissors
Eye protection such as goggles or safety glasses

Experiment 11.4
A 1.5 volt battery (Any AA-, C-, or D-cell battery will work. Do not use any battery other than one of those listed, though, because a higher voltage can make the experiment dangerous.)
Tape (Electrical tape works best, but cellophane tape will do.)
Large iron nail (at least 3 inches long)
Metal paper clip
2 feet of insulated wire (24 gauge wire works best. It should not be thicker than 18 gauge.)
Eye protection such as goggles or safety glasses.

MODULE 12

Experiment 12.1
A shallow pan (a pie pan, for example)
Cornstarch
Measuring cups
Water
Spoon for stirring
Eye protection such as goggles or safety glasses

Experiment 12.2
Water
Salt
Ice
Tablespoon
Small saucepan
Saucepan lid or frying pan lid larger than the
    saucepan used
Large bowl (It should not be plastic and heat
    safe, as it will get hot.)
Potholders
Zippered plastic sandwich bag
Stove
Eye protection such as goggles or safety glasses

You Do Science
A pumice stone
A zippered bag
Water

You Do Science
2 pieces of chalk
Some white vinegar or lemon juice
A medicine dropper
Water
2 plates or bowls

MODULE 13

Experiment 13.1
Thermometer (It needs to read from slightly
    lower than room temperature to slightly
    higher than room temperature.)
A large, zippered freezer bag (It needs to be
    large enough so that the thermometer can be
    fully zipped inside.)
Sunny windowsill (Perform this experiment on a
    sunny day.)
Bottle (a plastic 1 liter soft drink bottle, for
    example)
Vinegar
Baking soda
Teaspoon
Eye protection such as goggles or safety glasses

Experiment 13.2
Stove
Frying pan
2 empty, 12 ounce aluminum cans (like soft drink
    cans)
2 bowls
Tablespoon
Water

Ice cubes
Tongs
Eye protection such as goggles or safety glasses

You Do Science
A plastic cup
An index card
Water
A sink

Experiment 13.3
Ice
Water
Clean, dry plastic bottle (The best volume would
    be 1 quart or 1 liter, but any size will work.)
Balloon
Bowl (heat and cold safe)
Optional: rubber band
Eye protection such as goggles or safety glasses

MODULE 14

You Do Science
30 marshmallows
70 raisins (or craisins)
50 toothpicks

Experiment 14.1
Tincture of iodine—1 ounce bottle (You can find
    this at any drug store.)
Lemon juice
Apple juice
Orange juice
Grapefruit juice or pineapple juice (or another
    juice of your choosing)
100 mg vitamin C pill
Medicine dropper
A 1 quart jar
Measuring cup with milliliter markings
Water
Five 8 ounce clear plastic cups

You Do Science
A funnel (or an empty 2 liter soda bottle)
A ping-pong ball

INDEX

IMAGE CREDITS

<u>COVER & REPEATING IMAGES</u>
Green crystal © Nastya22 | Getty Images
Landscape © demerzel21 | Getty Images
Main Idea Lightbulb © Hilch | iStock/Getty Images Plus
graph paper: public domain
what to do clipboard icon: © LisLud | iStock / Getty Images Plus
chalk earth © ekazansk | iStock / Getty Images Plus
graph paper 2 © sidmay | iStock / Getty Images Plus
rocketship © Steppeua | iStock/Getty Images Plus
black chalkboard © STLLFX | iStock / Getty Images Plus
brain © erhui1979 | iStock/Getty Images Plus
You Do Science background paper © sidmay | iStock/Getty Images Plus

<u>INSTRUCTIONAL SUPPORT PAGE</u>
3d Metal icons   © bubaone | iStockphoto.com, modified
laptop, headphones, and social learner icons © Kittichais | iStockphoto.com, modified
book icon   © Wonderfulpixel | iStockphoto.com, modified

<u>MODULE 1</u>
Figure 1.3   phone 1 © doug4527 | E+/Getty Images
                 phone 4 © Jay Pierstorff | iStock/Getty Images Plus
                 phone 5 © Mark Swallows | E+/Getty Images
Figure 1.5   science icons, edited © Vecteezy.com
Figure 1.8   magnesium burn © OK Photography | iStock / Getty Images Plus
Figure 1.9   candle image created using hand © Milkos | iStock/Getty Images Plus
                 jar © WichienTep | iStock/Getty Images Plus
                 candle © RuslanDashinsky | iStock/Getty Images Plus
Figure 1.10   pendulum experiment © xefstock | E+/Getty Images
Figure 1.11   graphs and data © SeventyFour | iStock/Getty Images Plus
Figure 1.18   weight © LoKiLeCh [CC BY-SA 3.0 (http://creativecommons.org/licenses/by-sa/3.0/)]
                 scale © Lilly_M [CC BY-SA 3.0 (https://creativecommons.org/licenses/by-sa/3.0)]
                 salt © chictype | iStock/Getty Images Plus
Figure 1.19   dollar © neonbrand | Unsplash.com
                 soda can © karandaev | iStock/Getty Images Plus
Figure 1.20   runner © william stitt | Unsplash.com

<u>MODULE 2</u>
Figure 2.3   balloons, edited © audriusmerfeldas | iStock/Getty Images Plus
Figure 2.4   tea © domin_domin | E+/Getty Images Plus
Figure 2.5   aluminum can © Michael Burrell | iStock/Getty Images Plus
Figure 2.7   coal © Michael Burrell | iStock/Getty Images Plus
                 hydrogen © bentrussell | iStock/Getty Images Plus
                 oxygen © mrkevvzime | iStock/Getty Images Plus
Figure 2.9   mixtures in beakers © Turtle Rock Scientific/Science Source
Figure 2.10   mixtures in beakers © Turtle Rock Scientific/Science Source
Figure 2.11   infographic created using images from © Vecteezy.com
Figure 2.12   snow globe © TARIK KIZILKAYA | iStock/Getty Images Plus

Figure 4.26	Water, Ice, and Steam © Charles D. Winters/Science Source
Figure 4.27	structure of water © Gary Hincks/Science Source
Figure 4.30	meniscus © NatalieIme	iStock/Getty Images Plus
Figure 4.31	capillary © Martin Shields/Science Source
Figure 4.33	faucet © andhal	iStoc /Getty Images Plus

MODULE 5

Figure 5.1	reactions © Django	E+/Getty Images
Figure 5.2	iron oxide © Max.kit	CC BY-SA 4.0 (https://creativecommons.org/licenses/by-sa/4.0)
Figure 5.3	carbonate © Benjah-bmm27	wikimedia commons	Public domain
Figure 5.6	sodium chloride reaction © Charles D. Winters	www.sciencesource.com
Figure 5.7	peroxide © Joe_Potato	iStock/Getty Images Plus
Experiment 5.1	beaker, test tubes, bubbles, battery © Vecteezy.com, edited
Figure 5.9	airbag © uatp2	iStock/Getty Images Plus
Figure 5.11	potassium in water © Charles D. Winters/Science Source
Figure 5.12	copper and silver nitrate © Andrew Lambert Photography/Science Source
Figure 5.14	lead nitrate and potassium iodide © Turtle Rock Scientific/Science Source
Figure 5.15	burning marshmallows © Richard Bell	Unsplash.com
Figure 5.17	lighter © stocksnapper	iStock/Getty Images Plus
Figure 5.18	heat © Vecteezy.com, edited
Figure 5.20	mole of solids © SCIENCE PHOTO LIBRARY	Science Source
Figure 5.23	salad © SuwanPhoto	iStock/Getty Images Plus
Figure 5.25	elephant toothpaste © Passavitch	CC BY-SA 4.0 (https://creativecommons.org/licens

MODULE 6

Figure 6.4	roller coaster © Jupiter images	Stockbyte/Getty Images
Figure 6.15	parabolic trajectory © AntonO	CC BY 4.0 (https://creativecommons.org/licenses/by/4.0)] via wikimedia commons
Figure 6.16	carousel © mana5280	Unsplash.com
Figure 6.17	roller coaster © matt bowden	Unsplash.com

MODULE 7

Figure 7.2	man with umbrella © Chalabala	iStock/Getty Images Plus
	skateboard © jeff keplar	Unsplash.com
	tug of war © StockPlanets	E+/Getty Images
Figure 7.3	produce scale © Noel Hendrickson	DigitalVision/Getty Images
Figure 7.5	tug of war, both © ideabug	E+/Getty Images
Figure 7.6	skateboard © golobi	iStock/Getty Images Plus
Figure 7.7	friction diagram © ttsz	iStock/Getty Images Plus
	SEM of Car Paint Pigment © Eye of Science/Science Source
Figure 7.8	friction types © normaals	iStock/Getty Images Plus
Figure 7.9	man pushing child in box © PeopleImages	E+/Getty Images
Figure 7.10	hand truck © Clerkenwell	Vetta/Getty Images
Figure 7.12	Gravity Comparison © Ted Kinsman/Science Source
Figure 7.18	crash test dummies © RUSSELLTATEdotCOM	DigitalVision Vectors/Getty Images
Figure 7.19	pie pan, edited © alekseykolotvin28	iStock/Getty Images Plus
Figure 7.20	created using coin and jar from Pixabay.com, hand © catchlights_sg	iStock/Getty Images Plus
Figure 7.22	ear © abstractdesignlabs	DigitalVision Vectors/Getty Images
Figure 7.23	created using image of man © Ljupco	iStock/Getty Images Plus, dog © mphillips007	iStock/Getty Images Plus, and car via Pixabay.com
Figure 7.24	construction worker © Aleksander Kaczmarek	iStock/Getty Images Plus
	boulder © Barcin	E+/Getty Images

Figure 9.23	doppler effect © ttsz	iStock /Getty Images Plus
Figure 9.24	reflected wave © ttsz	iStock /Getty Images Plus
Figure 9.25	sonogram © SABarton	iStock /Getty Images Plus
Figure 9.26	sonar map © NOAA.gov
Figure 9.27	bat © Stephen Dalton/Science Source

MODULE 10

Figure 10.2	electromagnetic wave © KAMURAN AĞBABA	iStock /Getty Images Plus
Figure 10.7	cross waves © Michel Griffon	CC BY 3.0 (https://creativecommons.org/licenses/by/3.0)
Figure 10.8	light wave behavior/ double-slit experiment © Tim Brown/Science Source, left and center double-slit experiment © Dorling Kindersley	Getty Images, right
Figure 10.9	photoelectric effect © BSIP/Science Source
Figure 10.8	light wave behavior/ double-slit experiment © Tim Brown/Science Source
Figure 10.12	electromagnetic spectrum © normaals	iStock /Getty Images Plus
Figure 10.13	weather map © SpiffyJ	iStock /Getty Images Plus
Figure 10.15	thermogram © ivansmuk	iStock /Getty Images Plus
Figure 10.18	William Herschel © PHOTOS.com>> / Getty Images Plus
Figure 10.16	created by Andrea Kiser Martin using window, landscape, mirror, and table images from Pixabay.com and glass pan © Mubera Boskov	iStock /Getty Images Plus
Figure 10.17	visible spectrum © normaals	iStock /Getty Images Plus
Figure 10.20	Earth's ozone © Bigmouse108	iStock /Getty Images Plus
Figure 10.22	brain scan © BanksPhotos	E+/Getty Images
Figure 10.23	fishbowl © dem10	E+/Getty Images
Figure 10.24	translucent © Rene Böhmer	Unsplash.com
Figure 10.26	woman © Yuri_Arcurs	iStock/Getty Images Plus
Figure 10.28	man reflection © @plqml	@feliperizo.co on Unsplash
Figure 10.30	human head © a-r-t-i-s-t	DigitalVision Vectors/Getty Images
Figure 10.32	water droplet © SpicyTruffel	iStock/Getty Images Plus
Figure 10.33	spectrum © ttsz	iStock /Getty Images Plus
Figure 10.35	polarizing sunglasses © Charles D. Winters/Science Source
Figure 10.40	human eye © solar22	iStock/Getty Images Plus
Figure 10.41	human eye © ttsz	iStock/Getty Images Plus
Figure 10.42	retina © ttsz	iStock/Getty Images Plus
Study Guide, Q3	spear fishing © Daniel Eskridge	iStock/Getty Images Plus

MODULE 11

Figure 11.1	aurora © Joshua Earle	Unsplash.com
Figure 11.3	balloon hair © SPL/Science Source
Figure 11.5	photon © Claus Lunau/Science Source
Figure 11.7	atoms © ttsz	iStock/Getty Images Plus
Figure 11.9	static electricity © Ted Kinsman/Science Source
Figure 11.10	hand door knob © laymul	iStock/Getty Images Plus
Figure 11.11B	lid © Niteenrk	iStockphoto
Figure 11.11B	glass © ManuWe	iStockphoto
Figure 11.12	balloon © alekcey	iStockphoto
Figure 11.15	battery © Brett Jordan	Unsplash.com
Figure 11.16	circuit © GrigoriosMoraitis	E+/Getty Images
Figure 11.17	circuit symbols © frentusha	iStock/Getty Images Plus, edited
Figure 11.19	atoms © ttsz	iStock/Getty Images Plus
Figure 11.20	current © ttsz	iStock/Getty Images Plus
Figure 11.22	burner © gwmullis	E+/Getty Images
Figure 11.24	circuit © aryigit	iStock/Getty Images Plus

Figure 11.25	light bulb socket © dlerick	iStock/Getty Images Plus
Figure 11.25	light bulb © tr3gi	iStock/Getty Images Plus
Figure 11.26	light bulb socket © dlerick	iStock/Getty Images Plus
Figure 11.26	light bulb © tr3gi	iStock/Getty Images Plus
Figure 11.27	light bulb socket © dlerick	iStock/Getty Images Plus
Figure 11.27	light bulb © tr3gi	iStock/Getty Images Plus
Figure 11.30	refrigerator magnets © teddyandmia	iStock/Getty Images Plus
Figure 11.31	magnets repel © eliflamra	iStock/Getty Images Plus
Figure 11.34	magnetic filings, left © pippee	iStock/Getty Images Plus
Figure 11.34	magnetic field lines, right © anuwat meereewee	iStock/Getty Images Plus
Figure 11.35	magnetic poles © Photo Researchers/Science Source
Figure 11.35	magnetism © anuwat meereewee	iStock/Getty Images Plus

MODULE 12

Figure 12.2	seismic waves © Gary Hincks/Science Source
Figure 12.4	granite and basalt © James St. John	Flickr.com	CC BY 2.0 (https://creativecommons.org/licenses/by/2.0)
Figure 12.5	Earth layers © Spencer Sutton/Science Source
Figure 12.6	Earth's core © johan63	iStock/Getty Images Plus
Figure 12.7	Earth's magnetic field © Claus Lunau/Science Source
Figure 12.9	granite © James St. John	Flickr.com	CC BY 2.0 (https://creativecommons.org/licenses/by/2.0)
Figure 12.10	granite samples © MultimediaDean	iStock/Getty Images Plus
Infographic 12.1	rocks © James St. John	Flickr.com	CC BY 2.0 (https://creativecommons.org/licenses/by/2.0)
Infographic 12.2	amythest © kali-neri-NyapZuex	Unsplash.com
	pyrite © James St. John	Flickr.com	CC BY 2.0 (https://creativecommons.org/licenses/by/2.0)
	streak test © Joel Arem/Science Source
	talc © James St. John	Flickr.com	CC BY 2.0 (https://creativecommons.org/licenses/by/2.0)
	gypsum © Coldmoon_photo	iStock/Getty Images Plus
	apatite © nastya81	iStock/Getty Images Plus
	feldspar © VvoeVale	iStock/Getty Images Plus
	topaz © James St. John	Flickr.com	CC BY 2.0 (https://creativecommons.org/licenses/by/2.0)
	corundum © Coldmoon_photo	iStock/Getty Images Plus
	diamond © James St. John	Flickr.com	CC BY 2.0 (https://creativecommons.org/licenses/by/2.0)
	graphite © Ricpe	iStock/Getty Images Plus
Figure 12.12	the rock cycle © Spencer Sutton/Science Source
Figure 12.14	hydrologic cycle © stock_shoppe	iStock/Getty Images Plus
Experiment 12.2	created using bag, pan, lid, and burner from Vecteezy.com, ice and bowl from Pixabay.com
Figurte 12.15	Bryce Canyon © Bertrand Borie	Unsplash.com
Figure 12.16	rock formation © James Steinberg/Science Source
	pothole © State Farm CC BY 2.0 (https://creativecommons.org/licenses/by/2.0) via Flickr.com
Figure 12.20	pitted rocks © claffra	iStock /Getty Images Plus
	Monument Valley © Ilse Orsel	Unsplash.com
Figure 12.22	river © Kimson Doan	Unsplash.com
Figure 12.24	meanders © CLAUS LUNAU/Science Source
	NASA Earth Observatory images by Joshua Stevens